Hiking and Exploring the
Paria River

Including: The Story of John D. Lee and the
Mountain Meadows Massacre

4th Edition

Michael R. Kelsey

Kelsey Publishing
456 E. 100 N.
Provo, Utah, USA, 84606-3208
Tele & Fax 801(385 after 2005?)-373-3327
Email Addresses--one of these should work:
mrkelsey@quik.com
kelsey@canyoneering.com
kelseypublishing@hotmail.com
(Identify yourself with the name of a canyon or mountain)

For updates on the canyons in this book go to:
CANYONEERING.COM
Guidebook Updates - Canyon Conditions
Weather Forecasts - Desert Ecology
Open Forums - Canyoneering Techniques
Gear & Book Reviews
To post updates or changes in information since this book was printed,
go to: **http://www.canyoneering.com/books/index.html**
Please add changes or updates so others can view it.

Other websites which may have updated information
on canyons or hikes in this book:
americansouthwest.net
canyoneeringUSA.com
canyoneering.net
climb-utah.com
toddshikingguide.com

For a complete list of worldwide websites specializing in Canyoneering
use your computer's search engine to look up **Canyoneering**
or **Canyoning** for a list that may top 500.

First Edition November 1987
Updated Edition September 1991
3rd Edition January 1998
4th Edition July 2004
Copyright © 1987, 1991, 1998 & 2004 Michael R. Kelsey All Rights Reserved
Library of Congress Catalog Card Number 2004101663
ISBN 0-944510-21-3

Primary Distributors All (or most) of Michael R. Kelsey's books are sold by these distributors. Please call or write to one of these when ordering any of his guidebooks. A list of his titles is in the back of this book.
Alpenbooks, 4206 Chennault Beach Road, Suite B1, Mukilteo, Washington, USA, 98275, Website alpenbooks.com, Email cserve@alpenbooks.com, Tele. 206-290-8587, or 800-290-9898.
Brigham Distribution, 156 South, 800 West, Suit D, Brigham City, Utah, 84302, Tele. 435-723-6611, Fax 435-723-6644, Email brigdist@sisna.com.
Books West, 5757 Arapahoe Avenue, D-2, Boulder, Colorado, USA, 80303, Tele. 303-449-5995, or 800-378-4188, Fax 303-449-5951, Website bookswest.net.
Liberty Mountain, 4375 W. 980 S., Suite 100, Salt Lake City, Utah, 84104, Tele. 800-366-2666 or 801-954-0741, Fax 801-954-0766, Website libertymountain.com, Email sales@libertymountain.com.
Treasure Chest Books, 451 N. Bonita Avenue, Tucson Arizona, USA, 85745, Telc. 928-623-9558, or 800-969-9558, Website treasurechestbooks.com, Email info@treasurechestbooks.com.

Other Distributors
Anderson News, 1709 North, East Street, Flagstaff, Arizona, USA, 86004, Tele. 928-774-6171, Fax 928-779-1958.
Canyonlands Publications, 4860 North Ken Morey Drive, Bellemont, Arizona, USA, 86004, Tele. 928-779-3888 or 800-283-1983, Fax 928-779-3778, Email books@infomagic.com.
Crown West Books (Library Service), 575 E. 1000 S., Orem, Utah, USA, 84097, Tele. 801-224-1455, Fax 801-224-2662, Email jimproc@attbi.com.
High Peak Books, Box 703, Wilson, Wyoming, USA, 83014, Tele. 307-739-0147.
Recreational Equipment, Inc. (R.E.I.), 1700 45th Street East, Sumner, Washington, USA, 98390, Website rei.com, Mail Orders Tele. 800-426-4840 (or check at any of their local stores).
Online--Internet: amazon.com; adventuroustravelers.com; btol.com (Baker-Taylor); Ingrams.com; Bdaltons.com; borders.com (teamed with amazon.com).

For the **UK and Europe**, and the rest of the world contact: **Cordee,** 3a De Montfort Street, Leicester, England, UK, LE1 7HD, Website cordee.co.uk, Tele. Inter+44-116-254-3579, Fax Inter+44-116-247-1176.
For **Australia** and **New Zealand: Macstyle Media,** 20-22 Station Street, Sandringham, Victoria, Australia, 3191, Website macstyle.com.au, Email macstyle@netspace.net.au, Tele. Inter+61-39-521-6585, Fax Inter+61-39-521-0664.

Printed by Banta Book Group, 2600 North, Main Street, Spanish Fork, Utah.

All fotos by the author, unless otherwise stated.
All maps, charts, and cross sections drawn by the author.

Front Cover

Front Cover Fotos
1. Lower Buckskin Gulch
2. The Wave, Coyote Buttes
3. Yellow Rock, Cottonwood Wash
4. Paria Movie Set, near Old Pahreah Townsite

Back Cover

5	6
7	8
9	10

Back Cover Fotos
5. Aerial View, Cottonwood Wash & The Cockscomb
6. Upper Deer Creek Canyon, Rappel 2
7. Toadstools, The Rimrocks
8. Aerial View, Mollies Nipple
9. Hoodoos, Bryce Canyon National Park
10. Stone Donkey Canyon Slot

Table of Contents

Acknowledgments

Many people helped with information for this book, but special thanks should go to the following. The most important person, at least for the first 2 editions, was the late Rod Schipper (killed in a car wreck in September, 1997), more commonly known as "Skip". Until 1990, he was the BLM employee who lived and worked at the Paria Ranger Station. He began that job in 1980 and knew the lower Paria River Canyon better than anyone. Skip spent hours proofreading the hiking section of the first 2 editions of this book. See the small memorial to Skip in front of the Paria Ranger Station & Visitor Center.

Besides Skip, residents of Kanab the author interviewed were: Calvin C. Johnson, Jeff Johnson, Leola Scheonfeld, and the late Merrill MacDonald, Mason Meeks, Merrill Johnson and Dunk Findlay; also, the late Mel Schoppman and Bill Leach of Page, Arizona, and George Fisher of Las Vegas. There was also Bryce Canyon ranger Nate Inouye, plus Gayle L. Pollock of the Natural History Association; St. George BLM employees Tom Folks, Mike Small & Jennifer Jack; also the head of the newly-created Vermilion Cliffs National Monument which is headquartered out of St. George, Becky Hammond; plus BLM employees in Kanab Pete Kilborne, Bill Booker, Mary Dewitz & Mary Cassidy. Mike Salamanca, the one who replaced Skip as the Paria Ranger, proofread and helped update the 3rd Edition.

In the Bryce Valley towns, the author interviewed Ken Goulding Sr., Layton Smith, Marian Clark, Joe Dunham, Kay Clark and Herm Pollock (all deceased), and Ralph & Jack Chynoweth, Bob Ott, George Thompson, and Wallace Ott. Nearly all of these people were in their 70's or older when interviewed, while Marian Clark & Wallace Ott, were in their 90's; therefore lots of good information was gathered about the canyons, trails & old roads, early-day ranchers and oil wells.

Others who contributed with information or fotographs for this 4th Edition were Ken Goulding, Jr., Don Mangum, Fred Syrett, Charley Francisco, Ferrell Brinkerhoff, Desmond Twitchell, Mae Pollock Chynoweth, Jim Ott, Thayne Smith, Twila Mangum Irwin, Dale Mangum, Darrell Blackwell, Joe Thompson, Don Chynoweth, Mary Jane Chynoweth Fuller, LaKay Clark Quilter, Merrilyn Johnson Cornell, Tom H. Morris, JR Jones, Lula Chynoweth Moore, Iris Smith Bushnell, Afton Pollock, Hobart Feltner, Rhoda Henderson Shafer and Kay Sturdevant.

My mother Venetta B. Kelsey, was still able to watch after the business when the author was on the road.

The Author

The author, who was born in 1943, experienced his earliest years of life in eastern Utah's Uinta Basin, first on a farm east of Myton, then in or near Roosevelt. In 1954, the family moved to Provo and he attended Provo High School and later Brigham Young University, where he earned a B.S. degree in Sociology. Shortly thereafter, he discovered that was the wrong subject, so he attended the University of Utah, where he received his Master of Science degree in Geography (minoring in Geology), finishing classes in June, 1970.

It was then real life began, for on June 9, 1970, he put a pack on his back and started traveling for the first time. Since then he has seen 223 countries, republics, islands, or island groups. All this wandering has resulted in self-publishing 16 books. Here are his books as of 2004, listed in the order they were first published: *Climber's and Hiker's Guide to the World's Mountains & Volcanos (4th Edition); Utah Mountaineering Guide (3rd Edition); China on Your Own, and the Hiking Guide to China's Nine Sacred Mountains (3rd Ed.) Out of Print; Canyon Hiking Guide to the Colorado Plateau (4th Edition); Hiking and Exploring Utah's San Rafael Swell (3rd Edition); Hiking and Exploring Utah's Henry Mountains and Robbers Roost (Revised Edition); Hiking and Exploring the Paria River (4th Edition); Hiking and Climbing in the Great Basin National Park (Wheeler Peak, Nevada) Out of Print; Boater's Guide to Lake Powell (4th Edition); Climbing and Exploring Utah's Mt. Timpanogos; River Guide to Canyonlands National Park & Vicinity; Hiking, Biking and Exploring Canyonlands National Park & Vicinity; The Story of Black Rock, Utah; Hiking, Climbing and Exploring Western Utah's Jack Watson's Ibex Country; and Technical Slot Canyon Guide to the Colorado Plateau.*

He has also helped his mother Venetta Bond Kelsey write and publish a book about the one-horse town she was born & raised in, *Life on the Black Rock Desert--A History of Clear Lake, Utah.*

Grosvenor Arch as it appeared in 12/2003. Now there's a restroom and picnic tables next to the parking place, and a cement walk-way to the base of the arch.

Introduction to the Paria River Country

The Paria River begins at Bryce Canyon National Park and nearby high plateaus, and flows almost due south across the Utah-Arizona state line ending at the Colorado River and Lee's Ferry. After the Grand Canyon, Zion Narrows and the Escalante River system, this river basin has more visitors than any other canyon drainage on the Colorado Plateau. If you like narrow canyons, including the best slot canyon in the world, this is the place for you. One can take day-hikes in some of the shorter tributaries, or go on a week-long marathon walk in the lower end of the Paria Canyon. The northern half of the area covered by this book is now included in the western part of the Grand Staircase-Escalante National Monument (GSENM).

The Paria River drainage is located about halfway between Kanab, Utah, and Page, Arizona, and right in the middle of some of the best hiking parts of the Colorado Plateau. To the west is Kanab, St. George and Zion National Park; to the north is Richfield, Panguitch, and the Bryce Valley towns of Tropic, Cannonville, and Henrieville; to the northeast is Capitol Reef National Park, Torrey, Boulder and Escalante; to the south is Flagstaff, and to the southeast is Page and Lake Powell.

Local Towns and Facilities

In the last few years, since tourism has been so important to the local economies, better accommodations and roads have been built. Here's a rundown on what's where in the immediate area. Population figures are from **2000.**

Page, Arizona (population 6809) This town was built to house & accommodate the workers who built Glen Canyon Dam across the Colorado River creating Lake Powell. Today it's the southern gateway to Lake Powell and the local headquarters for the National Park Service, which administers Glen Canyon National Recreational Area. Page has 2 supermarkets, a good shopping center in the middle of town, and a new shopping mall south of town. Page is full of tourists, as well as Navajos from the reservation, and slows down only in about 3 months of winter. There are many motels and other facilities, and a good place to shop for about everything.

Kanab (population 3564) Kanab is a little smaller than Page, and it's more quiet--mainly because the reservation and lake are farther away. Kanab has one large supermarket, a smaller one, plus numerous convenience stores. Its facilities are similar to those of Page, with many motels, gas stations and restaurants. Kanab is the Kane County seat, and has 2 book stores, an airport, and golf course. Kanab has been the movie capital of southern Utah and is the jumping-off point to the north rim of the Grand Canyon, which is open from about mid-May until late October. Kanab has a BLM office (north end of town), the headquarters for the newly created GSENM (in the center of Kanab), and a new GSENM visitor center just east of town next to the golf course.

Panguitch (population 1623) This town is located just northwest of Bryce Canyon National Park and is half the size of Kanab. Panguitch is the Garfield County seat and has moderately good facilities, including one small supermarket, and many motels and restaurants. Panguitch still depends on farming and ranching for support, but in the warmer half of the year it's busy with tourists.

Bryce Canyon Facilities Along the highway between Panguitch and Bryce Canyon National Park, are many motels, convenience stores, gas stations and independent campsites. On the Paunsaugunt Plateau, and just north of the entrance to the park, is Ruby's Inn. This is a huge complex, with gas station & garage facilities, store (including curios and guidebooks), restaurant, laundry center, campground, horseback rides, a rodeo 3 nights a week in season, and helicopter rides into the park. The Bryce Canyon airport is just north of Ruby's Inn, and they have fixed-wing planes for tourist flights. Some of these facilities are now open year-round.

Inside the national park are 2 campgrounds, open in summers only. Bryce also has an historic old lodge and cabins for rent, and they're open from early April through October.

Tropic (population 508) This is the biggest town in Bryce Valley, and it's where the area's high school is located. Tropic has a gas station along with a small supermarket, several motels plus bed & breakfast establishments, a burger & malt shop (it's open from about Easter until after the deer hunt, at the end of October); and one garage, the only one in the valley. The burger stand, gas station and motels are open on Sundays, everything else is closed. As time goes on, Tropic is becoming more dependent on tourism, less dependent on farming & ranching.

Cannonville (population 148) This small town in Bryce Valley is located at the junction of Highway 12 and the paved road running to Kodachrome Basin, and the Cottonwood Wash Road. Cannonville has one business complex called the Grand Staircase Inn. This is a motel, store, restaurant and gas station all in one large building. One block west of that is a Koa Campground, and a block south of the inn is the new GSENM visitor center which is right on the road to Kodachrome Basin. This visitor center was first opened in 2003; it's closed in winter--Mid-November to roughly Mid-March (?).

Kodachrome Basin State Park In 1987, Bob Ott and family from Cannonville, opened a small camper's store in the state park just south of the campground. They now have full-service cabins, a new camper's store, plus horseback & wagon rides, and cater to senior citizens and campers. The campground has showers and a dump station. There's now a paved road all the way from Cannonville to Kodachrome Basin, and throughout the park.

Henrieville (population 159) Henrieville, which is also in Bryce Valley, no longer has any retail businesses in town. About the only public buildings there are the church and post office.

Escalante (population 818) A town full of ranchers, farmers, former sawmill workers, and a growing number of BLM, Forest Service and National Park Service personnel. It has at least 3 gas stations, several motels, 2 small supermarkets, several restaurants, and one burger stand, which does a good business in the spring, summer and fall, with the hikers heading into the Escalante River country.

5

There's a new multiagency visitor center on the west end of town, plus nearby offices for the BLM, Forest Service and the National Park Service.

Road Report

For the most part, access to most of the canyons in this book is reasonably good. If you're going down the Lower Paria River Gorge, you're in luck; you only have to drive about 3 kms on a graveled, all-weather road, and you're at the White House Trailhead. At the bottom end of the river, which is Lee's Ferry, you'll be on pavement all the way. For the rest of the hikes, with the exception of those inside Bryce Canyon National Park, you'll have to do some driving on dirt or sandy roads, but as a general rule, most of the hikes featured in this book are easy to get to with an ordinary car in dry weather.

Skutumpah Road This is a main link between the little community of Johnson, located about 16 kms (10 miles) due east of Kanab, and the Bryce Valley towns of Cannonville, Henrieville and Tropic. The Skutumpah Road itself begins at the head of Johnson Canyon, where the road divides and the pavement ends; at that point one road goes northwest to Alton, while the Skutumpah Road heads northeast to Cannonville. It's 99.5 kms (61.8 miles) from Kanab to Cannonville, first along Highway 89, then up Johnson Canyon, and finally along the Skutumpah Road.

The road up Johnson Canyon is paved up to the Alton--Skutumpah Junction, then it's graveled up to about the Deer Springs Ranch. After that it's maintained and graded, but made out of whatever material the road passes over. In places it's just ordinary dirt; other places it's gravely, and still other places it's made of clay. When it rains only lightly, it seldom affects the road. All you have to do is wait 'till the sun hits it a few minutes, and away you go. **When heavy rains soak the area, it may be a one or two-day wait in the warmer season before this road is passable; maybe a week's wait--or longer--during the winter seaon.**

For the most part, this road is closed in winter, but 4WD's sometimes do it, especially during dry spells, or in the morning hours when the road bed is frozen. However, on the dugway just south and above Willis Creek, is a seep next to the road. This sometimes makes the road icy in winter, and 4WD's occasionally slide off. For the most part, the Skutumpah Road is open for all traffic from sometime in March or the first part of April through mid-November, but each year is different. Because there are a number of ranches (and in recent years summer homes) along this road, it's well-maintained, and carries up to 40 or 50 cars a day during the warm season when it's dry. Expect traffic to increase because of the newly created national monument.

Cottonwood Wash Road The Cottonwood Wash Road runs south out of Cannonville, to and past Kodachrome Basin State Park, to Grosvenor Arch, down the Cockscomb Valley (Cottonwood Wash or Canyon), and eventually to Highway 89, at a point between mile posts 17 & 18.

The Cottonwood Wash Road was built in 1957 by a cooperative effort organized by then 72-year-old Sam Pollock of Tropic, who wasn't paid a dime for his efforts. It included people from Bryce Valley, Escalante and Antimony. That group of people wanted a shortcut to the Lake Powell area to increase tourism in their own little area.

For the job, Pollock leased a bulldozer from the Soil Conservation Service and it was operated by Harvey Liston; a road grader was borrowed from Garfield Country, and it was driven by Loral Barton; Byron Davis donated a compressor and helped run it (it was used for only 9 days, and they blasted in only 2 places). Doyle Clark also helped on the operation. It took 100 days for planning, engineering and construction, but only 70 days to complete once they got rolling. The project was started on June 28, and completed in early October of 1957. A dedication ceremony was held at Rush Bed Spring.

The state of Utah had surveyed 2 routes for a road to Page and the Glen Canyon Dam. They chose the route east from Kanab because it was cheaper and less complicated to build. The other more direct route through Cannonville and Cottonwood Wash would have cost $9.5 million. The road Sam Pollock built cost $5500. They got the money to build it from Garfield County, and from donations & sales of various kinds. Today it's a maintained county road.

That part of the Cottonwood Wash Road running from Cannonville to Kodachrome Basin is now paved. East of the Kodachrome Basin Turnoff (KBT), the road is made of sand, dirt and/or clay and in good weather is used by maybe 200-300 cars daily. Expect traffic to increase because of the new GSENM.

For the most part, this is a warm weather, summertime road, as there are slick spots in places whenever it rains hard making it impassable. When it's wet, not even 4WD's can make it! The spots that become extremely slick are made of the gray-colored clay beds of the Tropic Shale that are in the middle and lower end of the canyon. Whenever it rains hard, water flows across the road because there are few bridges or culverts, and no barrow pits or proper drainage. After floods, and after it dries a few days, a Kane County road crew out of Kanab (Tele. 435-644-5312) has to grade it again and again. Don't expect this road to be upgraded in the near future because it's in Kane County, and those people want tourists to drive through Kanab to reach Bryce Canyon National Park and Bryce Valley.

Nipple Ranch Road This is a maintained county road to the Nipple Ranch just northwest of Mollies Nipple. It begins at Highway 89, right at mile post 37, and runs north to an old oil well drill site north of Kitchen Canyon called Oil Well Hill. This is a graded road, but it gradually deteriorates the further north you drive. In its northern parts just west of Mollies Nipple, there are several big sand traps. If you don't have a 4WD, forget going over the pass and down to the Nipple Ranch. Beyond that pass, there is deep sand for 3-4 kms across the bottom of upper Kitchen Canyon. Because of the sand, this is one of the few roads which will be easier and safer to drive if the surface is wet, because sand sets-up and becomes more firm when wet. This road will get you close to the middle part of the Upper Paria River Gorge, plus Deer Creek and surrounding canyons.

House Rock Valley Road This maintained county road runs from Highway 89 just west of The Cockscomb (between mile posts 25 & 26), south to Highway 89A (between mile posts 565 & 566) where an old ranch called House Rock, is located. This is the approach road to the Buckskin Gulch and Wire Pass Trailheads, and to the several entry points to Coyote Buttes and the Sand Hills or Paria Plateau. The road runs for 48.1 kms (29.9 miles), from highway to highway. Normally it's open almost year-round, but in winter, or right after heavy rains, it will be slick in places. In recent years the state of Arizona has improved its half of the road by hauling in gravel to cover the clay beds, most of which are near the Utah-Arizona line (Arizona has made a campground immediately south of the state line). Road crews in Utah usually work the road over in April each year, or when there's a little moisture in the area. It's periodically closed during and right after flash floods. During the warmer half of the year it has moderately heavy traffic (including cars) for such an out-of-the-way road.

Pahreah Road The road to the Old Pahreah townsite and the Paria Movie Set leaves Highway 89 between mile posts 30 & 31 about halfway between Page & Kanab This is a good 10 km (6 mile) road, which is well-used in the warmer half of the year. In winter it may be slick in spots, because most of it runs along the Moenkopi clay beds. It is definitely impassable during or just after heavy rains, but ordinarily it's a good road for all vehicles.

Cedar Mountain Road This road leaves Highway 89 between mile posts 17 & 18, right across the highway from the beginning of the Cottonwood Wash Road, but heads south, then east to the top of East Clark Bench, Flat Top and Cedar Mountain. This is the area north of the Lower Paria River Gorge, and this road gives access to the north rim of that canyon. This is a sandy road all the way, but it's graded occasionally up to the communications facility near where the road passes under the power lines. After that it gets even more sandy and you'll normally need a HCV & 4WD to success-fully get through the sandier places along a loop on top of Cedar Mountain. Wet conditions makes this road better because it's sandy.

Here are some tips for driving the back roads of the Paria country. First, when you leave pavement, stop and **reduce the air pressure** in your tires. The author runs at about 38-40 lbs on the highways (for better fuel economy), then reduces it to about 20-25 lbs for dirt or gravel roads. If the road gets real sandy and getting stuck seems imminent, then tire pressure is reduced again to about 10 or 15 lbs. Reduced tire pressure puts more rubber to the road and increases traction. It also reduces the chance of sharp stones bruising or puncturing your tires, as well as gives you a smoother ride.

Emergency Provisions for your Car

Everyone reading this book should remember that once you leave the paved highways, some parts of the Paria River Country are very isolated. Special care should be taken in planning for a worse-case emergency situation. Perhaps the thing you need most is a **reliable vehicle,** one you can depend on. Besides that, here is a list of things everyone should have in their vehicle before ventur-ing out into remote areas. Take a **full tank of fuel**, and depending on where you're going and the size of your fuel tank, maybe extra fuel. Also, take most of the **tools** you own, plus a **tow rope** or **chain, battery jumper cable, shovel, tire pump & gauge, extra oil, matches** or **cigarette lighters,** some kind of **first aid kit, tire chains for winter driving**, and a **good spare tire** (check the air pressure before leaving home).

Also, take more **food** than you think you'll need, and if you're heading to a far away place, espe-cially in hot summer weather, take lots of **water and/or liquids**. This writer is always alone and dur-ing hot weather and in remote places, he starts out with as much as 35-40 liters of water, fruit juice and soda pop. That's about 10 gallons! In summer heat you'll drink about 3-4 times more than in the cooler months. Also, consider taking more clothing than you think you'll need. In spring or fall, weath-er can turn from summer to winter in a matter of hours. Also, always let someone know exactly where you're going and when you expect to return. The main thing to remember is, **GO PREPARED** for any problem that might arise!

Off Road Vehicles

Perhaps the most contentious issue on public lands policy involves the use of **off road vehicles**. These come in all sizes & shapes, from **motorcycles** to all terrain vehicles **(ATV's)** to **4WD's** of all kinds (pickups & SUV's). They're now everywhere on our public lands and running around free as birds; and no one seems to know what to do about it. These people and their vehicles are not only using public lands, but **abusing** them as well. This is the heart of the problem and at the center of all arguments about the use of public lands today.

In the Grand Staircase-Escalante National Monument (GSENM), which is run by the BLM, the fight has escalated with Monument BLM crews erecting signs of road or ATV track closures, and the local sheriff pulling them down. This battle over the definition of what is, and what is not a road, has been going on for a long time in southern Utah and will likely go on for a while longer. It's in the court sys-tem as this book goes to press.

At some time in the future, it's hoped that some homemade ATV or 4WD tracks will be closed per-manently. In the meantime, maybe we all need to think about the use of public lands, as opposed to the abuse of what little virgin country we have left. There's not a private landowner in this country or the world who would allow ORV enthusiasts to use his/her property like they've been using/abusing public lands for so many years! Before it's too late, **please keep your vehicle on an established and designated road.**

Best Time to Hike

For those heading into the Lower Paria River Gorge, the ideal time for hiking in the spring is from about late March through the end of May (but late May through June for the Buckskin Gulch). For some of the canyons higher in the drainage, April through mid-June is usually the best time. The biggest problem with going into the Lower Paria Canyon in cold weather is that you'll be wading in water most of the time, and in the early morning hours your feet will feel like blocks of ice!

In the fall season and in the lower gorge, mid or late September into late October is preferred, but higher in the drainage, early September through October is usually best, although snow can come dur-ing that time. For the high country hikes in Bryce Canyon and Table Cliff Plateau, the warmer months, or from about late May through October are usually the best, but early or late bad weather spells can shorten the season. If you're not wading, then late February and March, and November can be rea-sonably good times to hike in various parts of this canyon country.

The time of year when the flash flood danger in the narrow slot canyons is highest, is from about mid-July through August (the worst time) extending to mid or late September. Regardless of the time of year, one should always stay tuned to the local radio stations and have a generally good weather forecast before entering places like the Buckskin Gulch. The employee at the Paria Ranger Station & Visitor Center, always has the latest weather forecast posted in front of the ranger station **on the back side of the information board.** Always stop there and check things out before entering any narrow canyon.

With increased visitor use, especially during April & May, and October, consider going in the hotter summer months of June, July and August. There's a lot of good dry weather then, and if you're going into the slot canyons, the temperatures there are much cooler than out in the open.

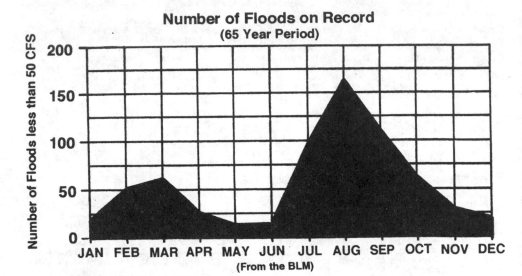

Number of Floods on Record
(65 Year Period)
(From the BLM)

Drinking Water

In recent years there seems to be great controversy over what is and what is not suitable drinking water in the backcountry. The US Public Health Service requires the National Park Service and the BLM to inform hikers to boil all surface water, including water coming directly from springs. This seems to leave little room for common sense. The chief reason they do it, is to save themselves from possible lawsuits.

Here are some steps the author has taken to prevent getting a bellyache while hiking in the Paria River country and elsewhere. On day hikes he always carries a plastic bottle full of tap or culinary water. However, if he passes a good spring, which is obviously unpolluted, he normally drinks from it because it's often colder. An unpolluted spring is basically one which cattle or other animals cannot get into. If it is free-flowing, comes right out of the ground or rock wall, and has no fresh signs of cattle nearby, then it should be at least reasonably safe to drink as-is (?).

When it comes to some of the small side-canyon streams, the thing you'll have to look for is any fresh sign of cattle. If there are cattle in the area, then you'd better purify or filter any running water. But if it's summer, and the cattle have been taken out of the canyons to higher summer ranges, and the water is free flowing, then the risks are lower. The Giardia cysts cannot swim; they can only float downstream. After a flash flood, most side-canyon streams have better water than before, because all the poop has been washed away.

The chief reason for taking precautions is to escape the intestinal disorder called **Giardiasis**. This is caused by the microscopic organism, Giardia Lamblia. Giardia are carried in the feces of humans and some domestic and wild animals. The cysts of Giardia may contaminate surface water supplies. The symptoms of this stomach problem include diarrhea, increased gas, loss of appetite, abdominal cramps and bloating. It is not life-threatening, but it can slow you down and make life miserable. If you take the precautions mentioned above and below, you'll surely miss out on this one.

If you're still not convinced, you can buy a water filter for $30-$40, and up. You can also buy small bottles of Iodine tablets for about $3-$4 (containing 50 tablets--one per liter). On all overnight hikes, the author carries a bottle of Iodine tablets, but rarely uses them.

Here's a tip for those who will spend several days in the Lower Paria Canyon Gorge camping. Take along one or more large water jugs--3.78 liters or one US gallon. This will enable you to carry water from a spring to your campsite, which may be a ways from a good water supply. Available water and possible hazards are discussed under each hike.

Insect Season

For the most part, insects are not a serious problem in the Paria River country. The insect season seems to begin in late May, and continues to about mid-July in most of the Paria River drainage. In the wider parts of the canyons above both Lee's Ferry and Old Pahreah, there are small **gnats** which get into your hair and bite. One remedy for this is to wear a hat of some kind. Sometimes insect repellent helps. In these same open areas there can be large gray deer or **horse flies** which bite the back of bare legs. Wearing long pants takes care of this problem. These horse flies are always found around areas where there's water and tamaracks and other brush. For some reason they mostly disappear in about mid-July, or about when the first monsoon rains begin. In the fall there seems to be a general absence of these pests, especially from mid-September on.

The author can't remember any of these pesky insects in the narrow canyons, such as the Buckskin; nor can he remember any mosquitoes, except in swampy places (or in some narrow slots after floods have left pools of water), such as around Adair Lake. Nor can he remember any mosquitoes in the Lower Paria River Gorge. He has been there no less than a dozen trips over the years, and in all seasons.

Equipment for Day-Hikes

For those with less experience, here's a list of things the author normally takes on day-hikes. You may want to add to this list. A small-to-medium-sized day-pack, a one or 2-liter bottle of water (up to 4 liters on hot summer days!), camera & lenses, extra film or digital memory card, extra batteries for digital cameras, a short piece of nylon rope or parachute cord, toilet paper, pen & small notebook, map, chapstick, compass, altimeter watch, pocket knife, a walking stick (in the Lower Paria River Gorge) for probing deep holes in the sometimes-murky water (perhaps a ski pole with a camera clamp on top which substitutes as a camera stand), a cap with a "sun shield" or "cancer curtain" sewn on around the back, a pair of long pants (for colder temperatures or possibly deer/horse flies or other insects) and a lunch for longer hikes.

In warmer weather, he wears shorts and a T-shirt; in cooler weather, long pants and a long-sleeved shirt, plus perhaps a jacket and gloves. In cooler weather and with more things to carry, a larger day-pack may be needed.

Equipment for Overnight Hikes

Here's a list of things the author normally takes on overnight hikes. You may add to this list as well. A large pack, sleeping bag, sleeping pad (Thermal Rest), tent--with rain sheet, small kerosene (your choice) stove, several lighters (no more matches!), 10m or more of nylon cord or light rope, camera & lenses, extra film or memory card & batteries for digital cameras, sometimes a walking stick for the Lower Paria, one large water jug, a one or 2 liter water bottle, a stitching awl & waxed thread, small pliers, canister with odds and ends (bandaids, needle & thread, patching kit for sleeping pad, wire, pens, etc.), maps, small notebook, reading book, chapstick, compass, altimeter watch, toilet paper, pocket knife, rain cover for pack, small alarm clock, candles for light & reading (or better still an LED headlamp), tooth brush & toothpaste, face lotion, sunscreen, cap with cancer curtain, soap, small flashlight, long pants and long-sleeved shirt, and maybe a lightweight coat and gloves. Also, a plastic bowl, cup, spoon, small cooking pot and extra fuel for the stove.

Food usually includes such items as oatmeal or cream of wheat cereal, coffee or chocolate drink, powdered milk, sugar, cookies, crackers, candy, oranges or apples, carrots, Ramen instant noodles, soups, macaroni, canned tuna fish or sardines, Vienna sausages, peanuts, instant puddings, bread, butter, peanut butter and salt & pepper.

Boots or Shoes

Because many of the canyons you'll be hiking in have running water, you'll want some kind of a boot or shoe which can be used when wet--some kind of a wading shoe. Most people just use an ordinary pair of running shoes, but here are some precautions: (1) If the shoes are too worn out, you may lose them before the hike ends, especially if taking in all of the Lower Paria Gorge. (2) If the running shoe is too old, it may lack proper support for the foot--a tip for older hikers. (3) A shoe made of canvas, rubber or nylon will last longer in a watery situation, than one with leather parts. (4) Leather shoes should be treated with oil after a trip with wading, such as through the Upper or Lower Paria Canyon. (5) You might consider starting with an older pair of shoes, but have an extra lightweight pair in your pack.

Hiking Rules and Regulations

Bryce Canyon National Park

There are some rules to backpacking in Bryce Canyon, as there are in any of our national parks. If you're planning to camp overnight in the backcountry, then you'll need a **camping permit**. Pick this up at the park visitor center, along with any other last minute information. You must camp in designated campsites only, and use a stove of some kind--no camp fires allowed. Camping is limited to 3 days in any one site. **If day-hiking, no permit is needed**. No wheeled vehicles of any kind are allowed on the backcountry trails. Get all the latest information at the visitor center just as you enter the park and just west of the Fee Gate. Or see their website at **www.nps.gov/brca**.

There aren't many hikers camping in the backcountry of Bryce Canyon. One big reason is, there is very little live running water in the park. Largely because of this, most people do day-hikes only.

Paria Canyon & Buckskin Gulch--Vermilion Cliffs Wilderness Area

Here's a list of regulations pertaining to the **Lower Paria River Gorge** between the **White House Trailhead** and **Lee's Ferry**. This also includes the popular **Buckskin Gulch**, the main tributary to the lower Paria.

Day Hiking

1. No Reservations needed for day-hiking. The **$5 fee** per person/per day may be paid, and hiking information obtained, at kiosks located at each trailhead. Be sure to have the **correct change** upon arrival. You are asked to obtain an envelope at the trailhead, fill in the blanks, tear off the stub placing that in the windshield area of your car; then place the $5 in the envelope and drop that in the metal box provided.
2. There is no quota on the number of day-hikers in these canyons. Everyone who comes, can hike.
3. Group size is limited to 10.
4. No overnight camping without a permit.
5. Dogs are not allowed within the permit areas of the Lower Paria River Canyon or the Buckskin Gulch.
6. Children under the age of 12 hike free.

Overnight Hiking & Camping
1. Permits Required: Reservations are most likely required in the busy seasons of spring & fall.
2. For overnight camping anywhere in the canyon(s), $5 per person, per night.
3. Only 20 people are allowed to enter the canyons per/day for camping.
4. If you arrive at the Paria Ranger Station & Visitor Center (or the BLM offices in St. George or Kanab--see addresses below) and there are slots available, then you can get a permit on the spot without reservations. Midsummer sees fewer hikers, and in winter (November through early March) there are few, if any hikers, so you can often pickup a permit on the spot for these time periods. Call or go to their website.
5. Maximum group size 10.
6. Dogs not allowed in the canyon.
7. No refunds or changes allowed to the permit

How to get a permit--Online Reservation Method
To quickly view available hiking dates, secure a reservation, and pay fees (credit card only), please consult the Paria Canyon Project Website at **www.az.blm.gov/paria**. If you do not have access to the Internet, or cannot obtain access at your local library, contact staff at the Arizona Strip Interpretive Association (ASIA) at 435-688-3246; or at the Kanab BLM Office at 435-644-4600, and they will access the website for you.

Or **Mail** your request and payment of fees to: ASIA, Paria Project, 345 East Riverside Drive, St. George, Utah, 84790; or the Kanab BLM Office, 318 North, 100 East, Kanab, Utah, 84741.

Or **Fax** your request and credit card payment to ASIA, Paria Permits, 435-688-3258; or Kanab BLM Office, 435-644-4620.

Once your hiking date is reserved, a permit & map will be mailed to you or you may choose to pick it up at one of the BLM offices listed above, or the Paria River Ranger Station & Visitor Center (by 2004 the visitor center may be hooked up to the internet?).

Other Information or Recommendations
1. Use existing campsites rather than creating new ones.
2. Trenching around tents is not needed in the canyons.
3. If camping in one of The Confluence campsites, please carry out your human waste in plastic bags. They may give you one at the Kanab BLM office, or at the Paria River Ranger Station & Visitor Center. For those going all the way downcanyon to Lee's Ferry, this isn't as critical--nobody will carry a bag of crap for 3 or 4 days anyway, so bury that waste in a cat hole and cover it. Try to defecate or urinate anywhere but near a regularly-used campsite.
4. Wash without soap to minimize water contamination or use a biodegradable soap away from water sources. Carry water away from the stream and wash dishes away from campsites.
5. Don't leave any food scraps (or any garbage of any kind) at campsites. It will only attract flies and make the next campers miserable.
6. There is no water at any trailhead so have some before you arrive, or get water at the well & tap 50m west of the Paria Ranger Station & Visitor Center.
7. If you plan to do the entire canyon hike from White House Trailhead (or walk through the Buckskin Gulch) to Lee's Ferry, call the BLM office in Kanab at 435-644-4600, and ask if they have a list of people who perform shuttle service between Whitehouse Trailhead and Lee's Ferry. Or better still, go to the website **www.az.blm.gov/paria**, and click on **Shuttles**. Here's what you may find: Barry Warren, PO Box 7041, Page, AZ, Tele. 928-640-0191; Betty Price, Tele. 928-355-2252; Canyon Country Outback Tours, Wally Thomson, Tele. 888-783-3807, or 435-644-3807; Marble Canyon Lodge, Catalina Martinez, Tele. 928-355-2295, or 928-355-2225; Paria Outpost, Susan & Stephen Dodson, PO Box 410075, Big Water, Utah, 84741, Tele. 928-691-1047.

Coyote Buttes Information
To get into Coyote Buttes, and more specifically to **The Wave**, the most popular destination around, you must get a permit and pay a $5 fee. Each day 20 permits are given out to the North Coyote Buttes & The Wave; 10 of which you have to make reservations for, 10 are given out as walk-ins (also 20 to the South Coyote Buttes, but these are very easy to get and reservations are not needed). Read more about the Coyote Buttes Special Management Area in the Hiking Section, **Map 35**, for all the rules & regulations.

Comments--This is your land, write letters--be heard
As this book goes to press, the BLM is in the never-ending process of retooling their management plan for the Paria River & Buckskin Gulch, as well as the Coyote Buttes & The Wave. If you have any disagreements with their policy and/or suggestions to offer on how they can improve the situation in this part of the Paria River drainage, you're urged to write to the **BLM--Paria River Project, 345 E. Riverside Drive, St. George, Utah, 84790, Tele. 435-688-3246; or BLM, 318 North 100 East, Kanab, Utah, 84741, Tele. 435-644-4600.**

This is your land, not theirs, and these people work for you & me. Generally speaking, the BLM is about as good as any government agency when it comes to listening to people's' concerns, which in the end, helps them set policy. The bean counters in St. George & Kanab do count letters, especially if the writer has legitimate and thoughtful proposals--not just complaints.

Here are some complaints this writer has regarding **Coyote Buttes & The Wave.** He has talked to no less than a dozen hikers in the last few years, and none have ever seen 20 permittees out there! One friend went there on December 26, 2002, and never saw a soul, even though the 10 reserved permits were filled. Some people think this may be the work of wilderness radicals just filling the slots with no intention of going there, just to keep others out. Or it may be professional photographers who reserve several days permits to insure they have a fighting chance to be there on a sunny day! Because of this, the author believes more permits can & should be issued on the spot as walk-ins, and maybe fewer reserved. Why not issue 25 or 30 walk-ins (or more), and only 5 or 10 permits with reservations? One argument for giving out so few permits is, the powers that be in the BLM, wants everybody to have a true wilderness experience! For that, there are a million other places in southern Utah you can be alone. Is going to some place with up to 19 other people a true wilderness experience?

Throughout the Coyote Buttes, it's nothing but sand & slickrock and the author has never seen any negative effects on the land due to hikers. With every rainstorm, or the passing of every cold front with subsequent winds, trails in the sand disappear in minutes. And you can't see any effects on the slickrock.

Apparently some fotographers claimed to have seen a slight gray smudging in the middle of The Wave due to people walking right on what everybody wants to take pictures of, but this writer has never seen it. If that should ever be a problem, then hikers can be asked to take off their shoes at the beginning of The Wave. Beside, with every rainstorm, any sole mark gets washed off--that's how canyons are made, by naturally weathering away.

Another point. BLM rangers who go to The Wave, regularly kick over stone cairns (piles of stones) that hikers erect so that others can more easily find the way. This is not an easy place to find, espe-cially right after a storm with lots of wind & rain! Since most people going there don't know how to rear a map or use a compass, why not erect a line of cairns to lead the way? There would be must less impact on the area if there was a single marked trail or route, instead of a dozen. This has to be the only place in the world where land managers want to eliminate any semblance of a trail. In every other wilderness area this writer has seen, rangers want everyone to stay on one narrow path, leaving everywhere else pristine.

Visitor Use in the Lower Paria River Gorge

The diagram below shows the number of visitors (those who volunteered to sign their names) to the Lower Paria River Gorge and the Buckskin Gulch during the 1994-1996 seasons. These figures should give you some idea of when to go to avoid the biggest crowds.

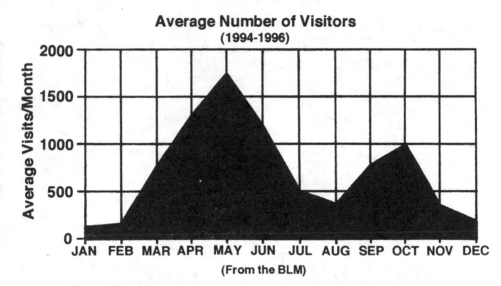

Average Number of Visitors
(1994-1996)

(From the BLM)

Hiking Maps for the Paria River Country

Shown on the next page is an index map showing most of the USGS topographic maps of the region. Any serious hiker should get one or several of the maps shown on this index.

There used to be 3 sets of maps for the area. They include: the USGS or BLM metric maps at **1:100,000 scale**; the mostly-new and highly detailed series at **1:24,000 scale (7 1/2' quads)**; and there used to be maps at **1:62,500 scale (15 minute)**, but they're no longer being printed. However, some may still be available.

For driving & orientation, the author prefers the newer metric maps, and uses these frequently. If you buy the 3 most important maps--**Kanab, Smoky Mountain,** and **Glen Canyon Dam,** you can hike and tour almost the entire region. Other than these, you'll need the **Escalante** map for a couple of hikes, and the **Panguitch** map covers the northern end of the Skutumpah Road and Bryce Canyon. Also, the **Fredonia** map covers the House Rock Valley Road and part of the Coyote Buttes. For those people who want to hike the Upper Paria River Gorge, Hackberry Canyon and The Cockscomb, then the Kanab & Smoky Mountain maps just about cover it all. Only one small corner of the Panguitch map might help with the Upper Paria River hike.

One reason the author likes the metric maps is they are relatively new, all dating after 1980, so nearly all present-day roads are shown. These maps are the best for driving. Some of the 1:24,000 scale maps date from the 1950's, and lack some of the newer roads, but if you want detail, these are the ones. The only disadvantage to these is that you may have to have several maps to cover one hike; whereas usually just one metric map covers several hikes. The metric maps also fold up and fit in your pocket.

For those who don't understand metrics, you can still get along with these maps because they're laid out in one square mile sections. Since all land was surveyed in these section & townships grids, it seems we will never get away from this old system entirely.

For the Lower Paria River Gorge, you might find 3 USGS maps at 1:62,500 scale, **Paria, Paria**

Plateau and **Lee's Ferry.** These are no longer being printed, so if you see any, buy them quick! For this hike, these maps are the very best. Or you might buy the USGS publication titled **MF-1475-- Miscellaneous Field Studies.** In this series of 4 maps, A, B, C & D, Geology, Geochemical Data, Mines & Prospects, and Mineral Resource Potential are covered . Map C or D might be the best for hiking the canyon. These maps are at 1:62,500 scale, and are based on the old USGS maps at the same scale. The great thing about these maps is, each one includes all the Lower Paria River Gorge, Lee's Ferry, the Sand Hills-Paria Plateau and the House Rock Valley Road. All on just one map.

Probably the single best map for those hiking from Whitehouse Trailhead to Lee's Ferry, if you can find it, is the old BLM publication, **Hiker's Guide to Paria Canyon.** This map is presently out of stock, but one BLM employee stated it will be reprinted again soon. It's based on the 1:62,500 scale maps, but concentrates on just the lower gorge with numbers indicating springs, abandoned meanders, campsites, etc., but omitting the Paria Plateau or Sand Hills. This map has been replaced by a newer plastic log-book-type booklet map titled, **Hiker's Guide to Paria Canyon.** It shows the entire canyon in 30 short segments. It has river miles, campsites, abandoned meanders and springs labeled. Its disadvantage is that it doesn't show the entire canyon on one map; that's the reason some would also like the return of the other BLM map mentioned above.

The last set of maps you'll want if you're a serious hiker, are the USGS maps at **1:24,000 scale or the 7 1/2' quads.** The maps needed to cover the area from Old Pahreah down to Lee's Ferry are: **Eightmile Pass, Fivemile Valley, Pine Hollow Canyon, West Clark Bench, Bridger Point, Glen Canyon City, Coyote Buttes, Poverty Flat, Wrather Arch, Water Pockets** and **Ferry Swale.** The Index to Topographic Maps (next page) shows the ones you'll need for all hikes in this book. Most of these maps are fairly new and of course very detailed. The only problem with this scale is, they cover a small area and you may have to carry several maps to do just one hike.

Fotography in Deep, Dark, Slot Canyons (Updated--3/2004)

Here are some tips on how to make your pictures better on your first, or next trip down a deep & dark slot canyon. Here's a list of some of the things that often happen. One is, your pictures turn out far too dark. The obvious reason is, the camera just doesn't have the capabilities to take a good foto in low light conditions. Another common result is, the pictures are blurred or out of focus. This is caused by a combination of low light, a slow shutter speed, and no tripod to hold it steady.

Another frequent occurrence is, half of a scene may be very bright or totally washed out; while the other half is dark, sometimes black and shows almost nothing. This is caused by taking a picture with half the scene in bright sunshine; the other half in shade or shadows. This is called a *high contrast scene.* These are the more common problems. Below are some suggestions on how to have a happy ending to your hike.

Cameras and Lenses--Digital and Film

As we all know by now, digital cameras are in the process of replacing film. However, regardless of whether you're shooting film or digitally, most if not all of the basic fotographic principles are the same. The buttons you push, or dials you turn, are a lot different in some cases, but the fundamentals of fotography are still there. Digitals are a new technology and have been prohibitively expensive until recently, but now the prices are coming down and quality going up, even with the low end of the market digitals. Below is about all a semiprofessional knows about cameras & fotography for both film and digital methods.

For the average person the recommended camera has always been a **35mm** with a through-the-lens metering system, along with 3 lenses; one the normal 50mm which used to come with all cameras, a moderately wide angle lens, such as a 24mm, 28mm or 35mm. A lens wider than about 24mm, will distort the foto more than most people want. And some kind of telefoto lens of 90mm up to 200mm or so.

However in recent years, **zoom lenses** have gotten better and today most cameras come with a zoom. People like zooms because one lens can do it all, but foto quality still isn't quite as good as with fixed-focal length lenses such as the standard 50mm. If you do decide on a zoom lens, a 28-80mm is the best for slot canyons. Most of the smaller digitals come with a 3X lens, which is the same as a 35-105mm zoom These appear to be very good quality.

Most of the older **mechanical 35mm film cameras** have a shutter speed ranging from one second up to 1/1000 of a second. With the author's Canon A60 digital, shutter speeds range from 15 seconds to 1/2000, with smaller increments than with film cameras. In darker slot canyons and without a tripod, you'll likely be using shutter speeds from 1/15 or 1/8 of a second or lower, depending on your film speed and lens. You can hand-hold a camera down to about 1/15 of a second if you're steady, or even 1/8 or 1/4 second if you lean your hand & camera against a wall or rock; however in this case the F-stop will be low (F2.8 or F3.5) and getting everything in focus isn't possible. *More on F-stops and focusing below.*

For many years, the author carried a Pentax K-1000, a totally mechanical camera, with a through-the-lens metering system and a screw-on self-timer. In 2001 he went to the newfangled Pentax ZX-30 and/or ZX-50 cameras (every camera company has models to match those from Pentax). These new models have an easy-to-use electronic self-timer and they automatically set shutter speeds from 30 seconds to 1/2000. The new film models are operated by a small computer which does a better job of metering light, especially in very dark conditions, than the older mechanical models. This was the primary reason (and advantage) the author switched film cameras--to get better results in dark slot canyons.

In 2003 and for the 4th Edition of this book, he finally bought a **digital, a Canon A60, 2 mega pixels (mp), F2.8 to F8** (it uses 4 AA batteries which can be bought anywhere). It is the bottom of the line as far as quality digital cameras go, but it's a good place to start and the foto quality at 2mp is good enough for any picture in this book. It has a good self-timer, but the time it gives you is a little short, so you have to run like hell to get in some pictures! It has a very good metering system and in smaller increments than film cameras. It has a dozen shooting modes, including Auto and Aperture Priority (Av), and dozens of other features this writer has yet to figure out! On the back side of his camera, there are several buttons--each digital has them in a different place, but they all seem to do the same thing or are set on the same principle. You'll have to let a sales person at a store specializing in cameras, help you out as far as which buttons do what, or read the operator's manual. Again,

Index to Topographic Maps--Paria River Country

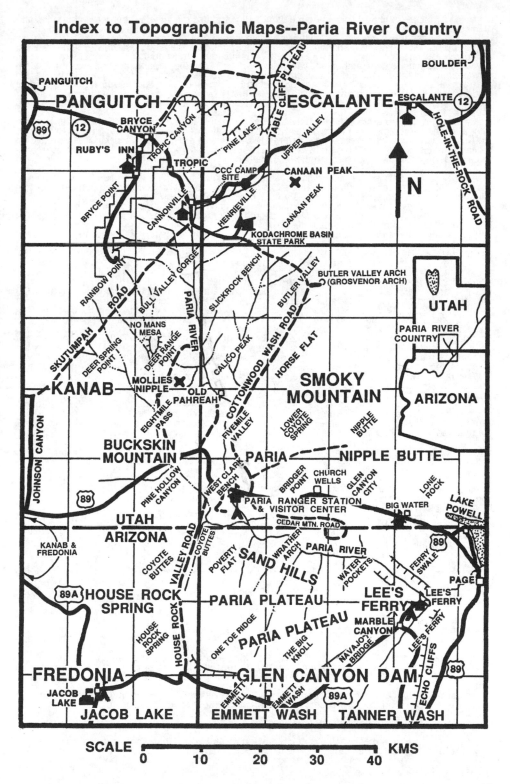

SCALE

| 0 | 10 | 20 | 30 | 40 | KMS |

the basic principles of film & digitals are the same. Buy and use the latest rechargeable batteries and experiment to learn.

Pictures or images taken with a digital camera are stored on small **memory cards** as tiny squares, dots or pixels. A 2mp camera shooting at the highest resolution has 2,000,000 dots per square inch. This gives you very good quality 10 x 15 cm (4"x 6") prints; but if you want to blow them up even more, say to 20 x 25 cms (8" x 10"), then you may want to go to a camera capable of shooting 3, 4 or 5mp. However, and in all honesty, the 20 x 25 cm prints the author has made using images from his Canon A60, are as sharp and clear as with any 35mm film he has tried. If it's detail you want, have prints made on glossy paper--never matt finish! Also, for better picture quality, always squeeze the trigger (shutter release button) slowly, never with a jerk! Remember, the camera dictates shutter release speed, not your finger!

Regarding dots per centimeter/inch, having more pixels means the dots are much smaller to begin with, and when you blow them up, quality remains good. If you want to make poster-size fotos, then the best quality large format film cameras are still the best, but digitals are closing the gap quickly. Digitals capable of shooting 6.3mp now cost about $1000 as this book goes to press. Digital cameras this expensive are SLR's with through-the-lens metering systems. Those shooting 4mp are less than $400. Prices are steadily coming down and quality and mp are constantly going up.

Memory cards coming with most digitals usually hold only 16 or 32mp, but you can buy others at 64, 128, 256, 500mp, or now up to one giga bite of storage. Shooting at 2mp, you can get about 24 fotos on the 16mp cards. The author has a couple of 256mp memory cards and he gets about 375 pictures on each at 2mp--even though the camera indicates you have space for 441. As of 2004, the most-widely used type of memory card was called the **Compact Flash**. Canon & Nikon, and some Fuji, Minolta and Pentax cameras use these.

If you want to make prints, just take your memory card to any foto shop or lab and they can develop just the prints you want from all the digital images. Or for friends, use your computer to burn images onto a CD--which are dirt cheap--then they can take that to a lab for processing.

The quality of the prints depends on which setting you use on your camera. The author's little Canon has 3 settings; 1.9 mp, .8 mp, and .3 mp. If set on the lowest number of pixels, you'll get about 4 times the number of pictures, but prints are of poorer quality.

There are several advantages digitals have over film cameras. The **best advantage** is the **LCD monitor.** The moment you take a picture, you'll see it on the small screen. If you don't like it, erase it, and shoot again. With film, you won't know what you've got until you get the film developed! That may be days or weeks later--and in most cases you can't go back and re-shoot the scene!

Another advantage for digitals, especially for this writer or anyone in the publishing business, is that the images are already in **digital form** and don't have to be scanned--which is the case for slides or print film. This way it's hard for someone to screw-up a good foto in the scanning process. In the computer some modifications to the image can be made easily, then it's sent to the printers on a DVD. All publishing and/or printing today starts with electronic files, instead of paste-ups with art boards that have to be shot with a film camera. The old way was called **camera ready**.

Other advantages are: If you want to email pictures to friends or family, this can be done without scanning them into your computer first. If you wish to share prints, they can be made on a home printer, or by most foto labs on regular fotographic paper. These prints can be made for about 25 cents each, and likely cheaper in the future. Digital cameras are generally smaller & more compact than film cameras, but other models are large and complicated--and still expensive as hell. Slowly but surely, the features you can buy on a digital camera are equal to those found on the expensive film cameras.

Advantages of the older **mechanical film cameras** are, they're more sturdy and can withstand more bumps, abuse, moisture, and sand or dust than the newer electronic models including digitals. Mechanical cameras are also more likely to work after they've been dropped in water than the new-fangled ones. They are also easier and less expensive to repair. Problems with a mechanical camera are easily diagnosed and repairs made quickly. With the newer **electronic film or digital cameras,** you may have a developing minor electrical short in the system, but which the repairman can't find or fix. Also, if an electronic film camera gets wet, repairmen normally just throw it away rather than fix it! More on this below.

Another kind of camera is the inexpensive **point & shoot** 35mm (this could include some cheap digitals without an LCD). Professionals won't touch these, but in some situations, and in the right hands, they produce surprisingly good pictures. If you're taking close-ups of people in dark slots, they automatically focus & flash and the results are unbeatable (a quick word of advice: in tight slots--turn your camera 90° and take vertical frames so the flash doesn't burnout the walls close to the camera). One disadvantage is, in a moderately dark slot, while they focus (if it's really dark, some cameras can't focus properly; in other words, they need something visible to focus on) & flash, they can't bring in the distant scenes which are always black. For that you need a camera with adjustable F-stops & shutter speeds like the ones mentioned above, and a tripod. If you're considering buying a point & shoot, be sure to get one with an electronic self-timer. For $40 to $50 you can get a pretty good film model; perhaps $100 to $150 for bottom-of-the-line digitals. The author used to use the Canon Sure Shot Owl Date model.

Lenses. A lens with an F-stop of 1.4, 1.7 (considered a **fast lens**, but there aren't many around anymore) or 2.0 has a larger opening when wide open and allows more light to reach the film or digital memory card. Older mechanical film cameras usually came with one of these. The F-stop on most zoom lenses is typically F3.5 up to F4.5 (these are **slow lens**). This means the aperture or opening in the lens doesn't open as large, so there's less light reaching the film or memory card. Naturally, a faster lens is better in dark slots because you can often hand-hold them and still get reasonably good results.

Almost all digital cameras have zoom lenses, and considering the price you pay, they seem as good, if not better, than the best zooms on film cameras. Most zooms on digitals are classed as 3X, or 35-105mm. Also, because of the nature of digitals, when you get these images on your computer (depends on computers), you can zoom in even more. Of course, when you do that, you'll be enlarging the dots and you lose detail.

Or, some or perhaps most, digital cameras have a **digital zoom** that works with the optical zoom. This also means you'll be enlarging the dots, and will lose detail. The problem with using a digital zoom is, if you have a 2mp camera and shooting at the highest resolution, when you zoom in digitally, the dots get big in a hurry, thus the quality goes down. To solve this little problem, you'd need a 4 or 5mp camera, then when you know you'll want to use the digital zoom to bring in a distant scene, you'll want to reset the camera to the highest resolution. After you zoom, then the final pixel tally or count, may be equal to a normal 2mp shot.

Film Type

For those with film cameras, besides using a fast lens (F1.4 or F1.7), you can also compensate for the darkness by using a faster film. Film speeds range from a **slow 25, 50, or 64 ASA (or ISO)**, up to a **fast 400 or 800 ASA/ISO**. If you're out on the ski slopes on a bright sunny day, you'll want film with a slow speed. But if you're in a dark slot, you'll want one of the faster films. One drawback to using some high speed film is, some cheaper brands can be grainy and don't give highly detailed fotographs. For many years, the author used a lot of 100 ASA/ISO color slide film (which is best out in the sunlight), but when he went with others and shared pictures, he used print film by Fuji called Superia X-Tra, or Kodak Max or Gold film, both at 400 ASA/ISO. Each of these films comes in 800 ASA/ISO, but foto lab employees think they're too grainy. Now with a digital, he simply burns all images onto a CD and sends that to hiking partners. This is the same as giving someone film negs and allows them to do as they please--making prints or seeing them on a computer.

Another technique you might try in very dark slots, is to **push the film or ASA/ISO**. For example, if you use 200 ASA/ISO Ektachrome (color slide film), you can set your camera ASA/ISO setting on 400 or 800 ASA/ISO, which is one or 2 full stops ahead. This higher setting (say 2 full stops) will change your shutter speed from 1/8 to 1/30 of a second. In this example, instead of using a tripod, you can hand hold the camera and still get decent results (but not everything will be in focus unless you can get the F-stop up to about F8 or higher. Read more about F-stops below).

When it comes time to develop the film, you'll have to take it to a lab which specializes in film finishing and tell them you pushed it one or 2 stops. They will then leave it in the developer longer, thus compensating for the adjustment you made with the ASA/ISO setting on the camera.

You can use this pushing technique on any film, but foto quality goes down--the bigger the push, the poorer the quality. Pushing tends to increase graininess. So before pushing the ASA/ISO, call a local lab first and ask their advice, especially on the type of film that works best.

Another thing to remember is, the lower the film's ASA/ISO, the sharper and more detailed the picture will be. If you plan to blowup your pictures to poster size, then the best film will be Kodachrome 25 or 64 ASA (Fuji also has a better film to match Kodak's). The author used to use a cheaper store brand 100 ASA/ISO color slide film from the 3MM Company, but it's not nearly as good as Fuji or Kodak. However, it seems to work OK for the small B+W prints in this book, partly because the printing process and cheaper paper usually negate the advantage of using more expensive film.

Tripod or Camera Stand

Carrying a tripod on a long canyon hike is asking too much for most people, but it will pay off with better results. Actually, if you have a fairly fast lens (F1.4 or F1.7), fast film (400 ASA/ISO), and compensate by pushing the film (one roll of film in the darkest narrows only) one or 2 full stops, or just hold your camera & hand against a wall or lay it on a pack or rock, you can usually get by without a tripod.

If your camera indicates the shutter speed is below 1/15 of a second, use a stand of some kind--either a rock, tripod, or backpack. Sometimes you can lean against a wall and get moderately good results by hand-holding it at 1/15 or maybe even 1/8 of a second--but squeeze the trigger slowly and in between heartbeats!

F-Stops--Film or Digital Cameras

Here's one of the most important things to remember if you want well-focused pictures from dark canyons--this is the same principal for film or digital cameras. The lower the F-stop setting on your lens, the smaller the field of focus will be. This means if shooting at F2.8, just a small part of your foto will be in focus, everything else either closer or further away, will be blurred. With a higher F-stop setting, then all or most of everything in your picture will be in focus. The advantage of using a tripod in a dark slot is, if you can get your F-stop up to between 11 & 16 (only up to F8 on the author's digital)--which means your shutter speed may be several seconds--then everything from one meter up to infinity will be in focus. This is the reason for a tripod. In many slots you'll want to put your camera on a tripod (or on a pack or rock), set the camera to **aperture priority** and the F-stop to between F-8 & F-16 (or as high as your camera will allow), then use the self-timer. In this situation, the camera's metering system will open the lens automatically for the length of time needed--usually from one to 3 or 4 seconds, and everything from about one meter to infinity will be in focus.

Some Tips for Film or Digital Cameras

When in a place like Buckskin Gulch, avoid taking a foto when there's some sunlight in your subject area. If you do, part of the picture will be washed out with too much light; the other part will be dark or totally black. Instead, take a picture where the sunlight is being bounced off an upper wall and diffused down into the dark corners. One exception to this rule would be if you're after special effects. In the case of Antelope Canyon (near Page, Arizona but not in this book), there is one place (The Crack) where a shaft of sunlight reaches the bottom at around high noon. Some fotographers set up their camera on a tripod, then throw sand in the air which creates dust in the shaft of light. This technique exaggerates the small sunny part making a pleasing affect to the picture.

Another way to get a foto with bright sun covering half your scene would be to wait for a cloud to cover the sun, then the light is diffused, thus eliminating the big difference between sun and shadow. The best time to take fotos in slot canyons is often in mid or late morning or mid-afternoon. This way you can easily find places where the sun isn't shining directly down into the narrows, but instead is shining on an upper wall, and the light is bounced or diffused down into the dark slot.

If you should slip while wading, or somehow drop your **mechanical camera** in water, here are the steps to take. Immediately take out the camera battery. Quickly roll the film back into the canister and remove it--if you can (this may be a problem with the newer electronic film models!). Open the camera and shake and blow out any water. Allow it to sit in the sun to dry, turning it occasionally to help evaporate any water inside. If you're near your car, start the engine, turn on the heater, and hang the camera in front of the vent. The warmer the camera gets, the better. This helps the water evaporate more quickly. The quicker the water evaporates, less corrosion there will be on the electrical system and less rust will be on metal parts. If you have a digital, the same general principal applies--get it dry as quickly as possible.

If your camera is under water for just a nano second or so, there will likely be little if any water deep inside. In this case, by following the above steps, you may be fotographing again in half an hour, especially if the water is clear, no sand has gotten into the camera, and if the sun is warm. The author had several of these little accidents with each of his older mechanical Pentax K-1000's. The last several times, no repair work was needed because he did the right things to get the camera dry fast.

Here's a sad story. While doing a hike on Lake Powell in 2002, the author's boat was swamped by big waves caused by passing boats in a narrow inlet. He returned to find that someone had rescued most of his stuff by placing it up on the slickrock out of the water. His backup film camera was sitting in 3 cms of water inside a box with half the film exposed. The next day, he rewound the film in a dark closet at home and took it to a lab. Every slide turned out good except one. This was the 3rd time he drowned a newer electronic film camera in 2 years; each time the camera was destroyed (and replaced with an extended warranty), but the film came out OK. So there is hope for the exposed film in your camera if you can remove it and/or rewind it in total darkness, and take it to a professional lab.

Who knows what will happen with a digital camera? Very likely the images you have on the memory card will be there because they seem to be well-sealed. So far the author hasn't had this experience.

If you're planning to go through some technical slot canyon, one that requires ropes, rappelling and **swimming,** then protect your camera by placing it in a **small plastic box made by Pelican or Otter** (or perhaps others?). The smaller the box, the better the chance it will keep the camera dry. The larger Pelican boxes are not totally waterproof! The smaller ones are. Buy and use a small camera for swimming through slot canyons! Another way to keep cameras dry is with a small drybag, but these are not as handy, and they offer less protection than a hard plastic box.

More thoughts for slot canyon fotographers. If you drop one of the newer electronic film models--the same for digital--into water, it likely won't be repairable, so they normally just throw it away. So if buying a new camera, pay a little more and get an **extended warranty**; that way if you drown a camera in the warranty period, say up to 5 years, they'll replace it free (read the small print!). Ritz camera stores offer such extended warranties, but the cost of the warranty for digital cameras is almost double that of film cameras. At this stage in fotographic history, it seems fewer people know how to fix digital cameras.

The Grand Staircase-Escalante National Monument (GSENM)

The GSENM is one of our newest national monuments; it was established September 18, 1996 by President Clinton and Interior Secretary Babbit. It's one of only 15 national monuments in America administered by the BLM.

Here are the approximate boundaries of the GSENM which is entirely in southern Utah. On the west is Johnson Valley or Canyon; on the south it's roughly US Highway 89 or the Utah-Arizona line and Lake Powell; on the north & northwest it's the Skutumpah Road which is real close to Bryce Canyon National Park, and Bryce Valley, Escalante & Boulder; while on the east it's Capitol Reef National Park and Glen Canyon National Recreation Area.

Commentary: In the time since this monument was created, the BLM has turned a quiet forgotten backwater into a bureaucratic nightmare. Management is now in the process of dreaming up reasons for you to come to one of their 5 visitor centers to pickup a camping permit! Even if you're just going to pull off the road--any road, including those for 4WD's only--and camp in places like the Rock Springs Bench, Cottonwood Wash, or in even more lonely outposts east of the Paria River drainage, they want you to come in and register--presumably for your own good!

In just the last couple of years, they've installed hiker's registers at some trailheads. The stated reason is, they want to know how many people are going there. It's assumed that if an area is being visited a lot, that allows them to fill out a requisition form and demand more money--which to this point has gone into building 5 brand new visitor centers (east Kanab, Paria River, Big Water, Cannonville & Escalante). By building these visitor centers, the people in charge of this shootin' match are going out of their way to attract customers (people) who otherwise would have no interest at all in this region. And of course the staff & budget is 7 or 8 times, maybe 10 times bigger, than it was in 1996 before the place was put on the map!

Most land in the GSENM, including just that part covered in this book--the Paria River drainage--is wild & rugged and accessible only by seasonal dirt roads that may be graded once a year--others never touched by a bulldozer! Yet management is going about their business as if this was in the Appalachian Mountains and surrounded by 100 million people!

One big question; what's the need for this rush into the black hole of bureaucracy? Basically nothing's changed since 1996, except that a few people have gotten it into their heads that they now have to keep track of how many people have come, and that they--the BLM--now has to worry about preventing people from walking on their cryptogamic soil, getting lost, or something (?). To you readers, this is your land, so if GSENM policies & policy makers burn your 3-letter A-word like they do mine, write letters and be heard. Policy is based on letters & comments.

Vermilion Cliffs National Monument-VCNM

America's newest national monument is the Vermilion Cliffs National Monument, created November 15, 2000 by President Clinton. It's boundaries are Highway 89A on the south and southeast, Glen Canyon National Recreation Area on the east & southeast, the Utah-Arizona state line on the north, and the Coyote & House Rock Valleys on the west.

As this book goes to press, this monument has no visitor center and it gets very little publicity. Hopefully it will remain that way instead of turning into another bureaucratic nightmare like the GSENM mentioned above.

Important BLM Offices--Colorado Plateau

Before starting any hike in the 4 Corners region, stop at one of these BLM offices and get the latest information on road, trail, water, flood or weather conditions. In some cases, the information in this book may be outdated the minute it goes to press! This is especially true in slot canyons where conditions can change dramatically with every flash flood. People at the BLM normally have good information on road conditions, and can go online to get an latest updated weather forecast. Here's a list of offices on the Colorado Plateau.

Utah
Cedar City, 176 East, D. L. Sargent Drive, 84720, Tele. 435-586-2401.
St. George, 345 East, Riverside Drive, 84790, Tele. 435-688-3200. Visitor Center, Tele. 435-688-3246.
Escalante, Visitor Center, Tele. 435-826-5499; BLM & Grand Staircase-Escalante N.M. office, Tele. 435-826-5600; Glen Canyon National Recreation Area office, Tele. 435-826-5651. These offices are in the same building complex located on Highway 12 on the west side of Escalante, 84726.
Kanab, BLM Office is at 318 North, 100 East, 84741, Tele. 435-644-4600. Read below for the various visitor centers in the Grand Staircase-Escalante National Monument (GSENM).
Richfield, 150 East, 900 North, Tele. 435-896-1500.
Hanksville, southwest part of town, P.O. Box 99, 84734, Tele. 435-542-3461.
Moab, 82 East, Dogwood, 84532, Tele. 435-259-2100.
   Multiagency Visitor Center, middle of Moab, Tele. 435-259-2468.
Price, 125 South, 600 West, 84501, Tele. 435-636-3600.
Monticello, 435 North, Main Street, 84535, Tele. 435-587-2141 or 1500.
Vernal, 170 South, 500 East, 84078, Tele. 435-781-4400.

Colorado
Grand Junction, 2815 H Road, 81506, Tele. 970-244-3000.
Montrose, 2505 South, Townsend Avenue, 81401, Tele. 970-249-5300.
Durango, 15 Burnett Court, 81301, Tele. 970-247-4874.
Dolores, 100 N. 6th Street, 81323, Tele. 970-882-7296.

New Mexico
Grants, 2001 E., Santa Fe Avenue, 87020, Tele. 505-285-5406. Or better still, stop at the new building nearby: **Northwest New Mexico Visitor Center,** 1900 E. Santa Fe Avenue, Tele. 505-876-2780.

Arizona
St. George, Utah (for the Arizona Strip District north of the Grand Canyon and Colorado River), 345 East, Riverside Drive, 84790, Tele. 435-688-3200. Visitor Center, Tele. 435-688-3246
Kingman, 2475 Beverly Avenue, 86401, Tele 928-692-4400.
Phoenix Field Office, 21605 N. 7th Avenue, 85027, Tele 623-580-5500.

National Park/Monument Offices & Visitor Centers in Southern Utah

Arches National Park, Visitor Center, North of Moab, Tele 435-719-2299.
Canyonlands National Park, Headquarters at 2282 S.W., Resource Blvd., Moab, Tele. 435-719-2100;. Visitor Information, Middle of Moab, Tele. 435-719-2313; Backcountry Reservations, Tele. 435-259-4351; Island in the Sky Visitor Center, Tele. 435-259-4712; Needles Visitor Center, Tele. 435-259-4711; Maze (Hans Flat) Visitor Center, Tele. 435-259-2652; or website **nps.gov/cany.**
Capitol Reef National Park, Visitor Center, Tele. 435-425-3791, or website **nps.gov/care.**
Grand Staircase-Escalante National Monument (run by the BLM), Escalante Interagency Visitor Center, West Side of Escalante, Utah, Tele. 435-826-5499; Kanab Visitor Center, 754 E, Highway 89, Kanab, Utah, Tele. 435-644-4680; GSENM Monument Headquarters, 190 East Center Street, Kanab, Tele. 435-644-4300; Cannonville Visitor Center, Cannonville, Utah, Tele. 435-679-8981; Big Water Visitor Center, 100 Upper Revolution Way (just south of Highway 89), Big Water, Utah, Tele. 435-675-5868, website **ut.blm.gov/monument.**
Natural Bridges National Monument, Mailing address HC-60, Box 1, Lake Powell, Utah, 84533, Visitor Center, Tele. 435-692-1234, Headquarters, Tele. 435-719-2100, website **nps.gov/nabr.**
Vermilion Cliffs National Monument, Interagency Information Center, 345 Riverside Drive, St. George, Utah, Tele. 435-688-3200, website **az.blm.gov.**
Zion National Park, Visitor Center, Tele. 435-772-3256; Backcountry Desk, Tele. 435-772-0170, website **nps.gov/zion**

Other Important Websites & Home Pages--US Government
Bureau of Land Management (BLM) -www.blm.gov
United State Forest Service (USFS) -www.fs.fed.us
National Park Service (NPS) -www.nps.gov

Canyoneering Information and Possible Updates

   One way to get updated information, or for you to update information in this book, is to contact one of the following websites. If it's up and running, Ben Bahlmann's **canyoneering.com** might be the best. If you go through any canyon in this book, but a flood has rearranged boulders, or taken out an anchor or bolt, then please post a bulletin on this website. First, click on guidebooks, then this guidebook, then the name of the canyon which needs comment. Type in changes that have taken place since this guidebook was printed. This way everyone has a chance to read it and go better prepared. Or you can use your computer's search engine to look up Canyoneering on the internet for a long list of websites. Here's a short list of websites that may be of help, or that have updated information on various canyons.

American Canyoning Association, club activities -canyoneering.net
Canyoneering Information & Updates -canyoneering.com
Climb Utah--Mountaineering & Canyoneering -climbutah.com
The American Southwest -americansouthwest.net
Todd's Desert Hiking Guide--Mostly Arizona -toddshikingguide.com
Tom's Utah Canyoneering Guide--Mostly Zion N.P. - - - - - - - - - - - - - - - - - - -canyoneeringUSA.com

Warning: Don't Blame Me!

People should keep a few things in mind when it comes to hiking in the canyons of the Paria River drainage. This writer has done his best to collect information and present it to readers as accurately as possible. He has drawn maps as carefully as possible, and encourages everyone to buy the USGS topo maps suggested for each hike. He has tried to inform hikers that canyons change with every flash flood, and that many of the hikes in this book are in isolated wilderness regions. He's also tried to tell hikers that some canyons are for experienced and tough hikers only. Some hikes discussed here are easy, but others are definitely not a Sunday picnic in the park!

For the first time, this edition presents several technically difficult canyons which involves serious downclimbing and/or rappelling to get all the way through. Some rappelling anchors are chokestones or trees, others are bolts in the canyon walls. If you choose to take on these challenges, it's your responsibility to check each anchor carefully, especially knots, slings, or webbing & bolts. Floods can alter, damage or wash away these sites, especially chokestones and webbing, so proper tools, equipment and supplies must be taken to insure you get through alive! No matter what, always take extra ropes or webbing to meet any kind of new situation or emergency. So for those who will somehow get lost, stranded, or have to spend an extra night in a canyon and be rescued, all I can say is, I've done my best. The rest is up to you, so don't blame me or this book for your mistakes, lack of preparedness--and yes, even your stupidity!

Before doing any hike, always stop at the nearest BLM office or visitor center, and get the latest information on road, trail, water, flood or weather conditions & forecast. Also, tell someone where you're going and when you expect to return. That way, friends can call for help if you don't return on time. One last thing; in some cases, the information in this book is different than in previous editions and can be outdated the minute it goes to press!

This is the lower end of Wall Street, one of the more interesting places in Bryce Canyon National Park. Not many branches on these tall thin douglas fir trees.

Metric Conversion Table

1 Centimeter = 0.39 Inch	1 Mile = 1.609 Kilometers	1 Ounce = 28.35 Grams
1 Inch = 2.54 Centimeters	100 Miles = 161 Kilometers	1 Pound = 453 Grams
1 Meter = 39.37 Inches	100 Kilometers = 62.1 miles	1 Quart (US) = 0.946 Liter
1 Foot = 0.3048 Meter/30.5 Cms	1 Liter = 1.056 Quarts (US)	1 Gallon (US) = 3.785 Liters
1 Kilometer = 0.621 Mile	1 Kilogram = 2.205 Pounds	1 Acre = 0.405 Hectare
1 Nautical Mile = 1.852 Kms	1 Metric Ton = 1000 Kgs	1 Hectare = 2.471 Acres
1 Kilometer = 3281 Feet	1 Mile = 1609 Meters	0.1 Mile = 161 Meters
1 Cubic/Liter = 61 Cubic/Inches	50 C/L = 3050 C/l	100 C/L = 6100 C/l

Meters to Feet (Meters x 3.2808 = Feet)

100 m = 328 ft.	2500 m = 8202 ft.	5000 m = 16404 ft.	7500 m = 24606 ft.
500 m = 1640 ft.	3000 m = 9842 ft.	5500 m = 18044 ft.	8000 m = 26246 ft.
1000 m = 3281 ft.	3500 m = 11483 ft.	6000 m = 19686 ft.	8500 m = 27887 ft.
1500 m = 4921 ft.	4000 m = 13124 ft.	6500 m = 21325 ft.	9000 m = 29525 ft.
2000 m = 6562 ft.	4500 m = 14764 ft.	7000 m = 22966 ft.	8848 m = 20029 ft.

Feet to Meters (Feet ÷ 3.2808 = Meters)

1000 ft. = 305 m	9000 ft. = 2743 m	16000 ft. = 4877 m	23000 ft. = 7010 m
2000 ft. = 610 m	10000 ft. = 3048 m	17000 ft. = 5182 m	24000 ft. = 7315 m
3000 ft. = 914 m	11000 ft. = 3353 m	18000 ft. = 5486 m	25000 ft. = 7620 m
4000 ft. = 1219 m	12000 ft. = 3658 m	19000 ft. = 5791 m	26000 ft. = 7925 m
5000 ft. = 1524 m	13000 ft. = 3962 m	20000 ft. = 6096 m	27000 ft. = 8230 m
6000 ft. = 1829 m	14000 ft. = 4268 m	21000 ft. = 6401 m	28000 ft. = 8535 m
7000 ft. = 2134 m	15000 ft. = 4572 m	22000 ft. = 6706 m	29000 ft. = 8839 m
8000 ft. = 2438 m			30000 ft. = 9144 m

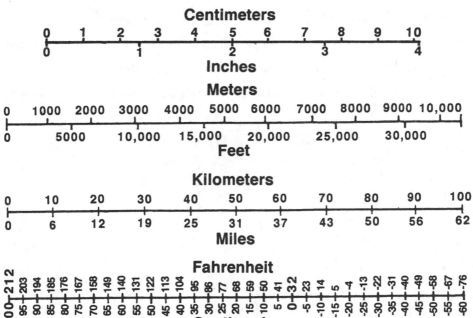

Centimeters / **Inches**

Meters / **Feet**

Kilometers / **Miles**

Fahrenheit / **Centigrade**

Map Symbols

Town or Community	▢ ▢	Peak & Prominent Ridge	━✖━
Building, Cabin or Home	▪	Stream or Creek, Desert	∼∼
Backcountry Campsite	▲	Stream or Creek, Mountain	∿
Campsite with Vehicle Access	⬢	Large River	▰▰
Campground	⋏	Dry Creek Bed or Channel	—…—
Cemetery or Gravesite	✚†	Canyon Narrows	⌇⌇
Ranger Station, Visitor Center	⚑⛪	Lake, Pond or Stock Pond	⬭ ◁
Hotel, Motel or Lodge	⬛	Large Pothole	⟳o
Airport or Landing Strip	✈	Waterfall or Dryfall	⊢⊣
U.S. Highway	⊞ (89) 20 21	Spring, Seep or Well	o
Utah State Highway	━(24)	Canyon Rim, Escarpment	⊥⊥⊥⊥
Road--Maintained	≡≡≡	Natural Bridge or Arch, Corral	∩ ⌒
Road--4 Wheel Drive (4WD)	⹀=====	Mine, Quarry, Adit or Prospect	⬦↗
Track--Old Road, Unusable	— ——	Geology Cross Section	⌐⌐
Trail, Foot or Horse	– – – –	Pass or Divide	≍
Route, No Trail	••••••	Rock Art--Pictograph	(PIC)
Cowboyglyph or Campground	(CG)	Rock Art--Petroglyphs	(PET)
Elevation in Meters	1490	Mile Posts (mp) Markers	⊞ 30 31
600 Meters	600m	Car-Park or Trailhead	(P)

Abbreviations

Canyon	C.	Campground & Cowboyglyphs	CG.
Lake	L.	Campsites	CS.
River	R.	Two Wheel Drive Vehicle or Road	2WD
Creek	Ck.	Four Wheel Drive Vehicle or Road	4WD
Peak	Pk.	High Clearance Vehicle or Road	HCV
Waterfall, Dryfall, Formation	F.	Off Road Vehicle	ORV
Kilometer(s)	km, kms	All Terrain Vehicle	ATV
North, North East	NNE	Spring	Sp.
South, West South	SWS	Sandstone	SS
Piñon/Juniper Forest	P/J	July, 2003	7/2003

United States Geological Survey	USGS
National Park Service	NPS
Bureau of Land Management	BLM
Grand Staircase-Escalante National Monument	GSENM
Vermilion Cliffs National Monument	VCNM
Civilian Conservation Corps	CCC's
National Geographic Society	NGS

Reference--Index Map of Hikes

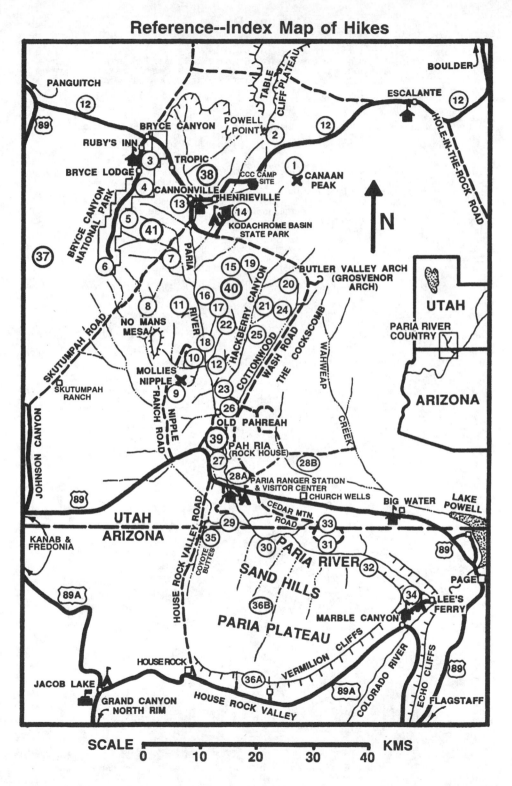

SCALE

0   10   20   30   40   KMS

Canaan Peak

Location & Access Canaan Peak at 2833m elevation, is located roughly halfway between the Bryce Valley towns of Tropic, Cannonville & Henrieville; and Escalante to the east. It's also just southeast of Highway 12 as you pass through the area. The original name for this was **Kaiparowits Peak** as shown on an 1884 map of Utah. The top part of Canaan is made of the same rock formations as in Bryce Canyon National Park and on Table Cliff Plateau, but its bright red limestone cap rock is almost eroded away. All other surrounding hills or mountains have lost this Claron (formerly known as the Wasatch) Formation cap except Table Cliff Plateau, which is located just to the northwest. See the next map.

To get to the trailhead, drive along Highway 12, the link between Bryce Canyon N. P. and Escalante. Just northeast of mile post 45, turn south at the sign stating, *South Hollow & Canaan Peak.* Drive south 7.7 kms (4.8 miles) on a good & well-maintained dirt road (#376). At that point you'll come to an open meadow and another sign on the right or south reading *Canaan Mtn. Loop Trail & Pole Spring.* Turn right off from the main road and continue along a faint vehicle track for 300m until you come to a metal watering trough. There you may see another sign, *Canaan Mtn. Loop Trail.* Park and/or camp in that area which has lots of shade from big pine trees. However, camp away from the watering trough because in summer lots of cows use it.

Trail/Route Use the little insert map to help locate the metal stock trough which is just below Pole Spring. From the watering trough, head south up an old road into a minor canyon towards the spring. After the dirt road peters out, watch closely for trail markers on trees, which look like an "i". On his 3rd hike to the summit in 2003, the author strayed to the right onto a well-used recently-made cow trail and got lost momentarily; so watch for the trail markers on douglas fir trees. Once on the trail, it's generally easy to follow, but the Forest Service doesn't remove deadfall very often, so you may have to jump over some downed trees occasionally. As you arrive on the west side of the main peak, and after you cross over a minor pass, the trail drops down to intersect a very old logging road, which is now unusable for vehicles. At about that point, you can walk straight up the slope to the top-most ridge, then head south to the summit; or continue around to the southeast side of the mountain and climb from there. The south face of Canaan Peak is very rugged and a nice place to take pictures.

Elevations Trailhead, about 2600m; Canaan Peak, 2833m.

Hike Length/Time Needed The hiking distance to the top is only about 3 kms, but will generally take 2-4 hours to climb, round-trip.

Water Take your own. Also at Pole Spring (questionable quality!), but none on the mountain above.

Maps USGS or BLM map Escalante (1:100,000) for driving & orientation; Canaan Peak & Upper Valley (1:24,000--7 1/2' quad) for hiking.

Main Attractions A short day-hike in a cool and little-known mountain region, with many good, free campsites. A nice place to visit on a hot summer day.

Ideal Time to Hike From about mid-May until the end of October, but each year is a little different. Get there too early in the spring, or too late in the fall, and you'll find muddy roads.

Boots/Shoes Any dry weather boots or shoes.

Author's Experience The author had to hunt for the trailhead on his first trip, but after locating it, went quickly up the trail to the summit from the southeast side. He came down the west slope and returned to his car in less than 3 hours. He re-hiked roughly the same route in about 2 hours on a 2nd trip in 1997. In 2003, he did the hike again with a digital camera, but got lost momentarily with lots of new cow trails. That one took 2 1/2 hours round-trip.

The summit of Canaan Peak from near the top of the southeast ridge.

Map 1, Canaan Peak

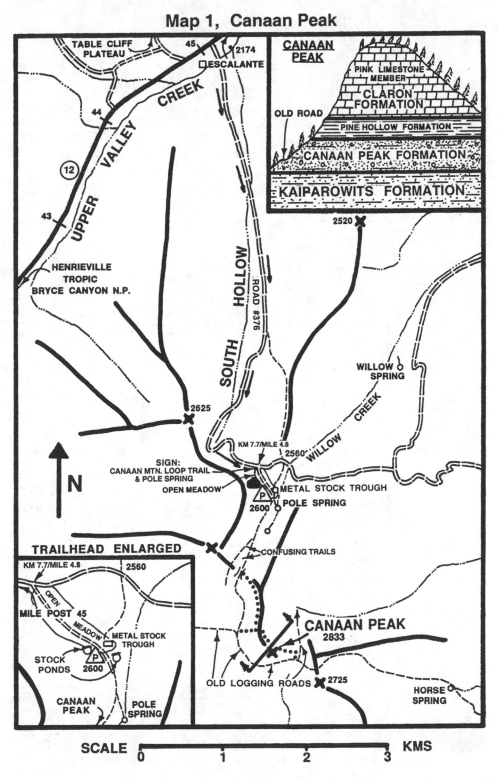

TABLE CLIFF
PLATEAU

45

2174

☐ESCALANTE

CREEK

44

UPPER

12

43

VALLEY

HENRIEVILLE
TROPIC
BRYCE CANYON N.P.

SOUTH HOLLOW

ROAD #376

CANAAN
PEAK

PINK LIMESTONE
MEMBER

CLARON
FORMATION

OLD ROAD

PINE HOLLOW FORMATION

CANAAN PEAK FORMATION

KAIPAROWITS FORMATION

2520 ✗

WILLOW
SPRING

WILLOW CREEK

✗ 2625

KM 7.7/MILE 4.8

2560

N

SIGN:
CANAAN MTN. LOOP TRAIL
& POLE SPRING

OPEN MEADOW

P
2600

METAL STOCK TROUGH

POLE SPRING

TRAILHEAD ENLARGED

✗

CONFUSING TRAILS

KM 7.7/MILE 4.8   2560

OPEN

MILE POST 45

MEADOW

METAL STOCK
TROUGH

STOCK
PONDS

P
2600

CANAAN
PEAK

POLE
SPRING

CANAAN PEAK

2833

OLD LOGGING ROADS ✗ 2725

HORSE
SPRING

SCALE   0   1   2   3   **KMS**

23

Table Cliff Plateau & Powell Point

Location & Access Table Cliff Plateau is located about halfway between Escalante and the Bryce Valley towns of Tropic, Cannonville & Henrieville. **Table Cliff Plateau,** or at least its very southern tip known as **Powell Point,** is one of the most prominent landmarks in southern Utah. On an 1874 map of the state of Utah, this high country already had a name, Summit of the Rim, and **Table Rock.** To get there, drive along Highway 12 between Henrieville & Escalante. The shortest route to Powell Point, can be found by leaving the highway very near mile post 44, and driving towards Pine Hollow as shown on the map; but that road is rough in places and you'll likely need a HCV of some kind to make it to the trailhead at 2400m.

To reach the best road and normal driving & hiking route to the top, continue along Highway 12 to near mile post 45, then head northwest on Forest Road #148. Follow the map. After 4.8 kms (3 miles) you'll come to a road junction near Garden Spring at 2390m altitude. Or another way to reach this same point is to leave the highway halfway between mile posts 46 & 47 and drive northwesterly 6.6 kms (4.1 miles) on Forest Road #144 to the same junction (this loop-road is in good condition for all vehicles). At the Garden Spring Junction is a sign pointing the way toward Water Canyon. Drive northwest another 1.45 kms (.9 mile) and park in a meadow 160m below the actual beginning of the trail. Most 2WD vehicles can make it up this old logging road to the trailhead at 2500m. This trail-head makes a nice campsite in the heat of summer.

Trail/Route From the trailhead, there's a well-marked trail to the top of Table Cliff Plateau. Once on this trail, it's easy to follow as it first runs up the bottom of Water Canyon with several nearby springs (in summer there are cows around, so purify the water before drinking!). This trail has ax marks on trees shaped like the letter "i". Higher up it zag zags up the steeper parts to the flat top. After about 5 1/2 kms, the Water Canyon Trail meets a rather good vehicle track running south to Powell Point. Once on this track, walk through white & douglas fir, limber & ponderosa pines and quaking aspen to where the road ends and a foot trail begins. Then it's a short walk through bristlecone pines to Powell Point. The west side of the Plateau is the most fotogenic, so arrive after midday for better pictures. A shorter, less-desirable route (no trail) runs up from Pine Hollow. There are a number of old logging roads in that area, so follow whichever one seems to lead in the right direction going west. The track leading towards *running water* (as shown on the map) is an easy route, then the steeper slope up the escarpment to the top, and finally by road & trail to Powell Point. Beginning in 2002, there is a new trail from Stump Spring around to the west side of Table Cliff which ends near Pine Lake.

Elevations Trailheads, 2390m, 2400m & 2500m; Table Cliff Plateau, 3125m; Powell Point, 3105m.

Hike Length/Time Needed One to 2 hours to reach the top of the Plateau, then the easy 3 km road-walk south to the end of the road, and another km to Powell Point. Round-trip will take from 4-7 hours.

Water Once in early June, the author found running water in upper Pine Hollow and other times in Water Canyon (a year-round flow). There's no water on top so always take some in your car and in your pack.

Maps USGS or BLM map Escalante (1:100,000) for driving & orientation; and Upper Valley & Pine Lake (1:24,000--7 1/2' quads) for hiking.

Main Attractions Splendid views, a cool summer hike, and cool quiet campsites.

Ideal Time to Hike From mid or late May to late October, but each year is a little different.

Boots/Shoes Any dry weather boots or shoes. Running-type shoes will work just fine.

Author's Experience On his first trip, the author walked up the Pine Hollow route from his car near the highway, then came down Water Canyon and road-walked back to his car, all in 5 hours. In 2003, he car-camped at the Water Canyon Trailhead and did the normal hike the next morning in just over 4 hours, round-trip.

Aerial view of Table Cliff Plateau & Powell Point in winter. Looking NNE

Map 2, Table Cliff Plateau & Powell Point

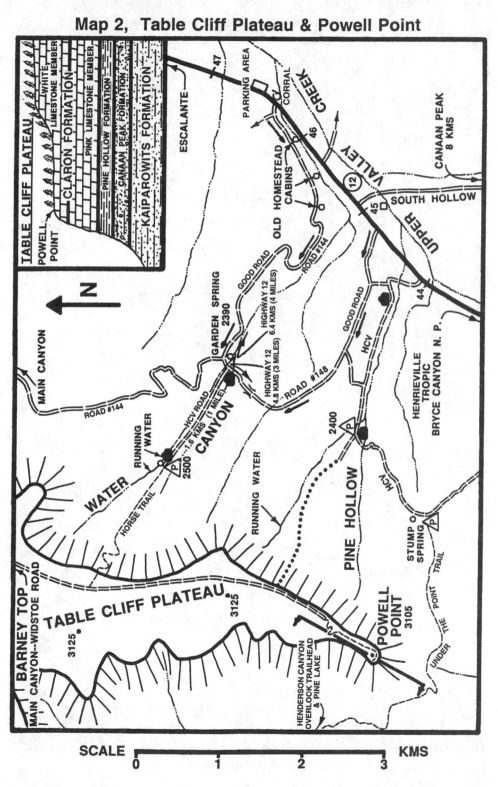

SCALE

KMS

0   1   2   3

Fairyland Trail, Bryce Canyon National Park

Location & Access Included in this book are 4 maps covering the trails in Bryce Canyon National Park. The Fairyland Trail is the most-northerly of the 4, and is the most-northerly of all footpaths in the park. This trail is located roughly due east of the park visitor center and North Campground. One place to begin hiking is at **Fairyland Point**. To get there, drive south from Ruby's Inn on the highway entering Bryce Canyon. From the national park boundary, which is marked by signs, continue south for .7 km (.4 mile) then turn east on the paved road signposted for *Fairyland Point*. Drive another 1.6 kms (one mile) and park. A 2nd place to begin hiking this loop trail is at **Sunrise Point**. To get there, first pass through the fee gate which is next to the visitor center, then continue south for about 800m (.5 mile) and turn left or east at the road signposted for *Sunrise Point*. Or continue south another short distance to near mile post 2, and turn east again at a 2nd access road. Just follow the signs to Sunrise Point using this or the free map they'll give you as you enter the park. A 3rd starting point is anywhere within the confines of the North Campground.

Trail/Route The Fairyland Trail, as with all trails in this national park, is a well-maintained walking path. You can't get lost, and all trail junctions and points of interest are signposted. This trail is easy walking but it's an up & down hike all the way. The better known points of interest along the way are the **Chinese Wall** and the London or **Tower Bridge** (this is actually an arch not a bridge). Depending on the time of day, you may have better light for fotographing this arch by walking around to the back side. At least from the south side you'll have lots more sun.

Elevations From a high point of about 2465m on the rim, down to about 2200m in Campbell Canyon.

Hike Length/Time Needed This hike is divided into 2 parts; the **Fairyland Trail,** running down into the canyons; and the **Rim Trail**. If you start at Sunrise Point and walk down along the Fairyland Trail, then it's just over 8 kms to Fairyland Point. From Fairyland Point back along the rim to Sunrise Point, is just over 5 kms. So the length of the loop is about 13 kms. Some people can do this loop-hike in as little as 3 hours, but for others it's a 4-5 hour walk. You can shorten it just a bit, if you begin at the campground or Fairyland Point, thus eliminating the short walk to or from Sunrise Point. Or, you could eliminate the Rim Trail part between trailheads by using a mtn. bike on the paved roads. Or, start at Sunrise Point, walk down to Tower Bridge and return the same way, which is the best part of the hike.

Water There are no springs or running water anywhere along this trail, so if it's summer with hot weather, be sure to take some water--up to 2-3 liters for some on a hot summer day. In cooler weather, and if you're a fast & fit hiker, you can likely make it OK without water or a lunch.

Maps Trails Illustrated/National Geographic map Paunsaugunt Plateau, Mount Dutton, Bryce Canyon (1:50,000); Bryce Canyon National Park (1:31,680); or the free map given to you upon entry to Bryce.

Main Attractions Easy access, a good & well-maintained trail, very little other foot traffic, and perhaps the second best area in the park to walk through and see the hoodoos. See the geology cross section.

Ideal Time to Hike May through October. Midsummer can be a bit warm as the altitude is only moderately high. A winter outing could be fun too, for the properly equipped hiker, but it's not marked for winter use. Snow cover is generally light in this section of the park during winter, but in some years it can be more than a meter deep.

Hiking Boots Any dry weather boots or shoes.

Author's Experience The author started at Sunrise Point and made the loop-hike in about 3 hours on a very cool May morning. On another trip from Sunrise Point, he went down to Tower Bridge and the Chinese Wall, waited a while for clouds to move, and returned in less than 2 hours.

Looking northward at the south side of Tower Bridge.

Map 3, Fairyland Trail, Bryce Canyon National Park

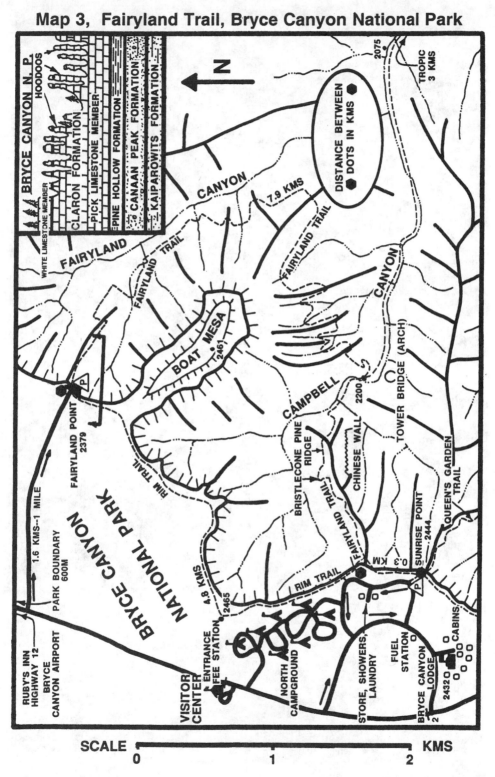

N

BRYCE CANYON N. P.

HOODOOS

CLARON FORMATION

WHITE LIMESTONE MEMBER

PICK LIMESTONE MEMBER

PINE HOLLOW FORMATION

CANAAN PEAK FORMATION

KAIPAROWITS FORMATION

2075

TROPIC 3 KMS

DISTANCE BETWEEN DOTS IN KMS

CANYON

7.9 KMS

FAIRYLAND TRAIL

FAIRYLAND TRAIL

FAIRYLAND

FAIRYLAND TRAIL

CANYON

BOAT MESA 2461

CAMPBELL

CHINESE WALL 2200

TOWER BRIDGE (ARCH)

FAIRYLAND POINT 2379

RIM TRAIL

BRISTLECONE PINE RIDGE

FAIRYLAND TRAIL

QUEEN'S GARDEN TRAIL

SUNRISE POINT 2444

0.3 KM

BRYCE CANYON

NATIONAL PARK

RUBY'S INN HIGHWAY 12

BRYCE CANYON AIRPORT

1.6 KMS—1 MILE

PARK BOUNDARY 600M

4.8 KMS

RIM TRAIL

P

2465

VISITOR CENTER

ENTRANCE FEE STATION

NORTH CAMPGROUND

STORE, SHOWERS, LAUNDRY

FUEL STATION

BRYCE CANYON LODGE

2432

CABINS

2

SCALE

0   1   2

KMS

The Tropic Ditch as seen immediately south of Ruby's Inn and next to the campground. This is just west of the highway running south into Bryce Canyon National Park

Viewing the Hoodoos for which Bryce Canyon is famous, from the top of the Navajo Loop Trail. Nearby is Wall Street, a narrow canyon within part of the Hoodoos.

Above A winter aerial view of the middle part of Bryce Canyon National Park. The upper middle part of this picture is of the Navajo Loop Hike and Wall Street.

Left Wall Street. This is part of the Navajo Loop Hike, which is right in the most popular section of Bryce Canyon National Park. The beginning of this trail is only 400m or so from the historic Bryce Canyon Lodge.

Navajo, Peekaboo & Queen's Garden Trails, Bryce Canyon N.P.

Location & Access The trails on this map are near the center of Bryce Canyon National Park, and in the part which has the best scenery and most visitors. It's here you can walk right through the narrow canyons of hoodoos, the erosional features so prominent in this section of the park and for which Bryce Canyon is famous. Just after entering the national park, you'll pass the fee station next to the visitor center. From there, continue south a ways and look for signs pointing out the access roads to Sunrise & Sunset Points on the left or east. A little further on (2.9 kms/1.8 miles from the visitor center/fee station) is the turnoff to Inspiration & Bryce Points. All the roads up to the turnoff to Bryce Point and the winter gate, are kept open year-round.

Trail/Route There are 3 possible starting points for hikes from the rim: **Sunrise, Sunset** and **Bryce Points.** The first 2 are the most used, since they're near the historic Bryce Canyon Lodge & cabins, and campgrounds. All trails on this map are heavily-used and well-maintained. All junctions are sign-posted, and in some places you'll find benches to sit on and rest. Walking is very easy and enjoyable. Most people here are tourists, not necessarily hikers, and for the most part they walk down one trail a ways and return the same way. The best trail in the park for taking pictures is the **Navajo Loop Trail.** It's a one-way hike that zig zags down & through a narrow, fotogenic gorge called **Wall Street.** This part has a couple of tall pine trees trying to reach the sun. Then it loops back up passing another little canyon with 2 bridges, before returning to the rim. From the top of this trail looking northeast toward Powell Point in the distance, is the best place in the park for taking fotos of **hoodoos.**

Elevations Sunset Point, 2431m; Sunrise Point, 2444m; Bryce Point, 2529m; and the lowest part of the Navajo Trail, about 2280m.

Hike Length/Time Needed On this map are some large dots with numbers in between. These numbers represent the kilometers between dots. None of the distances are very great. To walk down the Navajo, then along the Peekaboo Loop Trail, and finish the hike by walking up the Queen's Garden Trail to Sunrise Point, and finally back to the starting place at Sunset Point, is to walk about 10.5 kms. This can be done in as little as 2 hours by a fast hiker, but most would want about 4 hours, or about half a day for the trip. Some may want to take a lunch and spend more than half a day on this hike, especially if taking in some short side-trips, such as the walk into **Two Bridges Canyon.** A mtn. bike left at one trailhead would eliminate a tiresome road-walk, or rim trail hike back to your car, especially if you start or end at Bryce Point.

Water There is no running water anywhere in this area, so plan to take your own.

Maps Trails Illustrated/National Geographic map Paunsaugunt Plateau, Mount Dutton, Bryce Canyon (1:50,000); or Bryce Canyon National Park (1:31,680); or just use the simple free map given to you as you pass through the fee station. The first 2 maps can be bought at the visitor center.

Main Attractions The trails on this map give hikers the best opportunity of any location in the park to see at close quarters the famous bright red spires of Bryce Canyon called hoodoos.

Ideal Time to Hike May through October, but midsummer can be a little warm at lower altitudes. Because of relatively light snowfall, it's also possible to hike these trails in winter. However, in some winters the snow can pile up to more than a meter deep. Each year is different.

Boots/Shoes Any dry weather boots or shoes.

Author's Experience The author worked at Bryce Canyon Lodge in the summer of 1965, so he has been on these trails many times. Later, he walked the Queen's Garden & Navajo Loop in a couple of hours. In 2003, he re-hiked & fotographed the scenes along the Navajo Trail with a digital camera.

The historic Bryce Canyon Lodge is near the beginning of the Navajo Loop Trail.

Map 4, Navajo, Peekaboo & Queen's Garden Trails, B.C

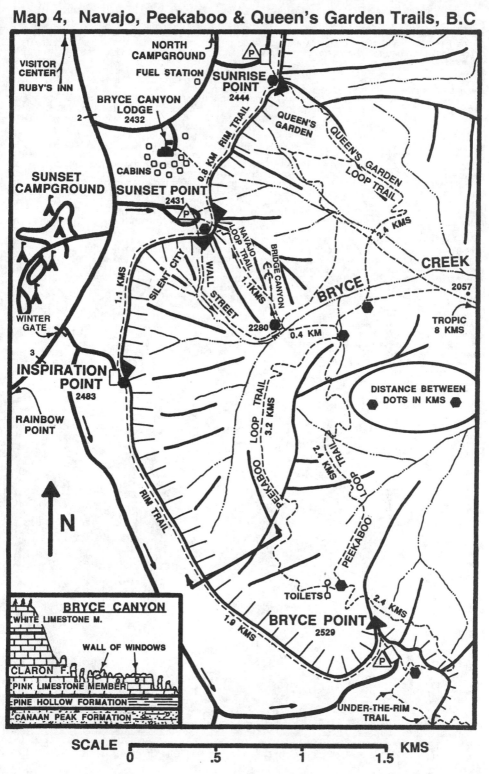

VISITOR
CENTER
RUBY'S INN

NORTH
CAMPGROUND

FUEL STATION

SUNRISE
POINT
2444

BRYCE CANYON
LODGE
2432

QUEEN'S
GARDEN

QUEEN'S GARDEN
LOOP TRAIL

0.8 KM RIM TRAIL

2

CABINS

SUNSET
CAMPGROUND

SUNSET POINT
2431

NAVAJO
LOOP TRAIL
1.1KMS

BRIDGE CANYON

BRYCE

CREEK

2.4 KMS

1.1 KMS

SILENT CITY

WALL STREET

2280

0.4 KM

2057

TROPIC
8 KMS

WINTER
GATE

3

INSPIRATION
POINT
2483

RAINBOW
POINT

DISTANCE BETWEEN
DOTS IN KMS

PEEKABOO LOOP TRAIL
3.2 KMS

LOOP TRAIL
2.4 KMS

RIM TRAIL

N

PEEKABOO

TOILETS

2.4 KMS

1.9 KMS

BRYCE POINT
2529

UNDER-THE-RIM
TRAIL

BRYCE CANYON
WHITE LIMESTONE M.

WALL OF WINDOWS

CLARON F.
PINK LIMESTONE MEMBER
PINE HOLLOW FORMATION
CANAAN PEAK FORMATION

SCALE

0   .5   1   1.5   KMS

Under-the-Rim Trail, Bryce Canyon National Park

Location & Access The Under-the-Rim Trail runs from **Bryce Point** near the center of Bryce Canyon, south to **Rainbow Point**, at the southern end of the park. It runs north-south along the eastern base of the Pink Cliffs, and offers both day and overnight hikes. In recent years, roads in the park up to Bryce Point have been kept open year-round. And if snow isn't too deep, and if graders are available, the road is sometimes plowed all the way to Rainbow Point. Before going anywhere, stop at the visitor center (VC), next to the fee station, for current information, maps, rules & regulation for campers, and if you're planning an overnight trip, pick up a free camping permit. From the VC, head south and follow signs to the trailhead you wish to hike from. The turnoff to Bryce Point is 2.6 kms (1.6 miles) from the VC; Rainbow Point is 27.5 kms (17.1 miles) from the VC (right at mile post 18). Three connecting trails are in-between. **Warning:** in 2003, they were reconstructing the road to Rainbow Point, so some trailhead parking places may be changed slightly. Also in 2003, and because of a long drought, drinking water was not available at Rainbow Point as it normally is.

Trail/Route The Under-the-Rim Trail is well-marked & maintained, so you can't get lost There are signs at all trail junctions, and at campsite locations. Because this hike is so long, it's necessary for most people to camp one night. There are 7 campsites along the way, all in the shade of ponderosa pines. Campsites are shown on the map. These campsites are never crowded, as very few people camp along the way. Water is scarce, which discourages camping. For this reason, most people hike it in stages, by using one of the connecting trails. This eliminates the need to carry water for camping. The connecting paths are called: **Sheep Creek, Swamp Canyon, Whiteman,** and **Agua Canyon Trails.** On this map, distances between dots are in kilometers (kms).

Elevations Bryce Point, 2529m; low point on the trail, about 2050m, Rainbow Point, 2776m.

Hike Length/Time Needed From Bryce Point to Rainbow Point is about 35 kms. This means the average person will need 1 1/2, or 2 days, and carry a large backpack. However, a fast hiker could do it in one long day with an early start and 2 cars (or perhaps a car & mtn. bike).

Water One major problem along this trail is lack of water. In the spring season, just after the snow melts, there's often some running water in most creek bottoms, but they dry up later on. Consult park rangers at the VC as to the whereabouts of water before hiking. Iron Spring has a good flow, but the water is undrinkable; Birch Spring has a small discharge and may be dry late in summer. Lack of good water is the reason this is not a popular place for backpacking.

Maps Trails Illustrated/National Geographic map Paunsaugunt Plateau, Mount Dutton, Bryce Canyon (1:50,000); Bryce Canyon National Park (1:31,680); or just use the little free map they give you upon entering the national park. Maps can be bought at the VC; also at Ruby's Inn.

Main Attractions A forested trail hike along the base of the Pink Cliffs.

Ideal Time to Hike May through October, but there will be more water available in May or June.

Boots/Shoes Any dry-weather boots or shoes. Running shoes work great on any trail in Bryce Canyon.

Author's Experience The author has hiked the entire trail, but in 4 stages, using all connecting trails. This took 2 days to complete. One stage from Bryce Point to Sheep Creek Trailhead, then the road-walk back to his car, took about 4 1/2 hours. A mtn. bike would eliminate a road-walk. All connecting trails were hiked a second time in 2003.

Looking north from the Agua Canyon Viewpoint. The Under-the-Rim Trail runs north-south along the eastern (right side) base of these Pink Cliffs in the pine trees.

Map 5, Under-the-Rim Trail, Bryce Canyon National Park

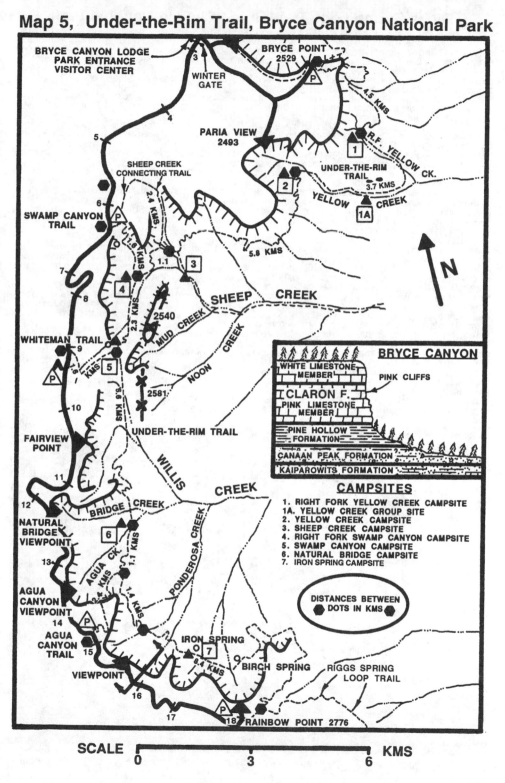

BRYCE CANYON LODGE
PARK ENTRANCE
VISITOR CENTER

WINTER
GATE

BRYCE POINT
2529

PARIA VIEW
2493

SHEEP CREEK
CONNECTING TRAIL

R.F. YELLOW CK.

1

UNDER-THE-RIM
TRAIL

YELLOW CREEK

4.5 KMS

2.4 KMS

1.6 KMS

2

3.7 KMS

1A

5.8 KMS

SWAMP CANYON
TRAIL

P

1.1

3

4

SHEEP CREEK

MUD CREEK

NOON CREEK

2540

2.3 KMS

WHITEMAN TRAIL

9

KMS

P

5

10

5.6 KMS

2581

UNDER-THE-RIM TRAIL

N

FAIRVIEW
POINT

11

WILLIS

CREEK

BRIDGE CREEK

12

6

NATURAL
BRIDGE
VIEWPOINT

AGUA CK.

PONDEROSA CREEK

2.4 KMS

1.1 KMS

13

1.4 KMS

AGUA
CANYON
VIEWPOINT

14

AGUA
CANYON
TRAIL

15

P

VIEWPOINT

IRON SPRING

7

8.4 KMS

BIRCH SPRING

RIGGS SPRING
LOOP TRAIL

16

17

P

18 RAINBOW POINT 2776

BRYCE CANYON

WHITE LIMESTONE
MEMBER

PINK CLIFFS

CLARON F.
PINK LIMESTONE
MEMBER

PINE HOLLOW
FORMATION

CANAAN PEAK FORMATION

KAIPAROWITS FORMATION

CAMPSITES

1. RIGHT FORK YELLOW CREEK CAMPSITE
1A. YELLOW CREEK GROUP SITE
2. YELLOW CREEK CAMPSITE
3. SHEEP CREEK CAMPSITE
4. RIGHT FORK SWAMP CANYON CAMPSITE
5. SWAMP CANYON CAMPSITE
6. NATURAL BRIDGE CAMPSITE
7. IRON SPRING CAMPSITE

DISTANCES BETWEEN
DOTS IN KMS

SCALE

0   3   6   KMS

Riggs Spring Loop Trail, Bryce Canyon National Park

Location & Access This is the last of 4 maps covering the trails of Bryce Canyon. Shown here is the Riggs Spring Loop Trail at the extreme southern end of the national park. The beginning & end of this hike is at **Rainbow Point,** which is at the end of the paved park road. In recent years, roads in Bryce Canyon up to Bryce Point have been kept open year-round; south of the winter gate it's normally closed (see Map 4). However, if the snow isn't too deep, the road to Rainbow Point is sometimes plowed, depending on availability of graders. At Rainbow Point there are toilets and sometimes drinking water (their spring was dry in the summer of 2003!). To get to the trailhead, drive south into the park from the Ruby's Inn area. It's best to stop at the visitor center located next to the fee station for any last minute information or maps. From there continue south for 27.5 kms (17.1 miles) and stop at the big parking lot next to mile post 18.

Trail/Route The Riggs Spring Loop Trail is well-maintained and because of the availability of water at 2 locations, it's one of the better hikes in the park, and certainly one of the better areas for backcountry camping. From Rainbow Point, you can do the loop-hike either clockwise or counter clockwise. From the parking lot look for any path heading south toward Yovimpa Point and the Bristlecone Loop Trail. At nearby trail junctions are signs pointing out the beginning of the Riggs Spring Trail. Once on it, head east or west. For this description, head west down toward Yovimpa Pass, a distance of about 2 1/2 kms. From there continue south on a good trail (actually an old road) to Riggs Spring and nearby campsite which is about 5 1/2 kms from your car. From there, head north, then east along the base of the escarpment. Along the way, you'll pass the Corral Hollow Campsite which has no water. From there continue easterly a ways, and south a little, then north & northwest back to the parking lot. If you're interested in a short walk, some of the nicest views around can be had from Yovimpa Point and from along the Bristlecone Loop Trail.

Elevations Rainbow Point, 2776m; Yovimpa Pass, 2548m; Riggs Spring, 2269m.

Hike Length/Time Needed The total length of the Riggs Spring Loop Trail is about 14 kms. Fast walkers can do this hike in about 3 hours, but for others it can take 4-6 hours. However, of all the trails in the park, this one has some of the nicest campsites, so you might consider spending a night on the trail. Riggs Spring is the best campsite, with good water and lots of shade & grass.

Water Riggs Spring is fenced off to keep cattle or deer away from where the water comes out of the ground in a pipe. It has a good, year-round flow, but of course the NPS insists you purify it first! Yovimpa Pass has a spring and maybe a little running water, some of which is pumped up to the parking lot at Rainbow Point (except during times of drought, as was the case in 2003!). The Corral Hollow Campsite is normally dry; unless you arrive in spring, when some water is available for a short period of time in the creek bed.

Maps Trails Illustrated/National Geographic map Paunsaugunt Plateau, Mount Dutton, Bryce Canyon (1:50,000); or Bryce Canyon National Park (1:31,680). Both maps can be bought at the visitor center. Or just use the little free map they give you when you pass through the fee station.

Main Attractions The highest & coolest part of the park is at Rainbow Point, making it a nice hideout in summer. The walk to Yovimpa Point is a good place to see old bristlecone pine trees.

Ideal Time to Hike From about early to mid-May, until the end of October. Each year is a little different.

Boots/Shoes Any dry-weather boots or shoes.

Author's Experience As usual, the author was in a hurry on this loop-hike, which usually included a short side-trip along the Bristlecone Loop Trail; round-trip was about 3 hours on 3 different hikes. His last trip in 2003 took 2 3/4 hours

This is the Riggs Spring Campsite with a tent in the background. The spring is off to the far right.

Map 6, Riggs Spring Loop Trail, Bryce Canyon N. P.

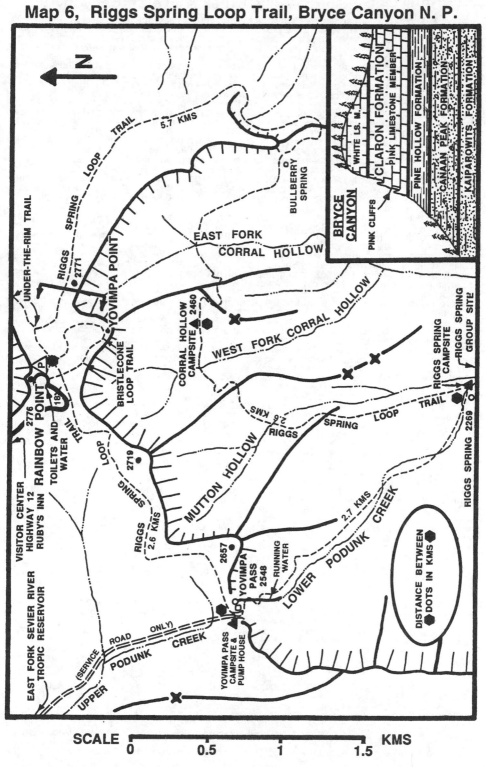

BRYCE CANYON

KAIPAROWITS FORMATION
CANAAN PEAK FORMATION
PINE HOLLOW FORMATION
CLARON FORMATION
PINK LIMESTONE MEMBER
WHITE LS. M.
PINK CLIFFS

N

5.7 KMS

SPRING LOOP TRAIL

UNDER-THE-RIM TRAIL

RIGGS 2771

YOVIMPA POINT

EAST FORK
CORRAL HOLLOW

BULLBERRY SPRING

CORRAL HOLLOW CAMPSITE 2460

WEST FORK CORRAL HOLLOW

BRISTLECONE LOOP TRAIL

2.6 KMS

RIGGS SPRING LOOP TRAIL

RIGGS SPRING CAMPSITE

RIGGS SPRING GROUP SITE

RIGGS SPRING 2269

RAINBOW POINT
TOILETS AND WATER
18

2776

VISITOR CENTER
HIGHWAY 12
RUBY'S INN

LOOP

SPRING

2719

MUTTON HOLLOW

RIGGS 2.6 KMS

2657

2.7 KMS

LOWER PODUNK CREEK

YOVIMPA PASS 2548

RUNNING WATER

DISTANCE BETWEEN DOTS IN KMS

EAST FORK SEVIER RIVER
TROPIC RESERVOIR

(SERVICE ROAD ONLY)

PODUNK CREEK

UPPER

YOVIMPA PASS CAMPSITE & PUMP HOUSE

SCALE
0   0.5   1   1.5   KMS

Bull Valley Gorge, Willis Creek & Averett Canyon

Location & Access This map shows 4 canyons located southwest of the small town of Cannonville. Get there via the **Skutumpah Road,** which runs from the area just south of Cannonville in a south-westerly direction towards these canyons, and on past the Swallow Park, Deer Spring & Skutumpah Ranches. The Skutumpah Road ends (or begins) at the upper end of Johnson Canyon northeast of Kanab. This is the shortest link between Kanab and Cannonville.

The Skutumpah Road is generally open to all vehicles from around the first of April until sometime in November. But each year is different. During years with dry winters, it's possible to travel it all the time, except for a week or so right after a storm. Parts of this road just south of the Bull Valley Gorge Bridge are made of clay, which becomes very slick when wet. Also the steep dugway just south of the old Clark Ranch on Willis Creek, is sometimes icy in the coldest part of the year. In the winter of 1986-87, two 4WD's slid off this part of the road and had to be pulled out. However, it's a better road now. In the warmer half of the year, the clay beds dry quickly after storms and it's a good road for all vehicles with a fair amount of spring, summer and fall traffic.

One way to get there is to drive east from Kanab on Highway 89. Between mile posts 54 & 55, turn left or north onto the paved Johnson Valley Road. At Km 26.6/Mile 16.5 is a junction at the head of Johnson Valley. Turn right or northeast onto the graveled & graded Skutumpah Road going toward Cannonville. You'll pass the Skutumpah, Deer Spring & Swallow Park Ranches, then at Km 67/Mile 41.6 (distance from Highway 89) will be the **Bull Valley Gorge Bridge.** Continue northeast to **Willis Creek** at Km 69.9/Mile 43.4; and to **Averett Canyon** at Km 72.4/Mile 44.9. If you continue northeast, you'll come to the paved Kodachrome Basin Road at Km 79.9/Mile 49.6. Cannonville is another 4.7 kms (2.9 miles) north.

If coming from Cannonville, head south on the Kodachrome Basin Road for 4.7 kms (2.9 miles) until you reach the Skutumpah Road, then turn south. From there, drive 7.6 kms (4.7 miles) to Averett Canyon; or to Willis Creek at Km 10/Mile 6.2; or on to the Bull Valley Gorge Bridge at Km 12.9/Mile 8.

Trail/Route There are no trails in these canyons; you simply walk down the dry creek bed or along a very small stream flowing through Willis Creek Gorge. If you make the loop-hike of Bull Valley Gorge & Willis Creek, using the middle part of Sheep Creek as a link between the two, then you'll walk along a seldom used 4WD track in the bottom of the dry wash of Sheep Creek. About twice a year, the graz-ing permit holders, take in or bring out cattle from the middle part of the Upper Paria River Gorge via Sheep Creek.

Averett Canyon & Monument To find the monument (read more about it below), walk from the Skutumpah Road down the dry creek bed a little less than one km; or 8 minutes at a fast walk. You'll know you're near the monument when you see an old trail running up the east side of the canyon. The monument is about 8m above, and 30m back from the dry creek bed on a low bench on the right or west side. It's in a small clearing, facing east and surrounded by piñon-juniper trees (be there in the morning hours to take pictures). If you continue downcanyon another km, you'll come to 3 dropoffs in about 100m. Walk along the west side of the canyon and just below the 3rd dropoff, climb down a ramp to the bottom. From there you can walk up Willis Creek to the road.

Willis Creek Simply walk in or out of the canyon with no obstacles. About 800m into the hike is a small waterfall; walk around it. The best narrows are about 300m before the junction with Averett Canyon. Below that the canyon slowly opens up and gets deeper.

Bull Valley Gorge Park on the north side of the bridge next to the fence, or at another site about 200m east, then walk along the north side of the narrow slot canyon west of the bridge about 350m. At that point you simply walk into the dry creek bed. Just below that there used to be a big log jam, but that's gone now (at least as of 2003), washed away in a big flood. In about the same area are now 2 short dropoffs of about 2m each caused by chokestones. Most people can get up or down these OK, but take a short rope to help less-experienced hikers. Near the bridge is another dropoff from a huge boulder; climb down a log on the right. Or maybe jump or slide. The best narrows in the canyon are in this upper part before coming to the bridge. When you reach the bridge, look up and you'll see the remains of the pickup which slid into the upper slot and took 3 lives. Read more below.

There's a steep route out of the gorge located about 100m or so below the bridge. The author went up this route once, but those unaccustomed to rock climbing may feel uneasy using this entry/exit (E/E). On the map are other possible E/E routes to the gorge; the best one may be about 1 1/2 kms below the bridge. Or just retreat back upcanyon the same way. If you like longer hikes, walk down to Sheep Creek, turn north a ways, then head west up Willis Creek and back to the road.

Elevations Bull Valley Gorge Bridge, 1850m; trailhead on Willis Creek, 1840m; the junction of Bull Valley Gorge and Sheep Creek, the low point on a loop-hike, about 1650m.

Hike Length/Time Needed Most people just hike down each canyon a km or so, see the best part, and return the same way. Doing this may take 1-3 hours. Or for long distance hikers, the length of the walk down Bull Valley Gorge, up Sheep & Willis Creeks back to the Skutumpah Road, is about 20 kms. Combine that with the 2 1/2 km walk along the road between the trailheads, and you have an all-day hike from 6-9 hours (a mtn. bike would eliminate the road-walk). It's also possible to do the hike in 2 days, making an overnight camp in the lower part of Sheep Creek, near where it enters the Upper Paria River Gorge. In that area you should find running water, presumably year-round (?), and good campsites. If taking in big packs, it'll be easier to go down Bull Valley Gorge, rather than up.

Water For short hikes take your own from a culinary source. But there's year-round running water in much of Willis Creek. You could probably drink this water as-is in winter, as the land above the road is summer range for cattle. It's best to purify it first however. Bull Valley Gorge is dry, as is most of Sheep Creek. Water does begin to flow out of seeps in the lower part of Sheep Creek as the red-col-ored lower parts of the Navajo Sandstone begins to be exposed. This should be good water in sum-mer, as the cattle are out of the canyons and in the mountains.

Maps USGS or BLM map Kanab (1:100,000) for driving & orientation; and Bull Valley Gorge (1:24,000--7 1/2' quad) for hiking.

Main Attractions The upper one or 2 kms of each canyon have some nice fotogenic slots similar to the Buckskin Gulch. The scenery in the lower part of Bull Valley Gorge, with the huge Navajo Sandstone walls dotted with pine trees, is worth seeing too. Also interesting is the unusual bridge over the upper part of Bull Valley Gorge, and the 1954 accident scene where 3 men were killed. Also, the Averett Monument discussed below.

Ideal Time to Hike From April through October. This time period offers the best chance for the

36

Map 7, Bull Valley Gorge, Willis Creek & Averett Canyon

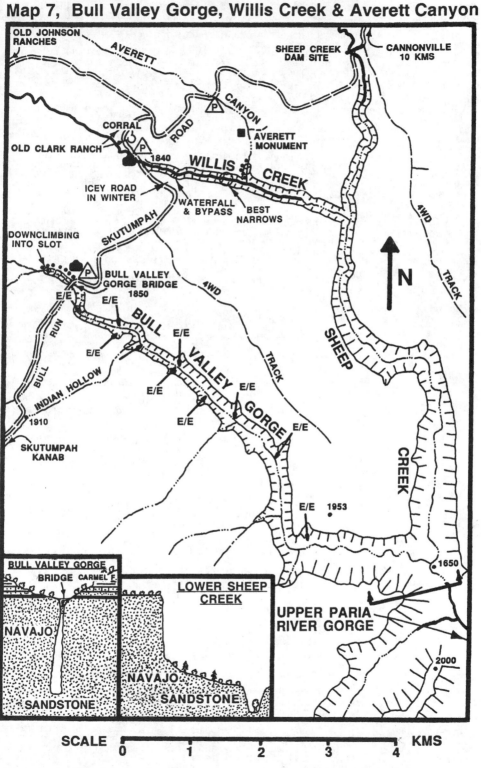

OLD JOHNSON RANCHES

AVERETT

SHEEP CREEK DAM SITE

CANNONVILLE 10 KMS

CANYON

P

ROAD

AVERETT MONUMENT

CORRAL

OLD CLARK RANCH

P

1840

WILLIS CREEK

4WD TRACK

ICEY ROAD IN WINTER

WATERFALL & BYPASS

BEST NARROWS

SKUTUMPAH

DOWNCLIMBING INTO SLOT

P

BULL VALLEY GORGE BRIDGE 1850

4WD

N

E/E

BULL

BULL RUN

E/E

E/E

VALLEY

TRACK

E/E

INDIAN HOLLOW

E/E

E/E

GORGE

SHEEP

1910

E/E

SKUTUMPAH KANAB

E/E 1953

CREEK

1650

BULL VALLEY GORGE

BRIDGE CARMEL F.

LOWER SHEEP CREEK

NAVAJO

SANDSTONE

NAVAJO

SANDSTONE

UPPER PARIA RIVER GORGE

2000

SCALE 0 1 2 3 4 KMS

Road to be open & dry. May or June, and September or October, might be the ideal time.

noes Willis Creek is small and you can hop right across, but it's best to have wading-type
or that part of the hike. Bull Valley Gorge has no running water, but just up from the bridge,
nay find pools which can hold water and mud for a few days or a week after each storm. For the
ure loop-hike, wading-type shoes may be best.

Author's Experience The author first tried hiking Bull Valley Gorge on a very cold mid-April morning,
but found big pools of water & mud near the bridge. A month later it was dry and he made 2 more
trips into the gorge at that time. Another time he went down Willis Creek on his way to Deer Creek in
the middle part of the Upper Paria River Gorge. His last trips were in 2003 with a digital camera.

History of the Bull Valley Gorge Bridge

One of the more spectacular and unusual bridges you'll ever see is the one spanning the upper part
of Bull Valley Gorge. The top part of this extremely narrow slot is only about one meter wide. One
reader, whose name has been lost, measured the depth of the slot from the top of the bridge to the
bottom at 44 meters. The rock involved is the ever-present Navajo Sandstone, the most prominent slot
canyon making formation on the Colorado Plateau.

This bridge was first built sometime in the mid-1940's by Marian Clark, Ammon Davis and Herm
Pollock. The first stage of that operation involved using a winch to drag several large logs across the
gap to serve as a foundation for the bridge. Then planks were laid across the logs, making a rather
simple bridge which was first used by local cattlemen. This was the first time Bryce Valley and the
Kanab & Johnson Canyon areas were linked. A later event forced the county to upgrade the bridge
which is safe & sound today.

That event was the accident which occurred sometime on Thursday, October 14, 1954. Three men
died as their pickup got out of control and slid off the bridge and wedged in the upper part of the gorge.
The victims were Max Henderson, 33, and Hart Johnson, 37, both of Cannonville; and Clark Smith,
32, of Henrieville. The Garfield County News carried the story in the October 21 edition.

Quoting from the newspaper report; *They started out Thursday to set up a deer hunting camp on
range land one of the men owned in Kane County. When they had not returned by Saturday, a search
was started for them.*

*A party led by Kendall Dutton of Cannonville, crossing the Bull Valley Gorge bridge, at 1 p.m.
Sunday, sighted the pickup truck lodged in the narrow gorge about 50 feet [15 meters] below the
bridge.*

*Bodies of two of the victims were still wedged into the truck, the third body had fallen clear and
crashed to the Gorge floor almost 200 feet [60 meters] lower down.*

*The Highway Patrol and county Sheriff were called in and the rescue operation started. Garfield
County Sheriff Deward Woodard was in charge of removing the bodies which was a hair-raising operation. His son, Paul Woodard, with a rope around his waist, worked for hours sawing away parts of
the truck--including the steering column--in order to free the bodies [Herm Pollock recalls they also
used an acetylene torch for awhile]. He worked at the dizzy height above the canyon floor, with the
swaying truck threatening to give [way] under him at any time [from the truck to the bottom of the gorge
is about 30 meters]. When one of the bodies was released from the truck, the weight almost pulled
22 men over the edge as the slack in the rope was suddenly snapped up.*

*According to the Sheriff, in reconstructing the accident, the light pickup truck the men were riding,
stalled on the south side of the bridge and rolled backwards and into the gorge, dropping 50 feet [15
meters] before the narrowing sides crushed the cab and the men inside it.*

Hart Johnson was buried in the Georgetown Cemetery south of Cannonville; Max Henderson was
buried in the Cannonville Cemetery north of Cannonville; and Clark Smith was buried in the Henrieville
Cemetery. All tombstones are dated October 14, 1954.

Since the accident, the Bull Valley Gorge Bridge has been rebuilt. It appears workers simply
pushed trees and large rocks down into the narrow chasm where they became lodged in the upper
narrow part. Then a bulldozer must have pushed more rock and debris on top of that, making a very
solid and much wider bridge than was first built.

When you stop there today, walk west from the bridge along the north side of the gorge and from
there you can see the pickup still lodged in the narrow slot. As you walk along the bottom of the gorge
you have an even better view of the truck from below. Because the pickup is sitting high and dry and
protected from rain and snow by the bridge, it will be there in the same position for a long time.

Averett Monument

Another interesting thing to see in the immediate area is the Averett Monument (some people spell
it Everett). First the story behind the grave.

In August of 1866, a Mormon cavalry company from the St. George area was ordered by Erastus
Snow, to go on an expedition to the Green River against the Indian Chief Black Hawk and his group.
This company, under the command of James Andrus, left the southern Utah settlements and went east
past Pipe Springs, Kanab, up Johnson Canyon, and northeast to the upper Paria River Valley. This
was before there were any settlements in the area and traveling was rough.

By the time they reached the spot where Cannonville is today, many men were sick. It was decided to send these men back home. So 6 men and 14 head of disabled horses headed back. Along the
way the small group was attacked by Indians. Elijah Averett Jr. was in the lead and he was shot and
killed. The rest of the group escaped and managed to circle around and return to the main unit in the
upper Paria. The Indians, presumably Navajos, were pursued, but escaped. Later, Averett was buried
on August 27, 1866, where he died. This is in the bottom of what is now called **Averett Canyon**. The
place is right on the old trail which was used by early-day stockmen and settlers before the present-
day road was built.

Later in 1871, Frederick S. Dellenbaugh wrote about visiting the place in his diary. He stated he
came across the grave marked by a sandstone slab with *EA 1866* cut on it, which the wolves had dug
out, leaving the human bones scattered around. Later, local cowboys reburied the bones and erected a cedar post with Averett's name on it. Many years later, the Boy Scouts of Tropic put that cedar
post in their little museum or scout hall in Tropic, and replaced it with a permanent stone marker that
you see there today. According to Wallace Ott of Tropic, the new monument, the larger of the two, was
dedicated in April, 1937. About 15 people showed up and James L. Hatch, the local Stake President
of the Mormon Church, conducted the dedication ceremony.

Both of these scenes are in the narrows of the upper part of Bull Valley Gorge not far above the historic bridge.

Above The narrows of Willis Creek. There's a small stream running through this canyon, but it's small and you can normally just step across it.

Right Bull Valley Gorge. This picture shows a hiker immediately below the Bull Valley Gorge Bridge. Just above the darkest part of this picture, can be seen the wheel of the pickup that's been there since October 14, 1954.

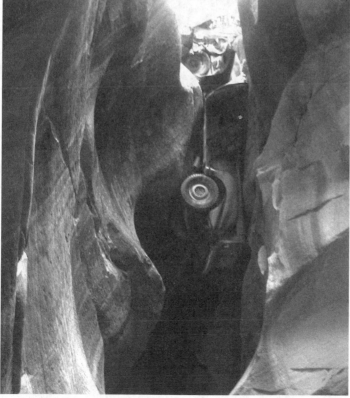

Above The Averett Monument in Averett Canyon. The smaller, rounded, and closer of the 2 monuments reads: *EA 1866*

Left A closeup telefoto look from below at the pickup lodged in the slot of the upper Bull Valley Gorge. It's now part of this historic bridge.

Above Looking southward at the historic dirt bridge over Bull Valley Gorge. To the right is upcanyon and the normal entry route.

Right The little waterfall in the upper end of Willis Creek. You can easily walk around this minor obstacle on the right or left.

In Bull Valley Gorge, just above the bridge and looking back upcanyon, is this boulder you'll have climb down over. This shouldn't be a problem as you can slide down, and help each other back up. Look for a log if there's none there. This place changes with every flood.

This is the little waterfall in the upper part of Willis Creek. Walk around this on the right or left.

Bullrush, Tank & Deer Range Canyons, Lick & Park Washes, and No Mans Mesa & the Jepson Goat Trail

Location & Access These 4 canyons are located about halfway between upper Johnson Valley (which is 16 kms/10 miles east of Kanab) and Cannonville. Before going, have the Kanab metric 1:100,000 scale map in hand. One way to get there is to drive along Highway 89 east of Kanab. Between mile posts 54 & 55, turn north onto the paved Johnson Valley Road. At the head of Johnson Valley and at Km 26.6/Mile 16.5, is a junction. Turn right or northeast onto the graveled & graded **Skutumpah Road** heading towards Cannonville. You'll pass the Skutumpah and Deer Spring Ranches, then at Km 50.5/Mile 31.4 (distance from Highway 89) is **Lick Wash**. Just before the dry creek bed, turn south onto a side-road and drive 100m to the trailhead parking & trail register. This should now be considered the place to park if you're going down Lick Wash to No Mans Mesa & the Jepson Goat Trail. Or, continue northeast past the Swallow Park Ranch on the right, to Km 55.4/Mile 34.4, then turn south and drive 1.3 kms (.8 mile) and park next to a gate & corral (when you arrive you may find a cattle guard instead of a gate). Beyond that point is private land belonging to James D. Ott of Kanab. If you want to see Adair Lake from that point, it might be best to call Ott first (Tele. 435-644-5000).

Or continue north on the Skutumpah Road to Km 57/Mile 35.4 and park at or near **Bullrush Hollow** (the gorge part is downstream a ways). This is the best place to park if you're planning to make a loop hike of both **Bullrush and Deer Range Canyons** if you have a **2WD** car. Or if you have a HCV/4WD, continue northeast to a junction at Km 60.2/Mile 37.4, then turn south toward **Deer Range and Tank Canyons**. Drive 400m (1/4 mile) to another junction with the most-used road veering left or east. Follow this pretty good road (sandy in places) for about another 3.2 kms (2 miles) and park next to a gate where 2 upper forks of Deer Range Canyon meet. By parking there, you can walk down Deer Range and up Tank Canyon. You could also head straight for the upper end of Tank Canyon but the vehicle tracks running there are seldom used so you'd need a 4WD for sure. The scenery and foto ops are much better in Tank & Deer Range Gorges than in Bullrush Canyon.

If you continue northeast on the Skutumpah Road, you'll come to the paved **Kodachrome Basin Road** at Km 79.9/Mile 49.6. Cannonville is another 4.7 kms (2.9 miles) to the north.

If coming from Cannonville, head south on the Kodachrome Basin Road for 4.7 kms (2.9 miles) until you reach the Skutumpah Road, then turn south. From there, drive 19.6 kms (12.2 miles) and turn south to the road junction near Deer Range Canyon mentioned above. Or for people with 2WD's, continue southwest to Bullrush Hollow at Km 22.9/Mile 14.2 (from the Kodachrome Basin Road) and park. Or drive 24.5 kms (15.2 miles) along the Skutumpah Road and turn south to the gate & corral mentioned above. Or better still, continue southwest to Lick Wash at Km 29.3/Mile 18.2 and park at the trailhead 100m to the south.

Trail/Route Starting from the **Lick Wash Trailhead**, walk down the dry creek bed. Soon you'll come to some short but interesting narrows in the upper part of the gorge, then use cattle trails near the bottom end, which will take you to the **LeFevre Cabin** and the **Jepson Goat Trail** (read more below). This old cabin, according to Ferrell Brinkerhoff of Tropic, was brought into the canyon from Ruby's Inn in about 1967. It had been one of the Inn's original rustic cabins. It was placed on a corner of what used to be a Utah state section. That state section has been horse-traded away since the monument was created. Because of the private land in Swallow Park, using Lick Wash is the best way to reach the LeFevre Cabin and the Jepson Goat Trail.

To hike up to **No Mans Mesa** along the **Jepson Goat Trail**, first make your way to the Lefevre Cabin. From there, walk eastward on the old road coming down from Swallow Park. As you reach the north end of No Mans Mesa, notice the talus slope coming down from the top. This is where the Jepson Goat Trail is located. To get on it, walk to the east side of a little hill at the northern base of the talus slope, then head straight up. You may go up halfway before finding the actual trail. Once on it, it's easy to follow. The upper part, which zig zags around some minor cliffs, is very obvious and is still in good condition. At the very top is a wire gate and short fence which kept the goats on the mesa. About 100m from the top of the trail on the east side, is another route up or down.

If you want to see Adair Lake, and if you've called James D. Ott and have permission, you could walk south from the corral & gate (or cattle guard) next to the historic Swallow Park Ranch. You'll be on a very sandy track that isn't used much. Soon you'll see **Adair Lake** to the west. You could also approach the lake by walking cross-country from the west and the Skutumpah Road as shown. Read more below.

Here's a loop-hike possibility. Walk down **Bullrush Hollow & Gorge**, then along the sandy road in Park Wash to very near the north end of No Mans Mesa & the Jepson Goat Trail, then turn northward into the dry wash coming out of **Deer Range Gorge or Canyon**. Walk north up the dry creek until you reach **Tank Canyon**; then veer left and continue to a very short slot & dryfall. To get around this, climb up an easy route on the left or west side, and exit Tank Canyon as shown. At about the junction marked 2075m altitude, turn left, and with compass in hand, walk west cross-country back to the Skutumpah Road.

However, a better plan for these latter 2 canyons would be to start in upper Deer Range Canyon. Simply walk downcanyon to where Tank comes in on the right, but continue down Deer Range for at least another 3 kms to see the best part of that drainage, then return and walk out of upper Tank Canyon. Upper Tank has some colorful rock as well. From somewhere in upper Tank, road-walk back to your car. With a 4WD (take a shovel), you can see Tank Canyon quicker. These 2 canyons with red & yellow streaked white Navajo Sandstone walls, plus blue skies & green ponderosa pines, offers some of the better foto ops around.

Elevations Trailheads; 1925m, 1950m, 2025m and 2002m, and down to 1850m at the old watering troughs north of the LeFevre Cabin near the base of No Mans Mesa.

Hike Length/Time Needed If you park on Bullrush Hollow, walk downcanyon and up Deer Range & Tank Canyons, then due west cross-country back to your car, it will be a long day for some, somewhere near 7-11 hours round-trip. If driving to upper Deer Range and hiking down that drainage and up Tank Canyon, you'll likely need 5-8 hours round-trip, but it will depend on how far down Deer Range Canyon you walk.

To walk down Lick Wash and to the top of the goat trail, will take most people all day, maybe 5-8 hours depending on how far you actually walk. Or for just Lick Wash, walk downcanyon 2-3 kms, see the best parts, and return the same way, all in a couple of hours.

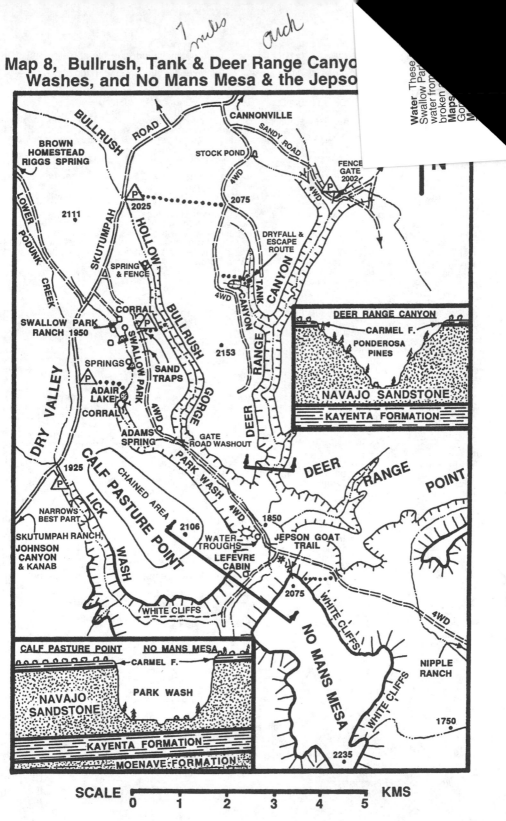

Map 8, Bullrush, Tank & Deer Range Canyo...
Washes, and No Mans Mesa & the Jepso...

7 miles *arch*

are all dry hikes so carry your own, and have plenty in your car. Nearby are springs in █ and in Bullrush Gorge, but with cattle there year-round, forget it! Cattlemen used to pipe █ Adams Spring down to around the LeFevre Cabin, but in the summer of 2003, the pipe was █ and uncared for. Don't expect water in the watering troughs in lower Park Wash.

█ USGS or BLM map Kanab (1:100,000) for driving & orientation; and Rainbow Point, Bull Valley █, Deer Spring Point & Deer Range Point (1:24,000--7 1/2' quads) for hiking.

█ **Attractions** Lick Wash has some pretty good narrows in its upper end. Or for scenery, see █ Tank & Deer Range Canyons. Those canyon walls have cracks allowing ponderosa pines to grow, making a unique scene. In some places, the colors are similar in some ways to the Coyote Buttes country. Also, Adair Lake, an old ranch, historic trail and grand views of the nearby parklands and White Cliffs from the top of No Mans Mesa.

Ideal Time to Hike Spring or fall, but it's also possible in summer because of the higher altitudes.

Boots/Shoes Any dry weather boots or shoes.

Author's Experience The author parked on the road at Bullrush Hollow, walked down the gorge, then up Deer Range & Tank Canyons, and finally cross-country back to his car, all in 6 1/2 hours. A 2nd trip in 2003 took 6 1/4 hours. He once walked down Lick Wash to the LeFevre Cabin, then around to the east side of No Mans Mesa, and climbed it along the route shown. He later came down the goat trail and returned via Park Wash and the Swallow Park Ranch. That took a little over 7 hours. Another time he parked at the corral & gate east of the ranch, walked down the road and up the goat trail, then checked out the cabin. After that he headed back, but climbed up the east side of Calf Pasture Point. That allowed some good views down on the LeFevre Cabin and No Mans Mesa. From there, it was back to his car, all in about 5 2/3 hours. In 2003, he actually drove his Tracker to the gate just beyond Adams Spring, rehiked the goat trail, saw the cabin, fotographed lower Deer Range Canyon and returned, all in 3 3/4 hours. It was after that trip that he talked to James Ott and it was agreed not to send hikers down from Swallow Park.

The History of Swallow Park Ranch

Swallow Park is a high valley just under 2000m elevation and located along the Skutumpah Road about halfway between the upper end of Johnson Valley and Cannonville. It's also just south of the southern end of Bryce Canyon National Park.

From the **Biography of John G. Kitchen**, it appears the first settler at Swallow Park was Frank Hamblin. This had to have been in the early 1870's because on an 1874 map of the state of Utah, Swallow Park and Adair Lake (also Molly's Nipple) are shown for the first time. Hamblin's occupancy extended into the 1890's to beyond the turn of the century. For several years, Hamblin was the only neighbor John G. Kitchen had while he lived at the Nipple Ranch. Read more about Kitchen in the chapter on Kitchen Canyon and the Nipple Ranch (Map 10).

If the memories of some of the old timers in Bryce Valley are correct, the second owner of the ranch was a man named George Adams. George married Minda, one of the daughters of Frank Hamblin, thus giving him a toehold on the ranch. George's name is on the spring located southeast of Adair Lake. Wallace Ott of Tropic believes Adams got there sometime in the early 1900's. Actually, it was November 23, 1917, when George first got the patent deed (first deed from the US Government) and official ownership under the homestead act. There are no other records of land ownership prior to that time, but most early settlers just squatted on the land without having a deed. It also took 5 full years of homesteading to gain official title. Frank Hamblin apparently never got the patent deed to the ranch.

Adams owned the ranch only a couple of years, then sold the lower part of the valley, around Adair Lake, to Jackson Riggs in December, 1919. Just prior to this sale, William Sears Riggs, settled and filed ownership on the northern part of the valley in November, 1919. In 1926, W. S. Riggs then bought more land from the federal government, which was an enlargement of his original 160 acres which is a quarter section. Sears Riggs is the one who built the first house at the ranch, which is still there today. His name is also on the good spring located near the head of Lower Podunk Creek, just south of the southern tip of Bryce Canyon and along the Riggs Spring Loop Trail.

Wallace Ott, who was born in 1911, bought the entire spread on December 11, 1940. He lived there part time, using it as a summer ranch until 1955. During his stay at Swallow Park, part of the property was sold to John H. Johnson in March, 1945. Then Wallace Ott sold out entirely to one of his relatives, Layton Ott, in December, 1955. Less than a month later, John H. Johnson sold his part of the Park to Calvin C. Johnson of Kanab. Many transitions have taken place over the years, but as of 2003, 3 Brinkerhoff brothers own the land north of the Skutumpah Road, while James D. Ott of Kanab owns the lower part of the old Swallow Park Ranch which includes Adair Lake.

In the middle of Swallow Park today (south of the Skutumpah Road), you'll see the old shack, built by Sears Riggs, and a newer larger house next to it. Regarding this home, and according to Ferrell Brinkerhoff of Tropic: *We tore down my Dad's old barn, and Les LeFevre constructed that house from the lumber. That would have been in about 1960.*

Also in this big pasture area are a couple of small dams and duck ponds which are nearly always full of water and are fed by several springs. Perhaps the most interesting thing to see is Adair Lake. It's been on early-day maps of the state of Utah as far back as 1874. It's at the southern end of the park, and right at the beginning of a little narrow section of upper Park Wash.

The lake is actually on a faultline, or just to the east of it. This faultline forms the cliffs you can see from upvalley. The west side has been raised, thus creating the lake just to the east. The lake and a swamp have always been there, but sometime prior to 1874, a very low dam was built, maybe a meter or less in height, to create a slightly larger and deeper lake.

One old-timer from Bryce Valley thought it was Frank Hamblin who built the dam, but a more likely scenario might be this. If you read the history of Pah Ria (Rock House), Pahreah and Adairville in the back of this book, it states that Jacob Hamblin and a small group of Mormons went to the Paria to settle in 1869 somewhere below The Box of the Paria. In the early 1870's they had floods & irrigation problems and part of that group, including Thomas Adair, went south and formed a small community later known as Adairville. It's very likely that Jacob & Frank Hamblin (?) and Tom Adair were together at Swallow Park and used that as a summer range for their cattle. It's almost certain that Adair built the lake which still bears his name.

The lake is there year-round; throughout wet and dry years (but it was dry in the summer of 2003!). On 2 occasions Wallace Ott attempted to plant bass there, but apparently it was too shallow to sustain them throughout the winter. Presently in the lake, and for as long as anyone can remember, are

46

salamanders, or what the locals call *water dogs.* The lake also has an abundant waterfowl population for much of the year.

Right on top of the low and almost invisible dam, is a corral. Wallace Ott used this corral to hold cattle for spraying, but other owners used it as a trap. They would herd cattle or horses up Park Wash from the area of No Mans Mesa. When they reached the corral, they were automatically trapped in one easy operation.

Adair Lake is easy to get to, and although it's on private land, it seems the owner shouldn't worry about visitors walking to it, because there's nothing there to disturb. Best to get there as suggested above, from the west and the Skutumpah Road.

No Mans Mesa and the Jepson Goat Trail

No Mans Mesa is a remnant of the former plateau to the north. At one time it was part of Calf Pasture and Deer Range Points, but erosion has left it high and dry, and surrounded by unclimbable cliffs. It's 6-7 kms long and about 2 kms wide. The walls you see are white Navajo Sandstone, which are part of the prominent feature across southern Utah known as the **White Cliffs.** The capstone is the Carmel Formation, a more erosion or weather resistant rock than the Navajo. The top of the mesa is flat, except it tilts down slightly to the north and northwest, as shown on the geology cross-section. The height of the cliffs range from 200m in the north, to about 400m at the south end. The altitude of the mesa top ranges from about 2075m on the north end, to 2235m to the south.

The author has found 2 routes to the top. One is up the east side of the northernmost point; the other is the nearby **Jepson Goat Trail.** In 1927, a local rancher by the name of Lewis Jepson built a trail up the extreme northern end of the mesa. He had 800 Wether goats on the mesa in the spring and summer of the first year, and 1300 to 1500 (one source states 3000) in the spring of 1928. One story says the goats were taken to the mesa top to hide them from the bankers who had a loan on their owner (?). The goats did fairly well for the short time they were there, but lack of water prevented it from becoming a good pasture, and has prevented any further grazing of livestock there since. For the most part, No Mans Mesa is untouched and is very pristine.

The very top part of the Jepson Goat Trail which winds it's way up the northern tip of No Mans Mesa. Right at the top is an old wire gate which kept goats from leaving this very pristine mesa.

Looking southeast at the northern end of No Mans Mesa. The Jepson Goat Trail zig zags up the obvious rockslide, then veers to the left near the top.

The LeFevre Cabin. It's located just across the valley from the beginning of the Jepson Goat Trail and the northern end of No Mans Mesa. This old cabin once housed tourists at Ruby's Inn.

Above Both pictures above were taken in the narrows of Lick Wash, as shown on the map. Using this gorge or canyon is now the preferred way to reach the Jepson Goat Trail and the top of No Mans Mesa.

Left Looking northwest from the top of the Jepson Goat Trail. In the far distance is the southern end of Bryce Canyon National Park; below that is Swallow Park, then Park Wash in the center of the foto. Off to the left a ways is the LeFevre Cabin; to the right and just out of sight, is the lower end of Deer Range Canyon.

Looking southeast with Adair Lake to the lower left. To the right of the lake is the corral & low dam, and the beginning of Park Wash. In the distance to the left in No Mans Mesa.

In the middle of Swallow Park is the old Sears Riggs shack on the left, the newer Brinkerhoff house in the center built by Les LeFevre in about 1960, and the southern end of Bryce Canyon National Park beyond. You can see the signature of Sears Riggs on the northwest face of Promise Rock. Read more about that place in the back of this book under, *Sheep and Sheep Shearing Corrals.*

Looking southwest from the top of the Jepson Goat Trail at Park Wash. In the background and to the right is where Lick Wash enters Park Wash. The LeFevre Cabin is hidden behind the buttress on the right

This is part of the fotogenic wall of upper Tank Canyon just below the dropoff.

Mollies Nipple, the Burch Ranch, and the Kitchen Corral Point/Telegraph Flat CCC Spike Camp

Location & Access Mollies Nipple is located just a few kms north of Highway 89, and about halfway between Page & Kanab. This peak is made of white Navajo Sandstone, but at the very summit is a brown and more erosion-resistant capstone. The author believes it could be the Carmel Formation; but it could also be a harder iron-rich layer within the upper Navajo. The name **Mollies Nipple,** supposedly comes from the wife of John G. Kitchen, whose name was Mollie. However, the name **Molly's Nipple** was first shown on an 1874 map of the state of Utah, which seems to be a little earlier than when Kitchen first arrived in this part of the country (?). Read more about Kitchen and his ranch under the next map, Kitchen Canyon and the Nipple Ranch.

To get there, drive along Highway 89. Right at mile post 37, turn north onto the **Nipple Ranch Road.** Drive north for 9.1 kms (5.65 miles) until you come to Kitchen Corral Point. There on the right or east side of the road will be a corral and stone building which was built by the CCC's who had a camp just up the road. If you want to visit the old **Burch Ranch,** park there. If you want to see where the old **Kitchen Corral Point/Telegraph Flat CCC Spike Camp** was situated, continue north on the Nipple Ranch Road to Km 11/Mile 6.8. Park on the right side of the road. From there, you should see a cement tank off to the east a ways--maybe 125m or so; and behind that a short canyon or indentation in the canyon wall with cottonwood trees.

To reach **Mollies Nipple,** continue north on the Nipple Ranch Road. At a junction known in the early days as **Five Pines,** which is 16.4 kms (10.2 miles) from the highway, veer right or northeast and drive through a gate (it it's closed when you arrive, close it behind you). Just beyond that gate is a shallow canyon and several pine trees, thus the name of the place below. At Km 18.2/Mile 11.3, turn right onto a sandy track. If you have a 2WD vehicle, drive about 100m and park next to 2 big round rocks & a juniper tree. If you have a 4WD, continue southeasterly on a very sandy track used mostly by ATV's. Most 4WD's can get up to a high point 1.9 kms (1.2 miles) from the Nipple Ranch Road. That place is marked 6152 on the *Deer Range Point 7 1/2' quad* (1875m on this map). From there you go down a very sandy slope; so only those who have lots of confidence in their vehicle should continue. In winter, or whenever there's moisture in the sand, any 4WD can make it to the base of Mollies Nipple; otherwise, park at one of these 2 suggested places.

To reach another possible starting point, continue northeast along the Nipple Ranch Road to a pass marked 1825m at Km 20.6/Mile 12.8. Up to this pass it's good for 2WD's. Park there. This improved Nipple Ranch Road was originally built by Pan American Petroleum which drilled a test hole near the high point marked 1937m on the *Kanab metric map.* That place is north of Kitchen Canyon and on top of **Oil Well Hill.** This road is now periodically graded by the county.

Trail/Route With so many 4WD's around these days, the most-used route to **Mollies Nipple** seems to be from along the very sandy track mentioned above. From wherever you start, just follow this track east to the base of The Nipple as shown on the map. This sandy track ends at the base of the peak where you'll see some ponderosa pines. Head straight up but veer a little to the left near the summit. There you should see a faint hiker's trail and after climbing a couple of steep pitches up the western side of the summit area, you'll be on top.

Or, from the pass marked 1825m, walk southeast up the slope to the top of a ridge. From there you'll see Mollies Nipple and your route in front of you. Walk east across the valley known as **South Swag,** and route-find up the south side of Mollies Nipple.

Elevations Mollies Nipple, 2216m; parking places, 1795m, 1875m, 2011m, and the pass at 1825m.

Hike Length/Time Needed From the pass on the Nipple Ranch Road, it's about 5 kms to the peak. A fit hiker can do this round-trip in about half a day; but for others, a full day, maybe 4-7 hours. However, it's a lot easier walking if you stay on the old sandy track all the way to the base of the Nipple. The distance will depend on where you park. It should take about the same time as going in from the pass.

Water Carry your own water.

Maps USGS or BLM map Kanab (1:100,000) for driving & orientation; and Deer Range Point (1:24,000--7 1/2' quad) for hiking.

Main Attractions A beautiful pyramide-shaped peak, an easy day-hike, and excellent views. Also the Kitchen Canyon cliff dwellings, along with an old abandoned ranch and remains of a CCC camp.

Ideal Time to Hike Spring or fall, but it can be climbed year-round.

Boots/Shoes Any dry-weather boots or shoes.

Author's Experience From the pass at 1825m, the author made it to the summit in 1 1/4 hours. He then went north down into Kitchen Canyon to the Monkey House, Nipple Lake & Ranch, then road-walked back to his car. Round-trip took 4 1/4 hours. In November, 1997, he walked from the Nipple Ranch Road along the sandy track to Mollies Nipple and explored upper Starlight Canyon & Cave. He returned the same way, all in 8 1/4 hours. In the summer of 2003, he drove his 4WD Chevy Tracker to the high point marked 1875m (6152') and stopped there because he was alone and the sand was very dry. He walked east along the sandy track and explored the peaks to the south along Pilot Ridge (some call this Starlight Ridge), then climbed Mollies for the 3rd time and returned, all in 5 1/4 hours.

The Burch Ranch

On your way to climb Mollies Nipple, you'll pass an abandoned ranch along the way. This is the **Burch Ranch,** one of the last to be built & occupied in the Paria River drainage. This old homestead is located in the northwestern corner of Section 33, T41S, R3W. Park beside the Nipple Ranch Road which is 9.1 kms (5.65 miles) from Highway 89 & mile post 37 and very near the old stone building.

Before going any further, remember part of the land you'll be walking over to see the Burch place is private and belonging to Calvin C. Johnson of Kanab. To rightfully explore the site, you should first telefon him and get permission. There's really nothing out there to disturb, but as a matter of respect, call him first at 435-644-2384. It was Cal Johnson who the author interviewed for this Burch Ranch story. Or you might also walk over to the CCC-build stone storage building east of the corral and talk to one of Calvin's hired hands and ask him if it's OK to proceed. In 2003, that was Chuck Beu who lived there in a small trailer house.

With permission or acknowledgment, walk across the main road from the corral to an old track running due west along a fence. Follow this track about 75m to a gate just before the Kitchen Corral Wash. Open, then close the gate behind you, and first walk southwest along this old road, then enter

Map 9, Mollies Nipple, the Burch Ranch, and Kitchen Corral Point/Telegraph Flat CCC Spike Camp

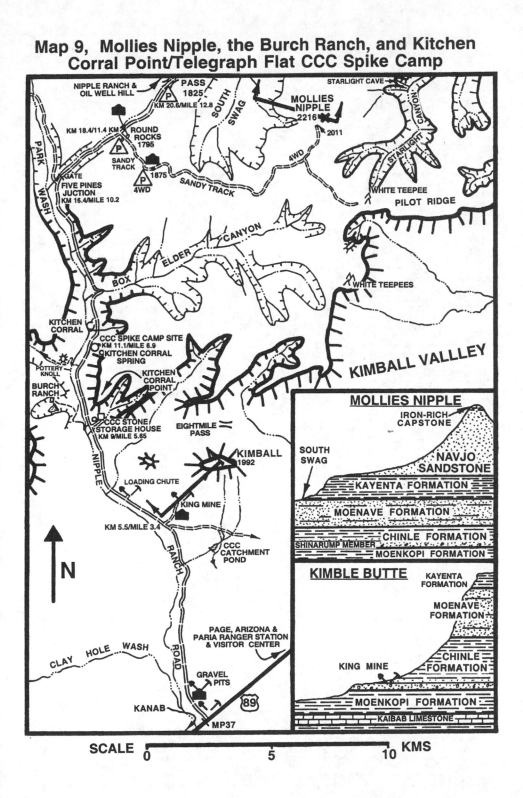

NIPPLE RANCH & OIL WELL HILL

PASS 1825
P
KM 20.6/MILE 12.8

STARLIGHT CAVE

SOUTH SWAG

MOLLIES NIPPLE 2216

STARLIGHT CANYON

KM 18.4/11.4 KM
ROUND ROCKS 1795
P

2011

4WD

PARK WASH

SANDY TRACK

1875
P
4WD

SANDY TRACK

WHITE TEEPEE
PILOT RIDGE

GATE
FIVE PINES JUCTION
KM 16.4/MILE 10.2

ELDER CANYON

BOX

WHITE TEEPEES

KITCHEN CORRAL

CCC SPIKE CAMP SITE
KM 11.1/MILE 6.9
KITCHEN CORRAL SPRING

KITCHEN CORRAL POINT

KIMBALL VALLLEY

POTTERY KNOLL

BURCH RANCH

CCC STONE STORAGE HOUSE
KM 9/MILE 5.65

EIGHTMILE PASS

MOLLIES NIPPLE

IRON-RICH CAPSTONE

NIPPLE

KIMBALL 1992

SOUTH SWAG

NAVJO SANDSTONE

KAYENTA FORMATION

LOADING CHUTE

KING MINE

MOENAVE FORMATION

CHINLE FORMATION

SHINARUMP MEMBER

MOENKOPI FORMATION

N

KM 5.5/MILE 3.4

CCC CATCHMENT POND

KIMBLE BUTTE

KAYENTA FORMATION

MOENAVE FORMATION

RANCH

PAGE, ARIZONA & PARIA RANGER STATION & VISITOR CENTER

CHINLE FORMATION

KING MINE

CLAY HOLE WASH

ROAD

GRAVEL PITS

89

MOENKOPI FORMATION

KANAB

KAIBAB LIMESTONE

MP37

SCALE
0   5   10 KMS

53

the gully and turn north for 75m in the dry wash bottom. Soon this old track veers up to the left out of the wash and heads west along another fence. After walking about 250m along the fence, turn right, pass through a 2nd gate and continue north along still another old road & fence. After 100m, veer northwest onto a cattle trail and walk another 500m to an old stock pond dam. The remains of the old Burch Ranch house is northwest of the dam about another 100m. This place is roughly 1 1/2 kms WNW of the Kitchen Corral Point.

In the early 1930's, Dood Burch, his wife, and 2 young sons, Robert & Omer, migrated from Texas to the House Rock Valley area, which is just south of the Vermilion Cliffs and Paria Plateau in northern Arizona. They lived there a couple of years, then homesteaded this ranch in about 1934 just below where Deer Spring Wash and Park Wash meet.

The first thing they did was build a small house out of lumber and a storage cellar behind the house. The cellar was dug out of the hillside, and lined with rocks. It was likely a place for food storage, but they may have lived in it too (?). They built several corrals, a small dam to hold back flood waters, and a blacksmith shop. Their water came from a small spring on the hillside about 200m south of the home & cellar. At one time they had water piped to the house where they raised a small garden.

One interesting feature of their home was that Mrs. Burch built a special floor, like nothing the author has ever heard of. When she had collected enough old fruit jars, she turned them upside down and placed them in the floor of the cabin. They must have been packed very close together so they wouldn't break. On top of the bottles, she laid goat hides. This is according the Calvin C. Johnson who later bought the place. When the author visited the site, there were a number of old bottles around, but apparently at a later date they installed another floor made of wood (?).

The Burches were horse & rodeo people. They apparently supplied some stock animals during the rodeo season in southern Utah and northern Arizona. They brought with them a number of quarter horses, and also ran goats in the hills around the ranch.

Evidently the Burches had marital problems. They never officially got a divorce, but he took off for Texas not too long after they had settled at this ranch. Sometime later he was killed when his horse stepped in a gopher hole and stumbled. Mrs. Burch ended up raising the boys by herself.

County courthouse records show the patent deed for the land was first obtained officially from the government in January, 1945. It was listed in the name of Omer Burch, the youngest of the 2 boys. Robert got married to a local girl and drove the mail truck for several years in the Kanab area before moving to Provo, where he lived for the rest of his life.

Omer and his mother moved to Oregon in 1947 after they sold the land to Johnson. Omer ended up as a brand inspector and continued in the rodeo stock business. After their departure, Johnson used the place as a kind of line cabin for several years afterwards, until the house and facilities literally fell apart and decayed. Parts of the house, cellar, and corrals are still there today.

The Kitchen Corral Point/Telegraph Flat CCC Spike Camp

From where you park right on the Nipple Ranch Road, 11 kms (6.8 miles) from Highway 89, look almost due east and you should see a cement structure about 125m away. This was a water storage tank for a Civilian Conservation Corps (CCC) spike camp. This was just one of hundreds of camps built throughout the west during the 1930's to do conservation projects of various kinds.

If you walk over there, you'll see some old pipe running up the short drainage behind it. Up that drainage a ways, near the cottonwood trees, is a pretty good spring which used to be piped down to the cement tank. About 60m or so northwest of the tank is a little depression which used to be a small pond. It looks like it was lined with rocks. About 50m southwest of that is a cement platform, likely part of the shower & toilet. Nearby is a small rock shelter. Other than these things there's nothing left to see of what was known to Kanab residents as the **Kitchen Corral Point Spike Camp**. But at least one of the boys who worked at the camp knew it as the **Telegraph Flat Spike Camp.**

The term spike camp, refers to a temporary camp the CCC's set up near some project they were working on. Workers at spike camps lived in tents, whereas in their main camps they were housed in army-style wood barracks. It was largely the US Army which organized, built and ran the main CCC camps. When the young men left their main camps to go out on work projects, they were supervised by either civilians and/or employees of the Grazing Service, which was the forerunner of today's BLM.

Calvin C. Johnson of Kanab, who was born in 1923, remembered a few things about this place:

That was just a little spike camp where the cement tank is. They set up their tents right there. They piped water from that spring up the canyon into the cement tank for their culinary supplies. They also honed out some logs for water troughs, and those troughs caught the overflow from the tank, then it would overflow into a little reservoir. They didn't have or use horses; they had convoy trucks, and they did all the work by hand. The guy who managed the spike camp was out of Tropic, which was my uncle John, a cousin to my grandad. John H. Johnson had a sheep permit out there and at one time owned the Nipple Ranch. Now in some way he organized that spike camp to do a lot of work in that Kitchen Point country.

That rock building the CCC's built was a sheepmen's supply house. It was located in the center of the winter sheep range and the sheepmen would take their herds down there in the fall & winter. All those sheep wintered around there and down below to the south. That was a 4-room supply depot for the sheepmen to store stuff in during the winter. It was made of native rock that the CCC's gathered up, then the sheepmen contributed money to buy lumber and other materials for the building; anything they had to buy was purchased by the sheepmen, but the CCC boys did the work.

Down south of there a couple of miles and to the east of the Nipple Ranch Road, they built quite a large stock pond, and rocked-it up. It's south & east of that King Manganese Mine about a mile [it's right on the line between Sections 11 &12, T42S, R3W]. They made a dike, then rocked-up the lower side of that, then they poured cement with rocks and made a spillway on the southeast side of that pond. At first it held water pretty good, but then it washed some of the sand away from the cement & rocks. The dike is still there but the spillway is partly washed out.

Hobart Feltner of Cannonville, who was one of the enrollees at the main Henrieville CCC camp just northeast of Henrieville, worked at this spike camp during the warmer half of 1937. He was a cook, and the cooks would rotate every 3 or 4 weeks with other cooks back at the main camp. Here's some of the things he remembered about the place, and an experiences or two:

*I'd say there was around 20 men there at that camp, maybe a few more. It wasn't a big camp. It was called the **Telegraph Flat Spike Camp**. There was 3 or 4 tents that the boys slept in and a cook tent. All the tents had wooden floors, and were boarded up around the sides, then they were capped*

54

with canvas. We cooked and ate in one big tent. We ate home style.

That cook stove burned coal. Them was great big long army cook stoves, and we had a little monkey stove in the back that you'd heat your water with, and we had an ice box to store food in. We could set our perishables in there and keep it cold. They'd bring ice in once a week. The supply truck came in once a week and it would bring supplies and we'd ship out laundry or whatever.

When the weather was good, the supply truck came right down the Piree (Paria) Crik and we'd stop at Crack Spring and get a good cold drink of water. In bad weather they'd have to go around by Kanab. When they took me in, we went right down the crik, but when I left, they took me around by Kanab.

There wasn't any army guys at the spike camps, it was just Grazing Service men and the enrollees. No flag raising or reveille! I was a cook and me and a helper got up and got everything ready for the boys and they ate their breakfast and they'd take the sandwiches we made for 'um and go out for the day. Then we'd have a damn good dinner for 'um when they came back in.

After we made lunches for the boys and they left to go to work for the day, then we'd have all this time to putter around, so we'd go over to **Pottery Knoll** and pick up broken pottery where they had dug them old boys up. That spike camp was just across the wash from Pottery Knoll, an old Indian village and burial ground.

We had a spring cemented-up into the side of the hill, then we had a cement tank that contained the water. Then there was a latrine tent where we could wash up and shower.

Chick Chidester was the head of the grazing end of the Henrieville camp, and he didn't like me and I didn't like him. So he was thinkin', I'll put him down at the spike camp and anchor him there! But of course I was workin' for the army and I didn't have to worry too much about ol' Chick Chidester! I didn't mind pullin' my time out there, at least something that was reasonable.

At that camp, a supply truck come in once a week and I told the driver, tell 'um to send a man out to replace me! But he didn't do it. So when the next truck come in, I said you tell them fellas up there--tell ol' Chick and that bunch--if he doesn't want these guys a cookin' for themselves, he'd better send somebody down here to take my place because this boy is comin' in on the next truck. Well, they had somebody to replace me on the next truck!

Pottery Knoll is located .6 km (.4 mile) back down the road (southwest) from the spike camp site. There you'll see a vehicle track running west into the **very sandy bottom** of Park Wash--park near the main road, then follow this track westward. At the southern end of a little ridge coming off the point between Park & Deer Spring Washes, is a high point called **Pottery Knoll**. Right on top is what is left of a small village. There are holes all over the top indicating it's been looted by local pot hunters. You'll also see small pottery fragments or potsherds all over the place, thus the name. If you take away even one piece of pottery, you'll be breaking Federal law. Please, just look around and leave everything as you find it.

For more information about other CCC camps in the area, read the chapter in the back of this book titled, **The Henrieville CCC Camp.**

Looking north at the south face of Mollies Nipple.

Above Kitchen Corral Point rises above the rock building built by the CCC's in the summer of 1937. This was once used by sheepmen for storing supplies during the winter season. The small house on the left was built later.

Right An old wood & coal burning kitchen stove and other junk litters the site of the old Burch Ranch. This place is located just west of Kitchen Corral Point.

Aerial view of Mollies Nipple. The north slope is in shadows on the left; south face on the right. In the background above the summit is lower Kitchen Canyon.

This is the old cement water tank at the Kitchen Corral Point/Telegraph Flat CCC Spike Camp site.

Right This sure looks like the Kitchen Corral Point/Telegraph Flat CCC Spike Camp which was situated next to the Nipple Ranch Road. These are army tents & cots, and an old coal oil (kerosene) lantern on the table. (Hasle Caudill foto)

This is the infirmary at the Henrieville CCC Camp in 1937. Looking north, the motorpool is to the right between the officer's quarters and the infirmary. Read more about the main CCC camp, and see more pictures, in the back of this book under *The Henrieville CCC Camp.* (Hasle Caudill foto)

Pieces of pottery, normally called potsherds, litter the ground all around the little butte called Pottery Knoll. This place is just west of the Kitchen Corral Point/Telegraph Flat CCC Spike Camp site.

CCC boys lining up for a meal at the mess tent at what appears to be the Kitchen Corral Point /Telegraph Flat Spike Camp. To the right out of sight is the cement water storage tank. Above that in a minor canyon is the spring. (Hasle Caudill foto).

Kitchen Canyon and the Nipple Ranch & Lake

Location & Access Kitchen Canyon is located in the area north of Highway 89 about halfway between Kanab & Page. One way to get there is to drive along Highway 89; between mile posts 30 & 31, turn north at the sign stating *Historic Marker*, with a parking place and a tall monument commemorating the old town of Pahreah. From there, the graded county road running northeast down to the **Paria Movie Set** is good for any 2WD car when conditions are dry. From the movie set, continue north for a total distance from the highway of 9.5 kms (5.9 miles) until you reach the Paria River in the area which was once the town site of Pahreah. Park at a convenient place in that area.

A 2nd way to Kitchen Canyon is to leave Highway 89 right at mile post 37, and drive north along the **Nipple Ranch Road.** At Km 9.1/Mile 5.65 you pass a stone building on the right at Kitchen Corral Point; at Km 16.4/Mile 10.2 is a road junction long known locally as **Five Pines**--turn right or northeast and close the gate behind you; at Km 20.6/Mile 12.8 is a pass marked 1825m on the map. 2WD's can make it up to that point, but that's where they must stop. Only 4WD's can go down the other side to the head of Kitchen Canyon and the Nipple Ranch. This last part is **extremely sandy!**

If you have a 4WD vehicle, continue north from the pass down to another junction at Km 24.5/Mile 15.2. From there, turn right and head southeast to the locked ranch gate which is 25.1 kms (15.6 miles) from Highway 89. Now if you're planning to use this route to get to Nipple Lake, the Monkey House and the old Kitchen Ranch Cabins, you must pass through private property. To get permission to walk along the upper part of Kitchen Canyon or Valley, call Calvin C. Johnson of Kanab at 435-644-2384. A simple telefon call will insure permission as he simply wants to know who is walking on his land. Even if you come using the Old Pahreah route to visit the Kitchen Ranch Cabins & Monkey House, Cal Johnson would prefer you call or let him know of your plans, as all these old historic sites are on his property.

Trail/Route After parking your car at the end of the road near the Paria River & Old Pahreah, simply walk upcanyon in the washed-out river bed. You'll be crossing the small Paria stream several times in the 8 kms or so to the mouth of Kitchen Canyon. Once inside Kitchen Canyon, you'll be walking west beside a small stream. When you arrive at Kitchen Falls (immediately beyond where Starlight Canyon enters--Starlight Canyon is discussed in the chapter with Hogeye Canyon, but the best map of it is here), route-find up the steep slope on the north side of the falls. You'll have to climb a little on all-4's because a big flood in the late 1990's caused the talus slope to slip. This wiped out part of the old trail which at one time was a wagon road down to Pahreah. Once above the falls, head west along cow trails. About 800m west of the falls (which is about where the private land begins), you can get out of the creek bed, and walk on cattle trails on either side of the "V" shaped erosional gullies so prominent in the lower end of Kitchen Valley. It's generally easy walking, but up to the old Kitchen Ranch Cabins & Monkey House, you'll have to navigate in & out of the big gullies on cow trails. Follow this map closely to locate these 2 historic sites.

If coming from the west, and with permission first, jump the fence at the locked gate, and walk along the sandy vehicle track on the north side of the big meadow in wetter times, is **Nipple Lake.** Near the low dam, which makes the lake bigger, you'll have a nice view of **Mollies Nipple** to the south. This old vehicle track ends at the **Monkey House** and another bigger dam Johnson bulldozed to stop further downcutting of the big meadow.

From the Monkey House, continue east on the south side of the big recently-made gully. If you stay on the south side, you'll have to weave your way around one canyon & gully coming in from the south, before you reach the Kitchen Ranch Cabins. Or head straight down inside one of these gullies, then after less than 1 1/2 kms, look for a cow trail heading up the embankment to the south. Simply said, you'll have to do some route-finding in this valley because of the new erosion gullies.

Elevations Old Pahreah, 1440m; the Kitchen Ranch Cabins,1642m; and Nipple Lake, 1693m.

Hike Length/Time Needed It's about 8 kms from Old Pahreah to the mouth of Kitchen Canyon, then another 5 kms to Nipple Lake. Plan on taking a lunch & water and spending the entire day seeing the Kitchen Valley historic sites. You could also camp in Starlight Canyon, where there's a good water supply--and no private land. With permission from Johnson, and a 4WD, you can see these historic sites in about half a day starting at the locked gate.

Water Take plenty in your car & pack. Lower Kitchen Valley & Canyon has running water, but there are cattle around throughout the year, so treat or purify all water. Lower Starlight Canyon has the best possibilities for a safe drink.

Maps USGS or BLM maps Kanab & Smoky Mountain (1:100,000) for driving & orientation; and Deer Range Point & Calico Peak (1:24,000--7 1/2' quads) for hiking.

Main Attractions Kitchen Falls, Nipple Lake, the stone Monkey House, and the ruins of the oldest ranch in the entire region, the John G. Kitchen Cabins and the Nipple Ranch. Once there, observe the unusual *ripgut or stake & rider fence.* Along the Paria are petroglyphs and the chimneys of the old Kirby Place and the Carlow Ranch, as well as the ruins of The Dugout Ranch. At or near the car-park along the Paria River is the Paria Movie Set, Old Pahreah townsite and the Pahreah cemetery.

Ideal Time to Hike Spring or fall. Or perhaps in winter warm spells, but if walking up from Old Pahreah you may want to use some waterproof rubber wading boots; otherwise your feet will turn to blocks of ice. Summers are pretty hot; too hot for most people to enjoy hiking.

Boots/Shoes Wading shoes along the Paria River route; dry-weather shoes if coming from the west.

Author's Experience He first visited the canyon on his first Mollies Nipple hike and from the pass at 1825m, then made 2 more foto trips into the canyon from Old Pahreah. One trip to Starlight, lower Kitchen and lower Hogeye Canyon, took about 9 1/2 hours round-trip. Another trip from Old Pahreah to Seven Mile Flat and the Monkey House, took 8 1/2 hours round-trip. In October, 1997, he parked at the pass marked 1825m, walked to the Anasazi ruins below, to the Kitchen Ranch Cabins and Monkey House, and returned, all in 4 1/4 hours. In 2003, he parked at the locked gate at the head of Kitchen Valley, walked down to the historic cabins, past Kitchen Falls, up to the cave in Starlight Canyon, then back to the valley and car, all in 6 1/2 hours.

History of the Kitchen or Nipple Ranch

One of the very first ranches to be built in this entire area is what most people call the Nipple Ranch. In researching the history of this old homestead, the author obtained a copy of the **Biography of John G. Kitchen,** from Adrian Kitchen (a great grandson) presently of Kanab. This short history of the original founder of the Nipple Ranch was compiled by Nephi Johnson of Mesquite, Nevada, and Ramona Kitchen Johnson of Kanab. They got the information from John G. Kitchen, Jr. The following is the his-

Map 10, Kitchen Canyon and the Nipple Ranch & Lake

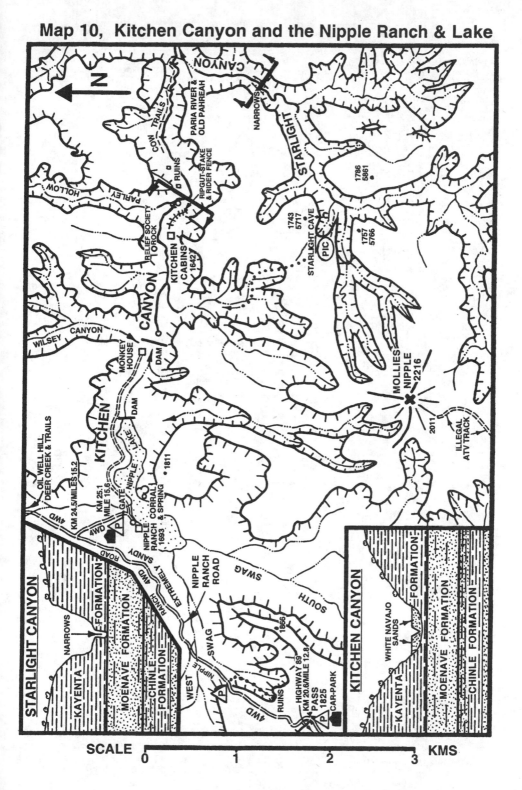

SCALE 0   1   2   3 KMS

tory of John G. Kitchen and the Nipple Ranch, which has been edited slightly for this book.

John G. Kitchen was born in Canada in 1830. Very little is known of his childhood or his early youth. The first anyone knows of him was during the gold rush days of California. There at the age of 19, his willingness to work and his determination to get along in the world began to assert itself. Money was plentiful at that time in California. A gold mine was to be had almost for the taking, but young Kitchen was not interested in a gold mine. His heart was set on a cattle ranch in the Rocky Mountains. So he worked at the job that paid the best and saved his $11.00 per day to make that cattle ranch dream come true.

In 1873 he arrived in Johnson, Utah [this is Johnson Valley east of Kanab], with a herd of heifer calves, which he had purchased in and around St. George. Sixtus Johnson was then running the Dairy Ranch, two miles [3 kms] north of Johnson, and he took the calves to manage while Kitchen went back to his job in California for the winter. This arrangement lasted for several years, with Kitchen returning each fall with more calves; or money to buy more.

In 1878 , he took a herd of steers to Nephi, Utah, to sell. While there and waiting for the train to load his steers, he became acquainted with Martha or Mollie Grice. She was waiting tables at the Seely Hotel, and keeping house for her uncle, William Grice. John married Martha and brought her back to the Dairy Ranch, which he had leased. There the couple lived until their first baby, Rose, was born. The following spring [1879] with the assistance of Nephi Johnson, they moved their cattle into Mollies Nipple Ranch.

The ranch received its name because of the peculiar shape and coloring of a large knoll or peak located to the south of the ranch and Kitchen Valley. Martha's nickname was Mollie, because it's common knowledge around the country this peak was named after Kitchen's wife. This peak of course, is named Mollies Nipple. When you see it, you'll understand how it got the name.

[Let's stop for a moment. On an 1874 map of the state of Utah, it shows among other places, **Molley's Nipple** for the first time. This means that Kitchen was actually there earlier than suggested above; or that the peak was not named after Mollie Grice Kitchen. Also, there are at least 2 ways of spelling this name. All the latest USGS maps spell it **Mollies Nipple.**]

Their life at the Nipple Ranch, though filled with hardships and disappointments, was successful. They started with meager beginnings and built slowly as time and means would permit, while faced with drought years, crop failures, and menaces such as gophers, squirrels, and chipmunks. For several years, Kitchen did all of his own riding on an old mare, "Dolly", upon which he carried food and a quilt for a bed when he was forced to camp away from home for a night or two. In later years he brought back a few blooded horses each fall or spring when he shipped his steers and thus built up a fine band of horses, along with his cattle.

Those first few years at Mollies Nipple Ranch were never to be forgotten by the Kitchens. They had a new country to conquer, land to clear, buildings and fences to be built, and cattle to tend. The cattle were so well taken care of, that other cattlemen said jokingly, that "Kitchen knew where every cow laid down each night." He knew his cattle so intimately that many of them were given names, such as Betsy, Posey, Kill Deer, Brin, Blue Neck, Red Rony, and Jennette.

The house or cabin built by John G. Kitchen. It has twin chimneys, a large rock cellar and smoke house behind. At least some of these structures must date from the 1880's.

Most of his cows were red Durham, branded with the box brand on the left ribs, and marked with a Kitchen Slit in each ear. The Kitchen Slit was a circular cut just above and following the vein in the lower part of the ear, and is so called because Kitchen was the first man in Southern Utah to use that mark.

To build up a better grade of cattle, he used to bring in blooded bulls each fall or spring when he returned from taking his steers to the railroad. One of these was a roan Durham named Paddy that cost him $500. The original cattle were Hereford stock.

A man named John Mangum helped the Kitchens with the buildings at Mollies Nipple Ranch. The corrals and fences were made of cedar logs and posts secured there in the valley and constructed in the stake & rider [sometimes called rip gut] style, which consisted of two posts set in the ground so as to form an X every 8 or 10 feet [2 or 3 meters] with a cedar pole rider placed in the saddle of the X to connect the pairs of posts. [Only those who have tried to chop down a cedar tree with an ax can appreciate the amount of work which went into this type of fence!]

The buildings were made of pine logs or native rocks laid up with mud. The roofs were of split pine logs. The split side was laid down, then covered with bark and about a foot [30 cms] of sand. It was on these roofs, warmed from the heat within, that the wild flowers first bloomed in the springtime.

The dwelling house, which consisted of two long rooms [actually two cabins and a store room placed next to each other], was constructed of hewed logs in the shape of a "T". One room served as a kitchen, living and dining room, and was heated by the cook stove and fireplace. The other room had a large fireplace and it served as a bedroom and a school room. The floors of both rooms were unplained lumber, but Mrs. Kitchen kept them scrubbed clean and white; "so clean you could eat off them", was a familiar family expression.

After their children became old enough, the Kitchens had a school teacher who boarded with the family every winter. These private tutors boarded with the family and assisted with the ranch labor when not teaching. Among these teachers were Robert Laws, Lydia Johnson, Jim Burrows, and a Mr. Ramsdale.

A little distance from, and at the back of the home, were the cellar and smoke house. These buildings were of much the same construction as the ranch house, except that the cellar was excavated about six feet [2 meters] in the ground. Here many bushels of fruit and vegetables were stored in winter, and milk and butter were kept cool in summer. The smoke house was constructed of rock, and here Kitchen cured beef, pork, and venison.

While their home was still being built, another child was born to them. For this occasion, Martha went to Pahreah, where she could have the assistance of other women during childbirth. The child was a boy and they named him John G. Kitchen, Jr. Their next two children were Rosena and Mattie, born at Nipple Ranch. Their fifth child, Una, was born in Kanab.

In addition to stock raising, Kitchen farmed and always had a garden to keep his family alive. There were several large springs that boiled up at the foot of the mountains creating a meadow land for several miles up and down the valley. These springs he dammed up and used for irrigation purposes. He would store the water for several days, until the ponds were full, then run the water off onto his crops. It was on the hillside just above the ditches that he used to build his hot beds. Early in the spring he would level off a small space on the mountain side, where the sun shone early and late and was pro-

This section of *rip gut or stake & rider fence* is southeast of the Kitchen House or Cabins.

tected from the cold. Here he would plant some of his seeds.

Before he began irrigating each spring he would carry water to the young plants. After he began irrigating, the hot beds were so located that he could scoop water from the ditches onto the plants with a shovel. He raised cabbage, cauliflower, squash, turnips, carrots, potatoes, corn, watermelon, rye, and hay. One year he raised over 800 bushels of corn. He had a span of oxen, Ben and Brady, to assist him with the farming, and other heavy work such as hauling wood and securing rocks for building.

Because of the lack of roads and long distances to any settlement, there was practically no demand for his produce, except what his own family, hired help, and what the livestock consumed. He delighted in taking a pack load of vegetables to his Hamblin friends at Swallow Park some 7 or 8 miles [11 or 12 kms] to the northwest. And each fall he enjoyed taking part of a beef to Pahreah, and distributing it among his less fortunate friends.

As his cattle increased and financial conditions improved, Kitchen purchased the Meadows Ranch from Chet Patrick. [In Dunk Findlay's history of his family's ranch, he states that Alexander Duncan Findlay sold his squatters rights of the Meadows to Kitchen for 50 head of steers]. This ranch was northwest of the Nipple, not far below the Pink Cliffs on Meadow Creek. It's just to the northwest of the present-day Deer Springs Ranch. That place was used primarily as a summer ranch. There he added dairying to his ranching activities. Some summers he milked as many as 50 cows. From the milk, they made butter and cheese, which were packed and stored for winters use at the Nipple. [The late Dunk Findlay stated that a man by the name of Joe Honey lived in a dugout Kitchen had built as a shelter at the Meadows for one winter, to preserve Kitchen's claim to the land].

At the Meadows Ranch, with the assistance of Edwin and John Ford, and Thomas Greenhalgh, Kitchen built a dugout shelter [it's still at the upper end of the Meadows today] and large corrals and fences. One night the cowboys had five hundred head of three and four year old steers ready to drive to the railroad the next morning. About two o'clock in the morning something frightened them, and they stampeded. The cowboys were camped only a short distance from the corral and when they heard the cattle running and bellowing, they rushed to the scene. The corral was built on a sidehill, and on the downhill side, the cattle were piling up and being trampled. Fear seized the cowboys, lest so many would die, so they spent the rest of the night fighting the steers back from the downhill side of the corral. The next morning revealed one steer dead, and several lame and bruised.

Another interesting event happened just south of Kitchen's Ranch. One winter Ira Hatch of Panguitch, Utah, had his sheep camp in the high country close to Mollies Nipple. One afternoon it began to storm, and it snowed all night. The next morning the sheep bunched up beneath cedar trees, unwilling to brave the deep, newly fallen snow. Still the storm continued. For three days it snowed and when the storm finally broke, Hatch and his sheep were virtually prisoners in four or five feet [about one and a half meters] of snow.

Hatch left his freezing, starving sheep and made his way to the Nipple Ranch for help. Kitchen took one team, Ned and Colonel, cut down a tree, and dragged it around to make trails for the sheep to follow into lower country where the snow wasn't so deep.

During the summer of 1895, Kitchen let Ebbin Brown dairy at the Meadows Ranch and paid him $1.00 per head for all the three and four year old steers he could roundup. He gathered 500 head. Then Kitchen and other cowboys gathered another 500 head and drove them to the railhead at Milford, Utah. There they were loaded on cattle cars and shipped to Kansas City, Missouri, and to Omaha, Nebraska. Young John Jr. accompanied his father on this trip, traveling with and tending the cattle until they reached their destination. It was on this trip, and while in Salt Lake City on their return journey, that his father gave him the gold watch which he still carries (1947) and treasures so much, and a bicycle, which was the first one ever owned in Kanab.

At the lower end of the canyon there were clumps of squawberry bushes. Every fall Piute Indians would come to the Nipple country to hunt deer and to gather squawberry brush to make baskets. Kitchen made it a practice to buy two baskets, two tanned deer hides, and several deer hams from them each fall. The baskets were used to haul laundry and for storing dried fruits and vegetables. The deer hides were used to make belts, saddle strings, harness parts and shoe laces. The deer hams were cured in the smoke house and eaten during the winter.

One interesting story is told about the "tally stick" method of keeping track of calves branded. Whenever Kitchen went out to brand calves, he would carry a short stick in his back pocket. When he branded a calf, he would whittle a notch in the stick. In the evenings after he had returned to the house, the notches were transferred to a much larger tally stick, which was 8 or 10 feet [2.5 or 3 meters] long and kept overhead on the rafters in the kitchen. Whenever he desired a count of the seasons branding, he would take down the tally stick and count the notches. One side represented the heifers; the other side the steers. It was when his branding count reached enormous figures that he became known as "The Cattle King of Southern Utah." It was estimated at one time that he owned about 5000 head of cattle, ranging from St. George on the west, Panguitch on the north, and to the Colorado River on the east and south. [When the late Dunk Findlay of Kanab heard about the 5000 head of cattle, he doubted very much the country could have sustained that many. Maybe 1000 would have been a closer figure, according to Dunk].

Kitchen was a great lover of knowledge, and so that the children might have an advantage of better schooling, and his family enjoy some of the finer things of life, he appointed George Adams foreman of his ranch, and moved the family to Kanab in the early 1890's. [It was during this time, 1894, that 18-year-old Will Chynoweth of Pahreah was hired to help with the cattle, which was reported to be 2000 head. He worked for Kitchen for 2 1/2 years, according to the Chynoweth family history compiled by Mary Jane Chynoweth Fuller] This move seemed to climax his career, and his star of success began waning. Liquor had always been his weakness, so while in Kanab and with plenty of leisure time and money, drinking got the upper hand. Trouble began brewing, which ended in the divorce courts.

The loss of his family was a great blow to Kitchen. Mollie ended up marrying Joe Honey, a man who once worked for Kitchen. Sorrowing, Kitchen made a liberal settlement both of alimony and for the education of his children, which Thomas Chamberlain faithfully administered. He sold his cattle to Scott Cutler and Hack Jolly, who moved them out of the country. The remnant of the box brand was sold to Johnny Findlay.

In 1898, Kitchen went to Lee's Ferry, where he lived only a short time. He died very suddenly, and under mysterious circumstances. A rider was dispatched to Kanab with the news. Young John rode *in haste all night, but the body was already buried when he reached the Ferry.*

Thus ended the career of a man with clouds of uncertainty hovering about the cause of his death as well as about the disposal of his property. In his will he bequeathed to each of his daughters $20,000, and to his sons $25,000, but through faulty administration, the fortune was dissipated. Although his family spent years in the inheritance courts, not a dollar was ever recovered.

In 1904, his children erected a monument to his memory at Lee's Ferry Cemetery. The monument which was there in 2003 read, "*John G. Kitchen, Born in Canada, March 25,1830, Died July 13, 1898.*"

After the death of Kitchen, there seems to be a gap in history of the Nipple Ranch. Evidently, it was in the courts for some time. Some of the old timers in the area thought it may have gotten into the hands of 2 men named Hunter and Clark, then after a time it may have been taken over by Jim Henderson. However, the first recorded transfer of the property (Kane County Courthouse) was on July 2, 1908. The land, part of a grant of 100,000 acres, was given to the state of Utah by the Federal government, for the use of the "Institution for the Blind".

The next transfer of ownership was on March 11, 1912, when the Cross Bar Land & Cattle Co. purchased the ranch from the state of Utah. Later, on May 7, 1927, John H. Johnson bought the land from Kane County, apparently for back taxes owed by the cattle company (?). The last time the land officially changed hands was on January 16, 1956, when present owner Calvin C. Johnson bought it from John H. Johnson.

At the ranch today, Calvin has a small cabin & windmill which pumps well water to a trough. It's located west of Nipple Lake, along with several corrals. Hikers are asked to stay away from this part of the ranch. About 1 1/2 kms west or upcanyon from Kitchen Falls are the ruins of an old chimney in one location, and a rock wall in another, as shown on the map. Calvin thinks these were built by the early white inhabitants of the valley.

Less than one km west of these ruins, and south of the 2 big gullies, are the Kitchen Ranch Houses or Cabins. These are in ruins, but in fair condition considering their age. The roofs have collapsed, but parts of log walls and the 2 chimneys are still standing. When the author first saw the twin chimneys and rooms, he thought it was the home of an old Mormon polygamist. Instead the second room was for the school and school teacher. Nearby is an old corral and a long fence running southeast, both of which are made in the *"rip gut or stake & rider"* fashion. The holes you'll see in the corral gate posts, are said to have been made by Kitchen who used a hot iron poker to run through the posts. Also the ruins of the rock smoke house & rock celler, and other structures.

From Kitchen's Ranch Cabins, route-find west in & out of 2 big gullies. After about a km, you'll see some of Calvin C. Johnson's work in erosion control. Crossing the valley is an earthen dam, and just to the northwest of it is a rock cabin called the Monkey House.

The Monkey House and Nipple Lake

According to Calvin C. Johnson, the Monkey House was built in 1896 by Dick Woolsey, at the mouth of what the USGS maps call Wilsey Hollow (it apparently should be "Woolsey" Hollow). It's made of stones, and it sits up against a large boulder. Here's an old tale about how this place came to be known as the Monkey House. When Woolsey and his wife first settled in at this location, they had with them a monkey. The monkey was kept in a box or cage on top of a pole near the cabin. When someone approached the homestead, the monkey would chatter loudly. However, Cal Johnson later talked to a descendent of Peter Shirts who lives in Escalante. He told Johnson the name comes from the shape of the rock which forms the back wall of the rock cabin.

Inside the cabin and on the wooden doorway structure, are many names of early-day cowboys. At least one new roof has been added, and the ramada or porch has been taken off from the original structure, evidently in the years John H. Johnson owned the land. The Monkey House is in quite good condition today. Behind the cabin is a small pen or corral in a small opening of the cliff.

About one km west of the Monkey House is Nipple Lake. Evidently there has always been a small shallow pond in this swampy area, but today you'll see a low dam, maybe a meter high, which backs up the clear blue water to form the lake. However, the flash floods of 1997 filled in about half of this lake; and in August of 2003, the lake was completely dry. This was the 5th year in a row with below average precipitation in Utah. As you walk through this valley, you'll see to the south, the ever-present Mollies Nipple, towering above the landscape.

Other Historic Sites

If you're coming into the area to climb Mollies Nipple from the west, there are several historic things to see along the way. Leave Highway 89 right at mile post 37, and drive north on the Nipple Ranch Road. See some of these historic sites under **Map 9** which includes the **King Manganese Mine, a CCC-built catchment pond & rock storage building, the old Burch Ranch, and the Kitchen Corral Point/Telegraph Flat CCC Spike Camp.**

Further along the Nipple Ranch Road at about Km 11.8/Mile 7.35 , is an **old stockade-type corral** (with the poles standing upright and stuck in the ground). This is called the Kitchen Corral, but he didn't build it. According to Calvin C. Johnson: *It was the old stockmen who ran cattle in there who built that Kitchen Corral. There was Kitchen & Findleys, and Swapps, Hamblins, and the people who had cattle, then they run a* **rip gut or stake & rider fence** *up there on the hill back of that corral. It goes from a natural ledge there on [a point next to] Box Elder Canyon, up to the natural ledge that drops into the Nipple Ranch.*

For those who like to explore, drive about another km north of the Kitchen Corral to the mouth of Box Elder Canyon coming down from the east (see the Kanab metric map). You can walk up this canyon to reach Mollies Nipple. Somewhere at the head of this canyon and before you reach the Nipple, is the old stake & rider or ripgut fence, mentioned above.

By parking at the pass marked 1825m, you can also include on your trip, a quick look at the only **cliff dwellings** in the immediate area. From the pass, walk or drive north down the very sandy road about 1000m (to about Km 21.7/Mile 13.5). There you'll be in what is known as the West Swag. Once there, walk due south in this valley to the head of what could be called the south arm of the West Swag. Right at the southern end, and under the overhang, are 2 cliff dwellings. These rock & mud structures have been partially damaged by time and cattle.

The strange thing about these dwellings is, they're under an overhang and facing north--the first of its kind this author has seen. The Indians who inhabited this site were likely a part of what archaeologists call the Virgin Anasazi. But the site is in the transition zone between the Sevier, Great Basin, or Fremont Culture area, and the Anasazi Cultures to the south. Just north of the ruins, and along the east-facing wall, are some minor petroglyphs. You'll have to look hard to find these.

The Monkey House got it's name because of the shape of the rock behind the stone cabin; it looks just like a monkey's face.

Old signatures can be seen on the doorways inside the Monkey House.

Left Old signatures (one dates from 1916) on the exterior doorway of the Monkey House.
Right This is a gatepost to the corral behind the ruins of the Kitchen Ranch house or cabins.

Near the end of Kitchen Canyon is a big dropoff and Kitchen Falls. To the right, out of sight, and coming off the bench above the waterfall, is the trail down to the old town of Pahreah.

Above The north facing Anasazi/Fremont ruins at the head of the South Swag.

Right Metate grooves (depressions where aborigines ground corn or maze, or other seeds) on top of a large rock next to the ruins in the South Swag.

Left John G. Kitchen died in 1898 at age 68, so this portrait is likely from the late 1880's, or more likely the 1890's. **Right** Mollie Grice Kitchen, perhaps from the 1890's. (Merrilyn Johnson Cornell foto)

This is Deer Range Point as seen from the southeast and from along the road running up to Oil Well Hill and the start of the hikes into the head of Deer Creek.

Deer Creek Slots and Oak Canyon

Location & Access At least one canyon on this map requires **ropes & rappelling gear** to get all the way through; this is the **Main or Southwest Fork of Deer Creek.** For those with no experience in technical canyoneering, it's recommended you go with someone who has the experience, equipment & skills needed. Or if you've done some rappelling, read parts of this writer's other book, **Technical Slot Canyon Guide to the Colorado Plateau** for a brief description of equipment & techniques.

Featured here is the **Main Fork of Deer Creek Canyon** and several tributaries including the **Left Hand Fork & Little Fork** (author's name), plus **Oak Canyon** which enters the middle part of the Upper Paria River Gorge just below Deer Creek and the CCC & Deer Trails Trails.

To get there, drive along Highway 89 about halfway between Page & Kanab. Right at mile post 37, turn north onto the **Nipple Ranch Road**; this is the same road that runs to the Burch Ranch, Mollies Nipple and Kitchen Canyon. Drive north past Kitchen Corral Point and the CCC-built sheepman's rock building on the right (Km 9.1/Mile 5.65), then at **Five Pines Junction** (Km 16.4/Mile 10.2), turn right or northeast and drive through a gate, closing it behind you. At Km 20.6/ Mile 12.8 is a pass between the Park Wash Drainage and Kitchen Canyon. From that point on **you must have a 4WD** with good clearance (if not, you'll have to park there and walk an extra 8 kms/5 miles). From the pass continue north downhill. At Km 24.5/Mile 15.2 is a turnoff to the right which takes you to Calvin C. Johnson's Nipple Ranch; but instead, continue north in deep sand across the head of upper Kitchen Canyon or Valley. In this area, you'll be in **deep sand** for about 2 kms, then as you start to climb up toward **Oil Well Hill**, small rocks are mixed with sand making driving easier. At Km 28.6/Mile 17.8, you'll be on top of a ridge where the road turns right and runs east to an oil well drill site. Stop at that curve where you see the very sandy ATV track heading northwest. Camp and/or park there.

Rating (From the American Canyoneering Association) Deer Creek **3A (this can be a B) III** or **IV**; Left Hand Fork, **3A III**; Little Fork, **3A II** or **III**; Oak Canyon, **3A III**.

Equipment For the **Main Fork of Deer Creek**, rappelling gear, one 60m rope, several meters of webbing or old rope for slings, several Rapide/Quik Links (R/QL) and bolt kit & 1 bolt just in case. If planning to rappel over all the dropoffs in the **Left Hand Fork & Little Fork of Deer Creek**, and **Oak Canyon**, rappelling gear, one 60m rope, lots of webbing & one shorter rope, and several R/QL's will be needed.

Trail/Route For the **Main Fork of Deer Creek** From the 4WD parking place, walk northwest along a very sandy illegal ATV track. After 600m, and about one cm northeast of elevation 6139 on the *Deer Range Point (DRP) 7 1/2' quad,* will be a cow trail heading due north downhill. This will be the end of the trail you'll use to get back to your car. But don't use it now; instead continue northwesterly on the sandy track toward DRP. Directly beneath this prominent peak, you'll cross a minor drainage, then veer northeast as the track fades. From there, continue north around the eastern base of DRP, then northwesterly on cow trails. When you're due north of the most-easterly peak on DRP, and at the head of Deer Creek's Left Hand Fork, you'll come to many *toadstool or mushroom-like rocks.* These features all have a piece of weather-resistent iron-rich caprock on top which shelters the softer Navajo Sandstone below leaving something that looks like a giant toadstool or mushroom. They're all over this region, but the best cluster seems to be north of DRP and at the head of the several forks of Deer Creek.

From the head of **Left Hand Fork,** continue west or northwest over a low divide near elevation mark 6273 and route-find down into the head of the **Main Fork.** Walk downcanyon. Soon you'll come to Rappel 1, a double drop of about 17m into a nice slot. Tie webbing around a nearby chokestone and rappel; just below that will be an interesting 7m downclimb in a vertical chute, then a short walk out of the **Upper Slot.** Below the Upper Slot are a couple of escape routes out to the east and several short narrows before coming to the **Lower Slot.** This is the good part. After about 400m of moderately cool dark slot, you'll come to R2, a drop of about 16m. There you should find one bolt & hanger (B&H) on the right. Rap down into a deep hole, then continue for another 30m to find a steep, tight 8m downclimb in the darkest part of the slot. Beginners may want to be belayed, but it's easier than it first appears. At the bottom is a pothole, possibly with water--no more than waist deep--and a 90° left turn, then a 2nd possible pool (could be a swimmer?), and a 90° right turn. After that, walk out through a 100m-long, 2m-3m-wide slot, after which it opens up into a gorge.

Below R2, you'll walk along a sandy wash inside an open gorge. After 500m will be the Northwest Fork coming in on the left. Walk up this 200m to find another nice straight slot before coming to a 7m dryfall. There should be more slot & rappels above that, but getting to the upper end of that fork would be time consuming.

In the 2 kms between the Northwest Fork and Rappel 3, you'll find one escape exit to the south onto **Cad Bench**, and several exists to the north up to **Asay Bench** as shown on the map. Immediately above R3 will be a 40m-long slot which you can downclimb into. At the end, you could arrange a chokestone to rappel from, but it will likely be an awkward start for a 30m rappel!

Or, climb upon the bench to the right or south side to find webbing around 2 bushes & a small rock buttress. There you'll have an easy start for the 30m rappel right off the nose of a larger buttress. At the bottom will be springs, running water & trees. Walk downcanyon in or beside the small creek--wading-type shoes will make the trip faster & easier. In the lower end of the canyon are many campsites, 2 panels of pictographs and a long panel of petroglyphs, as shown on the map. There's also a deer, cow & horse trail out of lower Deer Creek up to Cad Bench which you could use to return to your car. Read more about it under the *Left Hand Fork* below.

Less than one km below where Deer Creek meets the Paria, pay close attention on the right side to find a cairn marking the bottom end of the constructed **Deer Trails Trail** zig zagging up the west side of the Paria River Gorge (this trail begins about 100m below the beginning of the CCC Trail on the east side of the canyon). After zig zagging up about 100m, this old cattle trail levels some, then heads southwest up a sandy hogsback ridge between Oak Canyon and Little Fork. Soon it passes between 2 prominent round rocks as shown on this and the 7 1/2' quad. This trail eventually meets the sandy ATV track near the main road as described above. From there, it's 600m back to the main Nipple Ranch Road and your vehicle.

Left Hand Fork of Deer Creek This is the largest & longest of all the tributaries of Deer Creek except for the Main Fork. To get into it from the top, use the exact same route as if going to the Main Fork, but when you reach a point just east of DRP, follow that drainage (let's call it the **South Fork**) down to the north & northeast. Along the way are a number of dropoffs, all of which you can skirt around to the left or west. You could rappel these, but there doesn't seem to be any slots of conse-

Map 11, Deer Creek Slots and Oak Canyon

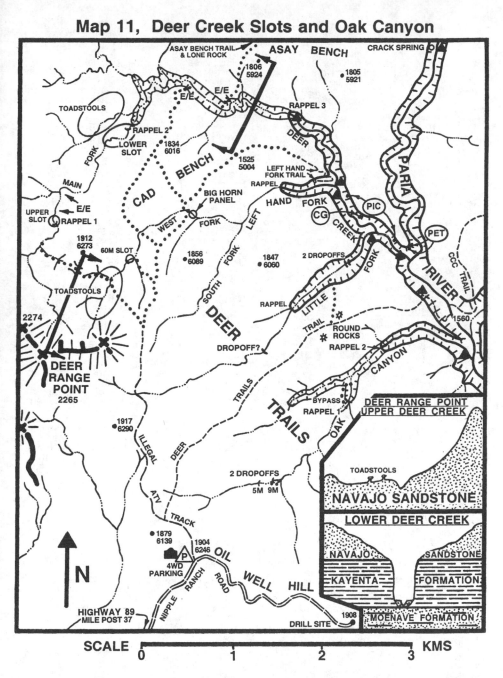

SCALE
0   1   2   3   KMS

quence, so rappelling seems pointless. When you reach the confluence of the **South & West Forks**, head up the West Fork skirting around 2 dropoffs. About 600m up the West Fork is one of the best petroglyph panels around. Wallace Ott of Tropic alerted the author to this. Read his story below. This **Big Horn Panel** is along the south side of a 2m-wide straight-sided slot. Most of the art is of big horn sheep which are 2m-3m above the dry wash. Some markings are up as high as 5m-6m. Those are much older than the lower ones.

You can also walk into the upper end of the **West Fork**, but after about 500m or so, you'll come to a 12m dropoff. The author still hasn't seen the top of this rappel, but has came up to it from below. Immediately below this rap is a nice tight 60m slot that's worth the effort. One full length rope and some webbing to tie to a log should set up this rappel. About one km below that will be the Big Horn

71

Panel.

Below the confluence of the West and South Forks, is one short slot a good climber can downclimb into, or skirt around it to the left and reenter just below. Finally, about 650m above Deer Creek, will be a big 30m-35m dropoff which you could rappel by using chokestones & webbing. That would put you into the lower canyon with water & trees.

Or, get out of the canyon on the left or north, and route-find east toward the point between the Main Fork and Left Hand Fork of Deer Creek. As you approach the end of that point, be looking for signs of an old trail which was first used by deer. Let's call this the **Left Hand Fork Trail**. Look for some stone cairns. This trail zig zags southeast right off the point, then one bench above the floor of the main canyon, it turns west and follows the same bench into the Left Hand Fork for about 225m before heading down through oak brush to the creek below. Wallace Ott & Wallace Henderson modified that old deer trail--read Ott's story below.

Little Fork This is the short canyon between the Left Hand Fork and Oak Creek. To do this canyon from the top end, start from the 4WD parking on Oil Well Hill, and walk down the Deer Trails Trail in the direction of the Paria. About one km above the 2 rounded rocks, turn left or north and work your way down into the upper end of the canyon. At the very beginning, you should come to at least one dropoff; you can either rig things up for a rappel--followed by some kind of slot or narrows--or skirt around this part on the right or left. About 750m below the first dropoff will be a big dryfall of 30m-35m or so. The author hasn't done this, but has seen it from below. You may need two 50m ropes, plus webbing & rappelling gear.

Below this big dropoff is a dry & uninteresting V-shaped canyon. There are several possible exits as shown, one of which the author used to escape south. One km below the big dropoff are 2 dryfalls of 7m-8m each, one after the other. You can downclimb the first, but it'll be tricky with crumbly-looking rocks on the right--so help each other. Or rap from boulders. Walk around the second drop on the left. From there it's 800m along a small steam to the mouth of the canyon and Deer Creek.

If you're in Deer Creek, you can walk up this short side-canyon and perhaps climb up the second dropoff on the left--it's tricking upclimbing too, as part of that rock wall looks like it's ready to fall! Once in the middle part of the drainage, there should be several escape routes out to the north, and at least one exit to the south up steep slickrock as shown. That's the one the author used.

Oak Creek To do this canyon from top to bottom, walk north and a little east from the 4WD parking at 1904m/6246. After about one km, you'll be in the main drainage. You'll soon come to a 5m drop; chimney 6m down a crack on the left side. About 300m below that will be a 9m dropoff; skirt around this on the right and scramble to the bottom. After about 1500m of easy walking, you'll come to a big dryfall of about 20m. If you wish to rappel, you can install webbing around some bushes or trees near the edge. If you don't want to rappel, then walk 200m along the left (northwest) rim and reenter the drainage just above a side-canyon. Below R1 is an easy walk of about 800m with at least one exit on the left or north, then R2, a drop of about 25m. You can of course exit and head down the Deer Trails Trail, and walk up the lower end of Oak Canyon from the bottom. Or if rappelling, there are nearby trees or rocks you can attach webbing to. At the bottom of this drop are springs, trees & running water all the way down to the Paria. Along the way, are old signs that beaver have been there, but nothing new as of 2003. If you see fresh signs of beaver, drink water from the spring source only; or purify it. Oak Canyon doesn't have any slot or real narrow parts, so most people won't be interested in rappelling through this drainage. The best part is the lower end.

Elevations 4WD trailhead, 1904m; bottom of Deer Trails Trail along the Paria River, about 1560m.

Hike Length/Time Needed To hike and rappel through the Main Fork and return via the Deer Trails Trail, will take from 9-12 hours. To go down the Left Hand Fork, view the Big Horn Panel, then rappel into the bottom--or walk down along the Left Hand Fork Trail--and return via the Deer Trails Trail, will take from 8-11 hours. The time it takes will depend on your fitness, route & side-trips. To explore Little Fork or Oak Canyon will take from 6-9 hours, depending on whether you actually rappel or skirt the dryfalls, or go on any side-trips.

Water Running water is found in the lower parts of each fork of Deer Creek & Oak Canyon, but take it directly from the spring source to avoid contamination from cattle or beaver. Or treat it. Cattle may be here during the winter grazing season--November 1 to May 1, depending on the ever-present drought conditions.

Maps USGS or BLM map Kanab (1:100,000) for driving & orientation; and Deer Range Point & Bull Valley Gorge (1:24,000--7 1/2' quad) for hiking.

Flash Flood Danger High in the lower slot (above R2) of the Main Fork of Deer Creek, low elsewhere.

Ideal Time to Hike Spring or fall, but you can hike year-round.

Boots/Shoes Normally, you can get by with dry-weather shoes in the upper canyons, waders in the lower end of each, and along the Paria River.

Author's Experience On one scouting trip, he went down the Main Fork as far as Rappel 2, then escape east and rim-walked other parts before going down Deer Trails Trail to the river, up Oak Canyon, up lower Deer Creek and back to his Chevy Tracker at the 4WD trailhead--round-trip took 9 1/2 hours. Another scout trip took him down Johnson Hole Canyon Trail (see Map 16) to Lone Rock, up Asay Canyon, onto Asay Bench, down into the middle part of Deer Creek, then returned, all in 10 1/4 hours. Another trip was with Nat Smale. We went down the Main Fork (setting up all rappelling stations), out the bottom end, up Deer Trails Trail and back to the Tracker in 9 3/4 hours. Your trip will likely go fast now the canyon has been prepared, but check the webbing closely, especially at the last rap because it's exposed to the sun. Later, the author explored the Left Hand Fork including the West Fork slot, the Big Horn Panel & Left Hand Fork Trail, plus explored Little Fork & parts of Oak Canyon, on 2 trips of about 8 hours each.

History of the Left Hand Fork Trail & the Discovery of the Big Horn Panel

Here's the story of the building of the Left Hand Fork Trail and the discovery of the Big Horn Panel of petroglyphs as told by Wallace Ott of Tropic:

Wallace Henderson and I built that trail in the 1930's. We took some powder down and done some blasting. He was 20 years older than me, but we worked and run cattle together, and we built that trail and fixed that waterin' hole. I fixed it so cows or horses could come down to water in that Left Hand Fork, then they'd go back out there on Cad Bench. I had a big log at the bottom so the horses couldn't go down the creek. It didn't work as good for cows as we thought it would, so later I run some horses out there and raised some colts. I'd only have to go out there about 3 times in the whole sum-

mer. Wallace Henderson has been dead for about 57 years (as of 2003), and I don't know of anybody else who ever run livestock on that trail--but there's been a few deer hunters use it. Wallace Henderson was the younger brother of Jim Henderson, the one who owned the old Nipple Ranch at one time.

Here's Wallace's story of how he found the Big Horn Panel: *It was deer season, and we had camped just off the Paria a little ways up Deer Creek. I had one of my older brothers and one of my brother-in-laws with me. We had gone up that Left Hand Fork Trail to look for deer on Cad Bench. I run out of canteen water; it had been stormin' a little, and I was lookin' for a little tank (pothole). And that's when I saw that panel. Joe Dunham, he lived there in Cannonville, is the only other guy I've talked to that's seen 'um, and he's been dead a long time. I saw that panel sometime between 1936 & 1940 after the CCC's was there. The CCC's was there at the mouth of Deer Creek Canyon in about 1935 & '36. That's when they built that CCC Trail out of the Paria on the east side.*

Deer Creek Rappelling Section

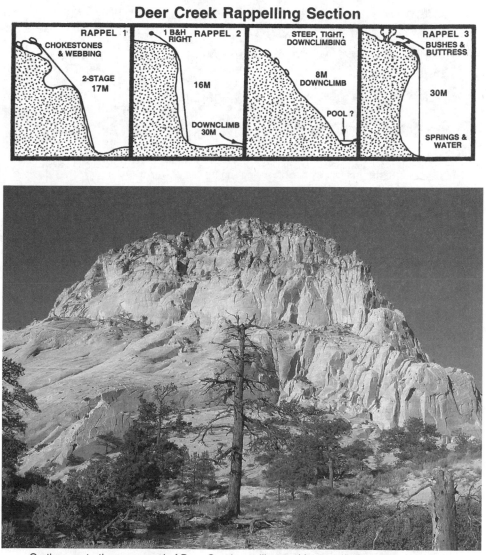

On the way to the upper end of Deer Creek, you'll pass this magnificent peak called Deer Range Point. Shown here is the eastern face. To the right is the upper end of the Main Fork of Deer Creek and the upper West Fork of the Left Hand Fork.

Left Looking south at the northern slopes of Deer Range Point. To the left is the upper end of the West Fork of the Left Hand Fork of Deer Creek, plus 2 of many toadstools in the area.
Right Another of many toadstools in the upper Deer Creek area.

Nat Smale making the 1st of 3 rappels in the upper end of the Main Fork of Deer Creek Canyon. This is a 2-stage rap of about 17m from webbing wrapped around a chokestone.

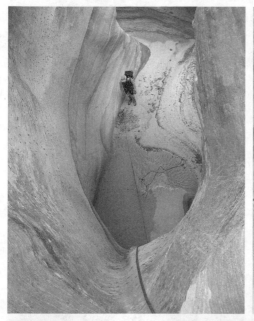

Above Left This is the 2nd half of the 1st Rappel in the Main Fork of Deer Creek Canyon. The total drop of this rappel is about 17m.

Above Right Immediately below the 1st Rap in the Main Fork of Deer Creek, comes this interesting 7m downclimb. It's normal dry at the bottom, but right after storms, you may find a pool. Downclimbing this is a little easier than it first appears.

Left This is the 7m downclimb just below Rappel 1 in the Main Fork of Deer Creek. See the foto above and to the right.

All fotos on this page were taken in the Lower Slot in the Main Fork of Deer Creek. This hike was on 10/5/2003, a day after some pretty good rains with minor flooding, so we wore wetsuits. In the middle of summer, and even after some rains & flooding, you likely won't need wetsuits.

Nat Smale using a hand drill to make a hole for a bolt. This is at the top of Rappel 2 in the lower end of the Lower Slot of the Main Fork of Deer Creek. Not far below this is a pretty good downclimb, perhaps into a pool. After that the canyon opens up wide.

Above Left Nat Smale has just finished the 16m Rappel 2 in the Lower Slot of the Main Fork of Deer Creek. This rappel is from a single bolt & hanger (B&H).

Above Right This is the last pool in the Lower Slot. Below this, it's a walkout of 100m to where the canyon opens wide.

Left From the canyon rim, looking SSW at the very end of the Lower Slot as it opens up wide. This begins the middle part of the Main Fork of Deer Creek Canyon.

Left Starting the 30m Rappel 3 into the lower part of Deer Creek. We attached webbing to a small rock buttress or outcrop, and a couple of bushes for added peace of mind. **Right** From below, and from the north side, you can see the top & bottom of Rappel 3 into lower Deer Creek Canyon.

Looking down on the spring at the head of the lower part of Oak Canyon. On the map this is labeled Rappel 2. If coming down from the upper end, you can exit up to the north side.

Left This is the Big Horn Panel in the West Fork of the Left Hand Fork of Deer Creek. This is one of the best petroglyph rock art panels around. **Right** Just one small part of the Big Horn Panel. Some etchings are 5m-6m off the ground; most are up 2m-3m.

This is the best part of the big pictograph panel in the lower end of Deer Creek Canyon not far above where it meets the Paria River.

Hogeye & Starlight Canyons, & Carlow Ridge

Location & Access This area is about halfway between Kanab & Page and north of Highway 89. Hogeye Canyon is located north of Old Pahreah & the Paria Movie Set. It drains into the Paria River from the east just north of where Kitchen Canyon enters from the west; Starlight Canyon is found just east of Mollies Nipple, northwest of Old Pahreah & the movie set, and not far north of Highway 89. The route to Starlight Canyon discussed here is from the southeast and the Paria River.

To get to the trailhead, turn north from Highway 89 between mile posts 30 & 31 at the sign stating *Historic Marker*. From this parking place & tall monument, drive northeast on a good dirt road. Even though this road is graded, it can be slick in wet weather because of the presence of the Chinle & Moenkopi clay beds. It's 7.6 kms (4.7 miles) to the Paria Movie Set; 8.4 kms (5.2 miles) to the Pahreah Cemetery; and 9.5 kms (5.9 miles) from the highway to a trailhead. You'll park on the west side of the Paria, while the townsite of Old Pahreah is on the east side of the river.

Trail/Route From where you park, simply walk north in the flood plain of the Paria River. You'll cross the creek many times. Along the way are ruins of old ranches and petroglyph & cowboyglyph panels as shown. Read more about the history of these sites under **Map 18, Upper Paria River Gorge**.

Starlight Canyon At the mouth of Kitchen Canyon, head west about 2 kms along a small stream. About 100m below Kitchen Falls, turn left or south and walk up Starlight. About 1200m into Starlight, the canyon constricts and you'll find a short narrow section; climb up a chute to a widening canyon above. Continue upcanyon about 2 more kms to the 2nd side-canyon coming in from the right. Walk up this short drainage about 200m to find **Starlight Cave**. In this deep alcove, you'll see where pot hunters or archeologists have been digging in the floor, as well as some pictographs inscribed with charcoal on the walls. The ceiling is black indicating aborigines used this cave for a long time in the distant past. On the ridge opposite the mouth of the cave, is a man-made cattle trail running uphill to the west. You could use this trail to get out on top of the mesa, then drop down into lower Kitchen Canyon and return from there (see **Map 10** for a possible route). There doesn't seem to be much to see further upcanyon, so most people will want to see the cave and return from there.

Hogeye Canyon From the mouth of Kitchen Canyon, continue north, perhaps stopping to see 2 panels of cowboy etchings & petroglyphs as shown on the map. Just over one km above Kitchen will be a rincon (abandon meander), an old ranch site, and the mouth of Hogeye Canyon. Just into this major canyon will be running water and lots of trees. About 1 1/2 kms upcanyon will be a mossy cataract with running water. About 300m above that will be a big wall collapse & boulders you'll have to climb around. For the next 800m or so you'll find a fairly narrow canyon with high walls, and tall slender cottonwood trees trying to reach the sun. These trees have branches on top--but none on their trunks.

About halfway up Hogeye is a dryfall you can easily climb. Beneath it is where water begins to flow. Above that, the canyon is totally different--it's dry with no cottonwood trees. This goes on for about one km, then for about another 500m will be more running water and cottonwoods. Beyond that it's dry again.

You could turn back there, or return to Old Pahreah via cow trails in Lower Death Valley and along the Carlow Ridge down to The Box and the Paria River. Near the upper end of Hogeye, you'll come to the confluence of 4 canyons. Turn right or SSE and walk up that drainage following this map. Just north of the butte that looks like a beehive, head east, then south and climb up just east of this bee-hive butte. Continue south but veer right or southwest and get upon a big hogsback ridge.

This ridge, the southern part of which is called **Carlow Ridge**, runs all the way south to where the Paria River cuts through The Cockscomb in what is called **The Box**. You could head southeast and visit Sam Pollock Arch, but that would make a very long day--so stay on the ridge line following various cows trails south. Further along you'll pass just east of what might be called a Rock Garden on Carlow Ridge. Soon after that, is a trail junction; the **Yellow Rock Trail** heads east into lower Cottonwood Wash, while The Box Trail continues south. Lots of stone cairns in this part marking the way. Once in The Box, turn right or northwest and walk up along the Paria again. Just south of where Old Pahreah once was, and on the far right or east side near the canyon wall, are the remains of 3 stone structures built by Charles H. Spencer in 1912. Spencer was trying to extract gold from the Chinle clay beds. Read more about this is the chapter, **Mining in the Paria River Drainage**, in the back of this book.

Elevations Old Pahreah townsite & trailhead, 1440m; lower Starlight & Hogeye Canyons,1525m; upper Hogeye, 1755m; high point along Carlow Ridge, 1856m.

Hike Length/Time Needed It's about 11 kms from Old Pahreah to the cave in Starlight Canyon; this might take 6-9 hours, depending on side-trips to the historic sites along the way. From Old Pahreah to the head of Hogeye is roughly 13 kms. This could take 8-11 hours round-trip, maybe a little longer if returning via Carlow Ridge & The Box (?). These are pretty long hikes, but walking is generally fast & easy.

Water There's running water year-round in the lower part of Starlight, but there may also be cattle around, so beware. There's no chance for cattle to get above the cataract in Hogeye, so above that, water should be reasonably good to drink (?), especially from the spring source.

Maps USGS or BLM maps Kanab & Smoky Mountain (1:100,000) for driving & orientation; Deer Range Point, Fivemile Valley & Calico Peak (1:24,000--7 1/2' quads) for hiking.

Main Attractions A short but interesting narrow section & pictographs in Starlight Canyon; cowboy etchings & petroglyphs and old ranch sites along the Paria; and in Hogeye, narrows, running water, total wilderness and great views from Carlow Ridge.

Ideal Time to Hike Spring or fall. Winter has ice water wading; summers are hot as a pistol.

Hiking Boots Wading boots along the Paria River; dry-weather shoes elsewhere.

Author's Experience Here are his major hikes in these parts. Years ago he walked from Old Pahreah, up to the Kitchen Cabins in Kitchen Canyon, up Starlight to where the water first begins to flow, then about halfway up Hogeye Canyon and back to his car, all in about 9 1/2 hours. A 1997 hike went up Starlight to the cave, then up into lower Hogeye Canyon and back to Old Pahreah in 8 hours. His last hike in 2003 was from Old Pahreah, up Hogeye and back via the Carlow Ridge to The Box, plus a quick peek at Spencer's stone cabins, all in 8 2/3 hours.

Map 12, Hogeye & Starlight Canyons, & Carlow Ridge

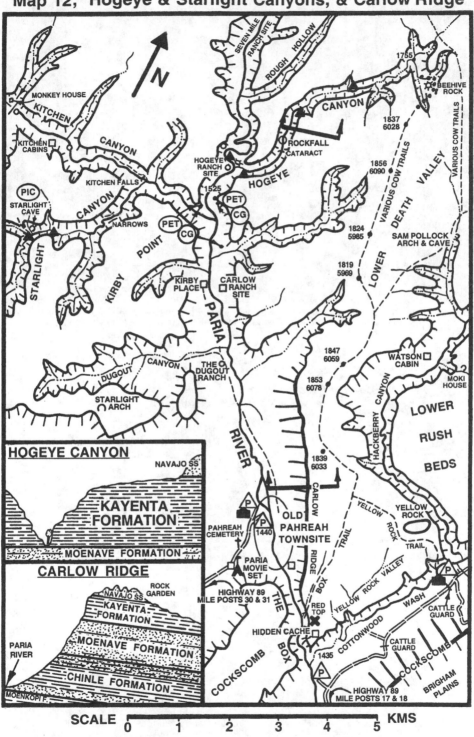

MONKEY HOUSE
KITCHEN
KITCHEN CABINS
CANYON
KITCHEN FALLS
PIC
STARLIGHT CAVE
STARLIGHT CANYON
NARROWS
POINT
KIRBY
1525
PET
CG
PET
CG
KIRBY PLACE
CARLOW RANCH SITE
STARLIGHT ARCH
DUGOUT
CANYON
THE DUGOUT RANCH

SEVEN MILE RANCH SITE
ROUGH HOLLOW
CANYON
ROCKFALL CATARACT
HOGEYE RANCH SITE
HOGEYE
1755
BEEHIVE ROCK
1837 6028
VARIOUS COW TRAILS
DEATH VALLEY
1856 6090
VARIOUS COW TRAILS
1824 5985
SAM POLLOCK ARCH & CAVE
LOWER
1819 5969

PARIA
RIVER

1847 6059
1853 6078
WATSON CABIN
MOKI HOUSE
HACKBERRY CANYON
LOWER
RUSH
BEDS
1839 6033

HOGEYE CANYON
NAVAJO SS
KAYENTA FORMATION
MOENAVE FORMATION

CARLOW RIDGE
ROCK GARDEN
NAVAJO SS
KAYENTA FORMATION
MOENAVE FORMATION
PARIA RIVER
CHINLE FORMATION
MOENKOPI F.

CARLOW
OLD PAHREAH TOWNSITE
CARLOW RIDGE
YELLOW ROCK
YELLOW ROCK
TRAIL
PAHREAH CEMETERY
1440
PARIA MOVIE SET
HIGHWAY 89 MILE POSTS 30 & 31
HIDDEN CACHE
RED TOP
THE BOX
COCKSCOMB
1435
YELLOW ROCK VALLEY
COTTONWOOD
WASH
CATTLE GUARD
CATTLE GUARD
COCKSCOMB
BRIGHAM PLAINS
HIGHWAY 89 MILE POSTS 17 & 18

SCALE 0 1 2 3 4 5 KMS

81

Both pictures above were taken in Hogeye Canyon above the cascades, and below the spring and the beginning of running water. Notice the long tall trunks on these cottonwood trees.

This is the cascade in lower Hogeye Canyon. This and a big rockfall not far above, keep cattle out of the middle part of the canyon.

The upper part of the narrows of Starlight Canyon.

Charcoal pictographs in Starlight Cave in Starlight Canyon.

Cannonville Slot Canyons

Location & Access The author was introduced to these 2 short slot canyons by Bob Ott of Cannonville, the man who runs the camper's concession at Kodachrome Basin. These slots are located very conveniently about one km southwest of the small town of Cannonville. All or most of these canyons are on public land, but the only way to get there is across Bob Ott's cow & horse pasture. As this book goes to press, Ott and GSENM personnel are working out details as to a satisfactory place for a trailhead parking area, and the route for a trail. The last proposal was to have an access road built starting about 400m south of the last house in Cannonville and running west a short distance from the paved Kodachrome Basin Road. From the parking place, a trail will be constructed by the GSENM into the mouths of each canyon. For the latest access information, please stop at the visitor center in Cannonville and talk to someone there, Tele. 435-679-8981. Also, as this book goes to press, the visitor center will be closed in the winter season, then opened sometime in early March and closed again sometime in November. It all depends on the amount of visitation.

So for now, drive south from the visitor center on the Kodachrome Basin Road about one km (.6 mile) and look for a new road turning right or west. There should be a sign or something (?). If they still haven't got a road & parking place built, the person at the visitor center should make a suggestion of where you can park and/or where you can enter. Or call Bob Ott at Kodachrome Basin, Tele. 435-679-8536. In the future, he may build some cabins or a camper's store somewhere near the trailhead. Bob is not against having people cross his property, he only wants it organized somehow. In fact, he seems to have been the one to propose this project to the monument BLM in the first place.

Trail/Route From wherever you park just follow the trail west or southwest into the drainage bottom of the first canyon. Walk up as far as you can; you'll be stopped by a dryfall. You can walk into either canyon from the bottom end. At the upper end of each, will be a short section of a narrow slot canyon.

These canyons are made from the same geologic formation as seen in Kodachrome Basin State Park to the east. The slots are in the lower levels of the **Entrada Sandstone Formation** called the **Gunsight Butte Member**. The color is red, and it's more of a hardened mud rather than sandstone--best to leave the "stone" off this one! When it rains, part of the outer surface melts away and ends up in the Paria, then the Colorado River. Inquire at the visitor center as to the best way to get up on top of the mesa just to the west for some interesting fotos looking down onto these red rocks.

Elevations Visitor center, Cannonville, 1792m; mouth of each slot canyon, same as in town, 1792m.

Hike Length/Time Needed To do a round-trip hike into each slot and return is to walk about 3 kms. This should take from one to 2 hours, maybe a little more if you want to set up a camera & tripod for pictures.

Water Take you own. There are water taps at the visitor center, town park, or the Grand Staircase gas station, store & motel.

Maps USGS or BLM map Panguitch (1:100,000) for driving; and Cannonville (1:24,000) for hiking.

Main Attractions Bright red-colored slot canyons that are easy to reach. No need for a 4WD here!

Ideal Time to Hike Spring or fall are the very best time periods, but these can be hiked 12 months a year.

Boots/Shoes Any comfortable boots or shoes. You'll never need wading-type shoes here.

Author's Experience At the invitation of Bob Ott, he parked at Bob's house and walked into each canyon. He set his camera up at the head of each of the 4 main forks, and took the time needed to come back with some pretty good shots. Round-trip took about 1 2/3 hours. If you're in a hurry you can do it faster than this.

Aerial view of the Cannonville Slots looking southeast. To the far left and out of sight is Cannonville.

Map 13, Cannonville Slot Canyons

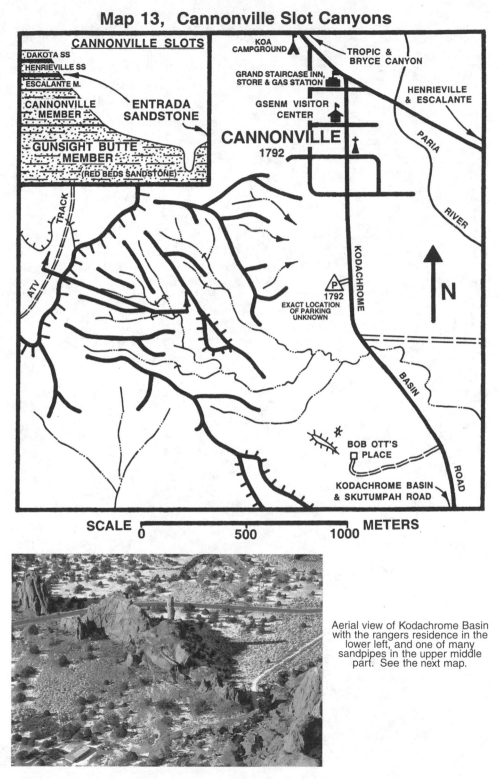

CANNONVILLE SLOTS

DAKOTA SS
HENRIEVILLE SS
ESCALANTE M.
CANNONVILLE MEMBER
GUNSIGHT BUTTE MEMBER
(RED BEDS SANDSTONE)

ENTRADA SANDSTONE

KOA CAMPGROUND

TROPIC & BRYCE CANYON

GRAND STAIRCASE INN, STORE & GAS STATION

GSENM VISITOR CENTER

HENRIEVILLE & ESCALANTE

CANNONVILLE
1792

PARIA

RIVER

TRACK

ATV

KODACHROME

P
1792
EXACT LOCATION OF PARKING UNKNOWN

N

BASIN

BOB OTT'S PLACE

KODACHROME BASIN & SKUTUMPAH ROAD

ROAD

SCALE

0   500   1000   METERS

Aerial view of Kodachrome Basin with the rangers residence in the lower left, and one of many sandpipes in the upper middle part. See the next map.

Kodachrome Basin Trails

Location & Access This map includes most of Kodachrome Basin (KB) State Park. It's located only about 3 or 4 kms directly south of Henrieville, but you can't approach it from there, except by trail. This park was first discovered by the outside world (National Geographic Magazine) in 1948 and was published in the September, 1949 edition. For about 60 years prior to that so-called expedition, Kodachrome Flat was known as Thorley's Pasture. Jack Breed forgot to ask the locals what the name of the place was.

To get there, drive south out of Cannonville & the newly-created visitor center, and follow the signs along the paved Kodachrome Basin Road. Drive a total of 11.7 kms (7.3 miles) to the Kodachrome Basin Turnoff (KBT). At that point, if you continue east, you'll be on the graded Cottonwood Wash Road--but instead turn left or north staying on the paved road going into KB. At the pay booth you must pay a fee of about US$6 to enter. Inside the park is a camper's store and fully-equipped cabins (with camping supplies and horseback rides), a campground with showers & dump station, a picnic site and several constructed trails. This state park is open year-round and there is an additional fee for camping and/or a shower. A national park service pass does not get you into KB. Frankly speaking, Kodachrome Basin is not worth the extra money, unless you're a geologist looking for Sand Pipes.

Trail/Route Most of the hiking trails are located northwest of the ranger's residence. Right next to the campground, is the beginning of the **Eagles View Trail**. It takes you up a steep path to Eagles View Pass, at 1935m. From there you have fine views of the basin below, making it worth the walk. South of the campground is the **Panorama Trail.** It's a constructed path which takes hikers into and through another section of the park. At this trail's western end is Panorama Point, an overlook situated on a rock outcropping, with a good view of the rock monoliths called **Sand Pipes**. In the last several years, this trail has been extended to the west and is called the **Big Bear Geyser Trail.** There are a couple of Sand Pipes out that way. As you enter the park, pick up a free map at the information & fee booth showing this new path. This walk is along a sandy trail and is well-signposted. On the eastern side of the park is a short trail through some low cliffs to the minor **Shakespeare Arch**. Another site to see, but which you can drive to, is **Chimney Rock**. Get there by driving northeast from the ranger station on a road which could be slick in wet weather.

Elevations Ranger's residence, 1765m; the Eagles View Trailhead, 1794m.

Hike Length/Time Needed The walk to Eagles View Pass is only about a km or less, and will take only 10-15 minutes, one way. The Panorama Trail, which makes a loop-hike, is something like 3 or 4 kms, round-trip. You could do this in about an hour, but you may want more time if you continue west on the Big Bear Geyser Trail. The distance to Shakespeare Arch is less than a km, and should take less than 10 minutes for the one-way walk. While there are no trails around most sand pipes west of the rangers residence, it can make an interesting walking area for someone looking for good fotos.

Water At the camper's store, the picnic site, and at the campground.

Maps USGS or BLM maps Panguitch & Escalante (1:100,000) for driving; and Cannonville & Henrieville (1:24,000--7 1/2' quads) for hiking; or any Utah State Highway map plus the sketch map from the fee booth.

Wintertime aerial view of Kodachrome Basin. This section is south of Eagles View Pass, and west of the campground. Notice the 2 sandpipes.

Map 14, Kodachrome Basin Trails

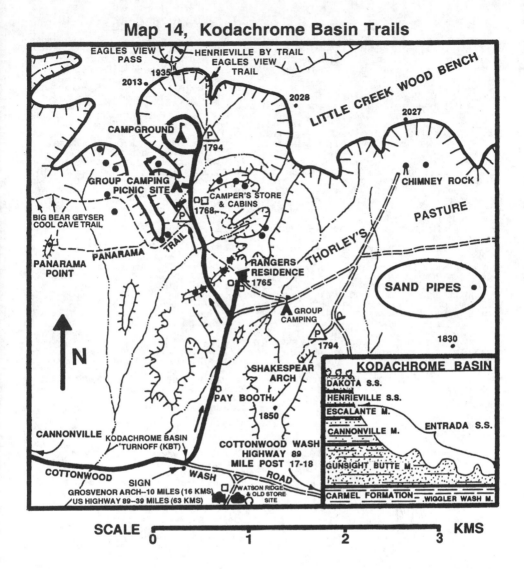

Main Attractions Red rock spires and cliffs, plus cabins and a developed campground, for those who enjoy that type of camping. Also, a rare geologic feature known as Sand Pipes. Read the explanation below.
Ideal Time to Hike Spring or fall, but the park is open and can be visited year-round.
Boots/Shoes Any dry-weather boots or shoes.
Author's Experience The author walked all but the newest trails on this map in about half a day.

Sand Pipes of Kodachrome Basin

Within this state park are some unusual geologic features called **Sand Pipes,** which occur almost nowhere else. In the park, they're found mostly in the red-colored Gunsight Butte Member of the Entrada Formation. They seem to be concentrated in the area west of the ranger's residences. These red rock spires are lighter colored and more weather resistant than the surrounding rock. They average about 20m in height and 3m-4m in diameter. The sand making up the pipes is normally much more coarse than the surrounding rock. It's been thought they were created by the injection of liquefied sand maybe from a tidal flat, perhaps triggered by an earthquake and possibly initiated by cold water springs. Later erosion left these pipes standing high and dry.

Road Map to Rock Springs Bench & Hikes

Location & Access Rock Springs Bench (RSB) is located southeast of Cannonville, immediately south of Kodachrome Basin State Park & the Cottonwood Wash Road, east of the upper Paria River drainage, and west of the upper part of Hackberry Canyon. From the north end and the Cottonwood Wash Road, the RSB slopes up to the south and ends at Rock Springs Point, which is part of the White Cliffs, a prominent feature running east-west across this part of southern Utah.

Use this map and driving information to gain access to: **(1)** Johnson Hole Canyon & Trail, including the Upper Paria River Gorge, Red Slot, Asay Bench & Canyon, and the middle part of Deer Creek Canyon; **(2)** Johnson Hole, Snake Creek & the CCC Trail into the Upper Paria River Gorge; **(3)** the technical slot in Stone Donkey Canyon; **(4)** Death Valley Draw, Upper Hackberry Canyon and/or the Upper Trail (Upper Death Valley Trail) into Hackberry. If conditions are right, a 2WD pickup can make it to all these trailheads, but it's best to have a HCV & 4WD.

To get to these RSB trailheads, drive south & east out of Cannonville (check road conditions at the new visitor center before leaving town) on the paved Kodachrome Basin Road. After 11.7 kms (7.3 miles) you'll come to the Kodachrome Basin Turnoff (KBT) with a pullout & information board on the right. Instead of turning left or north on the paved road going to KB; first set your tripometer at 0, **then head east on the unpaved but graded Cottonwood Wash Road.** After 1.3 kms (.8 mile) turn right or south onto Watson Ridge. After a ways, you'll pass the BLM or CCC corral on your far left, then will arrive at Rock Springs Creek (RSC) crossing (if there's been a flood in the previous day or two, this could be a problem even for 4WD's). About 200m past this normally dry creek bed, you'll arrive at Wallace Ott's Corral at Km 3.8/Mile 2.35.

To reach **(1) Johnson Hole Saddle & Trailhead,** make a hard right turn immediately south of the cattle guard & fence next Ott's Corral and continue west along the fence. Soon you'll cross RSC for the 2nd time, then will be heading west. Shortly you'll cross RSC for the 3rd time, this time with a little water. Just beyond that is where the old **Rock Springs Shearing Corral** used to be. Immediately to the north across the creek are 2 boulders leaning up against the canyon wall. There you'll find etchings of early-day sheepmen dating from the early 1900's. Read more about this place in the back of this book under **Sheep and Sheep Shearing Corrals.**

From the old corral site, head straight up the sandy track upon RSB. At Km 6.8/Mile 4.2 will be a road coming in on the left or east (If you have a 2WD, and are heading for the other 2 trailheads, turn left or east at this point as this is likely the easiest route). Finally, 10 kms (6.2 miles) from the KBT, you'll reach a low divide called here, **Johnson Hole Saddle,** and another road coming in on the left. At that road junction are big P/J trees you can park & camp under; or you can continue south past a very sandy area for another 300m or so to the beginning of the actual horse trail.

To reach the trailhead for **(2) Johnson Hole, Snake Creek, the CCC Trail** or **(3) Stone Donkey Canyon,** start at Ott's Corral 3.8 kms (2.35 miles) from the KBT. Drive on the main road southeast into what Wallace Ott calls **Rough Canyon.** At Km 5.4/Mile 3.35 is a junction. If you continue straight ahead, you'll come to a very rough & steep section which will challenge even 4WD's; so for most of us it's best to turn right and go west up a steep sandy ridge. In the past, the author has taken his old VW Rabbit & a newer Golf TDI up this section, but lately it's getting worse, so the last time up with his Chevy Tracker, he had to shift into 4WD. In the right conditions a 2WD can make this, but get a run on it.

Once out of Rough Canyon, you'll soon pass a gate & a chained area, then at Km 7.9/Mile 4.9 you'll come to a 4-way junction--turn left. After another 600m (.3 mile), is another junction--turn left again (if you turn right at this point, you'll end up at the Johnson Hole Saddle & Trailhead, #1 above). After another 400m (.25 mile), and at Km 8.9/Mile 5.5, is a 3-way intersection--turn right and drive south another 5.4 kms (3.35 miles) to the end of the road, which is 14.3 kms (8.9 miles) from the KBT. This last section of road runs straight south and straight up RSB and is rutted because flood water runs right down the track. In the past the author took his VW Rabbit & Golf up this, but both were high-centering a lot in sand. A HCV-2WD will handle this part OK.

To reach the **(4) Death Valley Draw Trailhead,** let's start at the junction just below the rough & steep section. With a good 4WD, head southeast; with luck, lots of clearance and in low range, you can make it up this bad place (most vehicles can come down this part without trouble; going up is a different story!). About 7 kms (4.35 miles) from KBT, is another junction--continue straight ahead to the southeast. After another 600m (.35 mile), and just beyond Sam Pollock's cabin & Wallace Ott's small trailer house on the left, the road veers left or east. Finally at the head of Death Valley Draw will be a junction and a fence & gate at Km 8.5/Mile 5.25--turn right or south and continue to where the road is blocked off at Km 9.1/Mile 5.65. Park there or nearby. In the future, the GSENM-BLM may change this parking place (?).

Regarding that old shack & small trailer house, here's what Wallace Ott of Tropic had to say: *That cabin was put there by Sam Pollock in about the late 1930's [Sam's son Afton Pollock says it was built in 1941]. He was a sheepman and he's the guy I bought the grazing rights from. I camped in that cabin quite a bit. I took that trailer in there in the 1960's.*

For those with a 2WD only, your best chance to reach all these trailheads would be to head west from Ott's Corral in the direction described above going toward the Johnson Hole Saddle Trailhead, then use the connecting roads shown on the map to reach the other 2 parking places. There's a fair amount of sand in this county, so keep moving when you see deep sand ahead. Also, **carry a shovel** at all times. In winter, or when the sand has some moisture, it's a lot easier to drive through; when it's extra dry, more difficult--even for 4WD's!

Also shown on this map are a couple of old mines. Halfway up Rock Springs Bench is the **George Johnson Copper Mine.** It has 2 shafts each going straight down about 30m or so. Get to that old mine by turn turning westward off the main road next to a 5m-high pinnacle-shaped rock.

Just before you cross RSC for the first time, look west about 15m and you will see some rocks and old boards. This was a squy or arasta which was used to grind lead ore into transportable consentrate. About 300m west of that is a tunnel in the south-facing cliff face called the **Nels Schow Mine.** Nothing was ever taken out of there. Another 100m or so north of that is an old shaft called the **Tom Farley/Wilford Clark Mine.** Some lead ore was taken out of that, but it was never mined commercially. Read more about both of these attempts at mining in the back of this book under Mining History of the Paria River Drainage.

Map 15, Road Map to Rock Springs Bench & Hikes

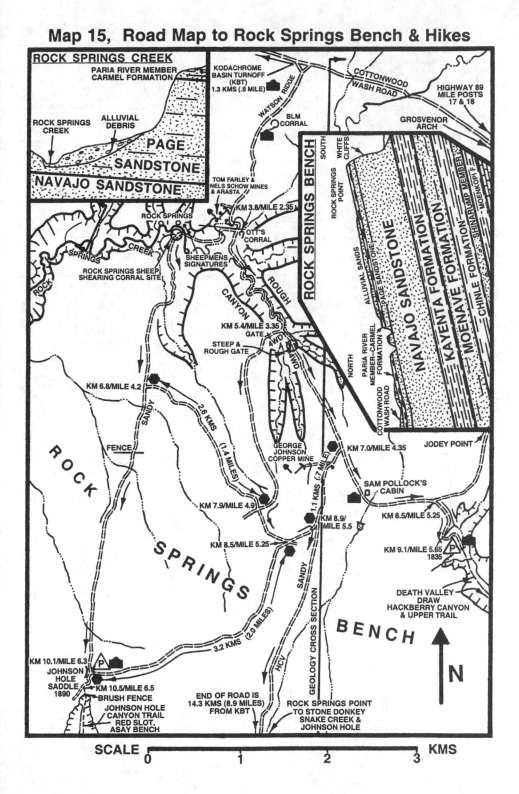

ROCK SPRINGS CREEK

PARIA RIVER MEMBER
CARMEL FORMATION

ROCK SPRINGS CREEK

ALLUVIAL DEBRIS

PAGE SANDSTONE

NAVAJO SANDSTONE

KODACHROME BASIN TURNOFF (KBT) 1.3 KMS (.8 MILE)

COTTONWOOD WASH ROAD

HIGHWAY 89 MILE POSTS 17 & 18

GROSVENOR ARCH

WATSON RIDGE

BLM CORRAL

ROCK SPRINGS BENCH

SOUTH

ROCK SPRINGS POINT

WHITE CLIFFS

TOM FARLEY & NELS SCHOW MINES & ARASTA

KM 3.8/MILE 2.35

ROCK SPRINGS

OTT'S CORRAL

SHEEPMENS SIGNATURES

ROCK SPRINGS SHEEP SHEARING CORRAL SITE

SPRINGS CREEK

ROCK CREEK

ALLUVIAL SANDS

PAGE SANDSTONE

PARIA RIVER MEMBER—CARMEL FORMATION

NAVAJO SANDSTONE

KAYENTA FORMATION

MOENAVE FORMATION

CHINLE FORMATION

SHINARUMP MEMBER

MOENKOPI F.

CANYON

ROUGH

KM 5.4/MILE 3.35 GATE

STEEP & ROUGH GATE

4WD

4WD

NORTH

COTTONWOOD WASH ROAD

JODEY POINT

KM 6.8/MILE 4.2

2.6 KMS (1.4 MILES)

SANDY

FENCE

R O C K

GEORGE JOHNSON COPPER MINE

KM 7.0/MILE 4.35

SAM POLLOCK'S CABIN

KM 8.5/MILE 5.25

1.1 KMS (.7 MILE)

KM 7.9/MILE 4.9

KM 8.9/ MILE 5.5

KM 8.5/MILE 5.25

KM 9.1/MILE 5.65 1835

P

S P R I N G S

SANDY

DEATH VALLEY DRAW HACKBERRY CANYON & UPPER TRAIL

3.2 KMS (2.0 MILES)

HCV

GEOLOGY CROSS SECTION

B E N C H

N

KM 10.1/MILE 6.3

P

JOHNSON HOLE SADDLE 1890

KM 10.5/MILE 6.5

BRUSH FENCE

JOHNSON HOLE CANYON TRAIL RED SLOT, ASAY BENCH

END OF ROAD IS 14.3 KMS (8.9 MILES) FROM KBT

ROCK SPRINGS POINT TO STONE DONKEY SNAKE CREEK & JOHNSON HOLE

SCALE

0   1   2   3   KMS

Johnson Hole Canyon & Trail; Asay Bench Trail & Canyon; the Red Slot; and the Middle Part of Deer Creek Canyon

Location & Access This area is due south of both Cannonville & Kodachrome Basin State Park, south & west of Rock Springs Bench, and also along both sides of the Upper Paria River Gorge. Read the driving instructions to this trailhead under **Map 15, Road Map to Rock Springs Bench & Hikes.**
Trail/Route From wherever you park, walk south down the shallow drainage on an emerging trail to the first little dropoff. There you'll find a brush & log fence and gate which is the beginning of the **Johnson Hole Canyon Trail.** This canyon & trail are named after an old-timer named **Sixtus Johnson.** Wallace Ott of Tropic had this to say: *That old trail through Johnson Hole Canyon was there for years & years, and it was named after Sixtus Johnson. But later I was the one who did most work on that trail. I took powder down in there, and in one place it was so slick, that the horses would slip. One old gray horse slipped and by the time he got down to the bottom he was dead. Then I blasted some up at the top and fixed it.*

Go through the gate and follow the well-used trail along the left side of the upper drainage. Further along, you'll drop down into the dry creek bed. Continue down the wash bottom until you come to a dropoff. Actually, if you're paying attention near that point, you may have seen one trail head south toward **Johnson Hole** about 125m above the dropoff. If you follow that one, it will take you past a small butte with the elevation marked 6188' (1886m) on the *Bull Valley Gorge 7 1/2' quad.* That trail is easy to follow until you reach a point halfway between Sugarloaf, and what this writer is calling Little Sugarloaf, then the path fades away to almost nothing.

However, don't take that route; instead, look for another trail bypassing the dropoff on the east side. Once back in the wash bottom, continue for another 300m or so, and be looking for the trail running up to the left. Hopefully you'll find a small stone cairn there. Once out of the drainage, the trail is easy to follow due south down a prominent hogsback ridge just west of the above-mentioned butte. Further down, you'll begin to veer to the right or southwest about 500m north of the elevation marked 5652' on the *7 1/2' quad.* This is where you'll have to watch closely for the trail as it runs southwest, then west down a smaller ridge (someone needs to put up some cairns in this part). If you want to see **Balanced Rock,** about halfway down this smaller ridge, and near a couple of cairns going due west, look SES about 300m. It's also about 200m WNW of elevation 5652'.

Soon the trail levels some, then makes an abrupt turn to the left 135° and heads southeast and off a minor point into the Paria River 15m below **Lone Rock**. Right at the bottom are willows & Russian olive trees, and the initials HS 1914. This stands for Harmon Shakespeare. According to Wallace Ott: *There's also an AD nearby, put there by Amond Davis. Harmon Shakespeare was my neighbor in Tropic, and he was down there in 1914 herding buck sheep. There used to be about 20 herds of sheep down here, and they'd take the bucks out alone, away from the ewes. And they took a herd of bucks down into Johnson Hole and Harmon and his brother was a herdin'um.*

Now before getting down into the Paria River at Lone Rock (which has some historic cowboyglyphs), let's head for a narrow section in the lower end of Johnson Hole Canyon, a place this writer is calling the **Red Slot.** From Lone Rock, retreat back up the trail about 200m and walk cross-country just about due north until you drop down into the lower end of Johnson Hole Canyon, then walk up the sandy wash bottom. Roughly 1 1/4 kms from Lone Rock you'll come to a slit in the wall in the bottom of the Navajo Sandstone, which in this area is bright red in color. Walk into the slot and after 30m you'll see Wallace Ott's signature on the right. After another 50m, the slot widens into what appears to be a tiny rincon immediately below where flood waters drop about 45m into the Red Slot. This is an interesting place, and well worth the visit.

Once at Lone Rock, you can head down the Paria River to Crack Spring (about 1 km and on the west side), or walk upcanyon. About 500m northwest of Lone Rock and on the left or west side will be the **Asay Bench Trail.** It will be behind some cottonwood trees and you may see an old fence around a section at the bottom of the trail. It's the only place around where the cliffs give way to a slope where a cattle trail can exist. This will be the way you come off Asay Bench and back to the Paria and to the Johnson Hole Canyon Trail.

According to Wallace Ott: *It was a rancher named Ed Asay who built that trail upon Asay Bench. He was my uncle and he lived in Woodenshoe. He was born in 1873, same as my Dad, and left the country in the 1910's, so it would have been built originally in the early 1900's.*

About one km upriver or north of the Asay Bench Trail, will be the mouth of **Asay Canyon.** Walk straight into this drainage and into a nice shallow narrows with perhaps a little running water. After about 200m, it slots-up into a crack and you'll have to chimney straight up about 2m to continue. With 2 or more people, this is easy--or you'll need long pants & long-sleeved shirt, or knee & elbow pads, to save skin! Just above this one little dropoff is a short slot, then the canyon opens some. Or, if you can't or don't want to chimney up, return to the mouth of the canyon, climb up on the bench to the north, and head upcanyon for 300m or so, then drop back down into the canyon bottom above the **lower slot.**

About one km above the mouth of Asay Canyon is a major fork; turn right into the longest of the 2 tributaries. After about another km, will be a short & sweet slot barely shoulder width. This **upper slot** is only about 50m long, but it's fotogenic. About 500m above this 2nd slot, the canyon narrows and you'll find a small stand of quaking aspen, the only ones the author's ever seen in such a low altitude semiarid environment! Just above these trees is a dryfall, so retreat to the last aspen and climb the wall on the northeast side. This has steep slickrock in a place or two. Once out on top, you could retreat back downcanyon; or walk across **Asay Bench** and down the cow trail to the Paria.

Or, walk south 600m and down a broad drainage into the middle part of **Upper Deer Creek Canyon**. You'll enter this drainage just above 2 gooseneck bends. Once down in, you can walk down to a 30m rappel into the lower end of the canyon. Hikers regularly walk up to the bottom of that big dryfall from the Paria. In Lower Deer Creek Canyon is running water, lots of cottonwood trees & campsites, and 2 panels of pictographs. Or you can head upcanyon and into the lower end of the **Northwest Fork.** There you'll find a nice 100m-long slot before coming to a dryfall. Or if you turn left instead, and into the **Southwest or Main Fork of Deer Creek,** you'll soon come to a 100m-long deep dark slot and perhaps a couple of pools. That will be the end of upcanyon travel. To do the entire length of the Main Fork of Deer Creek, read the information along with **Map 11.**

After your trip to the middle part of Deer Creek, head northeast a little more than 2 kms to the top of the Asay Bench Trail which drops off the northeast side of Asay Bench as shown on the map. You

Map 16, Johnson Hole Canyon & Trail; Asay Bench Trail & Canyon; the Red Slot; & Middle Deer Creek

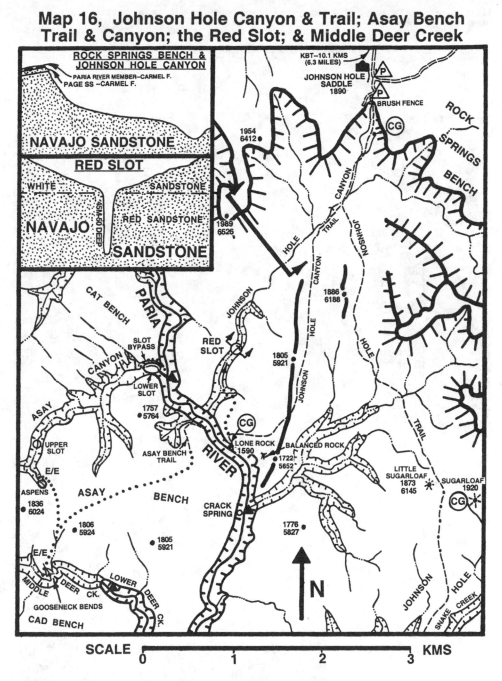

won't see this trail on top of the bench; only when it starts down from the top.
Elevations Trailhead, 1890m; Lone Rock & the Paria River, 1590m; top of Asay Bench, 1770m.
Hike Length/Time Needed To do the entire hike suggested above will take from 10-13 hours, maybe more for some people (?). A long all-day hike! Or you might backpack in and camp at Crack Spring or near the lower end of Asay Canyon and do it in 2 days.
Water Paria River water must be treated; water from lower Asay Canyon may be drinkable as is (?); and water from Crack Spring has been drank straight from a little pipe for more than a century.
Maps USGS or BLM maps Kanab, Panguitch & Smoky Mountain (1:100,000) for driving & orientation; and Bull Valley Gorge & Slickrock Bench (1:24,000--7 1/2' quads) for hiking.

Main Attractions Several short & sweet slots, historic cattle trails & cowboyglyphs.
Ideal Time to Hike Spring or fall, but can be done in summer or winter. This is sandy country, so the only place where wet roads can be a problem might be along the bottom of Rock Springs Creek with clay soil.
Boots/Shoes Along the Paria River, you'll need wading boots/shoes; elsewhere, dry-weather shoes.
Author's Experience He camped at the trailhead and did the described loop-hike in 10 1/4 hours.

Above Left Inside the Red Slot. You may have to crawl under a log or two to reach the upper end.

Above Right The entrance to the Red Slot. The name comes from the bottom layer of the Navajo Sandstone, which is this region is bright red. This slot is about 100m long and 40m-45m deep.

Right Sherrell Ott standing next to Balanced Rock. He's looking at the 1935 signature of Sam Pollock. Sherrell and his father Wallace Ott have the grazing rights to these canyons.

92

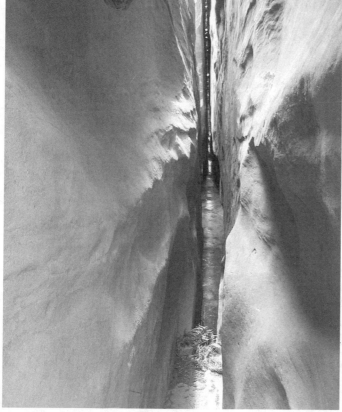

Above Just inside the Red Slot is this etching by Wallace Ott (born in 1911), who is still alive in Tropic in 2004. Wallace first ran cattle in these canyons in the 1930's.

Left The lower end of Asay Canyon where it gets real tight. Because it's so tight, you may need a boost from a friend to get up 2m or so. Or take the bypass route and get to it from above.

Left This is the Upper Slot in the upper end of Asay Canyon. **Right** Not far above the Upper Slot is a small grove of quakies or quaking aspen trees.

The lower end of Asay Canyon, just below the tightest part of the slot. There should be some running water in this part of the canyon not far above the Paria River.

Above An aerial view looking south at the northern slopes of Deer Range Point. This is the head of Deer Creek. The Canyon in the middle is the upper West Fork of the Left Hand Fork of Deer Creek. The 60m slot is in the lower part of the foto.

Left Another aerial view looking northwest down on the Upper Paria River Gorge. In the lower middle part of the picture you can see Lone Rock. Just to the right of it (not visible) is the lower end of the Johnson Hole Canyon Trail. Less than a km below Lone Rock is Crack Spring, the best water-hole in the entire canyon.

Johnson Hole, Snake Creek & the CCC Trail to the Paria River

Location & Access This area is due south of Kodachrome Basin State Park & Rock Springs Bench, and east of the Upper Paria River Gorge. Read the driving instructions for this hike under **Map 15, Road Map to Rock Springs Bench & Hikes.**

Trail/Route There are 2 possible ways into Johnson Hole & Snake Creek from the north. **Approach 1:** From the end of the road on Rock Springs Point, route-find due south with compass & map in hand, first along a faint winding ATV track, then along an emerging hiker's trail for about one km. About 200m before the actual end of the point, look for a cairn (single pointed standing rock) on the left marking a trail-of-sorts angling down over the rim heading southeast. This is **Wallace Ott's Horse Trail** (he only had a horse on it about 3 times!), but it's only visible in the upper part; further along, head straight down a sandslide. Consider caching a bottle of water at the bottom for the return hike--especially in hot weather. You'll hate climbing back up the sand!

Once in the drainage at the bottom of the sandslide, simply walk downcanyon--which happens to be the head of **Snake Creek.** After a ways, the drainage veers southwest, then in the area southeast of **Sugarloaf,** and near where 3 upper tributaries of Snake Creek meet, you'll come to a 40m dropoff. From there, turn back to the left about 50m and walk down in on the east side. Below the dryfall, the canyon gradually becomes more shallow again. Finally, you'll come to another dropoff of 40m-45m. From there, backtrack 100m to find a cow trail angling up to the south on the east side of the drainage. Get on it, walk south, and after another 300m, you'll start down several sections of constructed trail. This takes you down to where the main fork of **Upper Snake Creek** meets the **East Fork** (before going further, there are several other routes into the East Fork one or 2 kms east of this cattle trail as shown on the map). Wallace Ott of Tropic says this **Snake Creek Trail** was first built by Eli LeFevre and Layton Jolley during the 1930's, but after Ott bought their grazing rights in 1945, he upgraded it. His son Sherrell Ott now runs cows down Snake Creek during the cooler half of the year. Today you'll see fresh cut steps in the trail made with a cordless saw.

Approach 2: From Johnson Hole Saddle, at the head of Johnson Hole Canyon, start down the obvious trail heading south. After less than 2 kms and while walking in the upper drainage bottom, continue on a trail straight ahead to the south instead of following the dry creek bed southwest to a dryfall about 125m away (Read the information under **Map 16**). Follow the trail that runs south along the east side of a small butte labeled 6188 on the *Bull Valley Gorge 7 1/2' quad* and Map 16. Follow this well-used trail south, then southeast to between **Sugarloaf** and what this writer calls **Little Sugarloaf.** Watch carefully as the trail fades between these 2 peaks. From there, veer right or south and from the top of a low ridge, continue down a good trail into Upper Snake Creek as shown on this map. This is the trail the Ott's use to take cows into Johnson Hole & Snake Creek for water. This route, Approach 2, is the easiest, but a little longer.

Once into **Lower Snake Creek,** you have several route choices. One would be to go up the **East Fork** and explore 2 alcove-type caves. The 1st is about 400m up from the bottom of the trail and on the left or north side; the 2nd is about another 500m upcanyon and on the right. The back ends of both caves have black soot-covered ceilings, indicating they were used a lot in the distant past by fire-building aborigines. There seems to be no pictographs or petroglyphs around, but archeologists or pot hunters have been busy as beavers digging holes in the floor of each cave looking for something!

If you walk up each of the 3 main tributaries of East Fork, you'll come to dryfalls, or brush-choked narrows. Not so interesting, but you could route-find out of the canyon to the north and back to the Rock Springs Bench Trailhead as shown on this map.

About 125m downcanyon from where the 2 upper forks of Snake Creek meet, you'll come to the 1st of 3 dropoffs. Get around the 1st via a constructed cattle trail on the right or west side. Wallace Ott once did some cement work in this section so cows could get down to a spring and running water for a drink. Below this 1st dropoff is where cattle stop; and about 50m below that is a minor 7m-high waterfall. Route-find (no trail) around this 2nd dropoff on the right or west side.

About 500m below the 2nd dropoff is a big wall collapse which surely fell sometime around the year 2000 (?). The upcanyon-side of this dam is filled with sand and right after each flood will likely be a small temporary lake. About 250m below this rockfall dam is a 3rd dropoff which is a mossy cascade. Getting around this can be a problem so take a short rope or cord. Start on the left or east side. Walk 2m on a ledge, then help each other down, perhaps using a rope. For 2 or 3 people this shouldn't be a major obstacle. The author looped his pack rope around a small root and jumped down about a meter; the small rope kept him from sliding in the moss below. From there to the Paria you'll find an emerging hiker's trail coming upcanyon, running water & cottonwood trees and some campsites.

At the **Paria River,** look for a panel of cowboyglyphs behind willows on the left or east right where the 2 canyons meet. From there you could go all the way downcanyon to Old Pahreah and Highway 89, or head upstream. About 2 kms above Snake Creek on the left or west side is **Oak Canyon.** It has good running water in its lower end. About 500m above Oak, and again on the left or west side, is the bottom end of the **Deer Trails Trail.** This constructed cow path begins near the end of the Nipple Ranch Road on Oil Well Hill. This trail and Oak Canyon are discussed in detail under **Map 11, Deer Creek Slots and Oak Canyon.**

About 100m north or above the bottom of Deer Trails Trail, and on the right or east side of the Paria, is the lower end of the **CCC Trail.** At its beginning, this trail is well-constructed and was used to run cows from Upper Death Valley & Johnson Hole Country, down to water in the Paria Canyon. According to Wallace Ott, this trail was built by the CCC's sometime in the mid-1930's. At that time, they had their main camp northeast of Henrieville at the old Smith Ranch, but while doing various projects along the Upper Paria River Gorge, they may have had a temporary spike camp near the mouth of Deer Creek, which is another 300m upcanyon. If you have time, you could visit Deer Creek with its pictograph & petroglyph panels. But this may take an additional hour or two (?).

Or, for this hike, climb the CCC Trail which zig zags up and to the south along several benches. Soon it rounds a point just above the mouth of a short side-drainage Wallace Ott calls **Red Creek,** then just inside this minor drainage, it angles up to the left. It's easy to follow until it reaches the mesa rim, then it disappears in the sand. At that point, route-find north about 600m until you're above or north of the steep part of Red Creek, then turn east and walk about one km back to Snake Creek. At that point, you should be just above the big dropoff where the Snake Creek Trail begins. While in this area, you'll be passing through colorful teepee-shaped rocks which can be fotogenic. Once in Snake Creek, follow your tracks back to your vehicle, perhaps taking a look at the east side of Sugarloaf &

Map 17, Johnson Hole, Snake Creek & the CCC Trail to the Paria River

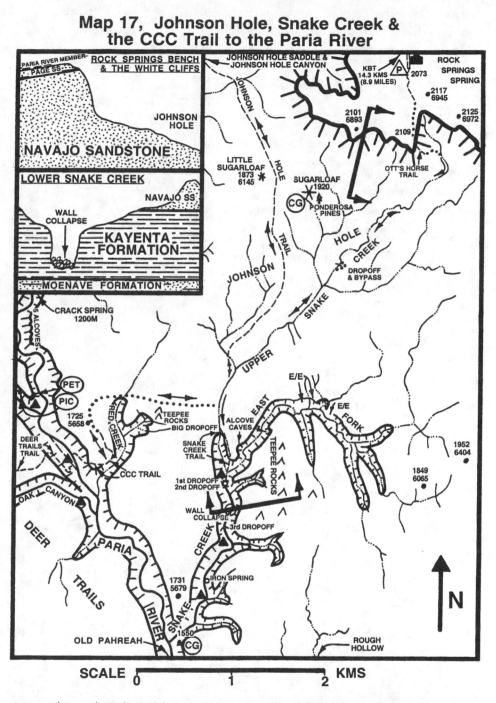

SCALE

0   1   2   KMS

some ponderosa pines situated there; another colorful scene. Or climb Sugarloaf and see more cowboy etchings right on top. That's where sheepherders spent time watching their flocks.

Or if you started hiking at the Johnson Hole Saddle, you could continue upcanyon along the Paria. About 3 kms above the bottom of the CCC Trail will be **Crack Spring** (good drinking water) on the left or west side. It comes from a crack in the wall behind some small cottonwood trees; look for clear water flowing from the bank, and grass. Also, look at all the **historic signatures** of cowboys and freighters who ran teams & wagons between Cannonville and Pahreah.

About one km north of Crack Spring is **Lone Rock** on the right or east. About 15m below it will be the beginning of the Johnson Hole Canyon Trail. Follow it as shown on **Map 16** back to your car at the Johnson Hole Saddle Trailhead. This is the same trail you use if going to Asay Canyon & Bench, and the Red Slot.

Elevations Trailheads, 2073m & 1890m; top of Wallace Ott's Horse Trail, 2109m; end of Snake Creek, about 1550m; Lone Rock & lower end of Johnson Hole Canyon Trail, 1590m.

Hike Length/Time Needed To do either of the loop-hikes suggested will take from 9-12 hours (longer if going via Lone Rock), but you can shorten the hike by going down Snake Creek only to the 3rd dropoff and returning; or make it longer by visiting Deer Creek Canyon. Or you can backpack in for 2 or 3 days, perhaps seeing Asay Canyon and coming out via Johnson Hole Canyon Trail. Lots of hiking options here.

Water Take plenty in your car & pack. Otherwise there's running water in Snake Creek and the Paria River (treat it). Also in Deer Creek, Crack Spring (best) & Asay Canyon, if you go that far.

Maps USGS or BLM maps Panguitch, Kanab & Smoky Mountain (1:100,000) for driving & orientation; Bull Valley Gorge, Slickrock Bench, Deer Range Point & Calico Peak (1:24,000--7 1/2' quads) for hiking.

Main Attractions Seldom-seen canyons, 2 interesting caves, an old CCC-built trail & cowboyglyphs.

Ideal Time to Hike As usual in spring or fall, but with the higher altitudes, hiking in summer isn't so hot. Winter hiking is also possible but with some frosty nights and possible wading!

Boot/Shoes Wading-type shoes in Snake Creek, Deer Creek and Paria River; dry-weather shoes elsewhere.

Author's Experience He's been in these parts many times, but the last 2 trips he car-camped at the end of the road on Rock Springs Point, then (1) hiked down Ott's horse trail to Sugarloaf, down into middle Snake Creek, explored all tributaries of the East Fork, visited the 2 caves, and returned basically the same way. Round-trip 7 1/3 hours. On his last trip (2), he went straight down Snake Creek to the Paria, upriver to the CCC Trail, then returned via Sugarloaf (and the lower end of the trail discussed under Approach 2--Johnson Hole Trail), all in 9 hours.

Looking west at the eastern side of Sugarloaf, located in the upper part of the Snake Creek drainage. After his last hike, the author learned of some etchings or signatures of sheepmen right on top. This would have been a good vantage point for sheepmen to look after their herds.

In the East Fork of Snake Creek, there are 2 alcove-type caves that have black soot-covered walls & ceilings indicating these were used by aboriginal Americans several hundred or thousand years ago. This is inside the 2nd, or most-easterly of the 2 caves.

This cow trail leads down between the 1st and 2nd dropoffs in Snake Creek where water begins to flow. This is as far as cows can go, but you can route-find around the 2nd dropoff.

This is the 2nd dropoff in Snake Creek Canyon. If going downstream, skirt around this minor obstacle on the right or west side. The camera is sitting near the top of the 2nd waterfall.

In the lower half of this picture, you can see parts of the CCC Trail. It was built by the CCC's in the late 1930's. They had their main camp about 11 kms above or northeast of Henrieville. To the left of this picture about 100m, is the beginning of the Deer Trails Trail which runs up to Oil Well Hill.

Looking west at the mouth of Deer Creek Canyon from high above near the upper end of the CCC Trail. The trails you see in the canyon bottom are roads made by the illegal use of ATV's in an otherwise very pristine canyon.

This picture was taken somewhere in Little Dry Valley (near Kodachrome Basin) on Christmas Day, 1936. That winter had some of the deepest snow in the history of the region. On the caterpillar is Hasle Caudill, in the snow is foreman Rex Thompson, both from the Henrieville CCC Camp. On that day, the cat cleared a road to Watson Ridge so the CCC boys could deliver 14 tons of cottonseed cake to a big tent at the CCC/BLM Corral. The cottonseed cake was for Sam Pollock's sheep herd, which was in the Upper Death Valley area at the time. (Hasle Caudill foto).

Upper Paria River Gorge

Location & Access The Upper Paria River Gorge is that part of the drainage between Cannonville and the Old Pahreah townsite. Some might extend this upper gorge on down to Highway 89. The Lower Paria River Gorge is from Highway 89 down to Lee's Ferry and the Colorado River. Like the Lower Gorge, this upper part has mostly easy access, but with some wild & wooly places in between.

You can start at either end of this section and walk all the way through, but you'd need 2 cars and a shuttle. Or you can park at either end and head for the middle part of the gorge, then return the same way. To reach the upper part, drive south out of Cannonville on the paved road in the direction of Kodachrome Basin. Cross the Paria River bridge going toward Kodachrome Basin, then park at one of several little side-canyons which can be used to reach the main drainage. Near **Shepherd Point** would be one entry; or walk down **Road Hollow**--which used to be the main wagon route until the road was built around Shepherd Point; down Little Dry Valley; or from Ott's Corral & Rock Springs Shearing Corral Site, then down Rock Springs Creek as shown. Other possible places to begin would be from along the Skutumpah Road where it crosses **Sheep Creek** or Willis Creek, or the more difficult and exciting Bull Valley Gorge.

To enter at the lower end of the gorge, drive along Highway 89 about halfway between Page & Kanab. Between mile posts 30 & 31, and at the sign stating *Historic Marker,* turn northeast and drive 9.5 kms (5.9 miles) to near the Old Pahreah townsite on a rather good dirt & clay road (which is slick as hell when wet!).

Another possible way into the middle of the upper gorge or canyon would be to drive along Highway 89, then right at mile post 37, turn north onto the **Nipple Ranch Road.** Drive northward to Oil Well Hill, but when the road turns east, stop and park where a very sandy ATV tracks heads northwest. This would be the beginning of the Deer Trails Trail. It takes you down to a point just below where Deer Creek enters the Paria. Read all about this under **Map 11**.

Elevations About 1750m along the Upper Paria trailheads; about 1850m at Willis Creek and Bull Valley Gorge; and 1440m at Old Pahreah.

Hike Length/Time Needed Old timers who talk about using the gorge as a road between Cannonville and Pahreah, say it was 30 miles (48 kms) between the 2 settlements. But you can shorten that a lot by beginning from one of the side-canyon drainages. This entire distance, say from Sheep Creek or near Shepherd Point, can be walked in one very long day, but you'd need a car at both ends. However, it's recommended you take several days because there are many side-canyons to see such as Asay Canyon, the Red Slot, Deer Creek, Snake Creek, and some old cattle trails to explore. In 3 or 4 days one could have a fun hike.

All of this Upper Paria River Gorge or Canyon is within the newly created GSENM, but since the main canyon corridor has been an old road since the 1870's, motor vehicles are presently allowed entry. This means you could take a 4WD, ATV or even a mtn. bike and save a lot of walking. It also means ATV drivers can & do leave the Paria River floodplain and make their own trails into side-canyons--which is definitely illegal. Hopefully this problem will be resolved in a few short years and ATV's totally banned. The GSENM arm of the BLM is recommending an emergency closure of the canyon to motorized vehicles, except for limited entry to stockmen who have cattle in the drainage during the winter months (approximately November 1 to May 1).

Water There is a year-round flow in the Paria, but during the irrigation season, which is from sometime in late April until about the first of October, there's little or no water flowing downcanyon past Cannonville. Each year is different. Most or all of the water in the gorge at that time, seeps out from the bottom of the Navajo Sandstone or the top layers of the Kayenta Formation. This is in the area below the White Cliffs, which begins near the bend of the river known as the **Devils Elbow.**

There are many small seeps in the upper part of this map and in the gorge near Devils Elbow, which should be drinkable as-is (?). Also, most major side-canyons have a small stream. If you walk up any of these canyons to where the spring or seep begins, then that water is normally drinkable as-is (?). In winter months there are cattle in the canyons, so some precautions should be taken, such as taking water directly from a spring, using Iodine tablets, or filtration. However, in the summer months, from about mid-May until the end of October or the first part of November, there are no cattle in the canyon. They are taken out during this time and put on higher summer ranges in the mountains. With the steeper gradient & monsoon floods, the stream flows fast and will wash out the microbes which can give hikers stomach troubles.

Throughout most of each year, and when there has been a long dry spell, the water in this upper gorge is as clear as any mountain stream and which the author has drank many times. About the only sediment entering the creek at this time is the small amount of sand being washed down by Kitchen Canyon Creek. However, when you get into mid or late summer, and with the presence of thunder shower activity, the water is often times very muddy.

For those who want to be on the safe side and drink only spring water, there are 2 fine springs on the west side of the canyon about straight across from the mouth of Hogeye Canyon. Another good source, perhaps the best in the gorge, is the historic **Crack Spring**. This spring is about 2-3 kms upstream from the mouth of Deer Creek Canyon and about 850m downcanyon from Lone Rock. Walk close to the west wall and look & listen carefully for the water coming out of a pipe in a cluster of small cottonwood trees.

Maps USGS or BLM maps Kanab & Smoky Mountain (and a small corner of Panguitch)(1:100,000); Calico Peak, Deer Range Point, Bull Valley Gorge, Slickrock Bench & Cannonville (1:24,000--7 1/2 quads). Be sure and carry either of these sets of maps, as this hand-drawn sketch is not that accurate. The 2 metric maps at 1:100,000 scale are recommended.

Main Attractions Sites of the old Dugout, Carlow, Kirby, Hogeye and Seven Mile Flat Ranches. Petroglyphs & cowboyglyphs or etchings are at the mouths of Kitchen Canyon, Deer Creek, Snake Creek and Rocks Springs Creek. Inside Deer Creek are the only pictograph panels in the area. Cowboyglyphs are at Crack Spring, Lone Rock and other sites. A number of old historic cattle trails, and many good campsites and solitude.

Ideal Time to Hike Spring or fall, with the very best times being from late March or early April to mid or late May, and from mid or late September to late October. Summers are hot, and late spring and early summer (late May through June and into July) usually brings small gnats and large horse or deer flies. If you go too early in the spring, or late in the fall, your feet will be blocks of ice.

Boots/Shoes Wading boots or shoes. If you're planning to do the entire gorge hike, which is rather long, take a sturdy pair of shoes. Many people take an old pair of shoes to "wear out" on a trip like

Map 18, Upper Paria River Gorge

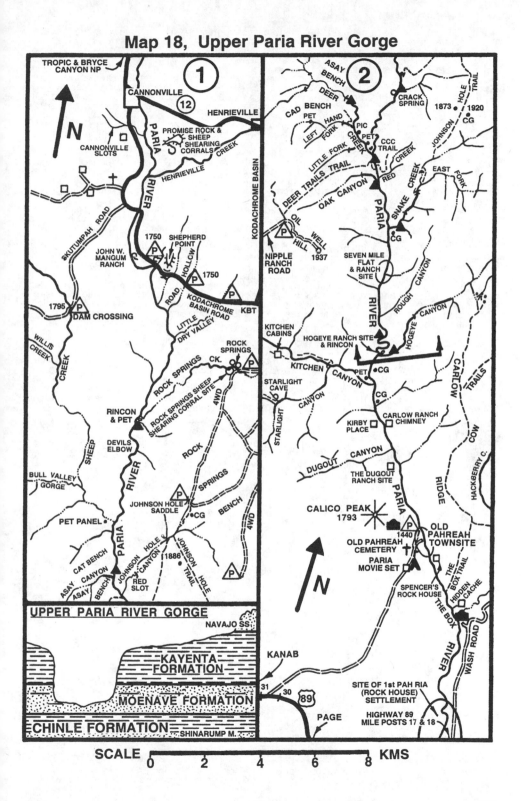

this, but if they're too old or battered, they fail to give support to the feet and may not last to the end of the hike. So take a pretty good pair of shoes, even though the wading will shorten their life.

Author's Experience The author has been upcanyon from Old Pahreah 6 or 7 times visiting the old ranches and trails, and Hogeye, Deer Creek and Kitchen Canyons. These were all day-hikes, which took from 8 to 9 1/2 hours. Another day he walked from Road Hollow down to Crack Spring, had lunch, and returned, in 7 1/2 hours. Another time he walked down Willis Creek to Deer Creek Canyon on a 2-day trip, which should have been at least 3 days. On one of his last visits, he walked from Old Pahreah to as far as Deer Creek and the cow trails in that area, in less than 8 hours, round-trip. One trip was a hike off Rock Springs Point. He walked down past Sugarloaf and into the middle part of Snake Creek, then over the hump west and down the CCC Trail, and up Deer Trails to the west side bench. Then he returned to his car on Rock Springs Bench, all in about 7 1/2 hours. In 2003, he was in this area with his 4WD Chevy Tracker and from Rock Springs Bench and Oil Well Hill to the south on no less than half a dozen hikes.

Trail/Route As you enter this canyon, you'll likely see some motor vehicle tracks (mostly ATV's) in the north & the south. In the lower end just above Old Pahreah, you'll likely be using some of the original old wagon roads which went from Pahreah to some of the ranches upcanyon. The *Smoky Mountain metric map* shows the old road accurately to where it ends below the Kirby Place. Today there's an occasional 4WD or ATV using this track, which are scarring parts of the canyon bottom and illegally entering side-canyons.

There are also grazing permit holders who go into the middle part of the canyon occasionally in 4WD's to take in or bring out cattle. This is usually about May 1, and in the first part of November. These permit holders have a reason to be there, and aren't just out joy riding, as most recreation vehicle owners are.

At about the Kirby Place and going north, these tracks fade away as the canyon narrows; then you'll be walking in the flood-gutted canyon bottom. Grazing permit holders now get into or out of the upper part of this gorge via Sheep Creek, but the early day wagon road was right down the Paria past Devils Elbow and Crack Spring. Walking is easy all along this creek bed.

Beginning now in the upper end of the gorge. You'll first be walking in a shallow canyon or drainage, but soon it narrows and deepens as the river begins to cut down into the Navajo Sandstone. Remember, while the river is downcutting, the walls are rising; that is, the top of the Navajo is higher in the south than to the north. In other words the rock formations slope down to the north.

At the mouth of **Rock Springs Creek**, you'll see an isolated, lone standing butte, which must be a part of an old abandoned meander or river channel. On the west side of this butte, and 6m-8m off the ground, you'll see some pretty good petroglyphs. They were apparently put there when the river bed was much higher.

Downriver from Rock Springs Creek, is a big bend in the canyon, which old timers call the **Devils Elbow**. At that point the canyon is getting deep and moderately narrow. The white sandstone walls are the Navajo Sandstone, which form the White Cliffs all across the region.

In the area of the Devils Elbow, you'll begin to see many small seeps along the sides of the stream channel, and the creek begins to grow in volume. In early summer, the upper part can be totally dry, or nearly so, and the water you see in the Paria downstream actually begins here.

Aerial view looking west at the butte or rincon at the junction of the Paria River and Rock Springs Creek. South or downstream is to the left. Look for rock art around this butte.

As you near where **Sheep Creek** enters from the west, you begin to see red sandstone in the canyon bottom. This is the lower part of the Navajo Sandstone. Then just a bit further downstream and in the area of Lone Rock, you'll see the top part of the Kayenta Formation emerging. The Kayenta forms little benches or terraces. As you walk south, the river continues to downcut, and the beds rise at the same time. From the Lone Rock area on down, most of the major side-canyons have some kind of water supply, either a flowing stream or good springs. If you walk up Sheep Creek a ways, maybe 300-400m, look for a nice panel of petroglyphs on the south side. Walk up a sandy slope to reach them.

Asay Canyon & Bench, Lone Rock, Red Slot & Crack Spring

About 2 kms below Sheep Creek will be **Asay Canyon** coming in on your right or west side. It will usually have some running water and there's a nice slot about 200m upcanyon. About one km below Asay Canyon is the **Asay Bench Trail**. It's an old cattle trail built in the early 1900's, and it's on the right or west side behind some cottonwood trees. It's the only place around where you can easily get upon Asay Bench. Read more about this canyon & trail along with **Map 16.**

About 400m downstream from the Asay Trail, and on your left is a big rock standing out in the river channel. This is what old timers called **Lone Rock.** Look closely on its sides and you'll see numerous old signatures or cowboyglyphs. Some of these date back to the late 1800's, but some of the older ones are now becoming indistinct. About 15m downstream from Lone Rock and up against the willows & Russian olives to the north, is the bottom of the **Johnson Hole Canyon Trail.** This begins at Johnson Hole Saddle and is discussed along with **Map 16.**

To see what the author is calling the **Red Slot,** walk north up this trail about 200m and where it starts to turn east, you continue in a northerly direction. After another 600m or so, you'll drop down into the lower end of Johnson Hole Canyon. Walk up this dry wash another 700m to find a nice slot in the lower red-colored Navajo Sandstone. This is also covered in more detail with **Map 16.**

About 850m below, or south, of Lone Rock, and on the west side of the canyon, is **Crack Spring.** You'll have to walk close to the west wall and watch carefully to be able to see or hear clear water coming out of a crack in the wall. It's on a narrow little bench with many small cottonwood trees, and is hard to see unless you're close by. In the old days, when wagoneers and freighters were running between Cannonville & Pahreah, they always made this place their lunch stop, thus making the whole trip in one long day.

Years ago someone placed a 5-cm pipe into the crack, making it easier to get a drink. The pipe is still there, and it always has a good flow. Since the space right at the spring is both wet & small, it's best to camp on the opposite side of the river and upcanyon about 100m under some big cottonwood trees. Camping there would also leave the spring clean and pristine.

The late Kay Clark of Henrieville, remembered a trip he took with his father in April, 1920. They started in Cannonville and headed for Pahreah. They were carrying several sacks of grain, evidently to be sold to sheep herders in the lower valleys. When they made their lunch stop at Crack Spring, there were several other wagons already there. Since they were riding in comfort in a white-topped buggy with fringes, some of the other drivers made comments as to how they were really traveling in style. In those days, a white-topped buggy was like a Mercedes; and ordinary wagons used by most local people, were like Model T Fords.

On either side of Crack Spring, are many very old **cowboyglyphs** or **signatures of travelers.** Those which are black in color, were made by placing axle grease on a finger, then writing a name. This grease prevented the sandstone from flaking away, so what you'll see there today are many raised

Left The bottom of the Asay Bench Trail looking east. **Right** Near the middle of the Red Slot.

Lone Rock, as it looked in the fall of 2003. On the sides of this pinnacle are many old signatures of sheepmen, cattlemen, and other people traveling along the Paria River between Pahreah to the south, and the Bryce Valley towns to the north. About 15m to the right of Lone Rock, and in the willows & Russian olives, is the beginning or end of the Johnson Hole Canyon Trail.

Crack Spring. This is where people always stopped for a good drink of cold water when they were traveling between Pahreah and the Bryce Valley towns to the north. This route has been used by cowboys and wagoners since about the late 1870's.

letters or signatures which literally stand out on the wall like Braille writing. Other people carved their names into the sandstone with a sharp metal instrument.

About 2 kms below Crack Spring are 5 big coves on the east side of the canyon high above. One seems to have developed into an arch. Just below these is the mouth of Deer Creek Canyon, one of the best side-trips you can take while hiking the Upper Paria River Gorge, so plan to camp and spend time in this one.

Deer Creek Canyon

Deer Creek Canyon is moderately narrow, with high vertical walls made of the red-colored lower Navajo Sandstone & Kayenta Formations. This canyon is similar to places in the Lower Paria River Gorge or even the lower end of the Buckskin Gulch, where the campsites are located.

Inside the canyon is a crystal clear, year-round stream, which begins flowing at the base of a 30m dryfall about 2 1/2 kms up from the Paria. Along the stream are many fine campsites under large cottonwood trees. The walls of the canyon are red, but the benches you'll be camping on are white Navajo sands, which have blown off from the White Cliffs above.

As far as Deer Creek water is concerned, cattle may be in this canyon from early November to May 1. By May the cows are taken to their summer ranges. After the cattle leave the water should be much better, but you'd better purify it anyway, unless you take it directly from the spring at the bottom of the big 30m dryfall.

If you're interested in petroglyphs & pictographs, this is one of the best canyons around to see them. Right at the mouth of the canyon is one long panel of **petroglyphs**, including one glyph which is like a tic-tac-toe box. You'll have to climb a cedar tree to have a close look at this one.

Just inside Deer Creek about 200m, and on the right or east side, are several **pictographs** and petroglyphs. At one time, it looks as though someone tried to chop one of them out of the wall with an ax--but was unsuccessful. About 200m above this panel is what the author calls **Little Fork** coming in on the left or west. You can walk up this drainage for about 650m, skirt one dryfall, and climb another. Above that are ways to climb completely out of the canyon.

About 400m above Little Fork and on the right or east wall are signatures of Kay Clark & Byron Davis from 1935. About 1200m upcanyon from the Paria, is the **best pictograph** panel around. There are actually 2 panels: one you can crawl up to and see close-up, the other is out of reach. The highest panel must have been made before part of the wall collapsed below it.

About 200m upcanyon from these pictographs, the **Left Hand Fork** of Deer Creek enters on the left or west. Walk west 225m into this well-watered canyon, turn right or north, scramble up a steep trail in the oak brush to the next ledge, and turn back east. This is the **Left Hand Fork Trail**. Right at the corner of the 2 canyons, and following stone cairns, turn northwest and walk up to Cad Bench. Read more about it under **Map 11, Deer Creek Slots & Oak Canyon.**

About 2 1/2 kms up Deer Creek Canyon you'll come to a blocking dryfall. This is as far as you go from inside the canyon. At the bottom of this 30m dryfall water begins to flow. It's in this upper part, that you'll find many white sand benches and large cottonwood trees, which combine to make some of the best campsites anywhere. Immediately below the dryfall is a large alcove-type cave on the north side which would make a good camp.

Continuing down the Paria Canyon now. About 850m below the mouth of Deer Creek, and on the east side, is the beginning of the **CCC Trail**. In the beginning, this trail is well-constructed, and was used to run cows from the Upper Death Valley, Johnson Hole and Snake Creek areas, down to water in the Paria Canyon. This one is easy to find and follow.

According to Wallace Ott of Tropic, this trail was built by the CCC's sometime in the mid-1930's. At that time, they had their main camp northeast of Henrieville at the old Smith Ranch. While doing various projects along the Upper Paria River, they may have had a spike camp near the mouth of Deer Creek Canyon. However, in talking to several of the enrollees of the Henrieville camp, none could remember a spike camp actually being in this canyon. They may have been driver there on day-trips out of their main camp (?).

About 100m below the beginning of the CCC Trail, and on the west side of the canyon, is the beginning of the **Deer Trails Trail**. Over the years, various cattlemen & sheepmen constructed this trail, at least that part up to the rim, then it's a well-worn cow path in the sand. Wallace Ott says Jim Henderson, who at one time owned the Nipple Ranch, was probably responsible for most of the rockwork you see there today. This trail was used as a link between the Bryce Valley towns and the Nipple Ranch. Henderson, who lived in Cannonville at the time, would take a wagon load of supplies down the Paria to Deer Trails, then transfer it to pack horses for the rest of the trip. This trail begins or ends on Oil Well Hill to the southwest. By using this trail, you can quickly get into this middle part of the Upper Paria River Gorge, but you'll need a 4WD vehicle to reach the trailhead. Read more about this trail along with **Map 11**.

Roughly 350m downcanyon from the Deer Trails Trail, **Red Creek** comes in on the left or east. This is a short drainage, and according to Wallace Ott, in the spring of some years, there used to be a little stream come out of it. In times of flood, the water came out red, thus the name. Just below the mouth of Red Creek, **Oak Canyon** comes in on the right or west. You can walk up Oak about one km to a big dryfall of about 25m. Below that is a good spring and that water runs all the way to the Paria. This is a deep narrow gorge with cottonwood trees and willows, but not a lot of room for camping. As of 2003, there were old signs of beaver in this gorge, but nothing new, so this water should be reasonably safe to drink (?), although to be sure, walk up to the dryfall and take it from the spring source (or purify it downcanyon).

Snake Creek Canyon

About 2 kms below Oak Canyon, and on the left or east, is the mouth of **Snake Creek**. Right there on the south side corner is a nice panel of cowboy signatures hidden behind some willows. Snake Creek has a good, year-round flowing stream for more than 2 kms along its lower course. This part has trees and campsites. You can walk up Snake Creek for about 2 kms along hiker & cow trails. After about 2 kms, you'll come to a waterfall or cascade. This one may be a little difficult to get around, but 2 or 3 people with a short rope should be able to help each other up. Above this first waterfall is a wall collapse and subsequent dam (it's easy to climb over). Beyond that is a section with more trees, then you'll come to 2 more dropoffs. Climb around the first on the left.

Between these 2 dropoffs, water begins to flow, and there's an old constructed cattle trail down between the two. Wallace Ott once did some cement work between these 2 dropoffs to enlarge one pothole and make a better trail.

About 125m above these dropoffs is where 2 upper tributaries of Snake Creek come together. Coming down the point between the 2 forks is another constructed cattle trail. Wallace Ott says this **Snake Creek Trail** was first built by Eli LeFevre and Layton Jolley during the 1930's, but after Ott bought their grazing rights in 1945, he upgraded it. If you walk up the East Fork of Snake Creek, you'll come to 2 big caves which were occupied by aborigines hundreds or thousands of years ago. See **Map 17** for more details.

There are 2 other ways you can enter this middle part of Snake Creek. One way is to walk up the CCC Trail from the Paria. Once that trail reaches the rim, it disappears going north. From there, and with a compass & map in hand, continue north for about 600m, then turn right or east and cross the upper part of Red Creek Canyon. When you come to the second drainage, which is the upper part of Snake Creek Canyon, turn right and head south downcanyon. When you reach a big dropoff, back up about 100m to find the Snake Creek Trail on the east side. Walk south on it and into the main canyon as described above.

The 3rd way into the middle and upper parts of Snake Creek, Johnson Hole and Stone Donkey Canyon is to drive to the end of the track on Rock Springs Point. If you're interested in that trip, see **Map 15, Road Map to Rock Springs Bench & Hikes** for more information.

Seven Mile Flat Ranch
About 2 kms below the mouth of Snake Creek is a place where the canyon opens up and becomes wider. This is **Seven Mile Flat**. It got its name because it was about 7 miles, or 11 kms, above the town of Pahreah. The late Kay Clark, an old-timer and cattleman from Henrieville, was too young to remember much, but was told this is where a man by the name of John Wesley Mangum had a small ranch which people referred to as the **Seven Mile Flat Ranch**. As the story goes, it was a summer-time place, with a cabin and corrals. At the ranch, they raised among other things, sugar cane, from which they made molasses. In winter the family lived in Pahreah for several years of its early history.

Kay Clark did remember that at the northern end of the flat area and on the west side of the river, he saw the remains of a small molasses mill. There was some kind of a foundation and the old rollers, which were used to squeeze juice out of the sugar cane. It's possible you might find something there today, although the author saw nothing.

No one can say for certain what the exact dates were when this ranch was occupied, but Kay thinks it must have been at about the same time Pahreah was prospering, which was in the late 1870's and up until about 1883 & '84. That's when the first big floods roared down the Paria which started the migration out of the valley. It must have been one of these first floods (later floods occurred in 1884 and 1896) which may have taken out the buildings at Seven Mile Ranch, and started washing farm-land away from Pahreah. Today at Seven Mile Flat, there's nothing more than a broad washed-out river flood plain.

Rough Hollow, and the Hogeye Ranch & Canyon
From the Seven Mile Flat area down to the mouth of Hogeye Canyon, there isn't much to see, except one side-canyon entering on the east. The author still hasn't been into this, but Wallace Ott says there's no water in it, so for a cow man, it wasn't very interesting. From the top end, it was too rough to get a horse into, although Wallace went in a couple of times on foot. For that reason he nick-

This chimney is all that remains of the Kirby Ranch

named it **Rough Hollow.**

At the very mouth of **Hogeye Canyon,** is a rincon (abandoned meander or river channel). Right in the middle of the rather flat area is a rounded butte, which apparently resembled a hog's eye, thus the name, Hogeye Canyon. Hogeye is another of the major side-canyons of the Paria River, which is discussed in more detail on another hike, see **Map 12**. It does have a good year-round running water supply and many good campsites upcanyon.

Right at the mouth of Hogeye Canyon and on the flats surrounding the Hogeye Butte, is the location of another old homestead known as the **Hogeye Ranch.** The late Marian Clark, who was in his 90's when interviewed in 1987, thought it was John Wesley Mangum who may have had some farmland and corrals there. The late Herm Pollock of Tropic thought Ernest Mangum, son of John Wesley Mangum, was there, which may be true, but Ernest wasn't born until January, 1894.

Both sources believed this summer ranch was occupied in the years after people started leaving Pahreah, but no one knows for certain when it was first used. Herm remembered a small wooden shack on the north side of Hogeye Butte, and Marian Clark remembered a small 2m-square stone storage building of some kind. Goats were raised, and some farming was done in summer. The big floods of 1883-84 and/or 1896 must have lowered the creek bed to the point they could no longer get water up to the farmland. Nothing remains today, except a lot of Cheat or June grass, indicating the place was heavily used by someone at some time in the past.

Just northwest of the Hogeye Butte is a good spring coming out of the west side of the canyon wall; and just southwest of the butte is another spring, which made the site a good one as far as water is concerned. About 800m south of Hogeye Butte, and on a point of land jutting out from the eastern canyon wall, are 2 panels of mostly **cowboyglyphs** or **signatures,** including Roy Twitchell and Arthur Chynoweth, a couple of early-day cowmen in this country.

About 1 1/2 kms below Hogeye is **Kitchen Canyon** coming in on the right or west. This is discussed in another hike, but right at the mouth of this canyon is a good panel of petroglyphs & cowboy signatures. Be careful of Kitchen Creek water; it drains the Nipple Ranch area which has cattle grazing year-round.

On the east side of the Paria Canyon, opposite the mouth of Kitchen Canyon, is where the Marian Mangum family may have had a dugout, and what must have been a garden and summer ranch area. The author was made aware of this place after his early hikes were finished, but as late as 2003, he saw nothing that would indicate a ranch was ever located there.

However, about one km below the mouth of Kitchen Canyon, and on the north side of the mouth of a side-canyon coming into the Paria from the east, is a large boulder with more cowboy etchings; *Arthur Chynoweth, Nov. 24, 1925, and X Land + Cattle Co., Jos. + Geo. Graf.* The Grafs were former Cannonville sheep & cattlemen; and Author Chynoweth came into this country in the fall of 1892 with his parents and 3 brothers; Will, Sam and Harvey. The Chynoweths are still one of the more prominent families of Bryce Valley today.

Kirby Ranch

About 1200m below the mouth of Kitchen Canyon, on a bench just west of the creek and under a cottonwood tree, are the ruins of the **Kirby Place or Ranch**. The only thing left to see is a rock chimney. The old cabin was either burned down or the logs were hauled away to build another house or barn someplace else.

As with the other ranches in the area north of Old Pahreah, not much is known for sure about this

Left Part of the petroglyph panel at the mouth of Kitchen Canyon. The late Herm Pollock's name is in the upper part. **Right** This chimney & stove is all that remains of the Carlow Ranch.

ranch site. But everyone agrees that it is the Kirby Place, and that it was first occupied from the years of about the mid-1870's on through about the time of the first flood to hit the valley. The late Kay Clark said it was the typical summer ranch site. Apparently the Kirby family lived in Pahreah during the winters, then had cows and a small garden at the ranch in summer. Herm Pollock believes the Kirby family left for Arizona after the 1883 & '84 floods, which left their irrigated land high & dry.

Carlow Ranch

About 300m due east of the Kirby Ranch house chimney on the opposite side of the canyon, and sitting out in the middle of a sagebrush flat, is the foundation and chimney of the **Carlow Ranch house**. Herm Pollock remembered this family when he was just a boy of 12.

The year was 1922 and it was Christmas time. For most of that fall Herm and his father Sam Pollock, had stayed in what was left of the town of Pahreah. The Pollocks lived in Tropic, but they were in the Pahreah area with a sheep camp, and were also in the business of supplying food & supplies to other sheep camps in the region.

On Christmas morning with nearly half a meter of snow on the ground, Sam loaded up 2 boxes of food and other supplies and put them on 2 mules. He instructed 12-year-old Herm to go up the canyon about 5 kms to the Carlow home, and present the family with the gifts of food. Herm vividly remembers the time, because it was the first time he ever played Santa Clause.

He also remembered the time well, because of how poor the Carlow family was. Their home was a one-roomed cabin made of logs & rocks. At that time it had no door, only a piece of canvas covering the opening. The only heat they had was from an open fireplace. When Herm first went in, he placed one hand on the inside of the door frame, which was covered with thick soot. When he pulled his hand back, it was black.

The several small children were dressed in rags, and were absolutely filthy. Their normally red hair was black, covered with soot from the open fire, and because they had gone so long without bathing. Mrs. Carlow was dressed in cloths made from flour sacks. Herm also remembered a story of one of the young boys. He had found an old blasting cap somewhere and was playing with it when it exploded. He lost 3 fingers on one hand.

Herm Pollock went back home a week after this experience, but his father helped the Carlow family get through the winter. When spring finally came, Sam took a wagon to the ranch, and helped them get out. Later in the spring of 1923, the family left the country, and no one remembers where they went or if their old cabin was ever occupied again.

If looking for the old Carlow Ranch site, first find the Kirby Place, which is easier to locate. Then walk 300m due east across the creek, which is a low flood plain, then upon a sagebrush-covered bench. It must be about 50m or so west from where the steeper canyon wall on the east comes down to the tall sagebrush.

Going downcanyon from the Kirby Place, and on the west side of the river, you can get onto one of 2 of the old original roads and walk most of the way to Old Pahreah. At the mouth of Dugout Canyon, the 2 tracks meet. If you continue on this single track about half a km south or below the mouth of Dugout, you'll see on the right, just as you go down a little decline, several old logs, posts and a depression in the ground. This is believed to be what is called The Dugout and the Dugout Ranch.

The Dugout (Dugout Ranch)

The Dugout is just one of several old ranch or homesteads along the Paria River just above the old townsite of Pahreah. The site was situated up against a low embankment; which was along the edge of an old river channel. First, earth was removed, then logs were built up on the sides and on the top. Dirt may or may not have been put on the roof, but inside it must have been cool in summer and warm in winter, because it was at least partly underground.

No one knows who first settled the Dugout Ranch, but in the life story of Sam Pollock (complied by Afton Pollock of Tropic) mention is made that William Swapp & his wife were living there in August of 1901. They helped a couple of young cowpokes with a bed and a little food as they were heading north back home to Bryce Valley.

Years after that, several old-timers from Tropic and Henrieville, remember the time John (Long John) William Mangum (another son of John Wesley Mangum) and family lived there. This was in the late 1920's and early 1930's, and may have extended to about 1934, according to Wallace Ott and the late Kay Clark. The wife of Long John Mangum was named Oma, and her maiden name was Carlow. Mr. Carlow of the Carlow Ranch was her brother.

As one story goes, in about 1934 the Mangums, either Long John (or brother Marian?), had a cabin at the mouth of Kitchen Canyon. At that place, they once had a fine corn field out on the flat. Herm Pollock remembered this time period well, because the Mangums lived there for 2 years, then were washed out by a big flood which rolled down Kitchen Canyon and the Paria on July 10, 1936. During this same flood, Pollock was stranded for 2 1/2 days on the Carlow Bench (surrounding the old cabin) with a herd of sheep. He had nothing to drink but muddy flood water. An interesting side-note to Mangum brothers, Long John and Marian; they married Carlow sisters, Oma and Edna.

Some time in the early or mid-1930's, Long John Mangum began working on a ranch in Fivemile Valley south of Pahreah, which he homesteaded. Long John's son Herman Mangum got title to it in June, 1937, according to courthouse records. This was at Cottonwood Spring and was called Fivemile Ranch by most people, but some called it Cottonwood Ranch. One or both of these Mangums lived there until 1942, then high-tailed-it for Idaho and greener pastures. See the **Hattie Green Mine story** along with **Map 27,** for the location of Fivemile Valley & Ranch, and how they got lumber for their ranch house.

Continuing south from The Dugout. Perhaps the last thing to see in the Lower Paria River Gorge, besides the Old Pahreah townsite, is the line of cottonwood trees marking what appears to be the original ditch or canal which provided water for Pahreah homes & gardens. This canal began about 1 1/2 kms below The Dugout, and about 2 kms above Pahreah on the east side of the river. It's where the stream is pushed to the west by a rocky buttress from the east. You can still see the very faint remains of the canal by following the broken line of cottonwood trees down to the townsite.

Left This is the monument to Old Pahreah on Highway 89 between mile posts 30 & 31. Turn northeast at this turnout and drive north to the Paria Movie Set, the Old Pahreah townsite and cemetery. **Right** Owen W. Clark and his wife Harriet in the early 1940's. (LaKay Clark Quilter foto)

Layton Smith and his sister Iris Smith Bushnell, standing in front of the last cabin to be lived in at Old Pahreah. This picture was taken in the 1970's. This cabin was taken apart and reassembled back from the river a ways in the early 1990's, then it burned down in the winter of 1994-95. (Iris Smith Bushnell foto)

Death Valley Draw, Upper Hackberry Canyon & the Upper Trail

Location & Access   Death Valley Draw (DVD) is one of the main tributaries to Upper Hackberry Canyon. If you're planning to hike all the way through Hackberry Canyon, you could use this upper side-canyon as the starting point; or the Slickrock Bench Trailhead discussed with the Round Valley Draw hike, **Map 20**. DVD is located west of Hackberry & Round Valley Draw, on the east side of Rock Springs Bench, and southeast of Kodachrome Basin State Park. Read the driving instructions for this hike under **Map 15, Road Map to Rock Springs Bench & Hikes.**

Trail/Route   From the end of the road, or wherever you park in upper DVD, walk south along an old road for roughly one km, then this vehicle track enters & disappears in the dry creek bed. For the next 1 1/2 kms, walk in the dry wash, or along a cow trail, then be watching carefully for the trail as it crosses the creek bed and climbs up the other side. Hopefully a cairn will still be there in the sand.

But let's stop there for a moment. If you want to enter Hackberry via the lower end of DVD, then continue downcanyon another km. There you'll find a chokestone and a 3m+ drop; chimney down and help others if necessary. This is the beginning of a short **50m slot**. Beyond that it opens up wide and after another 100m or so, is where flood waters drop into a **very tight crack** with a number of tree trunks wedged in its upper part. The top of that crack is more or less horizontal for about 30m with logs stuck on top and down inside. You can't get in at the very beginning of the crack, but if you have two 50m ropes, you might tie webbing to one of the logs near the end of the crack and rappel down to the bottom. Don't try to get in at or near the beginning of the crack--you won't make it through.

Or if you're not prepared to rappel, backtrack to the beginning of, or just above, the 50m slot. About 15m above that, is a walking route around the 50m slot just to the west Once in the area just west of the bottom of the 50m slot, turn right or west and route-find down into another little canyon that runs parallel to the tight crack. Getting through this little canyon requires downclimbing in 2 places, but anyone who calls him/herself a hiker should be able to handle it. Or help each other, and/or have a short rope to lower packs, then downclimb into and through this drainage. At the bottom, turn the corner to the left and view the lower end of the tight crack, then walk 350m to Hackberry Canyon which is a walkthrough from top to bottom.

Now back to the trail leaving DVD. Once out of the bottom of DVD, the trail heads nearly due south below big Navajo Sandstone cliffs to the west. Soon you'll cross a sizable side-canyon coming in from the right or west; not much to see up there. Beyond that, the trail passes west of a couple of monoliths or big round rocks on your left, then continues south into Upper Death Valley. It's in this region you'll see a prominent peak known locally by at least 3 different names; **Cottonwood** (USGS map name), **Buckhorn or Death Valley Peak.** This will be straight ahead as you walk south. Also, **Twin Knolls** will be ahead but to the left a little; and a peak that has no name on any map, but which Wallace Ott of Tropic calls **Little Mollies Nipple.** This is straight ahead but to the right a little.

Eventually you'll come to a fence running east-west. This separates grazing pastures. Walk through the gate and continue south and a little east toward Twin Knolls. Eventually the trail runs south along the west side of both knolls, crosses one shallow drainage with several big potholes, then south to another minor drainage where the **Upper Trail** or **Upper Death Valley Trail** runs down into Hackberry Canyon. When you arrive, you'll see some cairns, plus a path made smooth by the hooves of cattle & horses going down slickrock. In several places, steps are cut, then the trail turns left or northeast and runs along a ramp to the bottom. There you'll find a fence & gate and lots of cottonwood trees, water & shade.

Nearby are some cowboyglyphs: **E.M. Bolton 10/22/13, HS & JH 1913.** These stand for Harmon Shakespeare & Jim Henderson, and one of the Boltons from Tropic. Wallace Ott (born in 1911) remembered the Bolton family: *There was a Bolton family living here in Tropic about 2 blocks from where I'm living now. The old man died before I knew 'um, but I knew the family. And he had one son named Eplapapas, and another one named Lindonaflis, and the one that was my age was Wayne Bolton. It may have been the old man Bolton who put his signature there--or it could have been his son Eplapapas, because he run cattle and sheep down there too. Lindonaflis worked at the first sawmill which had power up here on the East Fork of the Sevier River. He was the first man that I know of that got killed at a sawmill. He got jerked into the saw and it sawed him right in two. He was just a teenager.*

Here's a little history on the Upper Death Valley Trail as told by Wallace Ott: *That Upper Trail was built by **Samson Chynoweth** [who arrived at Pahreah with his family in the fall of 1892], he was about the first one who ever used powder in this country. He had quite a herd of cattle--as many as 200 head of cows. He lived down at the Old Pahreah town, that's where he raised his family. He had his cattle in there and they had a terrible drought. There wasn't any way for the livestock to get down to Hackberry Creek, except for the Upper Trail. Then one cow dropped down and died right there on the trail, and the others was up on top and couldn't get by, and they figured between 80 & 100 head of cattle choked to death. That's why they now call it Death Valley.*

The late Herm Pollock of Tropic thought that originally some stockmen from Panguitch were the first to build & use this trail, but that anyone who ever ran cows in that country since then has made some improvements to it. Today it's a good trail and wide enough for 2 cows to pass.

Elevations   Death Valley Draw Trailhead, 1835m; bottom of Upper (Death Valley) Trail, 1622m.

Hike Length/Time Needed   Without any side-trips or much exploring, you could walk down DVD & Trail to the Upper Trail, then up Hackberry and back to your car via DVD in 8 -12 hours.

Water   Carry your own, but water begins flowing just above where the Upper Trail enters Hackberry.

Maps   USGS or BLM map Smoky Mountain (1:100,000) for driving & orientation; and Bull Valley Gorge & Calico Peak (1:24,000--7 1/2' quads) for hiking.

Main Attractions   An historic cattle trail, and 2 of several ways into upper Hackberry Canyon.

Ideal Time to Hike   Spring or fall. Pretty warm in summer, cold in winter.

Boots/Shoes   Dry-weather shoes--except if you hike down Hackberry beyond the Upper Trail, you'll need wading-type shoes as there's water throughout most of Hackberry.

Author's Experience   He hiked down Death Valley Draw, checked out the route around the big dropoff at the end of that canyon, continued south along the Upper Death Valley Trail to the Twin Knolls, then returned and explored the big side-canyon to Hackberry about 1/3 the way down to the Upper Trail. Round-trip took 9 3/4 hours. Next day he went down Wallace Ott's Horse Trail, and finished the hike to the Upper Trail, walked up to the beginning of running water, then returned--but did lots of exploring around all sides of Cottonwood Peak, and finally back to his Tracker in 9 2/3 hours.

Map 19, Death Valley Draw, Upper Hackberry Canyon, and the Upper Death Valley Trail

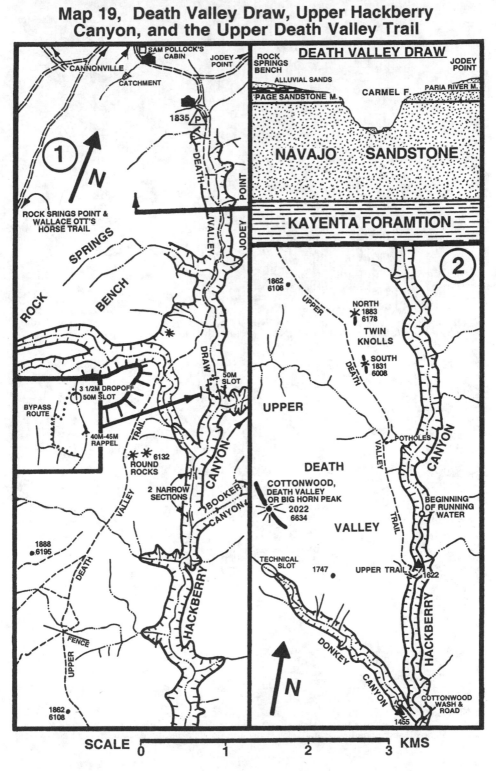

113

Left This is the 50m slot near the end of Death Valley Draw. **Right** This is Death Valley Draw as it drops down through a very tight crack for nearly 50m. It opens up wide below this.

This is the Upper Trail as it leaves Hackberry Canyon. It's wide enough now so 2 cows can pass. This trail begins at the head of Death Valley Draw and ends in Hackberry Canyon just below where water first begins to flow.

Left Looking at the northeast face of Little Mollies Nipple. Ponderosa pines like this slickrock country. **Right** Looking south from the Upper Trail into Hackberry Canyon. Pictures taken in 1987 show this as a flood-gutted wash. Today, it's full of young cottonwoods, willows and tamaracks.

The cabin built by Sam Pollock in 1941. It's located on Rock Springs Bench near the head of Death Valley Draw and the George Johnson Copper Mine. Sam's son Afton is on the left, along with his son Steve.

Round Valley Draw and Upper Entry to Hackberry Canyon

Location & Access Round Valley Draw is one of the main upper tributaries to the much larger Hackberry Canyon and is located about halfway between Kodachrome Basin (KB) and Grosvenor (Butler Valley) Arch. To get there from the Bryce Canyon area, drive south out of Cannonville (this town now has a new visitor center) on the paved KB Road. When you arrive at the KB Turnoff (11.7 kms/7.3 miles), continue straight east on the graded Cottonwood Wash Road. From the KB Turnoff, drive another 11.1 kms (6.9 kms), this should put you at the bottom of **Round Valley Draw.**

Or if you're coming from Highway 89, turn north onto the Cottonwood Wash Road between mile posts 17 & 18. Drive north for 54 kms (33.5 miles) to Round Valley Draw. Once there, turn south onto the Rush Bed Road, which is immediately east of the dry wash. After 2.7 kms (1.7 miles) you'll cross Round Valley Draw, then drive south up the hill 100m to a parking place & trail register. This is where most people park. If the BLM hasn't erected barriers, and if you have a HCV or 4WD, you might drive down the dry wash another 1.2 kms (.75 mile) and park next to a ponderosa pine on the left-side bench. This is 100m above where the Round Valley Draw Slot begins.

Trail/Route From the Round Valley Draw Car-park, walk down the dry creek bed 1200m to the ponderosa pine on the left bench. There you'll see the top layer of Navajo Sandstone (more likely the Page Sandstone?) exposed; and the beginning of the slot 100m beyond. Get down in the tight crack and chimney or downclimb right where the slot begins. Some less-experienced hikers may need a helping hand, so take a short rope just in case. Or you can bench-walk on the north side of the slot for about 300m until you come to a juniper tree which marks another steep route down into the depths. To some, this 2nd entry looks scarry, but it's easier than it first appears. Actually the **1st entry is easier & safer**, and recommended.

About 500m into the slot, and just past where the North Fork comes in on the right or north, you'll come to several large boulders. Every flash flood through this canyon rearranges the route through this section, so look for the footprints of others. You'll surely have to do some downclimbing in which some may need a helping hand. For some, this will be just difficult enough to be fun. Once through this little obstacle course, and after another 50m or so, you come to the deepest & darkest section. In the middle of this narrow part, you may have to wade between more boulders, as this part changes with every flood too! Continue downcanyon; there are still more narrows, but no more difficult obstacles. After passing through the narrows, you could return the same way back upcanyon; or climb out to the north toward the Slickrock Bench Car-park (the way to this car-park is discussed in detail along with **Map 23, Hackberry Canyon**), then rim-walk back to your car on a hiker-made trail as shown. This is now the normal return route.

Elevations The car-park or trailhead is about 1850m altitude, while it's about 1775m elevation at the bottom of the Slickrock Bench entry route.

Hike Length/Time Needed Hiking this slot, then exiting at the Slickrock Bench Route (a walk-up), and rim-walking back to your car, will take about half a day, depending on how long you want to enjoy the narrow slot.

Water Round Valley Seep is just up the road a ways from the trailhead, but it's not reliable. Best to take your own water and have a good supply in your car at all times. Sometime in the mid or late 1930's, a small **CCC spike camp** was located there while the boys worked on several projects in the area. If you look at the sandstone wall west of the spring & watering troughs, you'll see a hole that's been blasted out. This is where the camp stored perishable foods.

Maps USGS or BLM map Smoky Mountain (1:100,000) for driving & orientation; and Slickrock Bench (1:24,000--7 1/2' quad) for hiking.

Main Attractions Another deep, dark, narrow Navajo Sandstone canyon, more than a km of which is equal to or better than the Buckskin Gulch.

Ideal Time to Hike Spring or fall, but it's cool in the slot in summer, and usually dry in winter (?).

Boots/Shoes If you're there right after rains, take wading shoes. Otherwise use dry-weather footwear.

Author's Experience On one trip he went down in late March and found half a meter of snow on the narrow's floor. There was no water in any of the potholes then. He went down again in June, a week after heavy rains, and found some mud in the low places, but no pools of water. His last trip was in August, 2003, a few days after a flood, with mud everywhere and a few shallow pools. Round-trip took 3 1/2 hours.

This old 1930's foto shows the Round Valley Neck (or Draw) CCC Spike Camp. These watering troughs at Round Valley Seep (some locals call this Rush Bed Seeps) are in the same place as some newer troughs today. This site is about 600m south of the Round Valley Draw Trailhead. (Willy Bryant foto)

Map 20, Round Valley Draw and Upper Entry to Hackberry Canyon

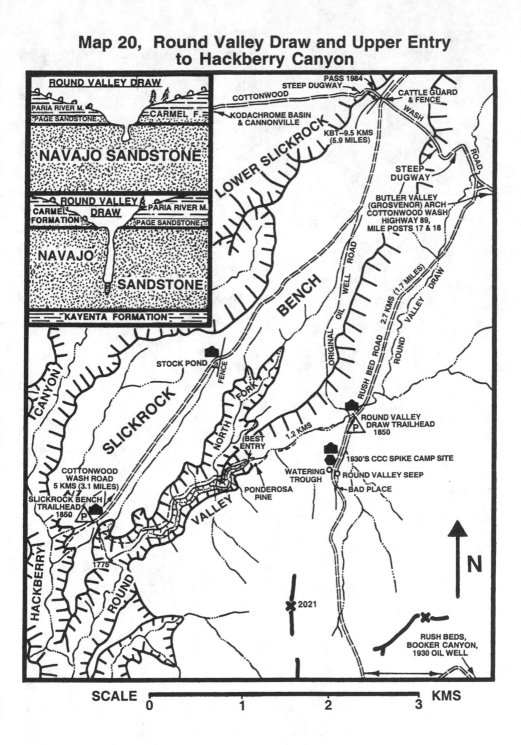

ROUND VALLEY DRAW

PARIA RIVER M.

CARMEL F.

PAGE SANDSTONE

NAVAJO SANDSTONE

ROUND VALLEY DRAW

CARMEL FORMATION

PARIA RIVER M.

PAGE SANDSTONE

NAVAJO SANDSTONE

KAYENTA FORMATION

PASS 1984

STEEP DUGWAY

COTTONWOOD

CATTLE GUARD & FENCE

WASH

KODACHROME BASIN & CANNONVILLE

KBT—9.5 KMS (5.9 MILES)

LOWER SLICKROCK

STEEP DUGWAY

ROAD

BUTLER VALLEY (GROSVENOR) ARCH COTTONWOOD WASH HIGHWAY 89, MILE POSTS 17 & 18

BENCH

ORIGINAL OIL WELL ROAD

RUSH BED ROAD

2.7 KMS (1.7 MILES)

ROUND VALLEY DRAW

CANYON

STOCK POND

FENCE

NORTH FORK

1.2 KMS

ROUND VALLEY DRAW TRAILHEAD 1850

P

SLICKROCK

BEST ENTRY

1930'S CCC SPIKE CAMP SITE

WATERING TROUGH

ROUND VALLEY SEEP

COTTONWOOD WASH ROAD 5 KMS (3.1 MILES)

PONDEROSA PINE

BAD PLACE

SLICKROCK BENCH TRAILHEAD 1850

P

VALLEY

N

HACKBERRY

1775

ROUND

2021

RUSH BEDS, BOOKER CANYON, 1930 OIL WELL

SCALE 0   1   2   3 **KMS**

Above Left This is the very beginning of the slot or narrows into Round Valley Draw. Here you'll find a drop of nearly 3m, but it's easy to downclimb. Some beginners may want a short rope or help from a friend.

Above Right This is the beginning of the slot into Round Valley Draw as seen from the bottom of the 3m dropoff.

Right A typical scene in the upper part of Round Valley Draw.

Above Left These are the boulders located just below where the North Fork enters the middle part of Round Valley Draw.

Above Right The deepest part of Round Valley Draw is in the lower end.

Left From the rim in the lower end of the narrows of Round Valley Draw, you can see where the canyon begins to open up.

Booker Canyon

Location & Access   The locals never had a name for this canyon but people at the BLM office in Kanab, once referred to it as Booker Canyon, after one of their staff, Bill Booker. It's the first canyon south of the narrows of Round Valley Draw, and is southwest of Grosvenor (Butler Valley) Arch. To get there from the Bryce Canyon area, drive east then south through Tropic to Cannonville (Cannonville now has a new GSENM visitor center), then continue south on the paved Kodachrome Basin Road for 11.7 kms (7.3 miles). At that point is an information sign on the right and the paved road turns left or north. This is the Kodachrome Basn Turnoff (KBT). From there, continue straight east on the graded **Cottonwood Wash Road.** Drive 11.1 kms (6.9 kms) from the KBT until you arrive at **Round Valley Draw.** Once there, turn south onto the **Rush Bed Road,** which is immediately east of the dry wash. After 2.7 kms (1.7 miles) you'll cross Round Valley Draw, but continue south uphill past the parking place & trail register for Round Valley Draw, then Round Valley Seep. Continue south. Not far from the Seep is a little wash cutting across the road--be sure to have a shovel handy because you may need to fill in that wash to get by--even with a 4WD!

About 5.8 kms (3.6 miles) from the Cottonwood Wash Road, stop and park where you can. You'll likely need a HCV or 4WD for this last section of road. While there are a number of ways to enter Booker Canyon, beginning at this place is the quickest and involves the least amount of driving.

If you're coming from the south and Highway 89, turn north onto the Cottonwood Wash Road between mile posts 17 & 18. Drive north for 54 kms (33.5 miles). At Round Valley Draw, head south along the Rush Bed Road past Round Valley Seep and to the parking place just described.

Trail/Route   From where you park, walk due south across one shallow valley. This will put you on a point between 2 upper drainages of Booker Canyon. Once there, walk southwest down the nose of the point. With a little zig zagging & route-finding, you can walk all the way down to the canyon floor. About 500m below where you reach the bottom, will be an 8m dropoff and a short narrows section. Skirt left and walk around the dryfall on the south side before reentering the dry creek bed. Continue downcanyon. About 2 kms below the 1st dropoff will be a 2nd dryfall of about 8m. To avoid this, walk along the right or north side and reenter the wash about 150m below. It's in this area you'll find some interesting foto ops with green ponderosa pines growing out of cracks in the white Navajo Sandstone slickrock, and hopefully with blue skies beyond.

From there to the beginning of the **Booker Canyon Slot** will be another km. This slot is less than one meter wide, so to get down in, simply span it--with one foot on one side, your other foot on the other. Do this for 10m-15m, then downclimb to the bottom just below several chokestones. Some beginners may feel a little uncomfortable here, so having an experienced hiker along may be helpful (for the experienced canyoneer it's nothing!). This shallow, but fairly tight slot, lasts for about 250m, then opens.

About 300m below the slot will be a 7m dryfall you cannot skirt around. This means you'll either have to stop there and return the same way; or rappel. There are 2 ways to rappel--**this will be for someone who has a little experience!** (1) Walk back upcanyon 75m and look for several fist-sized cobblestones to be jammed into a groove just above the dropoff. Once a cobblestone is wedged in, wrap a short piece of webbing around it, add a Rapide/Quick Link, and use a rope at least 20m long to rappel/or handline down. But doing it this way will be leaving trash in the canyon. (2) Or, take with you what climbers and canyoneers call an **Ibis Hook**, which you can buy in climbers supply stores. It's about 15cms long and shaped like a large fish hook. Tie a short rope to it, and place the hook somewhere in that groove. If it doesn't feel secure, use the hook's sharp point to create a small hole so the hook can't pop out, then rappel/handline from the hook. Once everyone is at the bottom, give the rope some slack, then flip it, and the hook should come right out, and you'll be on your way.

At the bottom of this simple rappel, you'll encounter a couple of minor dropoffs you can downclimb or slide down. About 1 1/2 kms below the rappel will be Hackberry Canyon. You can either continue down Hackberry to the Cottonwood Wash Road (this will likely involve spending one night in the

Halfway through Booker Canyon you'll see ponderosa pines growing out of cracks in the white Navajo Sandstone walls.

Map 21, Booker Canyon

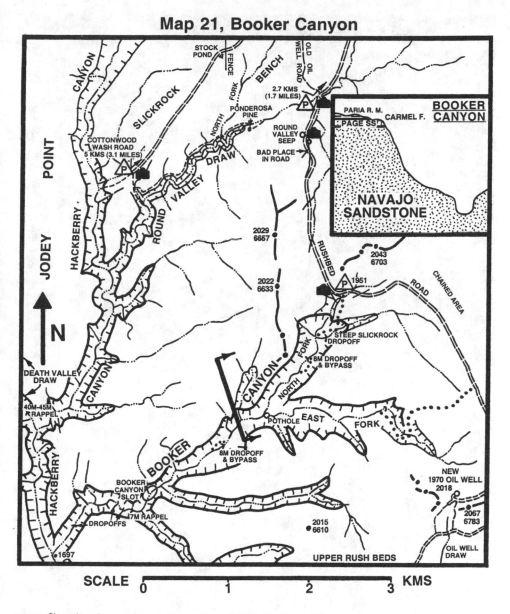

SCALE
0   1   2   3   KMS

canyon?); or head upcanyon and enter Round Valley Draw. If doing this, look at the previous map of Round Valley Draw to see how you can get back to the Rush Bed Road. You can do that by getting upon Slickrock Bench and rim-walking; or walk straight up the narrows of Round Valley Draw and eventually back to your car (a 2nd car would save 45 minutes walking).

Elevations Normal entry car-park, 1951m; junction of Hackberry & Booker Canyons, 1697m.

Hike Length/Time Needed If you walk down to the 3rd dropoff/rappel point & return the same way, about 4-6 hours round-trip. The 2nd option would be to make the simple rappel/handline into lower Booker, walk down to Hackberry, then up through Round Valley Draw and back to your car. This will likely take somewhere between 7-11 hours, a full day's hike.

Water This is a dry canyon, so take plenty of water in your car and pack.

Maps USGS or BLM map Smoky Mountain (1:100,000) for driving & orientation; and Slickrock Bench (1:24,000--7 1/2' quad) for hiking.

Main Attractions One short slot, possible rappel and solitude in a canyon that's never been grazed.

Ideal Time to Hike Spring or fall, but anytime the clay-based entry roads are dry.

Boots/Shoes Dry weather-type boots or shoes.

Author's Experience Once he came up from Hackberry Canyon and stopped at the 7m dryfall. His next trip was down from the top to the 7m dryfall/rappel, then back and out the East Fork as shown. That trip took less than 5 hours.

A scene in the middle part of Booker Canyon. Ponderosa pines growing out of cracks in the white Navajo Sandstone walls.

Left The Booker Canyon Slot in the lower part of the canyon. You can get down inside and crawl through; or span across the top and take the *high road* for a ways, then chimney down. **Right** Looking down on the 7m rappel. You can wrap webbing around a small stone set in the crack as shown. Or, rap from a ledge using an Ibis Hook. Lots of places to set a hook here.

This is Ilan Pollock, the son of Sam Pollock, and brother to Herm & Afton. This sheep camp is somewhere in Upper Death Valley just west of the upper end of Hackberry Canyon. The year was 1938. (Afton Pollock foto)

These 4 cooks are standing in front of the mess hall at the Henrieville CCC Camp. One or more of these enrollees likely worked at the spike camp located at Round Valley Seep, which is on the way to the Upper Rush Beds and Booker Canyon. From the late 1930's. (Hasle Caudill foto)

Stone Donkey Canyon

Location & Access Stone Donkey, which is unnamed on USGS maps, is an upper west-side tributary to Hackberry Canyon, which in turn is a tributary to the Upper Paria River. Stone Donkey Canyon is a technical slot requiring ropes & rappelling gear. It's located almost directly south of Kodachrome Basin, in between the Upper Paria River Gorge and Hackberry Canyon, as well as due north of the Old Pahreah ghost town.

Read the driving instructions along with **Map 15, Road Map to Rock Springs Bench & Trails** That map & description shows you the way to reach Stone Donkey from the upper or northern end and Rock Springs Bench. The author once got to the end of this track in his old VW Rabbit & newer Golf TDI, but since then, heavy rains have made the road even worse and now you'll likely need some kind of HCV, or better still, a 4WD. An alternate to driving this complicated route & bad road, is to drive north from Highway 89 on the Cottonwood Wash Road for 23.5 kms (14.6 miles) and park opposite the mouth of Hackberry Canyon. This will allow you to reach Stone Donkey from the lower end. See **Map 23**. This would make a slightly longer hike, but driving is much easier and less complicated.

Rating After a long hike you come to a tight slot with one or several rappels totaling about 40m, then some steep & tight downclimbing in a 250m-long slot. This rates a **3B III**.

Equipment Rappelling gear, one 60m & a 15m rope (if you intend to pull your ropes and drag them with you through the slot, then take two 60's and lots of webbing for slings), one 6m-8m rope/cord for lowering each pack, one headlamp per/person, and of course a compass & map, ascenders, etc.--as always! In warm weather, consider taking knee & elbow pads; in spring or fall, take a wet/drysuit-- there's always water in the slot.

Route From the end of the Rock Creek Bench Road, and with the two 7 1/2' maps listed below in hand, route-find due south about one km to the southern tip of Rock Springs Point as shown. About 200m before the actual end of the point, look for a cairn (single pointed rock) on the left marking a trail-of-sorts angling down over the rim heading southeast. This is **Wallace Ott's old horse trail** but is only visible in the upper part (he only took a horse up or down this route about 3 times!); further along, head straight down the sandy slope. Consider caching a bottle of water at the bottom of this steep slope for the return hike.

Once at the bottom of the big cliff & sandy slope, and with map & compass in hand, walk down the dry wash for about 5 minutes, then route-find SSE. After about 2 kms, you'll pass west of **Little Mollies Nipple** labeled 2080m (6825'). and immediately under the elevation marked 6444 on the *Slickrock Bench 7 1/2' quad*. Continue south along a hogsback ridge, but eventually veer southeast and drop down into the upper part of Stone Donkey. If you can't read a topo map, or compass, you're in the wrong place!

Once into upper Stone Donkey, walk about 4 kms with scattered ponderosa pines until you're almost exactly due south of **Cottonwood Peak** (other local names for this are **Buckhorn or Death Valley Peak**) marked 2022m (6634). When you reach the beginning of the slot, you'll have 3 choices of how to get started. (1) Tie a 15m rope to a small bush, then a 60m rope to the end of that. From there you can handline or rappel down over 2 dropoffs, then rappel over a chokestone and down another 20-25m to a walk-out pool. Leave ropes and pick them up later. (2) Or you can help each other down into the slot, set up handlines & D-rings on chokestones, then rappel down to the pool just mentioned. This way you'd be pulling your rope and dragging it down the remainder of a tight slot.

(3) Look southeast from the head of the slot to a cedar (juniper) tree which is about 30m from the edge of the slot. From it you can rappel in immediately below the pool mentioned above. To do that, first tie a short rope of about 15m to the tree, then attach the 60. Rap in from there, but tether your pack to the front of your harness and let it dangle down between your legs; this is because you'll have about 30m of free rappel. This will be a fast rap on a single rope, so better have a **variable speed control ATC,** or run the rope through an extra carabiner on a leg loop on your harness--anything to slow the descent! Leave the ropes in place to be picked up later on the way back to your vehicle.

At the bottom and just beyond the pool, remove your rappelling harness and tie it to the rope to be hauled up later--otherwise you'll scrape the hell out of it going downcanyon. After a short walk, comes several interesting downclimbs in a tight slot. This is where you'll want the **smallest pack possible.** This is also where either a wet/drysuit, or long pants & long sleeved shirt; or knee & elbow pads will save skin. Later, you'll come to a dark slot where **a headlamp is required.** This goes on for about 35m. There will always be deep water here, so chimney over the deep places to avoid swimming. A short distance below that, the canyon opens quickly. This entire slot is only about 250m long--but it's a good one.

About one km below the slot, turn left and exit the canyon at one of 2 or 3 places heading north. Once out, route-find northwest between the slot and Cottonwood Peak back to your ropes and return the same way back to your car. Or you could head downstream into Hackberry on a longer hike; in this case you'll want to lug your long ropes through the tight slot.

If coming up Hackberry, plan to backpack about 13 kms to the mouth of Stone Donkey, then walk 400m upcanyon to a spring. That's your waterhole. Camp near there. This should take half a day or so. From the spring, continue upcanyon just over a km, exit to the north as suggested above, route-find to the upper end of the slot and head downcanyon taking your ropes with you. Walk back to your car in the afternoon.

Elevations Crossing of Rock Springs Creek, 1725m; Rock Springs Bench Trailhead, 2073m; high point of hike on Rock Springs Point, 2109m; exit in Stone Donkey, 1627m; junction of Hackberry & Stone Donkey,1455m, end of Hackberry at Cottonwood Wash, 1440m.

Time Needed To insure success, camp at the Rock Springs Bench Trailhead, then take from 9-13 hours for the round-trip day-hike. If coming up Hackberry, you'll likely need about 1 1/2 days for the hike; but if you camp at the mouth of Hackberry, get an early start, then strong hikers may be able to do it in 12-14 hours round-trip (?). But maybe less (?). This would be for tough hombres only.

Water Take plenty in your car and pack. There's always some water in potholes and in the slot, and it's always at the spring in lower Stone Donkey. Take purification tabs for pothole water as there's always cow poop in the valley above the slot.

Maps USGS or BLM map Smoky Mountain (1:100,000) for driving & orientation; and Calico Peak & Slickrock Bench (1:24,000--7 1/2' quad) for hiking.

Flash Flood Danger High risk in the short 250m slot, but no danger elsewhere.

Best Time To Hike You can hike this canyon anytime between late March or early April through October. If going in the spring or fall, a wet/drysuit is required; this because any little shower puts water

Map 22, Stone Donkey Canyon

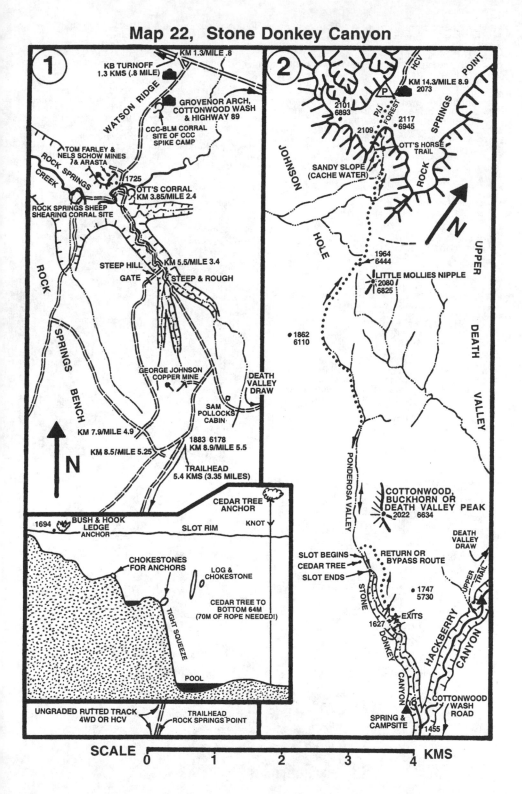

1

KM 1.3/MILE .8
KB TURNOFF
1.3 KMS (.8 MILE)

WATSON RIDGE

GROVENOR ARCH,
COTTONWOOD WASH
& HIGHWAY 89

CCC-BLM CORRAL
SITE OF CCC
SPIKE CAMP

ROCK SPRINGS

TOM FARLEY &
NELS SCHOW MINES
& ARASTA

ROCK CREEK

1725

OTT'S CORRAL
KM 3.85/MILE 2.4

ROCK SPRINGS SHEEP
SHEARING CORRAL SITE

ROCK SPRINGS BENCH

STEEP HILL
GATE

KM 5.5/MILE 3.4
STEEP & ROUGH

GEORGE JOHNSON
COPPER MINE

DEATH VALLEY DRAW

SAM POLLOCKS CABIN

KM 7.9/MILE 4.9

1883 6178
KM 8.9/MILE 5.5

KM 8.5/MILE 5.25

N

TRAILHEAD
5.4 KMS (3.35 MILES)

CEDAR TREE ANCHOR

1694 BUSH & HOOK
LEDGE ANCHOR

SLOT RIM

KNOT

CHOKESTONES
FOR ANCHORS

LOG & CHOKESTONE

CEDAR TREE TO
BOTTOM 64M
(70M OF ROPE NEEDED!)

TIGHT SQUEEZE

POOL

UNGRADED RUTTED TRACK
4WD OR HCV

TRAILHEAD
ROCK SPRINGS POINT

2

HCV

KM 14.3/MILE 8.9
2073

ROCK SPRINGS POINT

2101
6893

P

P/J FOREST

2117
6945

2109

OTT'S HORSE TRAIL

JOHNSON HOLE

SANDY SLOPE
(CACHE WATER)

ROCK SPRINGS

N

UPPER

1964
6444

LITTLE MOLLIES NIPPLE
2080
6825

DEATH

1862
6110

VALLEY

PONDEROSA VALLEY

COTTONWOOD,
BUCKHORN OR
DEATH VALLEY PEAK
2022 6634

DEATH VALLEY DRAW

SLOT BEGINS
CEDAR TREE
SLOT ENDS

RETURN OR
BYPASS ROUTE

1747
5730

UPPER TRAIL

STONE

EXITS

1627

DONKEY CANYON

HACKBERRY CANYON

COTTONWOOD WASH ROAD

SPRING & CAMPSITE

1455

SCALE   0   1   2   3   4   KMS

into the slot from the surrounding slickrock. Late spring/early summer is best because of longer days.
Boots/Shoes Wading boots or shoes for the slot, but any kind of shoe outside it.
Author's Experience On this first trip, he car-camped at Wallace Ott's Corral, then after an hour of wandering on top of Rock Springs Bench, he finally found the right road and got to the trailhead. His hike to the technical slot (but not down it) and into the canyon below to as far as the spring and back, took 8 hours.

On his second trip (9/23/2002), he carried a ton of ropes plus wetsuit, then attempted to go down from the head of the slot. He attached a 60m rope to the bush, backed up by an Ibis hook in a crack, then handlined down to the last big drop above the pool. He wasn't sure if the rope reached the bottom, so being alone he jumarred back up and went in from the south side as Scott Patterson & friends had done. After the slot, he retrieved his ropes (a 60m & 17m) and returned to his Chevy Tracker in 9 1/2 hours. He drank 4 liters of water on the hike which was an average day temperature-wise for September. On 8/31/2003, he hiked up Hackberry and climbed up the slot to the the pool & bottom of the rappel. On the way back, he left Hackberry Canyon at the Ken Goulding Trail and after trial & error and some backtracking, made his way to the west side of Castle Rock, then east along the drainage south of this peak. He finally got back to Cottonwood Wash Road and his car after 11 hours.

Right This is one of several permanent pools you'll find in the lower part of the slot in Stone Donkey Canyon.

Below Left The middle part of Stone Donkey's slot. There are lots of places in this section where you have to take off your pack and walk sideways.

Below Right This is the pool at the bottom of the rappelling or steep part of the slot. There will likely be water here all the time, because the valley above is totally slickrock, so any rainstorm of consequence will put water in this canyon. This was a summertime hike for the author, so there was no need for a wet/drysuit. However, if it's warm weather and you're waring shorts & T shirt, it's recommended you take knee & elbow pads, the kind volleyball players use. This will save lots of skin. They can be bought in any sporting goods store.

Left This is part of Stone Donkey's slot where you'll need a headlamp and be prepared to swim. Actually, you can spread your arms and legs and keep your shoulders above water. This foto was taken with a digital flash and is the darkest part of the canyon. **Right** One of several toadstool or mushroom-like rocks on the canyon walls above the slot in Stone Donkey Canyon.

This is part of the lower end of Stone Donkey Canyon, just below where water begins to flow. There are some nice campsites in this section plus running water all the time.

Hackberry Canyon & the Watson Cabin

Location & Access Hackberry is one of 3 long canyon hikes in this book, and it's one of the best when considering availability of water, good scenery, pleasant campsites and interesting things to see along the way. Hackberry lies just east of the Upper Paria River Gorge and runs south roughly parallel to it. The road you'll be using, whether you go in at the head of the canyon or enter from the bottom, is the Cottonwood Wash Road. For a better look at the lower end of the canyon, see **Map 26**.

To get there from the north & Bryce Valley area, drive south through Tropic to Cannonville. One block south of the Grand Staircase Inn & gas station is a new visitor center for the Grand Staircase-Escalante National Monument (GSENM). Stop there and check on the latest road conditions and other information. They are open from 8-4:30 every day during the 9 warmest months of the year (Tele. 435-679-8981). From Cannonville, head south & east on the paved Kodachrome Basin Road to the Kodachrome Basin Turnoff (KBT), a distance of 11.7 kms (7.3 miles). From the KBT, continue east on the graded & graveled **Cottonwood Wash Road** for 9.5 kms (5.9 miles). At that point you'll be on top of Slickrock Bench at a cattle guard & fence. See the **Map 20, Round Valley Draw** for a better look at the driving route to this trailhead.

If you're coming from the south & Highway 89, drive to a point roughly halfway between Page & Kanab. Between mile posts 17 & 18 turn north onto the same Cottonwood Wash Road (if coming from Page, stop at the new GSENM Visitor Center (Tele. 435-675-5868) in Big Water, Utah, between mile posts 7 & 8 for an update on the Cottonwood Wash Road). Most of this road has a clay base and when it's wet, it's impassible even for 4WD's! When dry it's fine for cars). Drive north up through Cottonwood Wash, past the mouth of Hackberry (this is 23.5 kms/14.6 miles from Highway 89; or 39.6 kms/24.6 miles from the KBT), past the turnoff to Butler Valley (Grosvenor) Arch, across Round Valley Draw and to the same cattle guard & fence mentioned above. This is 53.6 kms (33.3 miles) from Highway 89.

On the east side of the cattle guard & fence, turn south on a reasonably good 2WD track. Drive south & southwest past a fence & stock pond (Km 3.2/Mile 2) to the end of the road at Km 5/Mile 3.1.

Trail/Route From the Slickrock Bench Trailhead marked 1850m, and with compass in hand, **walk due south** on a minor trail about 150m or less; there you'll begin to drop down into a minor side-canyon of lower **Round Valley Draw** (don't head southwest on another faint trail which ends at the rim of Hackberry and some impassible cliffs!). This side-canyon entry gets a little steep in places, but should be easy even with a large backpack. Once at the bottom of Round Valley Draw, simply walk down-canyon.

About 2 kms below the trailhead, **Hackberry Canyon** comes in on the right or west side (at one time, you could drive down upper Hackberry about 4 kms to begin hiking, but that route seems to be washed out or blocked off and isn't used anymore). About 3 kms below the confluence with Hackberry, the lower end of **Death Valley Draw** comes in on the right or west. You can walk up this drainage about 300m; there you'll come to a crack where flood waters fall about 40m-45m to the canyon floor. There is a way up around this in a canyon to the left--read about it with **Map 19, Death Valley Draw.**

About 2 kms below Death Valley Draw, **Booker Canyon** comes in on the left or east. If you walk up Booker roughly 1 1/2 kms, you'll come to a couple of dryfalls, which you can bypass, then some pretty good narrows, and finally another dryfall you cannot climb. That's the end for people going up Booker Canyon. About 4-5 kms below Booker is another fairly long side-canyon coming in on the left or east side. Ken Goulding Jr. of Henrieville, the rancher who runs cows up on the Rush Beds, says there's a route somewhere near this canyon where you can ride a horse off the rim and down into Hackberry. So far, the author hasn't been in that canyon or on that route up to the east-side rim.

About 3 kms below that side-canyon, you should see water starting to seep into the creek bed. From that point on, all the way down to Cottonwood Wash, you'll have running water most of the way. About 800m below where water starts to flow, will be lots of cottonwood trees, willows and a bench on the right or west. On it you should see a fence, and behind it a constructed cow trail in and/or out of the canyon. This is called the **Upper Trail** or **Upper Death Valley Trail.** See **Map 19, Death Valley Draw** for more details.

The late Herm Pollock of Tropic, believed this Upper Trail was first made by a group of Panguitch cattlemen in the late 1800's (Wallace Ott thinks it was built by Samson Chynoweth?). It was on this very narrow path, as it runs along the rim of the canyon, that a cow once laid down on the trail and died. Because it was so narrow, the other cows wouldn't step over her body to get to water. The end result was the choking death of many cows in the area which is now called Upper Death Valley. Since that disaster, the trail has been improved by different cattlemen who ran stock in the Upper Death Valley area. Today it's a good trail.

A little over 2 kms below the Upper Trail, **Stone Donkey Canyon** comes in on the right or west side. This canyon divides the Upper from Lower Death Valley. Walk up this drainage about 400m to find a low dryfall with a potty-type arch above a spring. You can bypass this little dryfall on the left. If you continue up Stone Donkey, you'll come to a very good slot as described on **Map 22.** If coming from above, you'll have to rappel in, but if coming up from Hackberry, you can wade in from the bottom. If you have a headlamp, knee & elbow pads (and a wet/drysuit in spring or fall), and have the strength to chimney up a narrow crack, you can reach the pool at the bottom of the rappelling section. If you can make it to that point, you'll have seen about 95% of the slot. You can also get out of lower Stone Donkey on the north side, walk around to the upper end of the slot and rappel down in, as described in the separate chapter mentioned above.

Less than 2 kms below Stone Donkey, is another cow trail out of the canyon to the right or west. This is called the **Lower Trail** or **Lower Death Valley Trail.** As you near this area, you'll notice the wall on the right gets lower & lower with sand on top. Right at the bottom of the trail and high on the wall in front of you, are several cowboyglyphs. The best & most famous one reads, **W.M. Chynoweth, 1892.** It's about 3m above the creek and 20m from the bottom of the Lower Trail.

The Lower Trail is mostly along a natural break in the cliffs, but minor work has been done in the very lowest part. Just above the cliffs is a long sand slide where cows walk going to or from the creek for water. This is still used by cattle today in the Lower Death Valley area during the winter months.

About 400m below the Lower Trail and on the left or east side is another low bench. Get upon this at the north end to find the beginning of the **Goulding** (pronounced Golding) or **Ken Goulding Trail.** There should be a stone cairn at the beginning (?). This trail was likely first built by the **Chynoweths** beginning sometime after their arrival at Pahreah in the fall of 1892, but much more work was done on it by the late Ken Goulding, Sr. His son Ken Jr., still lives in Henrieville and still runs cow there.

The Goulding Trail zig zags back & forth up the east side of the canyon wall, then once on top, it

Map 23, Hackberry Canyon & the Watson Cabin

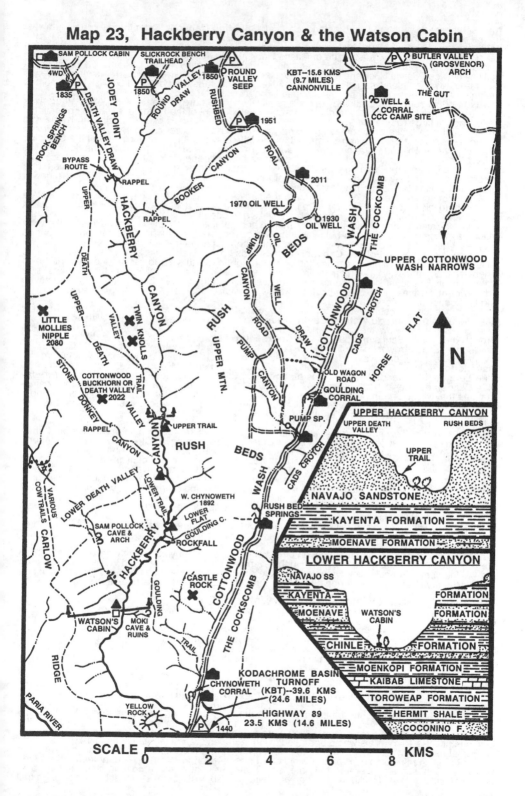

SCALE
0   2   4   6   8   KMS

runs southeast down into a little drainage we'll call **Goulding Canyon**. From there it runs southwest up the other side to the top of the mesa. You can follow it on the map. Once out of Hackberry, it runs south past the head of a little side-canyon with some Anasazi (perhaps Fremont?) Indian ruins (read below), then curves to the east south of Castle Rock. It's in this section you'll likely see a few stone cairns marking the trail. Finally, it zig zags down a little side-canyon into Cottonwood Wash about halfway between Castle Rock and the mouth of Hackberry. That last steep section was man-made, as was the part where it leaves Hackberry. In between, the trail runs through sand but it's visible most of the time. This trail and the ruins are described in detail with **Map 26.**

About 400m below the Goulding Trail is a relatively new feature in the canyon. Where there was once a minor 1m-high ledge & waterfall right at the contact point of the Kayenta & Navajo Formations, there's now a large **rockfall** in the canyon. On October 25 1987, part of the Navajo Sandstone wall on the west side broke away creating a dam across Hackberry Creek. This was heard by Ralph Chynoweth who was deer hunting & camped on the little bench at the very beginning of the Goulding Trail at the time. The dam is about 8m high and at first created a sizable lake above the dam for perhaps 100m or more upstream. However, the waters finally seeped through the debris and over the years has created a new stream course on the west side of the dam. Slowly over the years, flood waters have carried away most of the sediment that had backed up behind the dam. There's now a hiker's trail around the dam on the east side.

About 75m below the rockfall, is a route to the canyon rim up a steep gully on the east side. You can climb up this to meet the Goulding Trail, but it's choked full of unstable rocks & boulders, and isn't recommended. In places you have to climb on all-4's and one of the large rocks could dislodge at any time! Immediately opposite this steep gully, there's another little side-canyon coming in from the west which has a small stream. A km below that are 2 goosenecks bends where the canyon is about as deep as it gets. Just below that, you may see a nice spring on the right or west side.

Further along is **Sam Pollock Canyon**. About 3 kms up this drainage is an arch with Sam's name on it. At one point, you'll have to route-find up to the right or north side, to get around a dryfall which otherwise blocks the way. It's an easy climb. Once you reach the arch, which is on the northeast side of the canyon, look to the north or upcanyon side less than 100m to see a big alcove-type cave, maybe called **Pollock Cave (?)**. In the back are cowboy signatures such as Art [Arthur] Chynoweth, 1918, and black soot from aboriginal camp fires.

About one km downstream from the mouth of Sam Pollock Canyon, and on a bench on the west side of the creek, is the old **Watson Cabin.** Read the full story about it and Frank Watson below.

About 3-4 kms below the cabin and where the gorge turns east, Hackberry cuts dramatically through the Navajo Sandstone part of **The Cockscomb** before reaching Cottonwood Wash. This is the deepest and narrowest part of Hackberry Canyon. Just to the south of the mouth of Hackberry is a very colorful dome of Navajo Sandstone called **Yellow Rock**, which is discussed on another map.

Elevations Slickrock Bench Trailhead, about 1850m; bottom end of Hackberry Canyon, 1440m.

Hike Length/Time Needed This hike is around 28 to 30 kms long. It can be done in one long day with a car on each end, but most people normally take 2 or 3 days, depending on how many side-canyons they visit along the way. If you're going all the way through the canyon, consider leaving a mtn. bike at one end to substitute as a car shuttle. But riding a bike back to your car would take 3 or 4 hours--or more! Hitch hiking is another option. In October, 2003 there were 200-300 cars a day using Cottonwood Wash Road.

Water It begins to flow in the creek bed about 800m above where the Upper Trail comes in. It then flows nearly all the way to Cottonwood Wash. There's a good spring up Stone Donkey Canyon, and there are several seeps or springs just below the rockfall, including a side-canyon to the west.

From the first of November through April, there can be cattle in the canyon--depending on the drought, so take water directly from a spring, or purify it first. In summer when the cattle are gone, it should be better--a lot better after a flood has washed out all the cow pies and cleaned the canyon.

Maps USGS or BLM map Smoky Mountain (1:100,000) for driving & orientation; and Slickrock Bench & Calico Peak (1:24,000--7 1/2' quads) for hiking.

Main Attractions Good water, shady campsites, narrow side-canyons, old historic cattle trails, an old homesteader's cabin, and solitude.

Ideal Time to Hike Spring or fall. In late spring and early summer, you'll be plagued by deer flies (from late May into July). To survive these pests, wear long pants.

Boots/Shoes Wading boots or shoes.

Author's Experience He's made a dozen or more trips into the canyon, but only once did he walk all the way through. On that occasion, he left in the evening from the road to Round Valley Trailhead, then rim-walked above Round Valley Draw to the route down in, and finally camped near the confluence with Hackberry. Next day he hurried all the way through and hitched a ride back to his car.

The Story of Frank Watson and the Watson Cabin

There's a rather well-built and well-preserved cabin in the lower end of Hackberry Canyon and an interesting story behind it. It's called the Watson Cabin, after a man known locally as Frank Watson.

The man's real name was **Richard Welburn Thomas** who came from Wisconsin. As the story goes, Thomas apparently had a quarrel with his wife one night, then early the next morning, he got up, left the house and walked to the railway station where he boarded a train for the wild west. This is the story that's told, but he could also have been a fugitive from the law (?). Why else would he change his name?

After some wandering, it seems he ended up at Lee's Ferry under the employment of Charles H. Spencer. Spencer was the big-time mining promoter who got lots of money from investors and tried to find a way to separate gold from the Chinle clay beds at Lee's Ferry. Spencer worked at Lee's Ferry between 1910 and 1912. It was at this time Thomas changed his name to Frank Watson. Evidently, Watson was a good all-around handy man and mechanic. It's been said by several men in Bryce Valley, that Watson was involved in the running of the paddlewheel steamer *Charles H. Spencer* up the Colorado River to Warm Creek, where they were to load coal and ship it by barge down to the gold diggings at Lee's Ferry. This whole operation failed in the end, and the miners left in 1912.

From Lee's Ferry, Spencer and his men went up the Paria River to the old town of Pahreah, and were involved in mining gold from the Chinle clay beds off & on from 1912 to about the end of World War I. Watson was also there at that time, and it appears that at some point in time he went over Carlow Ridge into lower Hackberry Canyon and built this cabin. It's been said that he had a rough trail or route from the cabin, over the ridge, and down to Pahreah, but no one seems to know of its where-abouts today.

The late Herm Pollock, a rock hound from Tropic, remembered the Watson Cabin as being well-built. Watson made the wooden hinges on the door with only a pocket knife. About 150m-200m south of the cabin, Watson had a flume and a sluice box, both of which were painted bright yellow when Herm saw the place in 1922. Apparently, Watson had tried to do the same thing in lower Hackberry, as Spencer tried to do over the ridge at Pahreah, because the Chinle clays are exposed in both places. Frank's operation failed too.

George Thompson of Cannonville, remembered a little about the cabin and the time when his father, Jodey Thompson (Jodey Point between Death Valley Draw & upper Hackberry carries his name), tried to homestead the bench land where the cabin is located:

We used to go down there when I was just a little feller when he had water out there on the ground, then a big flood came down and lowered the wash 'till he couldn't get it out into the ditches anymore. So Dad gave it up. I was 4 or 5 when we were down there, about 1926 or '27, and it was soon after that that he decided it was a useless effort. After that, they went down several times and put the water back in the ditches--they hauled trees into the wash and made dikes, and got the water back up there, but the wash was so deep that every little flood would take it down and wash everything out on 'um, so they finally decided it wasn't worth the effort.

For a year or two, Dad planted corn. [They also attempted to grow peach trees.] I remember he brought up corn for the cows in winter. There was a road down there--not much of a road, but it was travelable. I do remember that we went in a wagon--he'd load the kids and away they'd go. I don't know how they got past that little jumpup, but there was a way around it in those days.

There's an interesting story about one dark night in the cabin, as told by several old-timers in Bryce Valley. Jodey and one of his brothers either got to the cabin late at night, or were sleeping there, when they heard rattlesnakes in the darkened room. With only a candle for light and a pitch fork with 5 prongs, they somehow managed to spear one rattler with each prong. In the morning they stood the pitchfork up against the cabin wall with the 5 snakes dangling from it. The longest nearly reached the ground.

According to the late Ken Goulding, Sr. of Henrieville, Watson was employed by the Goulding family off and on for several years herding sheep, apparently during the mid to late 1910's (?). At one time Watson lived in a tent, which was pitched behind the Goulding house in Henrieville. Ken recalled one winter, Watson tore down an old Model A Ford, and put it back together again the next spring.

At about the end of World War I, and after the time Watson built his Hackberry Cabin and had worked for the Gouldings, he built a small store on what is now known locally as Watson Ridge. Watson Ridge is south of Henrieville, and due south of Chimney Rock, which is in Kodachrome Basin State Park. The store was small, and catered to the sheepmen who were numerous in the area at that time. He sold all kinds of supplies, but Ken Goulding remembered him selling candy, Bull Durham tobacco, and a bootleg whisky everyone called *Jamaica Ginger.*

This was in the early days of prohibition, and selling this rot-gut whisky was forbidden. The lady who owned & operated the only store in Henrieville, bought it from someone, then it was transported out to Watson's store, where they used to have some wild parties. It was sold and drank openly at

The Watson Cabin in the lower end of Hackberry Canyon. It's believed this cabin was built by Frank Watson sometime in the 1910's

Watson's place, because it was so far away from the law.

To get to Watson's old store site, drive east from the Kodachrome Basin Turnoff on the Cottonwood Wash Road for 1.3 kms (.8 mile). At the first road running south, turn right, and drive another 150m, then turn right or west again. It's near the crest of the hill, but on the west side. Today there's only a few scattered tin cans, etc., marking the spot. Just beyond his old store site is a corral built by the CCC's in 1937 or '38. It's now called the BLM Corral. A CCC spike camp was located just south of the corral

The last time Goulding saw Watson was in about 1921. Herm Pollock and some of the Otts pick up the story from there. After leaving the store on Watson Ridge, he likely went to the bottom end of Heward Canyon, a tributary of Sheep Creek, which is just east of Bryce Canyon, and southwest of Cannonville. About 2 kms west of the old Johnson Ranch on Sheep Creek, is a very well-built stone house along the road running up Heward Creek. This may have been built by Watson, since it was so well-constructed and is still in very good condition except for the wooden roof, which has collapsed under its own weight. Watson lived there, or perhaps just downcanyon at the Johnson Ranch. While there, he apparently tried to develop a coal mine just west of the cabin for one or 2 winters (see **Map 41, Bryce Valley and Skutumpah Road Ranches**, in the back of this book for the location).

To get to the Heward Canyon rock house, drive south out of Cannonville on the Kodachrome Basin Road for 4.2 kms (2.6 miles), and turn west past the cemetery toward the old townsite of Georgetown. From the Yellow Creek Road just west of Georgetown, turn south and head for Sheep Creek and the sites of the old Henderson and Johnson Ranches, and Heward Creek. About 2 kms west of the old Johnson Ranch, which is now owned by Colorado City (Short Creek) people named Binion and Stubbs, is the rock house on the right side of the road. It's **12 kms (7.45 miles)** from the Kodachrome Basin Road and on the right. It's hard to see because of 2 cedar trees, so watch closely.

Later, Watson landed at the old W. J. Henderson Ranch, which is about 1 1/2 or 2 kms southwest of the Georgetown site, and just up the hill from where the James R. Ott Ranch was located. At this ranch, Watson lived with an old man named Hyrum "Hite" Elmer. Wallace Ott remembers when old Hite died, because Watson came down to their ranch to get a wagon to haul him off.

From the Henderson Ranch, Watson went back to Wisconsin to see his aging mother sometime in the mid-1920's. She was apparently very happy and surprised to see him, according to Ken Goulding Sr. Since he had been gone for so long, and had lost touch with the family, his mother thought he surely must have been killed by Indians.

Right Joseph (Jody) Wallace Thompson and his wife Rachel in about 1900. He was 5 years old when his parents settled in Bryce Valley in 1876. In about 1926, Jodey attempted to farm the area around the Frank Watson Cabin, but that scheme only lasted for a couple of summers before floods lowered the creek bed. Jodey Point, located just west of the upper end of Hackberry Canyon, is named after this man. He is the father of George Wallace Thompson, presently of Cannonville. (George & Joe Thompson foto)

Below This is the signature of Will Chynoweth, 1892, located at the bottom of the Lower Trail. It's 3m above the creek and about 20m or so southeast of the bottom of the trail.

Aerial foto looking west shows Yellow Rock to the left, and lower Hackberry Canyon. Hackberry enters Cottonwood Wash about 200m below the bottom of this picture. All lighter colored rock is Navajo Sandstone.

Sam Pollock Arch. About 50m to the left of this arch is an alcove-type cave. In the back end of it you'll find the ceiling covered with soot, and old cowboy signatures dating from the 1910's.

Upper Cottonwood Wash Narrows

Location & Access Featured here is a short narrow section in the upper end of Cottonwood Wash. These narrows aren't very long, but they are nearly as deep and narrow as parts of the Buckskin Gulch, against which many slot canyons are judged. This hike is located about 7 kms south of the Butler Valley Arch (this was the name of the arch before the National Geographic Society arrived in 1948 and changed the name to **Grosvenor Arch** after the NGS President). To get there, drive south from Bryce Canyon on Highway 12 through the towns of Tropic and Cannonville. From Cannonville head south & east on a paved road following the signs to Kodachrome Basin. At the Kodachrome Basin Turnoff (KBT), continue east (instead of going north to KB) on the graded **Cottonwood Wash Road.** From the KBT, drive 21.4 kms (13.3 miles). This will put you at the bottom of a steep dugway going south. Just in front of you will be some very colorful red & white rocks, and just beyond those a 2nd pass. Park there wherever you can. If coming up Cottonwood Wash from the south, turn north from Highway 89 between mile posts 17 & 18. From the highway to the above-mentioned passes, red & white rocks and parking place is 41.7 kms (25.9 miles). When this Cottonwood Wash Road is wet, stay away--it's impassable, even for 4WD's! However, it tends to dry quickly in summer after rains. Check the nearest visitor center for a road report. Or call the one at Cannonville (Tele. 435-679-8981) or the Big Water visitor center (Tele. 435-675-5868).

Trail/Route From near the culvert over Cads Crotch Wash, scramble down into the drainage. After just a few meters, you'll have a choice of going up Butler Valley Draw a ways, or down the Cottonwood Wash Creek bed. Go up first, as that part is perhaps the best. It's not as deep as the canyon to the south, but it's more narrow. Then head downcanyon. There are 2 very short side-canyons and some high dryfalls to see along the way. After about 2 kms, you'll come out the bottom end heading east back toward the road. From there, it's a 20 minute (1.6 kms/1 mile) road-walk back to your car. These narrows are formed by a strange twist of the dry stream channel which is further west than the road; which is where you'd think the normal water drainage should be. This is called an antecedent stream, which means the channel was there before The Cockscomb was fully uplifted.

Elevations Entry trailhead, 1735m; bottom of narrows, 1675m; picnic site at Grosvenor Arch, 1900m.

Hike Length/Time Needed There's about 600m-800m of interesting narrows up Butler Valley Draw, then about 2 kms of Cottonwood Wash narrows. You can do the whole hike in 1-3 hours.

Water Carry water in your car and pack. There's no water at the little newly developed picnic site (with toilet & paved trail to the arch) 300m from the base of Grosvenor Arch.

Maps USGS or BLM map Smoky Mountain (1:100,000) for driving & orientation; and Butler Valley (1:24,000--7 1/2' quad) for hiking.

Main Attractions A short, but interesting & easily accessible narrow canyon, plus Grosvenor Arch.

Ideal Time to Hike About anytime, but summers are a little warm, and cold winter weather prevents the road from drying quickly after storms (best to get there via Cannonville). Spring or fall are the ideal times.

Boots/Shoes Dry-weather boots or shoes.

Author's Experience Once in early April, and again in mid-October, the author did this entire hike in about 1 hour round-trip. On 8/29/2003, he entered the drainage about 2 kms north of the normal entry point and walked down Butler Valley Draw first, then the lower narrows. The best part of Butler Valley Draw is just above the normal entry point & trailhead. His last scouting hike and road-walk took 3 hours.

This is one of the short side-canyons inside the narrows of the Upper Cottonwood Wash.

Map 24, Upper Cottonwood Wash Narrows

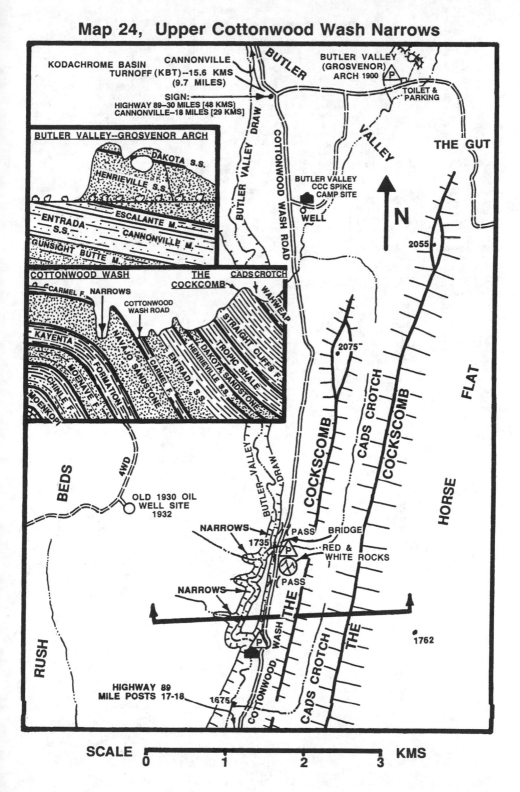

KODACHROME BASIN
TURNOFF (KBT)--15.6 KMS
(9.7 MILES)

CANNONVILLE

BUTLER VALLEY
(GROSVENOR)
ARCH 1900

BUTLER

P

SIGN:
HIGHWAY 89--30 MILES [48 KMS]
CANNONVILLE--18 MILES [29 KMS]

TOILET &
PARKING

BUTLER VALLEY--GROSVENOR ARCH

DAKOTA S.S.

HENRIEVILLE S.S.

ESCALANTE M.

CANNONVILLE M.

ENTRADA
S.S.

GUNSIGHT BUTTE M.

BUTLER VALLEY DRAW

COTTONWOOD WASH ROAD

THE GUT

VALLEY

N

BUTLER VALLEY
CCC SPIKE
CAMP SITE

WELL

2055

COTTONWOOD WASH

CARMEL F. NARROWS

COTTONWOOD
WASH ROAD

THE
COCKCOMB

CADS CROTCH

WAHWEAP

KAYENTA

MOENAVE F.

CHINLE F.

MOENKOPI

NAVAJO SANDSTONE

CARMEL F.

ENTRADA S.S.

HENRIEVILLE S.S.

DAKOTA SANDSTONE

TROPIC SHALE

STRAIGHT CLIFFS F.

2075

COCKSCOMB

CADS CROTCH

COCKSCOMB

HORSE

FLAT

BEDS

4WD

OLD 1930 OIL
WELL SITE
1932

BUTLER VALLEY DRAW

NARROWS

1735

PASS

P

BRIDGE

RED &
WHITE ROCKS

PASS

NARROWS

THE

COTTONWOOD WASH ROAD

CADS CROTCH

THE

1762

RUSH

P

HIGHWAY 89
MILE POSTS 17-18

1675

CADS CROTCH

SCALE

0   1   2   3 KMS

Upper Rush Beds Cattle Trails and the Old Oil Well

Location & Access   The high country south of Round Valley Draw, and in between Hackberry Canyon & Cottonwood Wash, is generally known as the **Rush Beds**. This information & map covers the northern or Upper Rush Beds from about the head of Booker Canyon south to Lower Flat & Rush Bed Spring, which is in Cottonwood Wash. Shown here is the road to the New Oil Well drill site, the Old 1930 Oil Well, the 4WD roads extending south from the oil wells, Upper Mountain, the Old Wagon Road, Pump Canyon & Trail, Rush Bed Spring & Trail and the Narrows of Upper Cottonwood Wash.

To get there, follow the signs south from Cannonville on the road running to Kodachrome Basin. At the junction or turnoff where the paved road heads north to Kodachrome Basin (KBT), you continue straight ahead to the east on the graded & graveled **Cottonwood Wash Road** (From the KBT (Km & Mile 0) to Highway 89 is 63.3 kms (39.2 miles). Or if coming from the south and Highway 89, turn north onto the Cottonwood Wash Road from between mile posts 17 & 18).

To reach the oil wells, drive east from the KBT to Round Valley Draw at Km 10.9/Mile 6.8 (54 kms/33.5 miles from Highway 89), and turn south on the Rush Bed Road as if going to Round Valley Draw (RVD) & Booker Canyon. You'll pass RVD Trailhead at Km 2.7/Mile 1.7, then south past RV Seep. Just after that is a partial road washout, the worst place on this drive. Having a shovel will help, even for 4WD's! After that the road is generally good, but has a rough place or two and is best to have a HCV. Continue south, then veer east & south around the head of Booker Canyon, which is along a chained & reseeded area. At Km 8.5/Mile 5.3 is a junction; to the left or east is the track running down to the Old 1930 Oil Well site, straight ahead is the road to the **New Oil Well**. If you turn left, after about one km will be a gate & rough place. Signs indicate this road may be blocked off there at some time in the future. About 1 1/2 kms from that gate, will be the **Old 1930 Oil Well** site down a short road to the left or east. From this well is an old 4WD track running down to Pump Canyon. Read more on the history below. In the future, if you want to go down to Pump Canyon from the Old Well, you may have to park at the well site, or back up the road at or near the gate, or even at the junction mentioned above (?). This will depend on future GSENM policy and lawsuit #2477 which will determine if they block off these roads or not. Stay tuned!

If you continue south toward the New Oil Well, at Km 9.5/Mile 5.9 will be a fence & gate (leave it as you find it--open or closed), then the road goes down to the southwest and ends in a sandy sagebrush flat at Km 10.5/Mile 6.5. Inscribed on the well's metal pole/plug is *"Butler Valley Gov. #1, Marathon Oil Co., Sept. 14, 1970, Sec. 22, T39S, R1W"*. From this site are 2 very sandy tracks heading south to join the track from the Old Well, but the BLM has them blocked off (ATV's are still driving past the signs illegally!). This will be one trailhead.

To reach the **cattle & oil well trails off the Rush Beds into the middle Cottonwood Wash**, drive east from the KBT to Grosvenor Arch Turnoff (Km 15.6/Mile 9.7) and veer south into Cottonwood Wash. Continue south past the Cottonwood Wash Narrows Hike to Km 26.2/Mile 16.3 (36.9 kms/22.9 miles from Highway 89) and park where you can right on the road. Just west of that point should be the bottom end of the **Old Wagon Road** (300m north of that will be the mouth of what this writer calls **Oil Well Draw**).

Or continue south to Km 28.7/Mile 17.8 (34.5 kms/21.4 miles from Highway 89) and turn west onto a little side road & camping place at the mouth of **Pump Canyon, Spring & Trail**. Park and/or camp in the little loop-road. Or continue downcanyon to **Rush Bed Spring & Trail** at Km 31.1/Mile 19.3 (32 kms/19.9 miles from Highway 89), and park at one of 2 pullouts on the west side of the road. Not far to the south of Rush Bed Spring is Castle Peak and other trails & hikes which are on the next map.

Trail/Route   Depending on monument policy, you will likely have to walk a short distance to the **Old Oil Well**, as described above, and below.

The **Old Wagon Road** is where wagons loaded with lumber from the Old Oil Well were taken off the Rush Beds into Cottonwood Wash. Ken Goulding, Jr. of Henrieville says: *I guess they put trees on 'um--put drags on 'um to hold 'um back, and went right off there. They must of had 'um fixed up pretty good, because it's steep!* From the bottom, John (Long John) W. Mangum & Jim Ed Smith, without a road, hauled the boards in wagons down to Old Pahreah & Fivemile Ranch (read more below).

From where you park on the Cottonwood Wash Road, look west at the steep slope where you'll see a long vertical mound of red dirt or clay sitting on top of the white Navajo Sandstone slickrock. Walk west about 200m to the southeast base of the red dirt mound and first look for a couple of small piles of old boards. Once you find those, walk northwest 75m to find the bottom of the Old Wagon Road which is on the south side of the long red dirt mound. This wagon trail wasn't used too much, but it's clearly visible. Walk up this to where it starts to level off, then it fades and disappears. If you continue cross-country to the west, you'll cross an old drift fence, which is now on the ground. About 200m west of that is the road the oil drillers used to get down to Pump Canyon and their water pumping operation.

According to Ken Goulding, Jr., there's another old cattle trail running east off the Rush Beds about 400m north of the Old Wagon Road. This one is on the north side of Oil Well Draw, but is barely visible in just a few place as it comes off the steeper slope.

From where you park near the mouth of **Pump Canyon**, cross Cottonwood Creek (usually with a little water) to the west to find the end of Pump's drainage. Climb out of it to the west and onto the lower end of an old unused & washed-out road. Follow it west to the bottom of the steep slope. From there, you can turn right or north, reenter Pump Canyon and walk up to the spring; but there's no sign of where the oil well's water pump & pond may have been. Or, you can continue west up the very steep **Lincoln Lyman or New Pump Canyon Road** along the south side of the canyon. At the top of the steep part is a fence & gate. This road runs west, then north to meet the original track running south to Pump Canyon as shown on the map. You can follow this north, then make a loop coming south on the north side of Pump Canyon where the road peters out next to the drift fence, which at that point is still standing. From there follow cow trails south down into Pump Canyon and up the other side back to the gate (or route-find down the steep slickrock to the spring).

Ken Goulding, Jr. remembers when the Pump Canyon Road was built: *I think the BLM built it. They had Lincoln Lyman go down there and blade it off with his Cat. About that time, I had an old 2-ton 4WD dump truck, and I took it off of there. And it was steep! You'd have to stand there with your feet on the brake & floor boards! It was built not long after we got the Rush Beds grazing rights, and that was in 1958. It must have been in about 1960 that Pump Canyon Road was built. That was Lincoln Lyman from Escalante, he was workin' for the BLM.*

There's another old cattle trail just west of **Rush Bed Spring**. From where you park, walk west

Map 25, Upper Rush Beds Cattle Trails & Old Oil Well

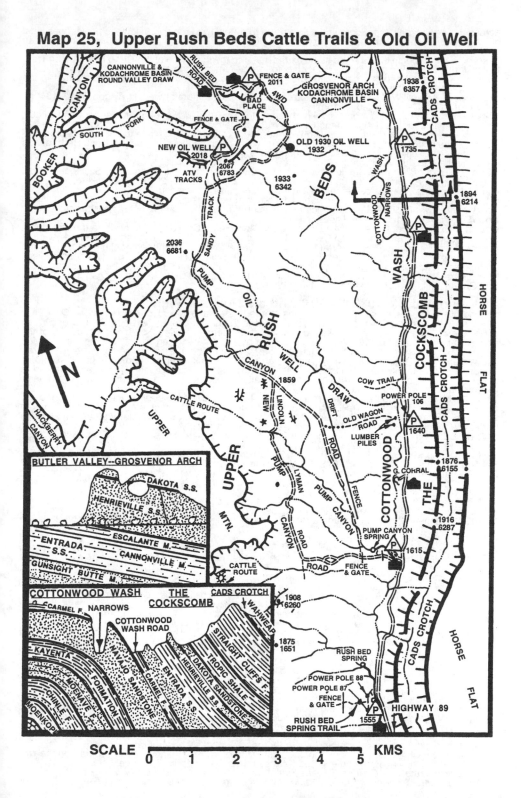

CANNONVILLE &
KODACHROME BASIN
ROUND VALLEY DRAW

RUSH BED ROAD

P

FENCE & GATE
2011

4WD

BAD PLACE

GROSVENOR ARCH
KODACHROME BASIN
CANNONVILLE

1938
6357

CADS CROTCH

SOUTH

FORK

CANYON

FENCE & GATE

NEW OIL WELL
2018

P

ATV TRACKS

2067
6783

P
1735

OLD 1930 OIL WELL
1932

BEDS

COTTONWOOD NARROWS

WASH

1894
6214

P

BOOKER

1933
6342

2036
6681

N

RUSH

OIL WELL

PUMP

SANDY TRACK

WASH

COCKSCOMB

HORSE

HACKBERRY CANYON

CATTLE ROUTE

UPPER

CANYON

1859

NEW

LINCOLN

DRAW

DRIFT

COW TRAIL

POWER POLE 106

OLD WAGON ROAD

LUMBER PILES

P
1640

CADS CROTCH

THE

1876
6155

G. CORRAL

BUTLER VALLEY--GROSVENOR ARCH

DAKOTA S.S.

HENRIEVILLE S.S.

ESCALANTE M.

ENTRADA S.S.

CANNONVILLE M.

GUNSIGHT BUTTE M.

UPPER

MTN.

PUMP CANYON

LYMAN CANYON

ROAD

PUMP CANYON

FENCE

COTTONWOOD

1916
6287

PUMP CANYON SPRING

P
1615

CATTLE ROUTE

ROAD

FENCE & GATE

COTTONWOOD WASH   **THE COCKSCOMB**

CADS CROTCH

Carmel F. NARROWS

COTTONWOOD WASH ROAD

KAYENTA FORMATION

NAVAJO SANDSTONE

MOENAVE F.

CARMEL F.

ENTRADA S.S.

HENRIEVILLE S.S.

DAKOTA SANDSTONE

TROPIC SHALE

STRAIGHT CLIFFS F.

WAHWEAP

CHINLE F.

MOENKOPI

1908
6260

1875
1651

RUSH BED SPRING

POWER POLE 88

POWER POLE 87

FENCE & GATE

P

RUSH BED SPRING TRAIL

1555

HIGHWAY 89

HORSE FLAT

SCALE   0   1   2   3   4   5   KMS

137

across the small creek, then route-find a little north to an old road running below the power lines west of the creek. Once on that track, head south past power pole #88. About 75m south of that and in an area that's seen some flooding, head west straight up the rocky & shaley slope. After another 200m or so, you should begin to see some stone cairns marking the lower end of the **Rush Bed Spring Trail**. Follow it up--the further you go, the easier it is to follow. Near the top of the steeper slope you'll be in a minor drainage, then you'll come to a drift fence & gate. Beyond that, the trail disappears in the sands of the Lower Rush Beds.

Elevations New Oil Well, 2018m; Old 1930 Oil Well, 1932m; bottom of the Old Wagon Road, 1640m; bottom of Pump Canyon Road, 1615m; Rush Bed Spring, 1555m.

Hike Length/Time Needed You can hike these historic trails in just an hour or two, or spend all day. You may be able to take a 4WD to the Old Oil Well, or maybe you'll have to walk in from the junction (?). You'll want an hour or two at the **Old Well**--it's the most interesting place to see on this map.

Water None on the Rush Beds, so take your own. Water can be found at Pump & Rush Bed Springs (2 parts--one in a little canyon, the other in the marshy grass across from the Cottonwood Wash Road). But you'll have to purify this water.

Maps USGS or BLM map Smoky Mountain (1:100,000) for driving & orientation; Slickrock Bench, Butler Valley, Horse Flat, Calico Peak & Fivemile Valley (1:24,000--7 1/2' quads) for hiking.

Main Attractions Historic cattle trails & old oil well in a little known country.

Ideal Time to Hike Spring or fall, but can be hiked anytime the roads are dry. The Cottonwood Wash Road is often wet & closed in winter--sometimes in summer. Check at the nearest visitor center.

Boot/Shoes Dry weather type shoes.

Author's Experience Once he hiked west up the New Pump Canyon Road, north to the road junction at 1859m, then down the Pump Canyon Road and back to Cottonwood Wash in about 2 1/2 hours. Another time, he parked his Tracker at the New Oil Well and hiked south then east on the track to the Old Oil Well while looking for a "Jeep Trail" shown on the Butler Valley quad. That road does not exit! Then it was road-walking back to his vehicle, all in 2 1/2 hours. Later, he found the old lumber at the base of the Old Wagon Road, along with the trail north of Oil Well Draw. Still later he found the Rush Bed Spring Trail. That hike lasted about 1 1/2 hours.

History of the Old 1930 Oil Well, and old Roads & Trails

One of the more interesting historic places to see in the Paria River Country is the Old Oil Well in the northern part of the Rush Beds. The Rush Beds is the higher country between Cottonwood Wash & Hackberry Canyon. At the well site, you'll find 4 large cement footings, one for each corner of the derrick, plus a metal pipe in the middle. Nearby is a pile of half-melted bricks which once lined the steam boiler, and several piles of hugh timbers which were part of the derrick. Also nearby is the rotting remains of a large wooden wheel, again part of the derrick complex, and some scattered junk. About 60m uphill to the west from the drill hole, is a large pile of wood cut into lengths just right for the boiler. About 200m north of the drill hole, are 3 smaller piles of wood (2 are almost covered by sand), in addition to what may have been a cellar (?).

In the **official records** about this well, a big mistake has evidently been made. According to the American Petroleum Institute (API), there were 2 drill holes very near each other in this area and both were done by the Midwest Oil Company. The first was called the **Midwest Butler Valley Well** and was in the SW1/4, SE1/4 of Section 14 (just to the north of the ruins you see today). According to their records, drilling began January 1, 1930 and ended on July 21, 1930. They reached 4436 ft. or 1352 meters. It's API number is 4302505000.

The second well was called the **Midwest Government #1**. It was located in the SW1/4, NE1/4 of Section 23. Both section were in T39S, R1W. For this so-called second well, drilling began on October 27, 1930 and ended December 15, 1930. It was reported to have reached 4436 ft or 1352 meters, same as the other one, but something isn't right! It's API number is 4302510726. This second well is the site with all the relics you actually see today.

After reading these records, the author returned to the site and walked through the area with map & compass in hand. However, there is no second oil well, the one supposedly in Section 14! Somehow, someway, someone made a mistake in recording the event. The well in Section 23 is the one you see today.

In 2003, there were several old-timers in the Bryce Valley area who knew something about this old oil well. One man was Desmond L. Twitchell of Cannonville. He was 8 years old when his father, Loren E. Twitchell was hired to haul some or most of the supplies & equipment to the well. Here's a few things Desmond remembered:

I rode out there on an old 1926 cat, a trawler cat. I rode on the seat with the driver. That was Midwest Oil Company's cat. They pushed the road out there and my Dad followed the cat. They had to hook the cat onto the truck to pull 'um for about 1/2 a mile before they got out to near the old well.

Dad had a 1927 White truck, and a 1929 White. He bought that 1929 White because he couldn't pull those hills with that '27. That was the fall of 1929. It took us 2 days to go from Cannonville to Marysvale, which was the end of the railway line, then out to the well, and back to Cannonville.

Once, they buried one truck out there in the creek, in the mud. We went down and tried to pull out #4--we called it #4, it was an old Jeffrey truck. It got in the flood and we tried to pull it out, but we couldn't with the other truck we had. Anyway, they finally got it out and stripped it down and used it for a trailer to haul supplies. The old chassis is still out there in Lower Slickrock north of the main road.

The 1929 White truck had duel wheels, and 2 transmissions, so it could pull up the hills. When we'd get to the bottom of some hill, we'd hook a cable from the duel-wheeled truck onto the other one and pull both of 'um over. They worked on the road in 1929, drilled in 1930, and hauled stuff out in 1931.

The bunkhouse was uphill from where that pile of wood is. They had a couple of guys, all they done was cut wood. The bunkhouse had 2 rooms; it housed their main crew that was there, the driller and a couple of helpers. They had a separate building for their tools and oil that they used on the rig. That big round wheel was on the top to the rig. It was used to hoist the material up. It was pretty well worn out so Dad didn't haul it out.

Another man who knew something about the operation was Charley Francisco of Tropic (his wife has a little bed & breakfast place on the southeast side of town). Charley's father worked on the well from start to finish. Here are some things Charley remembered about the place:

My Dad's name was Charles Edward Francisco. He came to this country from Kansas as a oil driller. He came down along the Colorado River to Wagon Box Mesa [by Capitol Reef N.P.]. They drilled a well over there on Wagon Box Mesa. My Dad fired a boiler for years. He was a fireman, then a driller. They drilled that one before my time. I was born in 1925. Then my Dad came here for I don't know how many years, but I can remember when they were drillin' out there on the Rush Beds. Dad lived here a while then met my mother and married her. He lived here for a few years before all this happened.

To begin, they built that road out there all the way by hand. A fellow out here in Cannonville by the name of Loren Twitchell had a big old White truck. He had a grocery store and he freighted for everybody in this part of the country at that time. And he went and bought another truck to haul all the equipment for that well in. I remember they said he got out here in Round Valley Neck [just north of Round Valley Seep] and buried one of those trucks in mud. And they had a hell of a time! I guess they had every man in this country trying to help lift that stuff off that truck so they could get it out of the mud. They brought that drillin' equipment down from the railroad in Marysvale, then through Panguitch-- about the same route as we have today.

Now they made that road from The Shepherd [Shepherd Point--the gap you drive through on the way to Kodachrome Basin] all the way out there. They worked everybody they could get when they was building that road. Every man that was available and had a team or had anything they could work with--they hired. They had fresnos & scrappers, and 2 or 3 guys was a usin' dynamite.

And everybody wanted to work. There was so such thing as a little cash down in this country! And them [oil company] guys paid good money according to what people was a makin' in this country, or could even think about makin'! I know them guys made more money out there in 5 months than they made in a year & a half herding sheep or cows or what ever they was doin'.

[After the road was built and all the equipment was hauled in], they had men a choppin' wood and a haulin' wood and cutting it in lengths. That was for the boiler because all the power they had for drillin' was steam. Everything was steam powered [they had a small gasoline engine which ran a generator for electric lights]. They used bricks in the fireplaces [boilers]. When those bricks would burn through, then you'd burn your metal out, so you had to replace the bricks to line the boiler.

The derrick was made of wood, and they had some steel for bracing, but it was made of great big heavy timbers. Them homes was back from the well a ways. Two or 3 of the crew lived there, where the other pile of wood is. Dad pumped water for a year up to the oil well site; he run that pump station at Pump Spring down in Cottonwood Wash.

Wallace Ott of Tropic had a little more information about the well and the pump in Pump Canyon, or at least in Cottonwood Wash: I went down there to get a job on that road when I was 18 years old. That was in 1929. They had quite a big camp, I ate with them; they had a cook and a kitchen outfit; it was quite a crew of guys. I'd say they had as many as 10 men altogether. I took a touring car out there a number of times--they had a pretty good road then. They had a gas engine pump in the canyon and you could hear it for miles around.

Now back to Charley Francisco's story: I was 7 or 8 years old when we went back out there after the drillin' had shut down. My Dad and a guy named Jack Seaton went out there to tear down all those buildings and stack up that lumber. We cleaned out all the nails--I pulled nails for days! Then they sold a lot of the lumber to Long John Mangum and Jim Ed Smith. I think they about got it for nothing. They hauled that stuff over and down over them ledges along the Old Wagon Road down into Cottonwood Wash and back up to Piaria [Old Pahreah], and took some down to Five Mile. Jim Ed Smith had some beautiful sheds and stables and corrals at Piaria. He built stables enough for 20 head of horses. [Long John Mangum took his share of lumber down to Five Mile and built a house. It's still standing today at the Five Mile Ranch which is just north of the Hattie Green Mine]

[After all the workers left], Carl Syrett hauled some of that wood up here to Ruby's Inn for several years. He had a great big truck and he hauled wood out of there--from those stacks at the old oil well. Ooh, there was ricks of wood! That was Ruby Syrett's boy Carl. Fred Syrett [Carl's son] told me they'd go out there and have a picnic and load a big load of wood on his truck and haul it home. It was still good wood, and it was all cut! They had a big fireplace at Ruby's Inn, and it was cut to the right length. At that time it was still a decent road, so it was easier doin' that than goin' out and choppin' it.

Wallace Ott again: When the oil well quit, the town of Tropic bought that pipe [which ran from Pump Canyon up to the well] and used it up here to pipe their water. I think it was a 4" metal pipe. A crew went down and brought it up. When I was mayor here in Tropic, they was using the same pipe.

This is one of the original White trucks Loren Twitchell used to haul drilling equipment from the end of the railway at Marysvale, to Bryce Valley and on to the oil well site in the Upper Rush Beds. Later Ruby Syret, the man who built Ruby's Inn, bought it to haul lumber. To see it, drive east from Ruby's Inn about 200m to the Bryce View Lodge. It and another old 1920's truck are sitting in front of the lodge's office.

Charley Francisco says this is the oil well in the Upper Rush Beds, but the background isn't quite the same--or perhaps the negative for this foto was flip-flopped (?). Or, could this be the well on Wagon Box Mesa? (Charley Francisco foto)

Charles Edward Francisco is one of the 2 drillers in the middle. This is supposed to be the drilling rig in the Upper Rush Beds, but the background doesn't seem to match. It looks like these men are waring some kind of masks, perhaps to protect themselves against dust (?). (Charley Francisco foto)

This appears to be the 1927 or 1929 White truck used by Loren Twitchell to haul this boiler, among other things, to the oil well in the Upper Rush Beds. It also appears to be the same one you can see at Ruby's Inn. See other picture on page 139. (Charley Francisco foto)

This is supposed to be the drilling rig in the Upper Rush Beds. (Charley Francisco foto)

These huge timbers were part of the drilling rig in the Upper Rush Beds. This picture was taken in the fall of 2003, 73 years after the rig was dismantled. About 200m off in the background is where the workers houses were sitting.

This is what remains of the biggest pile of wood at the Old Oil Well site in the Upper Rush Beds. In the upper left of this picture, you can see 2 of the cement corner supports for the drilling rig.

Lower Rush Beds Trails & Hikes: Castle Rock, Goulding Trail, Yellow Rock, Hidden Cache & The Cockscomb

Location & Access One of the most striking land forms of southern Utah is the feature known as **The Cockscomb.** The Cockscomb is a fold in the earth's crust, more properly called a monocline, which has created a rather sharp erosional ridge that runs north-south. It begins just south of Canaan Peak in the north, and continues south past Highway 89. The part shown on this map stands the highest, has the sharpest ridges, and is the most fotogenic.

This same feature continues south past Coyote Buttes and into Arizona. From Highway 89, you can follow it south along the east side of House Rock Valley Road. In the area of Highway 89A, in the House Rock Valley, you see it continuing south to Saddle Mountain and into the Grand Canyon. There it goes by the name of the East Kaibab Monocline.

Access to this area is via the **Cottonwood Wash Road.** It runs right down the middle of The Cockscomb Valley which is Cottonwood Wash; this begins just south of Grosvenor Arch and ends at the Paria River. While the highest and most rugged part of The Cockscomb is east of this road, there is also a less-dramatic ridgeline on the west side of The Cockscomb formed mostly by the Navajo Sandstone. The most prominent feature on the west side of The Cockscomb is **Castle Rock,** at 1850m elevation. It stands up like a sore thumb above all its neighbors. Another prominent feature is **Yellow Rock**. It's located just south of the mouth of Hackberry Canyon. Between Yellow Rock and **The Box** of the Paria, is a small valley right on top of the western ridge. Most of the rocks there are also yellow, but some peaks are capped with red sandstone. The author is calling this place **Yellow Rock Valley,** for lack of a better name.

All these places between Cottonwood Wash and Hackberry Canyon are on top of a plateau called the **Rush Beds.** In this case the Lower Rush Beds. The north or upper parts of the Rush Beds is discussed along with the previous map.

Besides all this scenic stuff, there are other interesting places to visit. Up on the lower or southern end of the Rush Beds is the **Ken Goulding Trail,** which was likely originally built by Sampson Chynoweth or his boys; Will, Sam, Arthur or Harvey (the family arrived in Pahreah in the fall of 1892). This good cattle trail connects the lower end of Cottonwood Wash with the middle parts of Hackberry Canyon. It also runs close to an alcove with Anasazi (or Fremont?) ruins--locally these are referred to as **Moki houses**. Just south of this trail is a short section of another trail or route sometimes called the **Chynoweth Trail,** which begins near what used to be the **Chynoweth Cabin** (before it burned down) **& Corral.**

There's one last interesting place to visit. The author is calling it the **Hidden Cache.** It's on top of the western side of The Cockscomb not far from where Cottonwood Wash and The Box of the Paria River meet. The story of this place is told below. Nearby and also inside The Box, is the beginning of **The Box Trail.**

To get to the Hidden Cache & The Box Trail, leave Highway 89 between mile post 17 & 18, and drive northwest on the Cottonwood Wash Road for 19.2 kms (11.9 miles). At that point (44 kms/27.4 miles from the Kodachrome Basin Turnoff--KBT), the road begins to run north along an eastern branch of the Cottonwood Wash. This will be just below where The Box and Cottonwood Wash meet which is just to the west. At that place, leave the main road and drive west along a side-road about 150m to where the river floods on occasions, and stop. By parking, and perhaps camping there, you'll have access to the Hidden Cache and The Box Trail.

If you continue north in Cottonwood Wash, you'll eventually pass 2 cattle guards. Just beyond, or north of the 2nd, and at Km 23.2/Mile 14.4, you'll come to the **Brigham Plains Road** on the right or east side (39.9 kms/24.8 miles from the KBT). This road zig zags eastward up the main Cockscomb Ridge to Brigham Plains on the other side. Walk or drive this steep road to access the top of The Cockscomb for great views & fotos. Or, you can park in the vicinity of this road junction and have access to the **Yellow Rock Trail.**

If getting into the lower end of **Hackberry** is your goal, then park just east of the mouth about 200m north of the Brigham Plains Road (23.5 kms/14.6 miles from Highway 89; or 39.6 kms/24.6 miles from the KBT). To see the **Chynoweth Cabin site, corral,** and the beginning of the **Chynoweth Trail,** turn west from the Cottonwood Wash Road 24.3 kms (15.1 miles) from Highway 89; or 38.8 kms (24.1 miles) from the KBT. To get to the **Ken Goulding Trail,** turn west off the main road 25.3 kms (15.7 miles) from Highway 89; or 37.8 kms (23.5 miles) from the KBT. You can park and camp at all of these trailhead parking places. Or if going to **Castle Rock,** continue north on this main road to a point 27.2 kms (16.9 miles) from Highway 89; or 35.9 kms (22.3 miles) from the KBT. Park right on the road.

Trail/Route From where you park just east of **Castle Rock**, head west across Cottonwood Wash, and walk into the prominent little canyon coming down from the south side of Castle. Just inside the bottom of the drainage, veer left and scramble up a steep slope to the southwest. Higher up, contour north across the upper face of the slope, go around a little corner or pass of sorts, then scramble down to the dry creek bed below. There is no trail--just route-finding. Continue west up this drainage until you can walk out on the right side onto the southeast buttress of Castle Rock. Once on this smooth, rounded buttress, head northwest up toward the summit area. This will involve a little route-finding. To get fotos of the back side of Castle, use the drainage on the south and west sides. There you'll find some pretty good cattle trails.

From where you park near the beginning of the **Ken Goulding Trail**, walk west 50m along a fence to the bottom of Cottonwood Wash and immediately turn northwest into a dry wash coming out of a minor canyon. Head that way for 200m; you may see a trail on the left. There at the very bottom of the steep part will be trail straight ahead and against the vertical wall on the right. This part has been constructed, but once on top and heading north, you'll just follow a trail marked with cairns. Soon you'll turn west a ways, then north again, then slowly it veers northwest and west again; in this area it's sandy, but the trail is still easy to follow. Just before you reach the high point marked 5770 on the *Calico Peak 7 1/2' quad*, the trail will be running north again along the ridge top. From that mark, it's 200m to a narrow little gap or pass.

From there, continue north on a fading trail for 400m, then if you want to see a **Moki house** or Anasazi ruins, turn down to the left or west & southwest and follow a shallow drainage. After about another 400m, you'll be in big Navajo Sandstone bluffs or domes, and a dropoff of a couple of meters. The author tied a short rope to a bush and got down, then back up OK, but with 2 or more people, you should be able to help each other down & back up without a rope, if you choose.

Map 26, Lower Rush Beds Trails & Hikes: Castle Rock, Goulding Trail, Yellow Rock, Hidden Cache & The Cockscomb

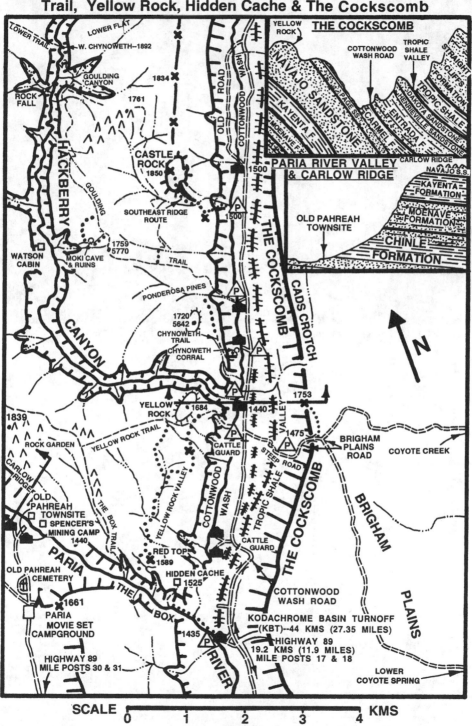

THE COCKSCOMB

YELLOW ROCK

COTTONWOOD WASH ROAD

TROPIC SHALE VALLEY

STRAIGHT CLIFFS FORMATION

NAVAJO SANDSTONE

KAYENTA F.

MOENAVE F.

PAGE SS.

CARMEL F.

ENTRADA F.

DAKOTA SANDSTONE

HENRIEVILLE SANDSTONE

TROPIC SHALE

CARLOW RIDGE

PARIA RIVER VALLEY & CARLOW RIDGE

NAVAJO S.S.

KAYENTA FORMATION

MOENAVE FORMATION

OLD PAHREAH TOWNSITE

CHINLE FORMATION

LOWER TRAIL

LOWER FLAT

W. CHYNOWETH—1892

1834

GOULDING CANYON

1761

ROCK FALL

HACKBERRY

CASTLE ROCK 1850

OLD ROAD

COTTONWOOD WASH

1500

GOULDING

SOUTHEAST RIDGE ROUTE

P

1500

WATSON CABIN

1759 5770

MOKI CAVE & RUINS

TRAIL

THE COCKSCOMB

CANYON

PONDEROSA PINES

P

CADS CROTCH

N

1720 5642

CHYNOWETH TRAIL

CHYNOWETH CORRAL

P

YELLOW ROCK

1684

1440

1753

1839

ROCK GARDEN

YELLOW ROCK TRAIL

P

CATTLE GUARD

1475

STEEP ROAD

BRIGHAM PLAINS ROAD

COYOTE CREEK

CARLOW RIDGE

OLD PAHREAH TOWNSITE

SPENCER'S MINING CAMP 1440

THE BOX TRAIL

YELLOW ROCK VALLEY

COTTONWOOD WASH

TROPIC SHALE VALLEY

THE COCKSCOMB

BRIGHAM

OLD PAHREAH CEMETERY

PARIA

RED TOP 1589

HIDDEN CACHE 1525

CATTLE GUARD

PLAINS

1661

THE BOX

1435

RIVER

COTTONWOOD WASH ROAD

PARIA MOVIE SET CAMPGROUND

P

KODACHROME BASIN TURNOFF (KBT)--44 KMS (27.35 MILES)

HIGHWAY 89 19.2 KMS (11.9 MILES) MILE POSTS 17 & 18

HIGHWAY 89 MILE POSTS 30 & 31

LOWER COYOTE SPRING

SCALE

0   1   2   3   4   KMS

From the top of The Cockscomb near the Brigham Plains Road, is one of the best views of the Cottonwood Wash and Castle Rock. In the far background can be seen Table Cliff Plateau.

Castle Rock from the west, and from the ridge where the Ken Goulding Trail runs. To the right or south a ways, is where you leave this trail to reach the ruins known to locals as Moki houses. Notice the toadstool or mushroom-like rocks in the foreground.

Castle Rock from the south and from the Ken Goulding Trail. The route to the summit begins in the middle right-hand side of the picture and angles up to the left along the Southeast Buttress.

From that little dropoff, walk northwest along a small canyon for 75m-100m and look to the right. There should be an alcove with one Moki house underneath. There are also a number of fairly recent signatures of cowboys *(Ken Goulding, June 1, 1929)* and other residences of Bryce Valley. This site is about 850m due east of Frank Watson's Cabin down in Hackberry Canyon. There is likely a route from the cabin to these ruins, but the author hasn't tried it yet. For sure, there are some big cliffs to route-find through. Also, from this site, you can get back to the Goulding Trail by walking north along the western face of some ledges for 500m, then veer east or northeast. This is the route taken by any-one riding horseback.

Now the Goulding Trail again. For the first little ways north of the Moki house area, it'll be a little hard to follow this trail in the sand, but it heads due north with a few turns in & out of gullies. As you near the **Rockfall**, the trail begins to veer a little to the northeast, then east as it drops down into what might be called **Goulding Canyon**. It's easy to follow in this region. At the bottom of the drainage, the trail immediately cuts back to the northwest on the north side. You'll see parts of a constructed trail there, then it runs north along a bench, and finally zig zags down the eastern wall of Hackberry Canyon on various benches. Several places have been rocked-up for cows. At the bottom, the trail veers north on the last or lowest bench and hits the creek almost exactly halfway between the **Rockfall & the Lower Trail** as shown (400m either way).

Going back up into Goulding Canyon for a moment. Right where the trail crosses the dry wash, if you walk upcanyon a little, you should see another constructed cow trail heading north and a little east-ward. Ken Goulding Sr. and his son Ken Jr., cobbled-up a trail there somewhere (the author wasn't aware of it on his last hike) which runs up through some ledges and out on top of what they call the **Lower Flat.** This continues to be a pasture for Ken Jr.'s cows during the winter months.

There's a good campsite right across the wash east of the **Chynoweth corral & old cabin site.** Just west of the corral is the foundation of a cabin. Here's what Ralph Chynoweth of Henrieville remembered about the first Cottonwood Wash Road, their family cabin & corral: *We used to camp there before we built that little house. And one time we had some wild cattle out there and we had this great big old steer and my dad told me I could have it if I'd go get 'im. We went down there and camped in a trailer that night--this would have been late November, 1957. That cabin wasn't there then, and that road goin' down Cottonwood wasn't very good either. In most of the places where it is now not where it was then. For most of the way above that old cabin, the road used to be on the west side of the wash, but over the years, they just kept improving it a little at a time. It was just a Jeep trail the first time they built it. We only had that trailer there about a year when we built that cabin. We had a ton and a half truck with a load of lumber on it--and I don't know how we ever got down there! It was my brothers Jack, Gene, Wade and myself who built the cabin. As near as I can remember, we built it in about 1958. We built the corral at the same time.*

I'd say that cabin burned down in the early 1980's. We don't know who burned it down, but it may have been the BLM, because they burned some others at the same time. Ours was burned down quite a while before those line cabins in the Escalante country were burned.

Regarding the building of the Cottonwood Wash Road, the best source is from the unpublished family history of Sam Pollock. His story went something like this. The road was built in 1957 by a coop-erative effort organized by then 72-year-old Sam Pollock of Tropic, who wasn't paid a dime for his efforts. It included people from Bryce Valley, Escalante and Antimony. That group of people wanted

This is the best preserved part of some Anasazi or Fremont Indian ruins under an alcove in the Lower Rush Beds not far east of the Frank Watson Cabin in Hackberry Canyon.

Looking SSW at the southern end of Cottonwood Wash as seen from the top of The Cockscomb just north of where the Brigham Plains Road levels out. That road is seen in the middle left part of this foto.

a shortcut to the Lake Powell area to increase tourism in their own little area.

For the job, Pollock leased a bulldozer from the Soil Conservation Service and it was operated by Harvey Liston; a road grader was borrowed from Garfield Country, and it was driven by Loral Barton; Byron Davis donated a compressor and helped run it (it was used for only 9 days, and they blasted in only 2 places). Doyle Clark also helped on the operation. It took 100 days for planning, engineering and construction, but only 70 days to complete once they got rolling. The project was started on June 28, and completed in early October of 1957. At that time, they had a dedication ceremony at Rush Bed Springs.

The state of Utah had surveyed 2 routes for a road to Page and the Glen Canyon Dam. They chose the route east from Kanab because it was cheaper. The other more direct route through Cannonville and Cottonwood Wash would have cost $9.5 million. The road Sam Pollock built cost $5500. They got the money to build it from Garfield County, and from donations & sales of various kinds. Today it's a maintained county road.

About 150m south of the cabin's foundation is the beginning of a very faint trail running west up to the top of the first little ridge. From the ridgetop, it heads north up on the Lower Rush Beds where it disappears. After about a km of no trail at all, one route heads west again. From there Ralph says: *That trail goes up a little canyon with lots of slickrock and some big ponderosa pines, then it heads north and connects with the Goulding Trail.* This trail/route isn't that good, so it's recommended you use the Goulding Trail to get upon the Rush Beds.

The Cockscomb If you've parked at the base of the steep part of the road going up toward Brigham Plains, then you have only to walk about 2 kms to the pass overlooking The Cockscomb Valley. Or you can drive up, but it's 1st gear all the way on a clay surface, so don't try it when it's wet! From the pass, walk north along the eastern base of the ridge for about 500m, then climb straight up to the west. You'll soon reach the highest part of the ridge In this immediate area marked 1753m. This is the easiest part of The Cockscomb to get to and fotograph from. This is due east of Yellow Rock.

To reach the area between Hackberry and The Box, which is **Yellow Rock Valley**, leave your car parked near the junction with the Brigham Plains Road, and walk west across Cottonwood Wash. Enter the first little drainage 450m south of the mouth of Hackberry. Once inside this tiny canyon, veer northwest and climb straight up an old horse trail. This is the beginning of the **Yellow Rock Trail**. Once on top, the trail is marked with stone cairns; so just head west toward the big dome which is **Yellow Rock**. It's made of the Navajo Sandstone, and is bright yellow with swirls of red, white & purple on the south side which resembles a *marble cake*. This is a marvelous place for color fotos. From the top of Yellow Rock, you'll have some great views looking north. There's another yellowish dome-like rock just to the north of lower Hackberry at 1720m altitude, and of course Castle Rock is off in the distance. Looking south, you'll see lots of mostly yellow dome rocks, plus the Red Top in the distance.

There are no trails down through **Yellow Rock Valley**, so pick the route that suits you best. Two possible routes are shown on the map. At the southern end just above The Box, is a another colorful sight. It's what this writer calls **Red Top**. The top is as red as the brightest autumn leaves, the lower parts are yellow--all varicolored Navajo Sandstone. Red Top soars above everything else in the immediate area. You can also get into the Yellow Rock Valley from the Paria River and The Box Trail, as shown on the map.

Now for the trail to the **Hidden Cache**. From the car-park near the confluence of the Paria & Cottonwood Wash, walk northwest along the Paria to the beginning of The Box. This is about 800m from the car-park. About 300m into The Box, and on your right or north, is a minor drainage. Head up and into this mini canyon on the left side. You should see some cairns. After a very short distance you'll see a trail heading straight up the drainage bottom. About 500m from the river, and just after you begin to level out, you'll see the first gray metal shelter, and just behind it 15m away, the remains of a second metal box and cave. The story is told below.

Less than one km from the beginning of the Hidden Cache Trail, you'll come to the beginning of **The Box Trail** (halfway between the two is a panel of cowboyglyphs & an old fence on the right or north side). It begins just above the middle of The Box and heads up an inclined ramp in a NNW direction. Once on top of the southernmost Rush Beds, this good trail heads north to a point due west of Yellow Rock. From there, one branch of this trail heads northwest, then north and follows Carlow Ridge all the way north to upper Hogeye Canyon. Read more about this trail under **Map 12**. But you can also turn east and walk along the **Yellow Rock Trail** back to Cottonwood Wash and the main road.

Elevations For The Cockscomb Hike, from 1475m altitude up to 1753m, or higher further north. Climbing Castle Rock, from just over 1500m where you park, up to 1850m on top. For Yellow Rock, you'll walk from 1440m up to 1684m, and for the Hidden Cache, it's from about 1435 m to 1525m.

Hike Length/Time Needed From the Cottonwood Wash Road to the pass in The Cockscomb, is less than 2 kms. From the pass to the high point is another 700m. The round-trip hike can be done easily in a 2-3 hours--much less if you drive up to the pass. For Castle Rock, it should take up to about 2 hours to climb, 3 or 4 hours round-trip--maybe more. To explore the country between Yellow Rock and Red Top, you'll need no less than half a day. If you're a color fotographer, you'll want to be there in the middle part of the day. It's only about 1 1/2 km from the car-park to the Hidden Cache, and can be done in 20-25 minutes, one-way, or a couple of hours round-trip.

Water Take your own, and always have extra water in your car. There's usually water in both Cottonwood Wash and the Paria which can be used for washing.

Maps USGS or BLM map Smoky Mountain (1:100,000) for driving & orientation; Calico Peak & Fivemile Valley (1:24,000--7 1/2' quads) for hiking.

Main Attractions An interesting look at an unusual geologic feature fully exposed. This is The Cockscomb. Geology students shouldn't miss this one, as these are some of the most interesting hikes in this book. The view from the top of The Cockscomb, Yellow Rock or Castle Rock is spectacular. It's also one of the most fotogenic places covered by this book. Also, a short hike to what has become a local legend at the Hidden Cache.

Ideal Time to Hike Spring or fall, but it can be climbed anytime the Cottonwood Wash Road is dry.

Boots/Shoes Any boots or shoes, but a rugged pair for climbing The Cockscomb Ridge. For the southeast buttress route up Castle Rock, and Yellow Rock Valley, use running-type shoes because of the slickrock. You'll have to wade the Paria several times on the way to the Hidden Cache, so go prepared for wading.

Author's Experience The author parked at the bottom of the ridge, then walked up the road to The Cockscomb. Round-trip was about 1 1/2 hours. He climbed Castle Rock 3 times, with a lot of explor-

Above From the top of The Cockscomb looking west at Yellow Rock, the mouth of Hackberry Canyon, and Mollies Nipple in the distance to the left. In the lower part of this picture is Cottonwood Wash.

Right The south side of Yellow Rock. Notice the swirling of red, white and purple in the yellow Navajo Sandstone. This place is for color fotography only!

ing along the way. He did some exploring around the west side on the second hike, and that took about 3 hours round-trip. One of his hikes was up to Yellow Rock, south through the Yellow Rock Valley to Red Top, and back the same way to his car; that took about 3 1/3 hours. On 2 trips to the Hidden Cache via The Box route, it took about one hour each, round-trip. Another time he hiked to the Hidden Cache, up The Box Trail to an overlook of Old Pahreah, down the Yellow Rock Trail and back to his car in about 5 1/2 hours.

The Story of the Hidden Cache

The last hike to be added to the 1st Edition of this book happened quite by accident. While interviewing one of the old timers in Tropic, the story about a possibly German spy and a cache of food and supplies was told. Later the author tracked down the people who originally found the cache, and got the full story.

It began on February 8, 1953. Harvey Chynoweth of Cannonville, his 4 sons, Jack, Gene, Wade & Ralph, and Harvey's oldest brother Will Chynoweth, were running cows in the lower Cottonwood Wash and out to the east of The Cockscomb on the flats called Brigham Plains. They had worked all day, and arrived back at camp late. Camp was on the lower Cottonwood Wash, not far above where it flows into the Paria River, at the bottom end of The Box.

Since the bottom of the valley had been grazed-out by cows and there wasn't much feed for the horses, it was common practice for cattlemen working in the area to run their riding stock up on top of the Carlow Ridge or Rush Beds to the west where they could pasture at night. Up there they couldn't go far because of rough terrain and there was plenty of grass. Since Ralph was the youngest of the boys, he was chosen to take the horses up above the cliffs.

It was after dark, but there was a full moon and the sky was clear. Ralph recalls having trouble with one little sorrel pony which was trying to run away or something. At any rate, when the horses were left in the upper pasture, they were always hobbled so they could be found and caught easy the next morning. When Ralph finally got a hold of the little sorrel, he began putting the hobbles on. But then something caught his eye. The moonlight was so bright, it reflected off something made of metal. He went over to investigate and found a couple of small metal sheds or boxes. He could see inside one of them and saw that somebody had lived there. He returned to camp a little spooked and told the story. No one believed him. They thought he was dreaming or just telling stories.

The next morning they all went back up to get the horses and saw in full light what was there. It was some kind of camp but hadn't been lived in for a long time. There were 2 galvanized metal boxes or shelters, measuring only about 1 1/4m x 2m x 2 1/2m each, and a cave which had the entrance

The Hidden Cache as of September, 2003. Behind is the cave with a cemented-up front wall. Fifty years after its discovery, it appears to be almost new. Nearer the camera is what's left of one of the 2 metal storage boxes that were used to store supplies. It's rusting away now, and there's not much left.

Part of the Hidden Cache in the lower end of the Rush Beds. About 20m southwest of the Cave is this 2nd metal box. This is the one which had a stove, sleeping cot, blankets & clothes, and a small .22 caliber rifle.

cemented-up with a little rock wall.

Inside one of the boxes was a bed with blankets on it, all tucked in neatly; a small metal wood burning stove which was new and apparently hadn't been used; and an old .22 rifle which hung above the door. The .22 was a hex-barreled single shot, which broke in the middle to load, like some single-shot shotguns. There were also several new denim shirts, underwear, socks, pajamas, 2 pair of boots, toothguns, toothpaste, and neatly folded napkins. The clothing items were neatly put together and folded, like what you'd find in the military. Besides these things, was some kind of a military uniform. One man swears it was from W.W.I.

In the other metal shelter near the cave, and all very neatly packed away, was a food cache of sizable proportions. The food cache included jars or buckets of peanut butter, canned & powered milk, chocolate, sugar, rice, flour, raisins, canned fish, sardines, corned beef, and other canned goods. Most of the cans had rusted badly, from the inside out, and had leaked, spoiling the contents. Indications were that it had been there for some time. One witness said they found one can of corned beef dated 1942.

Just behind the 2 metal shelters, was a small cave. The front of this cave, measuring about 1m x 2m, had been sealed up with a rock & mortar wall. The job was so well done, that in 2003 when the author last saw it, it appeared as if it could have been made only a month or so before. The entrance passage was a small metal-framed window, like the kind you see in some homes or buildings of W.W.II vintage. The inside of the cave had been dug out some, and it measured about 1 1/2m x 2m at the front end, and it tapered back to the rear about 4m. Not much headroom, but cozy.

Inside the cave, the Chynoweths found an electric hot plate and several 5-gallon (19 liter) glass storage jars full of water. The fact that they hadn't frozen and broken, indicates how well insulated the cave was in winter. There were also a bunch batteries of various kinds.

Right in the corner next to the entrance, are 3 wires which were built into the rock & mortar wall. These wires led outside to a windmill contraption and a generator mounted on a rock behind the cave. The single blade propeller was 4m-5m long, and mounted horizontally (instead of vertically as is usually the case with most windmills). The cave had built-in wiring so electricity from by the windmill generator outside, could be used for lights or cooking inside.

According to the newspaper report in the March 19, 1953, *Garfield County News* in Panguitch (a week later in the Kanab paper), all identifiable marks on the generator and other equipment found, had been scratched off. Even the numbers on a thermometer had been removed! Jack Chynoweth also stated that all labels from canned goods and from all clothes were also removed.

About 16 years after this story was told to the author, and in 2003, he went back to Ralph Chynoweth in Henrieville and asked more questions about the place, and he had this to say about what happened after they found the cache: *We went down there on horseback, down through Cottonwood, but my Dad, Harvey Chynoweth couldn't ride a horse, his hips was gone. So he came on down there in the Jeep so he could be with us. There wasn't no road in there then, not down Cottonwood Wash. He came right down through the Piree Crik, past Old Pahreah and through the Paria Box and up to our camp. If there would have been a road, we would have fed the horses hay; that's the reason we took the horses up on top to feed.*

We got all that stuff out of there and down to camp--we hauled it off with a pack horse. We carried everything that we thought was of any value at all, and carried it out of there, Dad carried some of it out in the Jeep, and we hauled some of it on pack horses. And we went down there several times to haul that stuff off. We had an agreement between the bunch of us that we'd never say nothin' to nobody. We were going to keep it a secret, because we wanted to go back and look around more. Maybe find something else (?).

Now, Dad and my Uncle Will and brothers, felt like them people had robbed a bank, or got into something like that, and they were going to come back there and have a place to stay. Well, we brought this stuff home and had it stored here for quite a long period of time before we told anybody about it. We kept that stuff in my Dad's shed down here. I didn't get to go after that first trip because I was just 16 and still going to school; but my brothers [Darrel Blackwell & George Thompson] and my Uncle and Dad, they all went down and they spent several days down there and searched that whole area. But it was some length of time after that before anybody else knew anything about it.

It was about a month and a half after they found the cache--Ralph thought it was longer--that they finally called the Sheriff of Kane County, Mason Meeks, and told him the story. Shortly thereafter, the Sheriff and Highway Patrolman Merrill Johnson, Merle (Peaches) Beard, and others, went to the Chynoweths place in Henrieville and took all the booty away.

At the time, Ralph told the Sheriff, that he had found the cache, including the .22 rifle, and that he wanted it back. That was the only thing he cared about. OK, no problem! But in the end nothing was ever returned to the Chynoweths--and this has been a burr under Ralph's saddle ever since.

Sheriff Meeks sent a report to the FBI. Later those investigating the case contacted Meeks and it was their speculation that whoever set up the place had likely been a spy of some kind from the W.W.II era (?).

But there were several different theories advanced as to who built the cache: (1) Who ever built it was a deserter from the army and on the run; (2) That he was a draft dodger; (3) He was just an old hermit, who happened to have been in WW I; (4) He had worked for Charles H. Spencer in the gold diggings at Pahreah, and had returned to hide out; (5) And because some of the clothing items had foreign labels (French), some thought he may have been a spy of some kind. The radio and generator equipment prompted this idea.

There was also endless speculation as to how this person may have gotten all the equipment and food there without being detected At the time the man was there, which must have been in the early to mid-1940's, there were no roads into the area except the one to Old Pahreah. When this story finally came to light, there was all kinds of talk about it, and then people started remembering events that had happened in the previous years, which may have had a connection with the cache.

The one which seems to hold the most credibility is the story told by Calvin C. Johnson of Kanab, the man who owns the Nipple Ranch. He remembered the time as being in 1944 or '45. On several occasions he and other cattlemen in the area of Old Pahreah, had seen a Willeys Jeep parked inside The Box, and at the bottom of the cliffs where the cache was later found. Calvin also remembers: *My brother and I were the first ones who knew of him when he was out there. My brother knew him better than I did. He would occasionally come to town in his old Jeep. Out there we would wave at 'im and he'd stop and say hello, but he had a heavy accent and we kinda figured he was a German spy* or something. He was just a real odd, quiet type of fellow. All he'd do is stop and we'd say hi--we did-n't ask him any question, and he just wouldn't answer--he wouldn't talk. We just talked about the time of day, or the weather, how he was doin'. He really had a real heavy German accent. I think he was maybe 30-35 years old at that time. He had army camouflage-type clothing with a hood. He had a heavy beard with a medium complexion. He was about 6 foot [183 cms] tall and weighed about 180 lbs [82 kgs]. Calvin also recalls the boys he rode with on the range used to call this fellow, *our little German spy!* Apparently this had more meaning in 1953 after the cache was discovered, than it did earlier.

Another event happened in 1963, which may have had a connection with this place. At that time, the Sheriff of Kane County was Leonard Johnson. His family lived in the polygamist community of Short Creek, now called Colorado City, Arizona, and/or Hildale, Utah. He had a pilot's license and once, while flying in the area between Hurricane Mesa and Short Creek, spotted something from the air. Later, they went to it on the ground, and found another small metal cabin full of food similar to the cache near Old Pahreah. Nothing else was found in that cache, but everyone familiar with the 2 sites, seemed to think there was a connection.

Left The Hidden Cache in February of 1953. L to R-- Will Chynoweth, Harvey Chynoweth (behind), George Thompson, Jack & Glen Chynoweth. This metal box is still in pretty good condition today.

Below Aerial view looking northward from the lower end of Cottonwood Wash. The Cockscomb is to the right; Yellow Rock and Castle Rock to the left. In the far distance is Table Cliff Plateau & Powell Point.

From in front of the cave at the Hidden Cache. **Left** Harvey Chynoweth inside the cave pulling stuff out. There's a generator, big battery, jugs with water, a crock pot, etc. **Right** L to R--Jack Chynoweth, his father Harvey, and brother Glen.

Above This is the metal box situated about 20m southwest of the cave. It's the one that housed the cot, stove, clothes & .22 rifle. It also had a shelf above the bed, and a small window at the back, as shown. Today, this box is still in good condition. **Above Right** This shows the inside of 2nd metal box nearest the cave. You can pick out lots of oatmeal, powdered milk, spices, and probably coal oil (kerosene) in the Sunoco can.

Right Having lunch down in Cottonwood Wash. These are the guys who carried all the supplies out of the Hidden Cache in late February,1953. L to R are Harvey Chynoweth, Glen Chynoweth, Darrel (Browny) Blackwell, Jack Chynoweth and Will Chynoweth. George Thompson took this picture. All old pictures on these 2 pages are from Darrel Blackwell, former CCC enrollee, now of Layton, Utah.

These are members of the Thompkins Expedition of 1939, who rode horses all the way from the Bryce Valley area into what locals call the *lower country*, which is Wahweap and the Lake Powell area. From left to right are: Earl Smith, Thompkins, the leader and organizer of the expedition, Tom W. Smith (Earl's brother, and son of the 2nd and last Mormon Bishop of Pahreah), Kay Clark and Byron Davies. This picture is in the possession of LaKay Clark Quilter of Henrieville. She is Kay's daughter and was born after the group went on this trip, but she can't remember the purpose of the expedition. A good guess is, Thompkins was after fotographs of the canyon country, as the camera that took this picture was a good one.

Walking southeast down the Box Trail toward the Paria River. Up the Paria about 2 kms is the townsite of Old Pahreah, and nearby, the ruins of Charles H. Spencer's gold mining operation.

Hattie Green Mine & the Fivemile Ranch

Location & Access Perhaps the easiest hike, and the one with the easiest access in this book, is the trail to the Hattie Green Mine. The Hattie Green is an old copper mine sitting right on top of The Cockscomb, sometimes known further south as the East Kaibab Monocline. This mine consists of 2 tunnels and 3 other pits, prospects or adits. The first claim on the site was filed in 1893. Get more information on this mine under **Mining History of the Paria River Drainage**, in the back of this book.

The location of this hike is just off Highway 89 about halfway between Kanab & Page. It's also about 11 kms (7 miles) northwest of the Paria Ranger Station & Visitor Center. One place to park would be right on Highway 89 about 600m south of mile post 28. Or stop at the parking place next to the highway & gate immediately east of mile post 28. That gate marks the beginning of the road to the mine. If you have a low clearance car, it might be best to park at one of these places and walk.

Or with a HCV or car, and if the gate near the highway is not locked, drive through and shut the gate behind you. Proceed across the dry sandy wash heading south, then east & south again, then veer southeast at the first road running eastward. Follow this fairly well-used track into the small north-south running canyon leading to the mine. After 1.4 kms (0.9 mile) park under a big piñon pine (this makes a good campsite as well). To reach this place you'll be **crossing a small piece of private land**, so if you see any **Private Land** or **No Trespassing signs**, park on the highway instead, and walk--hopefully that won't bother anyone (?).

Trail/Route From the 1st suggested parking place on the highway, walk due east, cross a fence, then a shallow drainage. In the middle of a meadow surrounded by sagebrush, look for the vehicle track running east & southeast. Or follow the road from the parking place & gate at mile post 28. Follow the track as described above around the southern end of a low minor sub-ridge of The Cockscomb. Once around this point, the road heads north in a short little valley within The Cockscomb.

From where the road ends at the piñon pine & campsite, walk north about 750m, then be looking to the left or west for a small man-made stone structure (a pile of rocks). About 25m north of that stone pile, look uphill to the east for some cairns marking the lower part of the trail. Further up, you'll see a real trail, which may have been an old wagon road. This 1st trail takes you to the top of The Cockscomb where some of the mining activity took place, including one tunnel, located 50m down the east side, and a pile of copper ore.

A 2nd trail runs up to the western tunnel. It begins about 25m north of where the 1st trail takes off. The bottom of this trail is marked by cairns, but a little further up, it turns into a real trail as well. At the entrance to the western tunnel is a pile of what looks like old stove pipes, but which must have been used to circulate air inside the tunnel (?).

To explore the tunnels, take a headlamp and a camera with a flash. About 25m inside the **eastern tunnel** is a wooden doorway with 1920 inscribed on it; just beyond that is a 4m-deep vertical shaft. Above it is a wooden hand-cranked hoist which brought ore from a 2nd lower tunnel up to the main passage. Both tunnels go back only about 10m beyond the hoist. Inside the **western tunnel** are wooden rails for small ore cars, then after maybe 40m, one tunnel goes left or north a short distance only, another heads straight ahead another 25m or so, and the one going right or south, goes on for a long ways, but to reach the end you'll have to crawl as it's caved in further along. This one has some old miner's signatures on the walls going back to the 1940's, maybe older (?). If you go inside, you will be visiting these tunnels at your own risk!

Elevations Highway trailheads, 1500m; end of HCV road, 1550m; the ridge-top ore heap, about 1675m.

Hike Length/Time Needed From the highway to the mine is only about 2 kms, and should take 2-3 hours, round-trip. If hiking from the piñon pine & campsite, only 1-2 hours will be needed, round-trip.

Water There's none around so take water in your car & pack.

Maps USGS or BLM map Smoky Mountain (1:100,000) for driving & orientation; and Fivemile Valley (1:24,000--7 1/2' quad) for hiking.

Main Attractions The Cockscomb, some interesting tunnels and one old heap of copper ore.

Ideal Time to Hike Spring or fall, but can be done 12 months of the year.

Boots/Shoes Any dry weather boots or shoes.

Author's Experience The author has been there 5 times.

The Fivemile Ranch

Added to the Hattie Green Mine hike is a little history on one of the nearby ranches. The Fivemile Ranch is one of the least-known outposts mentioned in this book. It's also one of the very last places to have been homesteaded in the entire region. The ranch is located in what is called Hattie Green Valley, about 8 kms (5 miles) due south of Old Pahreah--thus the name Fivemile. At least one old-timer from Tropic says the original name of the place was the Cottonwood Ranch, as it's located just below **Cottonwood Spring.** The ranch is located west of The Cockscomb and east of Highway 89.

To get there, turn off Highway 89, between mile posts 28 & 29, and park at or near the gate where the road enters the electric substation site. If you drive through the gate, always close it behind you. If driving a car, walk from the substation; with a 4WD, you can get closer to either spring.

The earliest written record the Kane County courthouse has on the Fivemile Ranch is dated May 11, 1913. That's when William J. Henderson filed a claim on the water rights to one or both of the springs involved with the Fivemile Ranch spread. To the north is the Fivemile Spring; to the south about one km is Cottonwood Spring--this is where the old ranch house is located.

The next recorded information about Fivemile Ranch was on June 17, 1937. This was when Herman Mangum got a patent deed on it from the government under the Homestead Act. To have gotten it under the Homestead Act, he would have had to live there, or made improvements to the place for 5 years, before getting title to the land, which apparently came in 1937. Herman was the son of Long John W. Mangum.

The John Mangum family lived in or around Old Pahreah after it was mostly abandoned in the early 1900's. Later on, Herm Pollock, Wallace Ott, and Kay Clark remembered the family when they lived in The Dugout, 2-3 kms north of Old Pahreah. That was in the late 1920's and early 1930's (?).

Here's a short history of the little house located just west or below Cottonwood Spring. In 1930, a crew of roughnecks from the Midwest Oil Company was drilling a test hole in the northern end of the Rush Beds, in the area south of Round Valley Draw, and south and a little west of Grosvenor (Butler Valley) Arch. That outfit pumped water to their camp & drill site from what has been called ever since,

Map 27, Hattie Green Mine & Fivemile Ranch

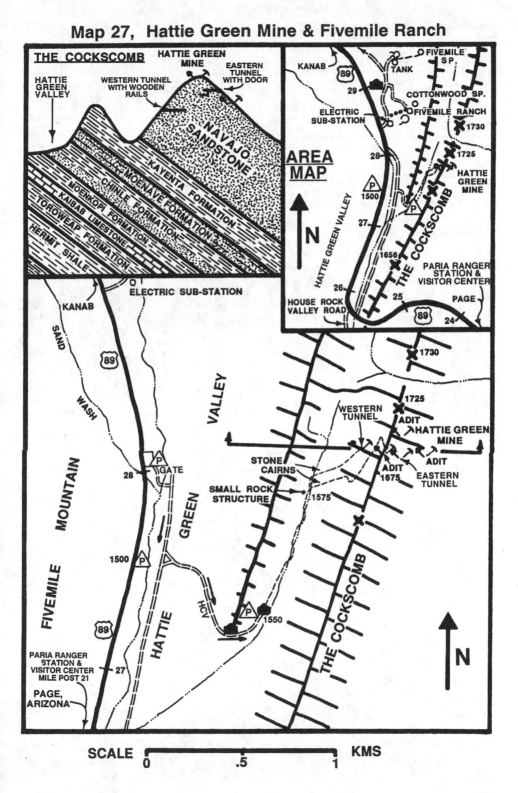

SCALE

KMS

0 .5 1

Pump House Spring & Canyon. That place is located in upper Cottonwood Wash where the water begins to flow. When their hole came up dry, they abandoned the site and sold parts, equipment and lumber to various local people. One of those people was Long John W. Mangum, who bought one or more wagon loads of used lumber.

Long John and his son Herman, along with Jim Ed Smith and his son Layton, hauled the lumber off the Rush Beds along the Old Wagon Road and down Cottonwood Wash to Cottonwood Spring in the Hattie Creek Valley, before a road was built. That was sometime between 1932 & 1935. Just southwest of the Cottonwood Spring, they built a small house out of the used lumber. It's a 2-room house, not too fancy, and without insulation. The back room wall used to be papered; not with wall-paper, but with pages from 1930's magazines. This homemade wallpaper job is gone today, but before, you could read up on events from the 1930's. The author once saw an advertisement for new Dodge cars selling for $640.

Throughout the years, the area around the Fivemile Homestead has been owned by 2 individuals. Apparently the Fivemile Spring was held by Jim Henderson through 1945, but before that, Delmar G. Robinson of Kanab, bought out the Fivemile Ranch and Cottonwood Spring from the Mangums in May, 1942. The Mangums then headed for Idaho.

Later on, in September 1959, it was deeded over to Delmar's son, Don R. Robinson. Finally in 1963, the Litchfield Company obtained a Quit Claim Deed on at least part of the property around the spring and ranch house. In the late 1980's, Jeff Johnson of Kanab leased the place and ran cows there. If you park at the substation, and walk to Fivemile or Cottonwood Spring, no one should care. Just don't go in hunting for some kind of souvenirs because both are on private land. There's not much to see around there anyway, just the shack and fences at the ranch site. If you see any **No Trespassing** signs, **Stop.**

Right The entrance to the western tunnel at the Hattie Green Mine. Notice the pipe on the left. This was surely used to pump fresh air into the mine.

Below This picture shows a hand-operated wooden hoist near the end of the eastern tunnel which was used to lift ore up a shaft from a second tunnel about 4m below. The foto on the opposite page shows a ladder which is immediately below this hoist.

Left Above The ore dump right on top of The Cockscomb Ridge at the Hattie Green Mine. Almost every rock has some turquoise-colored stains of copper. Just below this is the entrance to the eastern tunnel.

Left Below This is the 4m-deep shaft immediately below the hand-operated wooden hoist as shown on the opposite page. The lower tunnel runs for another 5m or so and ends.

Below This is the old wooden house at the Five Mile Ranch. This is located just Northwest of the Hattie Green Mine. This house was built in the early 1930's by John (Long John) W. Mangum and his son Herman. The lumber came from the Old Oil Well in the Upper Rush Beds just south and east of Booker Canyon and Round Valley Draw. The lumber was loaded onto wagons and brought down the Old Wagon Road off the Rush Beds into Cottonwood Wash before there was a road in the canyon. The Mangums left for Idaho in the mid or late 1930's.

The Rimrocks and Wahweap Toadstools

Location & Access Featured here are some short hikes to several groups of toadstool (TD) or mush-room-like rocks. Several groups of these are located immediately north of Highway 89, north & east of the Paria Ranger Station & Visitor Center, and in the area known as **The Rimrocks**. To get to this area, drive along Highway 89 about halfway between Page & Kanab. Between mile posts 19 & 21 are 4 minor valleys running north from the highway into The Rimrocks. Use this map to locate the various parking places. The most popular hike, and most-used starting point, is at the bottom **Valley 4**. This parking place is halfway between mile posts 19 & 20. Another starting point begins just north & across the highway from the Visitor Center called here **Valley 1**. For closeup views of the 2 best groups of TD in this area, drive along Highway 89 to between mile posts 17 & 18, then turn north onto the Cottonwood Wash Road. After 4.8 kms (3.0 miles), stop & park right on the road as shown.

Another area with perhaps the most-interesting group of TD is located just outside the boundaries of the Paria River along **Wahweap Creek**. To get there, drive along Highway 89. Between mile posts 17 & 18 turn north onto the Cottonwood Wash Road (Km & Mile 0). Drive 2.25 kms (1.4 miles) and turn right or east onto another good graded road. If weather is threatening, or the roads already wet, stay out of this area--**this is clay country which means slick roads when wet!**

Almost immediately you'll pass under some big power lines heading northeast. At Km 6.1 (Mile 3.8) is a road turning off to the right; this 4WD track runs south along Coyote Creek to some TD or chimney-like towers above. But continue eastward; you'll soon cross Coyote Creek which is the only real rough place on this road, then at Km 7.3 (Mile 4.55) is a large catchment called **Blue Cove Stock Pond**. At Km 13 (Mile 8.1) the White Sands Road turns south toward Big Water--but it's sandy as hell in places! At Km 15 (Mile 9.3) is a fence & gate just beyond another stock pond; just beyond that is a steep dugway made of gray Tropic Shale. Finally at Km 17.1 (Mile 10.6) you'll come to Wahweap Creek and a gate in the fence on the right. If things are dry and you have a HCV, you can continue south along Wahweap from there, but that gate in Section 8 is the end of the road. Be aware, if you drive south down the creek bed, you'll be in a wilderness study area (WSA), which is illegal.

Trail/Route From the bottom of **Valley 1**, hop the fence carefully and walk north or northeast for a lit-tle over one km. The area northeast of the trailhead has many TD rocks high on the shoulder of a but-tress. In Valley 2, you can just barely see some TD high above, while Valley 3 has nothing of interest. From the trailhead in **Valley 4**, walk through a hiker's gate heading north on a well-used trail; this is the most popular TD hike in the area. You'll soon pass a trail register. At the head of this valley is one very prominent red TD, then several more just beyond that. Other TD can be seen to the west.

If coming from the north & the Cottonwood Wash Road, walk southwest for one km in the direction of the highest point on the horizon--better have a compass to do this! Once on the rim, one group of TD should be just below and to the left (east). Follow the map--there's an easy way down to the next level or bench. From that group, you can bench-walk southwest and around the corner of a jutting point to see a 2nd group which is the same bunch you see if walking northeast up Valley 1. There are likely other TD in the area.

From the gate on Wahweap Creek, walk or drive south along the right or west side of the dry wash. After 2 kms, you'll come to the first group of TD on the right or west in a little hollow formed by the white cliffs of the Gunsight Butte Member of the Entrada Formation. This is the best group. Around the corner 400m in the next indentation of the canyon wall is another really good group. These are both in the NE 1/4 of Section 17, T42S, R2E. Others are just south of that. No doubt there are still more in the prominent canyon just west of Wahweap Creek, and elsewhere.

Elevations Highway trailheads,1335m; Cottonwood Wash Road parking, 1470m, Wahweap Creek, 1310m.

Hike Length/Time Needed In The Rimrocks, about 45 minutes to an hour round-trip for each hike--maybe longer for photographers. Along Wahweap Creek, maybe 2 hours, perhaps longer for foto hounds.

Water There's a well & tap about 50m west of the Visitor Center. Take plenty if going to Wahweap Creek.

Maps USGS or BLM maps Kanab & Smoky Mountain (1:100,000) for driving & orientation; West Clark Bench, Bridger Point, Lower Coyote Spring & Nipple Butte (1:24,000--7 1/2' quads) for hiking.

Main Attractions These fotogenic Toadstool/Mushroom-like features were created by 2 types of rocks with contrasting erosional characteristics. The pedestal part of the TD is white sandstone and believed to be the Gunsight Butte Member of the Entrada Sandstone Formation. This is the white fine-grained massive sandstone with a red layer at the bottom, forming most of the higher cliffs in The Rimrocks. The capstone in The Rimrocks is a gray more weather-resistent sandstone with some limestone--at least the erosional features look like limy sandstone (?). This could be from an upper layer of the Entrada or Henrieville Formations, or is perhaps part of the Dakota Sandstone. For sure, it's from one of the layers above the Gunsight Butte, and below the Tropic Shale. See the Geology Cross-Section of the Paria in the back of this book.

The Wahweap Creek TD have reddish conglomerate capstone or topknots. On the canyon wall this is the layer immediately above the white Gunsight Butte Member. This white fine-grained friable (which means the grains of sand can be rubbed off easily) sandstone is the pedestal. The unique thing about this rock is, when it rains and the outer surface of the pedestal gets wet, gravity pulls the outer one centimeter down and it looks just like flowstone in most limestone caves. It's as if these pedestals are made of sugar and with each rainstorm are slowly melting away. This is truly a unique place.

BYU geologist Tom Morris, says this sandstone appears to fall into the category of **Quartz arenite** (more than 90% of the grains are derived from quartzite). The cement or matrix holding the grains together is calcium carbonate, a kind of limestone.

Over thousands of years, parts of the limy sandstone or conglomerate caprock broke off and rolled downhill to rest on top of a bench or a more eroded part of the Gunsight Butte Member. Then the caprock, being more weather-resistent, shielded the softer white fine-grained sandstone below from eroding away. After many more years, all that's left is a pedestal and a chunk of capstone balanced on top.

Ideal Time to Hike Spring or fall, or anytime the roads are dry.

Boots/Shoes Any comfortable shoe will do as these are very short & easy hikes.

Author's Experience He spent about one hour in Valley 1, about 45 minutes going up Valley 4, and 1 1/4 hours exploring the best groups from the Cottonwood Wash Road. Also, he was about 1 1/2 hours at the Wahweap site.

Map 28A, The Rimrocks Toadstools

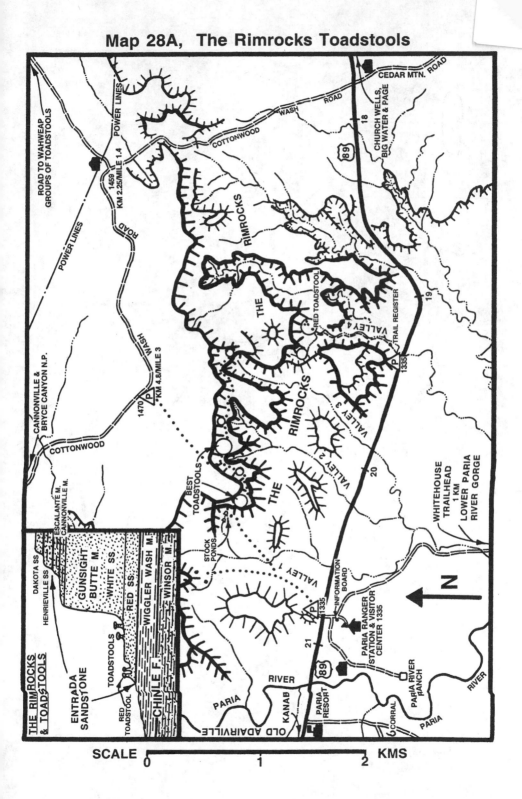

SCALE

0   1   2   KMS

Map 28B, The Wahweap Toadstools

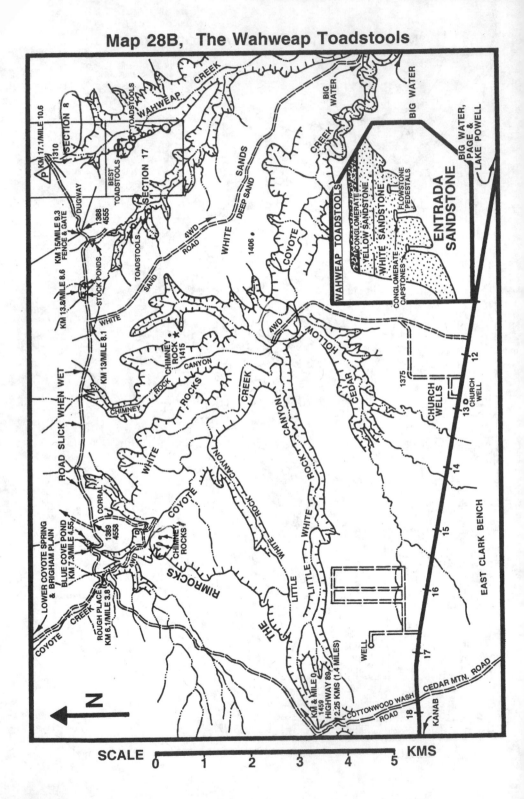

SCALE

0   1   2   3   4   5   KMS

Both of these toadstool or mushroom-like rocks are located at the head of what the author calls Valley 4 near mile post 19 in The Rimrocks. The one on the right has been featured on a poster; the author calls this the Red Toadstool. The one on the left is about 100m behind or northeast of the Red Toadstool.

Left These twin toadstools are located on a bench at the head of Valley 2. To reach these, you must use the route coming from the Cottonwood Wash Road. **Right** This is just one of many toadstools seen along Wahweap Creek. This one is in the group featured in the geology cross-section.

Left This is in the northeast part of what this writer is calling Valley 1. It shows a stock pond, cottonwood trees, and high above on a bench or shoulder, a group of toadstools. **Right** This is one of many toadstools found at the head of Valley 2. This group is labeled *Best Toadstools* on The Rimrocks map. Approach this group from the Cottonwood Wash Road, as shown.

Looking down from the rim on what is labeled the *Best Toadstools* at the head of Valley 2 on The Rimrocks map. The tallest toadstools here are in the range of 10-12 meters in height. Approach this group from the Cottonwood Wash Road.

This site is labeled *Best Toadstools* on the Wahweap Toadstools map (the group in the geology cross-section). Notice how this white fine-grained friable Entrada Sandstone looks like flowstone in limestone caves. The topknots or capstones are made of a course reddish conglomerate.

An aerial view of Castle Rock looking northwest. The southeast buttress starts at the lower right. On the east side are lots of fins and towers. In the upper right side is Cottonwood Wash.

The Buckskin Gulch & Paria River Loop Hike

Location & Access This section, **Map 29 and Part 1,** includes the upper part of what is traditionally known as the Paria River hike, and its best-known tributary, the Buckskin Gulch. This map covers the upper part of the Lower Paria River Gorge down to The Confluence which is where the Buckskin Gulch enters from the west. It also shows the entire Buckskin Gulch and its 3 trailhead entry points.

Map 30 and Part 2 begins at The Confluence and includes that part of the Paria River Gorge down to Wrather Canyon & Arch. This is the best part of the Paria, because it has many springs, good narrows, excellent campsites, an old historic trail to the rim, and at least one good panel of petroglyphs.

Map 31 and Part 3 shows the Paria River from Wrather Canyon down to Bush Head Canyon. This is where the gorge begins to open up and becomes wider. This is also where it begins to look more like the Grand Canyon. This section has one of the best arches in the world, 4 routes to the rim for fine views of the canyon below, more good springs & water, campsites, and more petroglyphs.

The last part of the Paria River Gorge is shown on **Map 32 and Part 4.** It begins at Bush Head Canyon and ends at Lee's Ferry on the Colorado River. The canyon in this section opens up wide and has old ranches, some abandoned uranium prospects, adits or mines, and some of the best petroglyphs or rock art on boulders the author has seen. Each of these segments could be a one-day hike, but to see all the side-canyons, and do side-trips, it may take 5 or 6 days. Most people do the entire hike in 3 or 4 days.

In 1984, all of this Lower Paria River Canyon and the Vermilion Cliffs, was put aside as a wilderness area. Now this one large crescent-shaped region is officially called the **Paria Canyon--Vermilion Cliffs Wilderness Area.** It includes all of the Paria Canyon from the power lines below the White House Trailhead, and the Buckskin Gulch, down to near Lee's Ferry, then west following the Vermilion Cliffs to the House Rock Valley to the west. Then in 2000, the **Vermilion Cliffs National Monument** was created. It includes all of the Sand Hills and/or the Paria Plateau, the wilderness area mentioned above, plus almost all land between the House Rock & Coyote Valleys on the west, Highway 89A on the south, Paria River Canyon on the east & northeast, and the Utah-Arizona state line on the north.

There are 4 ways to get into this gorge, all of which are from Highway 89, which runs between Page & Kanab. The normal entry point for the Paria is the **White House Trailhead.** It's the easiest to access and can be used regardless of the weather conditions, as it's at the end of a graveled road. The other 3 entries are into and through the Buckskin Gulch. They are; the **Middle Trail/Route** on top of West Clark Bench, **The Buckskin,** and the most-used, the **Wire Pass.** All these are discussed later.

The real starting point for all hikes in the Paria River & Buckskin Gulch is at the **Paria Ranger Station & Visitor Center.** It's located about halfway between Kanab & Page, between mile posts 20 & 21, and about 200m south of Highway 89. Be sure to stop there before entering the canyons and talk to a BLM employee or volunteer. They now sell books, maps and post cards, etc. It's open from 8:30 am to 5 pm daily from March 15 to November 15. At some time in the future, and because of the new Grand Staircase-Escalante National Monument (GSENM), it may remain open year-round (but not as of 2004). Usually someone lives behind the office in a trailer house, and they keep the latest information on weather & hiking conditions posted outside on an **information board.** That information comes from the Kanab BLM office, Tele. 435-644-4600. The visitor center has a radio telefon but it's used for emergencies only.

If a ranger is not at the visitor center, you can pickup & fill out the Recreation Fee Permit Envelope at the self-service pay station or information board. After filling it out, drop it in the metal box provided. As of 2004, day-hikes down the Paria and/or Buckskin cost $5 per day; as well as $5 a night for camping in the canyons. Reservations are required to camp in either canyon. See more details and the **latest regulations in the introduction to this book.** But for the very latest information, go to the website **www.az.blm.gov/paria.** Every year the BLM makes some kind of change in policy and the internet is the best place to be current.

Also, after leaving the visitor center, you're requested (voluntary) to sign in at any of the 4 trailheads, whether you're going on an overnight trip, or day-hiking. Because of the heavy visitor use around The Confluence of the Paria & Buckskin, everyone is urged to day-hike only, rather than camp in that area. If you need to **fill water bottles,** do that at the tap 50m west of the visitor center, as all the trailheads are dry.

Now, to reach the normal trailhead for entry to the Paria River--turn east then south right at the Paria Ranger Station, and drive 3.4 kms (2.1 miles) on a good gravel road to the **White House Trailhead.** This place has picnic tables, fire pits, toilets, and can be used as a campsite--but for a fee! It's $5 a night. However, for a quiet & uninterrupted night's sleep, it's recommended you camp anywhere but there! Best to pull off the highway on any side-road in the region. This area is almost all public land.

If you arrive at the trailhead without water, go back to the ranger station; or walk across the river and downstream about 450m and up a short side-canyon to the west where the White House Spring is located. This water is very good if taken directly from the spring. Nearby are lots of old cowboy signatures. If you have time, you can visit some petroglyphs just across the river to the west and up 2 minor draws. The white sandstone seen at this trailhead is the Thousand Pockets Tongue of the Page Sandstone (although almost all maps still show it as the upper part of the Navajo Sandstone).

The White House or Clark Cabin Ruins

The story behind the name of this trailhead, and the White House Cabin & Spring, was told to the author by the late Kay Clark, formerly of Henrieville. The story begins in the Luna Valley of New Mexico. In February, 1887, Wilford Clark (Kay's father) was born to Herriet & Owen Washington Clark. Soon after Wilford was born, and Herriet strong enough to travel, the small family moved from Luna Valley to southern Utah and set up a homestead on the Paria River just downstream from where the White House Trailhead is today.

They arrived in June, 1887, and immediately built a small cabin. The family lived there only about one year, then in 1888, moved upriver a ways to the Adairville site (Adairville existed only from about 1873 until 1878, then was abandoned because of lack of summertime water). Largely because of water problems, that place didn't work out either, so in 1889 the family moved further upstream to Pahreah, which at that time was in the process of losing population. The first big floods to come down the Paria River, which caused many people to have second thoughts about living at Pahreah, roared down the canyon in 1883 & '84. Another big flood came in 1896.

In 1892, Owen W. Clark moved the whole family once again, this time to a safer and more promis-

164

Map 29, The Lower Paria River Gorge--Part 1
The Buckskin Gulch & Paria River Loop Hike

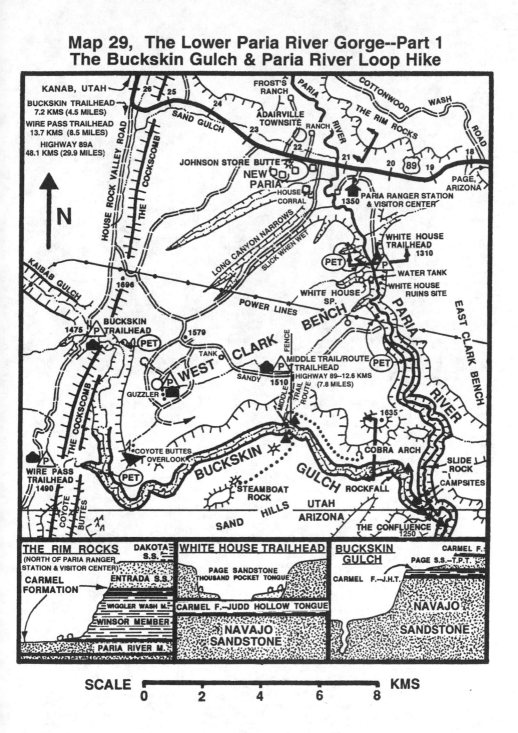

Owen W. Clark (picture taken in the early 1900's) and his family arrived in southern Utah in June of 1887 and built a cabin just downstream from the White House Trailhead. A pile of stones from that cabin's chimney is all that remains of the cabin. (LaKay Quilter foto--daughter of Kay Clark)

ing land around the town of Cannonville. The family has been in Bryce Valley ever since.

Back now to the name of White House. After the Clarks left their original cabin, sheepherders used the place as a camp and a supply depot when they had their flocks out on top of East Clark Bench just to the southeast (both the East Clark and West Clark Benches appear to be named after Owen W. Clark?). Sometime in the 1890's, the cabin burned down, apparently due to carelessness on the part of a sheepman.

It was the sheepmen who gave the place the name, **White House Cabin** and **White House Spring**. When they were out on the range for a long time, and had to drink any water they could get, they always enjoyed going back to the Clark Cabin because of the good-tasting water they could get from the little spring located just upstream and into a little draw to the west. As the story goes, someone commented that this water was so good, it could have come directly from the White House (in Washington DC). Thus the name stuck on both the cabin & spring; and later the trailhead.

To find the White House Ruins today, walk south from the parking lot along the east side of the Paria River flood plain. After almost exactly 1000m or one km, and 400m southeast of the metal water tank which is located just below the White House Spring, get up on the low bench on the east side. Once there, look for an inconspicuous pile of rocks. This is said to be the remains of the cabin's fireplace. There were at one time some corrals just north of the ruins, but they were washed away long ago by floods. About 40m east of the pile of stones, and at the base of the cliffs, is a cowboyglyph or etching which looks like someone's brand.

Buckskin Gulch Trailheads

The other 3 trailheads are for entry into the best slot canyon on the Colorado Plateau and the world--the Buckskin Gulch. To reach the **Buckskin Trailhead,** drive west from the Paria Ranger Station & Visitor Center on Highway 89 and through The Cockscomb. Just west of where the highway cuts through the monocline, and between mile posts 25 & 26, turn south on the House Rock Valley Road (HRVR). This road is well-traveled, well-maintained and generally good for any car even in light rains. If you drive this road south, you'll end up on Highway 89A between mile posts 565 & 566 in the House Rock Valley. Highway to highway the distance is 48.1 kms (29.9 miles). From Highway 89 south to the first car-park, the Buckskin Trailhead, is 7.2 kms (4.5 miles); or 40.9 kms (25.4 miles) from the south & Highway 89A. At that point, turn east and drive 250m and park and/or camp at the trailhead which is just behind a low hill. This is where Kaibab Gulch cuts through The Cockscomb.

From the Buckskin Trailhead, continue south for a total of 13.7 kms (8.5 miles) from Highway 89, to the **Wire Pass Trailhead** (34.5 kms/21.4 miles from the south & Highway 89A). This is the more popular starting point of the 2 entries at the head of the Buckskin Gulch, because it shortens the walk by a couple of hours. The Wire Pass Trailhead is located in the lower end of Coyote Wash or Valley, but for some reason that part of the drainage below the trailhead is not called Coyote Wash. Instead, it's just called the Wire Pass. You can camp at either trailhead, but both are dry, so take plenty of water with you. The BLM has installed a pit toilet at each of these trailheads.

The 4th and last entry possibility into the Buckskin, is from the West Clark Bench and the **Middle Trail/Route.** Until recently it was really more of a route than a trail. Get there by driving along Highway 89 between mile posts 21 & 22. Immediately east of the Paria River Guest Ranch turn south onto a good graded road. This is public access, but you pass through some private land and 2 gates in the first 1 1/2 kms. Leave the gates as you find them; either open or closed, then drive southwest up **Long Canyon** (which has some moderately good narrows) on a maintained road which can be slick & muddy in wet weather. At the head of the canyon, stay on the most-used road, the one which veers left at 2 junctions, then continues south, then east. The last part will be down a very shallow & broad drainage towards the Middle Trail/Route Trailhead near a fence & gate, as shown. In the last km or so before the trailhead, **beware of deep sand!** If the sand has a little moisture, 2WD's can make it OK. If the sand is dry, it's for 4WD's only! The author made it several times in his VW Rabbit, but 4WD's are recommended. If you're driving a 2WD car, stop a little ways before the trailhead. In June, the driest month, sandy roads tend to be their worst, so a shovel in the trunk should be standard equipment! The trailhead is 12.6 kms (7.8 miles) from Highway 89.

This trailhead and the Middle Trail/Route is the least-used of the entries to the Buckskin, but it affords a different view of the country you'll be walking through, and the access road is generally good for all vehicles. It also allows you access to Cobra Arch, one of the most unique around.

Trail/Route--FROM WHITE HOUSE TRAILHEAD Most people going down the Paria just to the lower

Buckskin and back, or all the way to Lee's Ferry, usually begin at the **White House Trailhead**. Many people walk down to The Confluence, up the Buckskin Gulch a ways, then return the same way. This part of the hike down the Paria is very easy, and normally there are no obstacles.

In the first 2 kms or so, the bed of the Paria is wide with the creek meandering all over, then the Navajo Sandstone walls slowly come closer together. You'll have to cross the creek several times in this first part, so get used to the idea of wet shoes! After about 2 kms will be a short side-canyon coming in from the right or west. About one km below that, and again on the right or west, will be a big rounded curve with a high smooth wall that's covered with desert varnish. All around that wall will be scattered etchings of **rock art,** but the biggest & best panel will be on the south side.

A little over 2 kms below these petroglyphs, and as the river is running southeast in a straight line, will be more rock art on the right or west side. Look for a crack in the wall opening to the north about 200m from the river. Walk inside this crack to find more **etchings** 3m-4m above on the east facing wall. Another km below these, and again on the right or west side, and up 4m-5m, will be more hard-to-see petroglyphs. About 50m below these is a paleface-made + & 1/4 high on the wall. Just above that is a big horn sheep.

About 5-6 kms below these last petroglyphs will be **Slide Rock.** This is where a section of the Navajo Sandstone wall was undercut, then broken off and slid straight down into the river. Presently, the river flows behind it, making a short tunnel or bridge. Below Slide Rock, the canyon constricts and in 2 places, and the creek fills the slot from wall to wall. These 2 places are about 50m & 300m from The Confluence with the Buckskin Gulch.

Please be aware, that in the past, and after some floods--but not all--these 2 short sections can be extra deep. Having at least one air mattress with your group would help ferry packs across deep water. For this reason, be sure to stop and look at the **back side of the information board** located in front of the Paria Ranger Station & Visitor Center. Rangers will alert you to any problem areas in the canyon on that chalkboard; however, 99% of the time there's little or nothing to worry about. Now let's stop at The Confluence and go to the trailheads for the Buckskin Gulch.

FROM BUCKSKIN TRAILHEAD From the **Buckskin Trailhead,** you have an unobstructed walk into the Gulch. About one km from the trailhead, and just after you walk through a gate-like narrow constriction, veer left and look almost due east. About 125m away is a good panel of big horn sheep **petroglyphs** on a wall on the bench above the creek bed. After the petroglyphs, the canyon is open for a ways then begins to narrow as you near the confluence of the Buckskin & Wire Pass drainages. There's not a lot to see before you arrive at the Wire Pass drainage.

FROM WIRE PASS TRAILHEAD In the first km, you'll first pass through open country and the trail going up to the right to the Coyote Buttes and The Wave. Read about this with **Map 35.** From there, the wash narrows quickly. Soon you'll come to the place where there can be a minor obstacle, a chokestone or two, which can create one or more dropoffs of one to 3m. This situation changes with every flood. If there's a problem here, the rangers will let you know by posting a message on the back side of the information board in front of the Visitor Center. Right where the Wire Pass & Buckskin Gulch meet, are a number of **etchings** of big horn sheep on your right-hand or south side.

From the Wire Pass/Buckskin Confluence, the real Buckskin Gulch begins, and doesn't end until The Confluence with the Paria. This part of the canyon is nearly 20 kms long, and averages 4m-5m in width for its entire length. At times the gorge may open to 8m-10m in width, then narrow down to no more than a meter wide. The author recalls something like 40 to 50 places in the Buckskin where

This is the Wirepass drainage just above where it meets the Buckskin Gulch. It's in this section that chokestones periodically wash into the slot and create minor dropoffs.

logs were seen wedged into the slot high above--mute evidence of nature on the rampage, and a grim reminder of the danger of walking this gorge. One last word of caution: **HAVE A GOOD WEATHER FORECAST BEFORE ENTERING THIS CANYON!** Normally this slot's depth is somewhere between 20m & 30m, but downcanyon near the Paria, the walls are nearing 100m in height! This is the longest slot canyon in the world.

For the most part, walking down the Buckskin is uneventful, but normally there are several small pools of water or mud you must wade through. These pools occur where the slot constricts and flood waters gush through and scour out holes. Most of these are concentrated in the 3 or 4 kms upcanyon from where the Middle Trail/Route enters. There's no running water in the Buckskin Gulch, except in times of flood. Since the bottom is so hidden from the sun, and the temperatures so cool, there is little evaporation, even in the heat of the summer, therefore muddy pools are usually there all the time. One such place is called the **Cesspool.** It's about one km upcanyon from the Middle Trail/Route. Right after any big flood, you may have to float your pack across this pool, so taking an air mattress is a good idea. Once again, check for messages on the back side of the information board at the Paria Ranger Station for the latest word concerning the depth of this pool and others. Then at the last minute make the decision to take an air mattress or possibly an inner tube.

FROM THE MIDDLE TRAIL/ROUTE From the parking place, follow the fence due south to some minor cliffs. Hop the fence to the west side, then follow footprints down and to the right. A trail is slowly developing along a drainage veering a little southwest from the trailhead. This takes you right to the rim of the Buckskin. From there turn east for 200m-300m for the final route into the bottom of the slot. **WARNING:** From the lip of the narrows, you'll have to downclimb about 30m over fairly steep downsloping slickrock that's always covered with loose windblown sand. This means you'll have to remove packs and lower them by hand to a companion, or use a short rope. *Short people, inexperienced hikers and anyone carrying a large pack, may find it difficult getting up or down (especially down!) this last 30m.* On the author's last trip, it had been raining, the sand was wet and sticking to the soles of his shoes. This was the worst he has ever seen it! He slipped near the bottom and slid a couple of meters, and although no harm was done, it was a wakeup call that this route can be risky! If using this Middle Trail/Route as an entry point, be sure to take a short rope and help each other down.

For anyone hiking the Buckskin in 2 days, this is a good place to camp, as it allows you to take another look at the weather situation halfway through the gorge. This is obviously a hike you don't want to do in a monsoon weather pattern. The Middle Trail/Route also allows you to exit and take a 3-km side-trip to **Cobra Arch** (best to do that on a separate hike). From this entry/exit point, you can also scramble up a steep slope to the south rim for a possible hike to the fotogenic **Steamboat Rock** (please don't walk on the delicate erosional fins!) and other landmarks on top the Sand Hills/Paria Plateau.

A couple of hours downcanyon from the Middle Trail/Route entry/exit point, is what is normally the only obstacle in the Buckskin. This is **The Rockfall,** created by some large boulders falling off the canyon wall about 3 kms up from The Confluence. The worst part is a 3m-high climb or descent, over one of these boulders. During the 1980's, someone chopped several steps into one of the boulders which you might use, but you'll normally find a rope nearby as well that you can handline down. BLM

Looking down on the last part of the Middle Trail/Route. You must climb down on the left, which can be tricky with a large pack or if there's lots of wind-blown sand on the slickrock. Take a short rope to lower large packs, or to help beginners. On this day, the Buckskin was flooding.

rangers normally cut out ropes that appear to be unsafe, so be prepared to install a new one (with knots or loops) to help you get down and/or to lower packs. To insure you have no problems, take **a rope 10m long.** Without packs, hikers can sometimes slide, jump or wiggle down through this dryfall but it's a little risky without a rope.

In 1991, there was an unusual short-lived obstacle in the lower Buckskin between The Rockfall and the campsites in the lower end. This was a rare swimming pool. Apparently a bigger-than-normal flood roared down the Buckskin in the fall or winter of 1990-91 and scoured out deep holes where the walls constrict. At the deepest pool, the author had to hold onto a log with one hand, while holding his daypack up with the other to keep it dry. People taking big packs down had to float them across, while others just swam. Later floods filled in these holes and by 1997 and in 2003, everything was back to normal, with ankle-deep water. Expect big changes with every flood and go prepared!

About 300m above The Confluence with the Paria River, there are several campsites in the lower Buckskin on a couple of sandy benches high above the creek bed. This is a heavily-used area, and at times in the past has been closed to camping. The reason for the closures was to allow the vegetation to recover, and the toilet poop to disintegrate. If you're camping there, please tread lightly and use existing paths and tent sites. Also, be careful where you use the toilet and dispose of waste. **The toilet problem in the lower Buckskin is the primary reason the BLM instigated the policy of allowing only 20 hikers per/day to backpack & camp in the Buckskin/Paria drainage.** If camping or day-hiking, try to do your toilet duties anywhere but at this site in the lower Buckskin. Here's an option. One campsite that's seldom if ever used is about 750m below The Rockfall. You'll have to carry water back up from downcanyon, but it will lessen the impact on The Confluence campsite.

Elevations The White House Trailhead, 1310m; Buckskin Trailhead, 1475m; Wire Pass Trailhead, 1490m; Middle Trail/Route Trailhead, about 1510m; The Confluence of the Buckskin & Paria, about 1250m.

Hike Length/Time Needed The distance from the Buckskin Trailhead to the confluence of Wire Pass is about 7 kms. From the Wire Pass Trailhead to this same confluence is about 3 kms. From that point to The Confluence with the Paria is another 19 kms. From The Confluence back up to the White House Trailhead is another 11 kms or so. This makes the total distance from the Buckskin to the White House Trailhead about 38 kms. From Wire Pass to White House is about 33 kms. This can be done in one long day, but it's not recommended for everyone. You'll need 2 cars; or a car & mtn. bike to be used as a shuttle.

The author once left a mtn. bike at White House, then drove to Wire Pass. He walked down the Buckskin and up the Paria to White House in 8 hours 13 min. This wasn't too bad, but the bike ride back to Wire Pass was--being at the end of an otherwise long day and peddling against the wind. It turned out to be a very tiring 10-hour day. Despite its length, it's recommended you do this in one day to cut down on the number of campers near The Confluence.

Or you can do this same hike in 2 days; but the problem with camping (likely at the **Middle Trail/Route**) would be that you'd have to carry at least a gallon (3.785 liters) jug full of water; perhaps more in hot weather, less in cooler conditions. Most people however, make it all the way through the Buckskin in one day and end up camping near The Confluence where there's a permanent water supply.

Water The Buckskin is normally bone-dry, but with an occasional pool of water or mud to wade through. Since most people don't have the courage to drink this, count on it being a dry hike. Carry all the water you'll need. Normally, about 2 kms up the Buckskin from The Confluence, you'll begin to

Looking north at Cobra Arch, one of the most unique around.

see pools of water; and about one km from the Paria, and just above the campsites, water begins to flow. This seep is a year-round water supply. But since this campsite area and the lower part of the Buckskin is so heavily used, with people walking in the water all the time, especially in the spring and fall months, plan to filter or purify it first.

Another option for those camping near The Confluence is to take empty jugs (always have plenty of empty jugs, as they weigh almost nothing) down the Paria a ways, and fill them up at **Wall Spring** or at the spring just above it (see the next map of the Paria, Part 2). This is about 3 1/2 kms below The Confluence. Still another alternative is to purify or filter the Paria River water. Since most of this water seeps out of the bottom layers of the Navajo Sandstone in the Upper Paria River Gorge and below the town of Cannonville, it's really not that bad; it's just a little muddy at times, especially if there's any storm activity upcanyon. The author has never used filters, but it seems they would clog-up badly if used in muddy water. So let muddy water settle overnight first, then filter it. A bottle of Iodine tablets might be the best idea.

The Paria below The Confluence flows year-round, but between the White House Trailhead and the Buckskin it's often dry in the early summer. The stockman who leases a ranch just north of Highway 89 near the site of old Adairville, uses a bulldozer to make a small temporary dam across the creek during part of the summer, and uses the Paria water for irrigation. This is usually in May and June. However, in the heat of the summer, water in the Paria doesn't even reach the old Adairville site. In July, and after the first storm or flood of the season, the Paria River then flows again, usually until the next spring or summer. To check on the Paria water, just glance at the creek bed as you drive across the bridge on Highway 89 near mile post 21. Also, it's important to check on the water situation at the ranger station, or ask other hikers of its whereabouts.

Maps USGS or BLM maps **Kanab** and especially **Smoky Mountain** (for the Buckskin Gulch only), and to these add **Glen Canyon Dam,** which shows the Paria River from the state line, or The Confluence, down to Lee's Ferry (all at 1:100,000 scale). The Glen Canyon Dam map also shows the Vermilion Cliffs. Or you might try the 1:62,500 scale maps Paria, Paria Plateau, and Lee's Ferry. These are now out of print, but there may be a few still around in some sales outlets.

The BLM has recently published a new map/guide called **Hiker's Guide to Paria Canyon.** It's in book form with 30 small maps covering the Paria and Buckskin down to Lee's Ferry. But it's not just one map showing the entire canyon. Their old map with the same title at 1:62,500 scale is a good one if you can find it. One BLM employee stated in 3/2004, they were working to reprint this map.

Another excellent map is one of the series of 4 field study maps which were prepared by the BLM, USGS, and others, covering the Paria Plateau or Sand Hills. These maps are in the series titled **MF-1475, A, B, C & D.** Each map is at 1:62,500 scale, and very much the same, except each has a different emphasi such as (A) geology, (B) geochemical data, (C) mines & prospects, and (D) mineral resource potential. Get these maps from any USGS outlet. Each of these covers the entire Lower Paria River Hike from White House to Lee's Ferry, also the Vermilion Cliffs and all of the House Rock Valley Road.

Those who want something with greater detail, consider buying the 5 or 6 maps at 1:24,000 scale (7 1/2' quads). See the **Index to TopoGraphic Maps--Paria River Country** on page 13. All these quads can be bought at the BLM office in Kanab, or at the Paria Ranger Station & Visitor Center.

Main Attraction The best slot canyon hike in the world. Also, with an exit at the Middle Trail/Route, you can have a look at Cobra Arch, one of the most unique around. Be sure you read the part on Fotography in Slot Canyons in the Introduction, which will help you take home better fotos of this very dark chasm.

Ideal Time to Hike Because of possible cold water in the pools of the Buckskin, May & June have become the most popular time to visit this canyon. It's getting hot by June, but once inside the narrows, it's very cool. You'll seldom see the sun; and it's that way for 19 kms! So the heat of the outside world doesn't really matter, except for the walk back up the Paria to the White House Trailhead.

June is the driest month of the year, not only for this region, but for the entire state of Utah. Kanab receives about 31 cms (12 in.) of rainfall annually, most of it in winter. With the low temps and lack of sun in the gorge, the pools of water, especially the Cesspool, simply don't evaporate. Pools seem to stay in the Buckskin most of each winter, and often times until about June, then sometimes may be dry for a time. Each year is different. If you were to go down the Buckskin right after a summer storm, you may have to float your pack across one or more pools on an air mattress or inner tube. See the information board at the Paria Ranger Station for the latest word on the Cesspool situation and hiking conditions in the Buckskin.

You can hike the Buckskin throughout the summer, but you'd want a good weather forecast. If you're there in a dry spell, then fine. But if you arrive in a wet period, with showers around, stay out of this canyon! Southern Utah has 2 or 3 very wet monsoon periods each summer, each lasting a few days or a week or so. These periods usually occur sometime between mid-July to mid-September. This is the period you should be most cautious with the threat of flash floods.

Actually, as narrow as the place is, there are still many high places you could crawl up to and away from raging flood waters. But when the floods do come, they usually come in a surge, and you may not have time to look for a hideout. Always listen to the local radio stations for the latest weather forecasts as you drive into the area. Remember, the Buckskin Gulch is the worst place in the world to be in a flash flood!

Boots/Shoes Best to take wading-type boots or shoes for the entire hike.

Author's Experience The author has been all the way through the Buckskin twice, and at least part way through on a dozen other occasions, and from each trailhead. On one trip he made it from The Confluence campsite to the Wire Pass Trailhead, with a large pack, in less than 6 1/2 hours. On 4 or 5 trips, he walked from the White House Trailhead, down the Paria, up the Buckskin to The Rockfall, then back the same way, all in about 7 hours. Another time he left the Middle Trail/Route parking, walked down to the bottom of the entry/exit point, then to Cobra Arch, and back to his car, all in 3 1/2 hours. Another hike was down the Middle Trail/Route and up the other side to Steamboat Rock. Round-trip was about 4 hours. Most people will want more time than that taken by the author. Some may want to almost double the author's hike times.

Above The route down through the Rockfall in the lower end of the Buckskin Gulch. To the right of center are some steps cut in the wall. To the left is a log with a rope attached. If all else fails, you could slide down on the left, or help each other. But it's best to take a rope, just in case.

Left From below, you see the rope as shown in the foto above. This is the only place in the Buckskin Gulch that presents any problem at all--and it's not that difficult. Two people can help each other up or down.

Above Left Immediately below the Rockfall is this large boulder you'll have to crawl under.

Above Right A hiker in the lower part of the Buckskin Gulch below the Rockfall.

Right Another scene in the lower end of the Buckskin not far above the campsites and The Confluence with the Paria River.

Above Left The lower Buckskin Gulch. This is the deepest part of the entire canyon.

Above Right A Boy Scout troop about 100m below The Confluence of the Buckskin Gulch and the Paria River.

Left This is the Paria River about 50m above The Confluence with the Buckskin Gulch. Water normally fills this narrow section from wall to wall. If this place has been scoured out and made deeper by big floods, the rangers will inform you by leaving a message on the *back side of the Information Board in front of the Visitor Center.*

Lower Paria River Gorge--The Confluence to Lee's Ferry

Location & Access The Lower Paria River Gorge is so long and has so many interesting sites to see, it's been broken down into 4 parts with 4 different maps. Part 1, covers mainly the Buckskin Gulch and the trailheads leading into it; and the upper part of the Lower Paria River Gorge or Canyon. The second, third and fourth maps cover the canyon from The Confluence of the Buckskin Gulch and the Paria River all the way down to Lee's Ferry. This is where the Paria empties into the Colorado River.

If you plan to do this entire canyon hike from top to bottom, call the BLM office in Kanab, 435-644-4600, and ask if they have a list of people who perform shuttle service between Whitehouse Trailhead (or any of the Buckskin Gulch trailheads) and Lee's Ferry. Or better still, go to the website **www.az.blm.gov/paria/,** and click on **Shuttles.** Here's what you may find: Barry Warren, PO Box 7041, Page, AZ, 928-640-0191; Betty Price, 928-355-2252; Canyon Country Outback Tours, Wally Thomson, 888-783-3807 or 435-644-3807; Marble Canyon Lodge, Catalina Martinez, 928-355-2295 or 928-355-2225; Paria Outpost, Susan & Stephen Dodson, PO Box 410075, Big Water, Utah, 84741, 928-691-1047.

Once you get someone lined up, the normal procedure is for you to drive to Lee's Ferry and park in the **Long Term Parking Lot** which is 300m from the boat launching site at the end of the road. There's a sign telling the right parking place. Then your shuttle drives you to Whitehouse or Wirepass, and you hike back to your car at your own pace.

Most people who do the entire Paria River hike, start at the White House Trailhead. To get there, leave Highway 89 between mile posts 20 & 21, and drive south for 3.4 kms (2.1 miles) on an all-weather gravel road. Read more about this and the 3 other entry points under Part 1, The Buckskin Gulch.
Elevations The White House Trailhead, 1310m; The Confluence, 1250m; Paria River at the bottom of Wrather Canyon, 1165m; the mouth of Bush Head Canyon, about 1100m; and Lee's Ferry, 950m.
Hike Length/Time Needed Here are the latest BLM calculations for distances in the Paria River Canyon. From the White House Trailhead to Lee's Ferry, is about 39 miles--62 kms. From the Buckskin Trailhead to Lee's Ferry, about 48 miles--77 kms. From Wire Pass Trailhead to Lee's Ferry, around 45 miles--72 kms. A long hike anyway you look at it, but a fun one, and one which has several side-canyons, or routes to the canyon rim to explore.

An extra fast walker could get through the canyon in 2 long days, but some people have trouble doing it in 3 or 4 days. Most do it in about 3, but this book introduces some new hikes out of the canyon and up to the rim, so some may want 5 or 6 days. It you're the type who likes to take it easy, do a lot of exploring, and likes to set up nice camps and relax, then a week isn't too long. However, the longer you plan to stay, the heavier your pack will be!
Water From The Confluence to Lee's Ferry, you'll have year-round water all the way, but you can only drink river water if you purify it with Iodine tablets or filter it. During the irrigation season in the Bryce Valley (Tropic, Henrieville & Cannonville), which extends from about mid-April through the beginning of October, there's very little water flowing down the Paria below Cannonville. Most of the water you see entering this Lower Paria Gorge during this time period, seeps out of the bottom layers of the Navajo Sandstone as the river cuts through the White Cliffs below Cannonville. So it's pretty good water, but there are cows in the canyon, usually in the cooler 6 months of the year, so therein lies the danger.

In the heat of most summers, or at least in June and July, the water in the upper gorge (between The Box, where the Paria cuts through The Cockscomb, and Highway 89) disappears in the sands. Then it begins flowing again in the lower canyon at the bottom end of the Buckskin Gulch near The

Left Unusual petroglyphs located west of the White House Trailhead and upstream a ways. **Right** Slide Rock is located not far above The Confluence of the Paria River and the Buckskin Gulch.

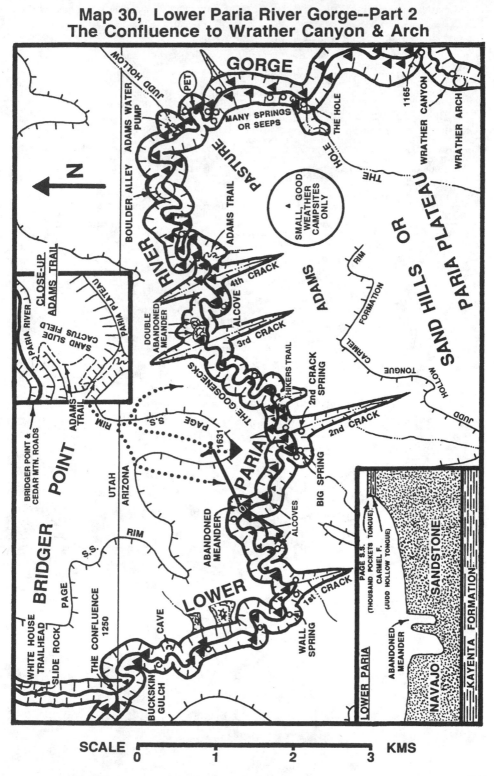

Map 30, Lower Paria River Gorge--Part 2
The Confluence to Wrather Canyon & Arch

GORGE

JUDD HOLLOW

PET

ADAMS WATER PUMP

MANY SPRINGS OR SEEPS

THE HOLE

1165

WRATHER CANYON

WRATHER ARCH

BOULDER ALLEY

ADAMS TRAIL

PASTURE

SMALL, GOOD WEATHER CAMPSITES ONLY

RIVER

SAND HILLS OR PARIA PLATEAU

RIM

CARMEL FORMATION

CLOSE-UP ADAMS TRAIL

PARIA RIVER

SAND SLIDE

PARIA PLATEAU

CACTUS FIELD

DOUBLE ABANDONED MEANDER

4th CRACK

ALCOVE

3rd CRACK

ADAMS

JUDD HOLLOW TONGUE

THE GOOSENECKS

HIKERS TRAIL

2nd CRACK SPRING

2nd CRACK

JUDD

PAGE S.S.

•1631

ADAMS TRAIL

RIM

BRIDGER POINT & CEDAR MTN. ROADS

BIG SPRING

UTAH
ARIZONA

PARIA

PAGE S.S. (THOUSAND POCKETS TONGUE)

POINT

ABANDONED MEANDER

ALCOVES

CARMEL F. (JUDD HOLLOW TONGUE)

RIM

SANDSTONE

BRIDGER

S.S.

PAGE

LOWER

1st CRACK

ABANDONED MEANDER

NAVAJO

KAYENTA FORMATION

WHITE HOUSE TRAILHEAD

SLIDE ROCK

THE CONFLUENCE
1250

CAVE

WALL SPRING

LOWER PARIA

BUCKSKIN GULCH

N

SCALE 0   1   2   3   KMS

175

Confluence. It then flows year-round to Lee's Ferry. The extent and amount of flow changes from year to year.

For those who prefer to drink good spring water without filtration or chemicals, take it from **Wall, Big, and Shower Springs,** and from springs inside Wrather and Bush Head Canyons. However, between The Confluence and Bush Head, are a number of minor seeps, which likely will have flowing water most of the time. The author always carries a small $4 bottle of Iodine tablets in his pack for emergency situations.

The alternative to chemicals is filtration. The latest REI catalog lists filters designed for hikers ranging in price from $35 to $130, but there are cheaper ones than that. Some manufactures are making a fistful of dollars on the scare tactics of some people, but the BLM and the NPS are required to tell hikers to boil or treat all water--even spring water, to stay away from possible lawsuits. The author prefers spring water, and Iodine tablets as an emergency backup.

Another thing to remember, carry several empty water bottles or plastic jugs. They don't weigh much, and can be thrown away at the end of the trip. By having a couple of gallon (3.785 liters) jugs, you can carry good water from springs to unoccupied camps sites.

Maps Read about maps under the previous chapter, **The Buckskin Gulch & Paria River Loop-Hike.**

Main Attractions A deep and narrow canyon, several places to climb out to the rim, interesting side-canyons, one of the best arches in the world, a chance to see desert big horn sheep, and many good campsites and petroglyphs. It's a great trip for those who have time off work in the spring or fall. More later under **Trail/Route.**

Ideal Time to Hike If you're doing this hike from the White House Trailhead straight down the Paria to Lee's Ferry with just a quick look into the bottom of the Buckskin, then spring or fall is best. More specifically, the best time is from about the first of April through May; and again from about mid-September through mid or late October. If you go too early or late in the season, the icy water you'll be wading in all the time will make your feet feel like blocks of ice! The author prefers the spring months because the days are longer. Remember, March 21, has the same amount of daylight as does September 21.

By June 1st, the temperatures are getting up there to around 30°C (86°F) on average, and that's pretty warm while walking in the sun all day with a big pack. You can count on temps of about 40°C (104°F) all through July and into August at Lee's Ferry. In the narrowest parts, and when wading in the creek, the heat doesn't affect you so much; but in the lower end of the canyon near Lee's Ferry, the altitude is only about 950m, and you'll be walking in the sun constantly.

Another reason to stay out of the area in about June, is because there are big deer or **horse flies** which bite the back of bare legs. The solution; wear long pants. They seem to congregate in the more open areas in the bottom end of the canyon, with water and tamaracks around. You'll also be hindered by very small gnats which get in your hair and bite. In the spring and fall, these 2 pests don't exist. Neither do they seem to exist in the narrow parts of the canyon at any time; instead, just in the more open places.

Boots/Shoes You'll be walking in or crossing the Paria River hundreds of times on your way to Lee's Ferry. In the narrower places you'll be hiking right in the stream continually. Your footwear will be wet all the time, so some kind of wading boots or shoes is recommended.

In the last few years, a number of new hiking boots or shoes have been on the market, designed especially for this type of hike. The very best kind is something that isn't affected by water. In other

A group of older hikers just below The Confluence of the Paria and Buckskin.

words, a shoe that's not made of leather. For use in places like the Zion Narrows in Zion NP, shoes by the name of 5-10's are really the best, but they're expensive. The Converse All Star basketball shoes, made of rubber and canvas, are good, but they have a thin sole and low heel. Then there are the plain ordinary running shoes. They are very good, but they have leather parts which shrink after they've been wet. This means you may want to apply boot oil to the leather parts after the hike.

Another tip, since this is such a long hike, start with a pair of shoes in good condition. Or if you have an old pair, and are trying to put them out of their misery, it might pay to take along a newer and light weight pair as a back-up. This is an especially good suggestion if you intend to climb out of the canyon. It takes a lot out of footwear to be used under strenuous conditions when wet all the time.

Author's Experience The author has been into the canyon from the White House Trailhead on 6 or 8 occasions, up from Lee's Ferry on more than half a dozen other trips. On each trip, he went to somewhere in the middle of the canyon, and returned the same way to his car, thus avoiding a car shuttle or hitch hiking. In addition, in 2003, he entered twice from the north rim via the old Indian route. Once he went upcanyon as far as the 2nd Crack; the next day he went down to Bush Head Canyon, climbed out, rim-walked to Wrather Canyon and returned from there. Later he walked all the way from White House Trailhead down to the 2nd Crack and back in one day.

Trail/Route--from The Confluence to Lee's Ferry The first half of the way between The Confluence and Lee's Ferry is narrow, but it's not the slot-type canyon you find in the Buckskin Gulch. There are many springs, campsites, running water year-round, and no obstacles. If you were caught by a flash flood in this section, you would have very little trouble finding a high place out of the way of the torrent. There are many good campsites, and always one site near each of the good springs. Taking fotos is in some ways easier here than in the darker Buckskin, because here you'll see the sun part of the time. There are several abandoned meanders (abandoned stream channels) to explore, and there are some petroglyphs, an historic pumping site, and several trails or routes to the canyon rim.

If you arrive at The Confluence, near mile P7 on the BLM log-type map, and find the campsites just inside the lower Buckskin too crowded or noisy, then you could walk downstream about one km to find several other places, high and dry and safe--near mile P8. Some might prefer this campsite to the Buckskin sites anyway, as it's closer to the springs located another 2-3 kms downcanyon. Just a couple of bends downriver from this campsite are a couple of alcove-type caves.

About 3 1/2 or 4 kms below The Confluence, is a nice campsite and a usually good spring the author calls **Wall Spring**--near mile P9. It's had a good flow of water each time the author was there, but Skip, the former Paria Ranger, recalled times where its flow was so low, it was hard to get a safe drink. But normally you can rely on this spring.

About 500m below Wall Spring is a good campsite and another spring, which may in the long run be more reliable than its neighbor upstream. This spring, near mile P10, is at or near a side-canyon this author calls the **1st Crack**. It's the result of a minor fault, as are all 4 of the Crack Canyons shown on **Map 30.**

From Wall Spring, the canyon runs a little northeast, then southeast. Between the 1st & 2nd Crack Canyons, you'll pass 3 large alcoves or overhangs. These undercuts are similar to those found in West Canyon, Coyote Gulch and elsewhere. A km or so beyond the first overhang or alcove, is another overhang where the river undercuts the Navajo Sandstone wall. About 800m beyond that is a feature known as an **abandoned meander**, or an abandoned stream channel--near mile P11. A few thousand years ago, the Paria River ran through this channel, but it slowly undercut one of its walls in

Taking water from Wall Spring. The river is just to the left.

the process of making a gooseneck turn. It finally abandoned the old loop for a new one. The former stream channel is 5m-6m above the present level of the river. It may be worthwhile to take a break from wading the river and check this out. The access is easy and there are camping possibilities on the north side of the meander. About 350m below this is the last of the 3 undercuts and the possibility of a minor seep.

Just before you arrive at the **2nd Crack**, you'll come to the best spring in the canyon. This one is called **Big Spring**. Across the river is another good, very popular campsite--near mile P12. If that site is full when you arrive, just go downstream a ways to find still more camping places and springs--near mile P13.

Right at the very end of what the author calls the 2nd Crack, is another possible spring. It flows out of this little side-canyon with a good discharge--at least when the author saw it the first time. If you're a rock climber, it might be fun to look for a route out of the canyon to the south and up this 2nd Crack. Someone who is experienced with chimneying might be able to get out of or beyond the first set of ledges, and find a way up this crack canyon to the south rim. It looked promising, for a real tough climber.

Beyond the 2nd Crack, the Paria tends to the northeast again, and you enter a section of the canyon where there are few if any springs. Between 2nd Crack and the Adams Pump, there are no springs of any consequence, just river water. The author has placed several springs on the map, but they are mostly just minor seeps, and may or may not be of any use. This part of the canyon has some very tight turns, very high walls and it's as narrow as any part of the Paria River below the area just above The Confluence. The author has labeled this section **The Goosenecks**--even though the entire gorge is one gooseneck bend after another! You'll be walking in the stream as often there as anywhere along the hike.

About 600m below the 2nd Crack, is a bench on the right or south, and a big horn sheep & hiker's trail going up into what is likely yet another abandoned meander high above the present stream channel. Here's another corner the author didn't fully explore, but there could be a way out of the canyon higher up.

Near the end of The Goosenecks is the **3rd Crack**--mile P14. It, like the other 2 upstream, is a little inconspicuous. It's hard at times to follow the river channel on the map; that's part of the reason these crack canyons are not easily seen. It's also a little difficult to keep your orientation (north-south) as you walk down this narrow gorge. A compass is helpful.

Just beyond the 3rd Crack and on your left, is another **abandoned stream channel.** It's maybe 10m-15m above the river level, and easy to get into. The author followed it for a ways, then returned the same way. But it appears on the *Wrather Arch 7 1/2' quad*, to be a kind of double abandoned meander--that's just below mile P14. It might be worthwhile to take the time to check this one out. It could also make an interesting campsite if you can get up inside it.

Less than 2 kms below the 3rd Crack you'll come to the **4th Crack**--near mile P15. This one is more obvious than the previous 3, partly because the canyon is beginning to open up and become wider. From the rim above, it appeared that a good climber could possibly make it out of the canyon to the north, using this very narrow slit in the wall, but the author didn't take the time to try it. In the 4th Crack running south, there are some ledges to skirt and a little climbing, but from the top of the **Adams Trail,** where the author looked down on it, it appeared to be climbable, at least for an experienced person.

Big Spring has 2 parts, right and left. Each has a nice flow and it's easy to fill water bottles.

Above Both pictures were taken below Big Spring. The foto on the right shows one of 3 big alcoves or undercuts in this section.

Left A typical scene along the Paria in the area of the 4 crack canyons. This wall is covered with desert varnish. This is caused by rainwater running down the wall and leaving behind mineral deposits rich in iron.

About 500m beyond the 4th About 500m beyond the 4th Crack, and on the south side of the creek bed, is the beginning of the old Adams Trail. More interesting than the trail itself, is the hard-luck story behind it.

The Adams Trail and Water Pump

The area south of this middle part of the Lower Paria River Gorge is called the Sand Hills by all the local cattlemen; the Paria Plateau by others. The name Sand Hills is very fitting, as the topmost layer of rock is made up mostly of the Navajo Sandstone. When it weathers away, it forms very sandy conditions. Because of the sand, the only way to get around the plateau is to walk, ride a horse or use a 4WD.

Despite the poor travel conditions, the area has been used for cattle and sheep & goat grazing since about the mid-1880's. It's fairly high, rising to 2043m on the southern edge at Powell's Monument and elsewhere above the Vermilion Cliffs. This means it has good pasturage, and it's surrounded on 3 sides by impassable cliffs or canyons. To the north is the Buckskin Gulch, on the north & east is the Paria River Gorge, and on the south are the Vermilion Cliffs, which rise up 500m or 600m above the valley floor. The only easy way onto the plateau is from the west and the Coyote or House Rock Valleys.

Throughout the years, cattlemen slowly but surely began to develop water facilities in the Sand Hills, as there is no running water, and not one good reliable spring on the Plateau. They built small dams below exposed slickrock slopes to catch whatever rain fell. They blasted holes in the slickrock to make stock tanks, and of course there were already natural potholes or tanks in the slickrock. The number of cattle was always small and limited by the available water. Despite all the hardships, things went well for 50 years or so. Then a long drought began in the early 1930's which coincided with the Great Depression.

During this drought period, there were several different cattlemen who had livestock on the Sand Hills range. The northeast quarter of the plateau was used by a man named Johnny Adams. As he began to see his cattle die of thirst, he started looking down into the Paria Canyon for water. He must have pondered long and hard as to how he might get his cattle down to the year-round flowing river-- or how he might get some of that water up to his cows.

Finally he thought he had the problem solved. He investigated pumping equipment and had come to the conclusion that with available technology and pumps, he could move water from the river to the rim, a vertical distance at one point of about 215m. So in the winter of 1938-39, he made the decision to build a rough access trail to install pumping equipment. After searching the rim, he found a place, which with a little dynamite and work, could be used.

The **Adams Trail** was hacked out of the canyon wall in the spring of 1939, and the pump, gasoline engine, and 300m of 5-cm (2") pipe were trucked in over the Sand Hills access road. For the last part of the journey, pack animals were used to haul the equipment in.

According to P.T. Reilly, the man who researched the history of this pumping station (which is written in the **Utah Historical Quarterly, #2, 1977**), it was Dean Cutler who straw-bossed the job for Adams who was rather elderly at the time. The remaining crew members were Lorin Broadbent, Eugene McAllister, and Lynn Ford. The country was very rough, and getting the equipment to the rim was a major undertaking. Water and food were packed in, and the most luxurious comfort was one's

Left The beginning of the Adams Trail which is an easy scramble. **Right** Looking back upcanyon at the sandslide, part of the cactus patch, and the Adams Trail (right side).

to warm up.

Their first job was to construct a rough trail to get the motor and pump down to the river. It was never intended to be a good trail, only good enough for men to scramble up & down. Horses were apparently never taken up or down the trail. The men lowered the pump and motor down the cliffs with ropes, one step at a time. Finally the pump and engine were in place, then pipe was carried down one section at a time and attached.

It was well into summer when they installed the last section of pipe. They had intended to fill several potholes which were just above the rim. When the pipe was finally in place, they climbed down to the river to give it a try. But the river was very muddy, the result of storms upstream. They decided to abandon any pumping until the creek cleared. But that night it rained. It filled all the stock tanks and potholes. The drought was over, and the pump was never even tested. There it sat for 2 years.

In 1941, Adams sold the pump to another cattlemen, A. T. Spence. But Spence never used it. He ended up selling it to Merle Findlay in 1944. The pump continued to sit and gather dust & rust. Findlay owned the unused pump for 4 years, then sold it to Gerald Swapp in 1948.

Gerald Swapp's cattle range was the area north of the Paria, called the Flat Top and East Clark Bench. It was, and still is, a good grazing country, but lack of a good water supply has always restricted the potential of the range. After mulling over the idea of pumping water from the Paria up to the benchland for 10 years, Swapp finally bought the unused and untested pumping rig to give it a try. His intention was to pump water into the lower end of **Judd Hollow**, which is about 3 kms downstream from where the pump was originally set up at the bottom of the Adams Trail.

To do the job, Swapp hired Eugene McAllister, who was one of the original members of the crew who put the pipe & pump in place, and Tony Woolley. In December, 1948, the 3 men walked down into the canyon along the trail, got the engine running and got a good flow of water out the upper end of the pipe.

Later, in January of 1949, under some rather cold conditions, Woolley rode a horse down the Paria Canyon, in similar fashion to the feat performed by John D. Lee in 1871. The pipe was all disconnected and placed in bundles, then tied together at one end. A rope was tied to the cross-tree of the saddle, and the pipe was dragged down the partially frozen stream to Judd Hollow. The 4 cylinder, Fairbanks--Morris flathead engine and the pump, were carried on horseback downstream, one at a time.

To avoid damaging the pump by using it with muddy water, the crew dug a sump at the edge of the north bank of the stream. It was a hole, lined with rocks, which would allow water to filter in slowly, thus avoiding the muddy water when the stream was running high. Their intention was to run the pipe directly up to the bottom of Judd Hollow, a rise of 300m. Then they hoped to run it northeast for another 3 kms to a tank in the area where cattle were located. This would require much more pipe. So Woolley rode the horse downcanyon to Lee's Ferry, while Swapp and McAllister hiked back up the Adams Trail to the truck and drove back to Kanab, to get more pipe and a booster for the pump.

But things just didn't work out for Swapp. He had been ill throughout the ordeal of replacing the pump & pipe, so he decided to remain in Kanab until he felt better. However, he got worse instead. Finally he was taken to the hospital in Cedar City, where he died on March 28, 1949.

After this second effort to pump Paria River water upon the benchland surrounding the canyon, no one ever tried the feat again. And there it sits today; the engine, pump and one length of pipe running

The upper part of the Adams Trail as it runs up the cliff face from lower right to upper left.

one ever tried the feat again. And there it sits today; the engine, pump and one length of pipe running into the ground where the sump was dug. You can still see it on the north side of the stream, on a low bench, at the mouth of Judd Hollow between miles P17 & P18 on the BLM log map. More on this later.

Now back to hiking. To find the **Adams Trail**, walk downstream about 300m from where the south arm of 4th Crack drains into the canyon. On the south side of the creek, on a minor bench, and in an area which is rather broad, look for yet another rounded bench rising about 10m above the embankment. You may first notice some moki steps notched into the sandstone wall. It's possible these could be old Indian-made steps, because they're very smooth and worn today. The author never did make it up the steep part using these steps. But just to the east or left (as you look at the sloping rock wall), is a near-vertical 1m-2m-wide crack in the sandstone bench. You have to use all-4's to make it up, but it's easy climbing. For a closer look at this trail, see the little insert on **Map 30, Lower Paria River Gorge--Part 2.**

Once you arrive on this first bench, walk east along a good trail, gradually turning to the right or south. Almost immediately you begin to walk up a steep sandslide covered with cactus. To avoid damaging this pristine cactus field, follow the established hiker's trail as it veers to the right and southwest, then turn south into a minor drainage. Further up you'll come to the base of a talus & sandy slope on the right. Head straight up this slope which comes down from where a minor drainage comes off the wall in front of you. As you arrive near the top of this sandy slope, you begin to see part of the original constructed trail. Near the top, and almost next to the canyon wall, turn right or northwest, and walk along the base of the cliff. After about 100m, you come to more cliffs and at first it appears to be a dead-end. At that point, look to the left, or south along the cliff face, and you'll just be able to make out a faint line indicating the trail angling up along the cliff face. Walk up this ramp, which is a little steep in a place or two, but which is easy walking. An unloaded burro may or may not make it up, but a big horn sheep or deer would have no trouble.

Further along you come to a level section, then less than 100m away, you'll again come to what is obviously a constructed trail. It zig zags up one last steep place to the southwest before running due south up the minor drainage you saw from below. At the top of this draw, the trail vanishes in the sand.

This is an easy walk, and it seems a pity no one took the time to finish the trail. Just a little more work, and it would be good enough for a horse to use. Once you get on the trail, anyone can make it to the top in about half an hour. From the top, you can walk along the rim in either direction for some fine views of the canyon below.

Now going downriver again. Between the Adams Trail and the mouth of Judd Hollow, the river makes several tight bends and is again enclosed in high walls. After about 1 1/2 kms, you'll come to a 250m section where several large boulders have fallen off the canyon wall and landed in the stream channel. In this part, the river meanders back and forth between rocks. In times of flood and high water, deep holes are scoured out next to some of these boulders. If you're there not long after a flood, you may encounter the deepest water of the entire hike. A walking stick would be helpful, but on the author's last trip in 2003, there was a trail of sorts around all these boulders mostly on the north bank, so deep wading may be a thing of the past.

The Adams Pump. Motor on the right, the pump & pipe to the river is on the left.

Aerial view looking west at The Confluence of the Paria River & Buckskin Gulch. The Buckskin Gulch is in the upper and right-hand side of this foto.

Aerial view looking southward at the Double Abandoned Meander near the 3rd Crack.

An Episode of Military Explorations and Surveys--October, 1872

This place, which the author calls **Boulder Alley,** may have been the place which inspired a story to be written about the Paria Canyon by a member of the October, 1872, military expedition to the region. The author found this story, **An Episode of Military Explorations and Surveys,** in the **October, 1881** issue of **The United Service.** It was written nearly a decade after the event, and for obvious reasons. The author is identified only as T. V. B., and it goes like this (edited slightly for this book).

I know that the hero of the following narrative would rather lose his tongue than speak of a noble deed performed by himself. Nevertheless, every noble action deserves to be known. I beg the Lieutenant's Pardon.

In the month of October, 1872, the different field-parties composing "explorations and surveys west of the one hundredth meridian," rendezvoused near St. George, in Southern Utah, and after a week spent in preparations for the final work of the season again broke camp, the writer being assigned to the "party of the southeast," of which Lieutenant W. L. M., of the corps of engineers, had charge. The duty assigned to this "party" was the exploration of the "rim of the Great Basin" of Southern Utah, thence to go to the Colorado River, ascend and explore the Canyon of the Paria, and return.

After a couple of days' march, the greater number of packers and escort were left in camp, as it was thought that a smaller party could do more effective work, and the number of explorers was reduced to ten,--Lieutenant M., Mr. W., topographer, a cook, two packers, two soldiers, a Mormon, a Pah-Ute, and myself. The Indian was to be our guide, but as he only knew enough English to ask for whisky, the Mormon was taken along as interpreter.

In those high regions the nights were already disagreeably cold, so that after making camp we would pile up half a dozen dead pine-trees and start a fire that lit up the pine woods for miles, and sometimes even compelled us to shift camp, much to the disgust of our Pah-Ute, who was fearful of a visit from his dreaded foes, the Navajos, and did his best to convince us that one could warm himself better over a small fire than a large one, generally finishing the pantomime by telling us that "whitey man big fool!"

In due time we struck the "Great Navajo Trail," used by the Navajo Indians in their annual trading expeditions to the settlements of Southern Utah, and here our Indian became quite frantic with anxiety to go back to his own hunting-grounds, pleading that "his father never went farther;" but he had to stay with us, and every morning, without fail, he mysteriously showed us the footprints of savage enemies who had been lurking about the camp through the night--though we failed to see an Indian during the entire trip, or had even a mule stolen.

The party derived considerable amusement from the repugnance of the mule ridden by Lieutenant M. for the Pah-Ute: neither did time do much towards reconciling the two. Whenever the Indian made his appearance unexpectedly before the lieutenant's charger, off came the lieutenant and away went the mule, a maneuver to which our chief at last became so accustomed that rather than be violently ejected from the saddle, he would gracefully slide off when he saw "coming events cast their shadows before," and he owned, good-naturedly, that when that mule wanted him off he might as well come. So the Indian was quite as much a trial to the lieutenant as to the mule.

We encamped on the Paria River two miles from its junction with the Colorado. I speak of the Paria as a river because it is honored with that rank on the maps, but feel as though I owe the reader an apology for deceiving him, for in a less arid country it would scarcely be dignified with the name of creek. But in this respect the pilgrim of the great trans-Rocky Southwest cannot afford to be fastidious. In these water-scarce regions everything having the appearance of running water is at least a creek, and the imagination delights in exalting a creek into a river. So on all the maps of New Mexico and Arizona the Rio Colorado Chiquito [Little Colorado River] figures prominently, and would readily impose itself upon the unwary as a second Mississippi, yet memory vividly and lugubriously recalls the times when, not in one particular locality but in many, I boldly straddled it with my legs, and in that position washed my soiled undergarments; and worse, for too often it contained no water to wash with at all.

Two miles from our camp, at the junction of the Colorado and Paria, amid that weird scenery, isolated from all the world, was the ranch of John D. Lee, late bishop and major in the Mormon Church. The martial bishop was not often at home, and Mrs. Lee No. 17, with her nine children, garrisoned the ranch and battled with the elements for a livelihood.

In the mean time we had lost our Indian and his adjutant, the Mormon, much to the relief of Lieutenant M.'s charger. The two worthies had, from the beginning, overloaded their stomachs with ham and bacon, articles of diet to which the Indian and Mormon stomach is not accustomed, and had brought upon themselves severe bilious attacks.

The canyon of the Paria, which we were now to explore, was estimated to be about thirty two miles in length, and it was said that no human being had ever succeeded in getting through it. A flock of geese, the Mormons told us, had swam through the canyon, from the Mormon settlement of Paria to the Colorado River, and though we did not succeed in getting through it ourselves, our very failure, me-thinks proves that we were not geese.

Early on the morning of November 20 [1872] we started on the performance of what we all knew would be a difficult and dangerous task. At first the gorge was several hundred yards wide, the walls of the canyon sloping and not more than seven hundred feet in height; but with every mile the canyon narrowed and its walls became higher and more vertical, until at the end of five miles it did not average more than thirty yards in width, while the walls had attained a vertical height of fifteen hundred feet. The creek occupied the middle of the chasm, and often the entire space, from wall to wall, so that we were obliged continually to cross and recross it, as well as ride against the stream, a task which was rendered more difficult by oft-recurring patches of quicksand in which our animals became mired, obliging us to make frequent halts to dig them out. In this way we accomplished ten miles the first day, camping in a cottonwood grove where the canyon had widened, and where enough grass grew to feed our animals.

The next day the difficulties increased. Occasionally the walls met overhead forming caverns dark as night, through which we waded and half swam, often compelled to bend over the saddle, so low was the rocky ceiling. Nor was the labor of urging the bewildered mules through these dark passages an easy one. That night we encamped, wet and chilled, on a peninsula of rocks large enough to accommodate ourselves and our animals.

The third day was bitter cold. Soon after starting the mule, ridden by the cook, Kittelman, a mid-

dle-aged German, whose duty on the march it was to lead the burdenless bell-horse, sank, belly-deep, in quicksand, and stuck fast, keeling over on his side and lying on Kittelman. We were occupied half an hour digging out the mule, during which time it required the strength of two men to keep the mule's head above water, and of one to perform a similar office for the poor cook. The mule, in his struggles, frequently struck Kittelman in the face, so that the latter, when extricated, was badly bruised and stupid from cold and excitement. No time was to be lost, however, and in his half-frozen condition the man had to mount the bell-horse and follow the party.

We now found ice formed in localities where the water was deeper and less rapid. This increased in thickness from one-eighth to one-half inch, when our mules refused to take to it farther, and we found ourselves compelled to dismount, wade up the icy stream, often to our armpits in water, and here and there break the crust of ice by means of our carbines, rocks, etc. This task was performed by Lieutenant M. and myself, for which purpose we kept a few hundred yards ahead of the party, leading our mules.

About 3 P.M. we came to a sharp bend in the canyon, where the water had cut into and undermined a portion of the wall, forming a large and deep pool about fifty feet wide and forty feet long, which was also covered with a crust of ice, half an inch thick. This pool we must needs cross. After breaking up the ice with large rocks, I attempted to wade through it, but when about ten feet from the edge sunk knee-deep in quicksand and was fain to scramble back. I then mounted my mule and attempted to ride him in, but no amount of either urging or coaxing would induce the otherwise tractable animal to take to the water. Lieutenant M. then made the attempt with his mule, with the same result; the animals instinctively shrank back. By this time the remainder of the party had come up. The bell-horse had been ridden by the cook since the accident of the morning, and was saddled. I was about to mount him to ride him through the pool, knowing that he would obey under all circumstances, when Kittelman, though shivering with cold and scarcely more than half conscious, anticipated the movement, saying that he was not afraid to ride his horse where any other man was willing to go. The animal entered the pool without hesitation, and had gotten nearly halfway across when, as if sucked down, man and horse disappeared. In about twenty seconds the man's head again came to the surface, as well as that of the horse, Kittelman no longer on the horse but evidently still clutching the bridle,--his gaze vacant. After a few seconds, to our horror, man and horse again disappeared, and now it was that we began to realize that a human being, our companion and servitor during months of exploring, was about to perish before our eyes--almost within reach of our hands--and we utterly powerless to help, for who would plunge into that ice-covered pool, occupied as it was by a horse struggling for life?

Among the party was a packer by the name of Evans, a large, powerful man. He had passed most of his life in Oregon, and his swimming-feats on the Columbia River, as related by himself, surpassed those performed by Leander and Byron. To him all eyes were now turned and there he stood, the picture of sickening fear and cowardice. Lieutenant M. now called out in agonized tones, "My God! will nobody save that man?" and hearing no response, without waiting to disencumber himself of overcoat or boots, he plunged, head foremost, into the awful hole. After fifteen seconds of terrible suspense, during which the horse had regained the surface and crawled to the rocks on which we were assembled, Lieutenant M. reappeared, holding the body of Kittelman in his arms. The latter was still alive, but only drew breath four or five times after leaving the water. We at once placed him on a pile of blankets, and four of the party chafed him vigorously for an hour and used other means of resuscitation, but in vain--he was dead.

In the mean time one of our packers had scaled a crevice in the rocks, to a point where a lot of stunted cedars could be seen, of which he threw down a sufficient quantity to keep up a fire during the night. Though not unused to hardships and stirring scenes, I shall never forget that night's camp. We were upon a peninsula of rocks, just large enough to accommodate the party; beside us flowed the dark stream; over us rose to a vertical height of over three thousand feet the rocky walls of the chasm, but a few stars being visible. The body of Kittelman lay a few feet from the fire, covered by a blanket. The glare of the fire served only to intensify the weirdness of the scene. Added to this was the knowledge that should tomorrow be an unusually warm day the snow would melt in the mountains, the stream would rise, and we should be drowned like rats in a cage before the end of the canyon could again be reached.

So we waited anxiously for morning. The body of Kittelman was sewed up, sailor-fashion, in a piece of canvas and packed on a mule, the frozen bones cracking horribly during the process. We carried the body with us for about two hours, when we came upon a crevice in the rocks, some twelve feet above low water, and into that we laid the remains and covered them with rocks, assured that no human hands would ever disturb them.

And though we returned to the mouth of the canyon unsuccessful, and with a life less, we had gained a hero more.

T. V. B.

Portions of this military episode in the Paria Gorge are obviously exaggerated and were written to entertain. Very seldom is there quicksand in the canyon, but horses could easily get quagmired. Their feet cover less area than do humans, but they might have 10 times more body weight. John D. Lee however did take a herd of cows down this same canyon, almost exactly one year before this military expedition, and it took him 8 days to get from Pah Ria (Rock House) to the Colorado River.

Going downstream again. About 700m below Boulder Alley, where the big rocks are in the stream channel, you'll come to the **Adams Water Pump** on the left, about 5m above the creek. Just behind the pump is another of many abandoned meanders in the canyon. Less than one km below the pump and on a sharp bend in the river, are several good campsites, possibly a good spring and one panel of petroglyphs--between miles P18 & P19.

Just below the petroglyphs, you'll normally begin to see seeps along the stream's edge. Along the river between the petroglyphs and The Hole are many places where you can camp and get water--just above mile P19. Each time the author visited this part of the canyon they were flowing.

The next feature of interest is **The Hole,** which is near mile P19 on the new BLM map. The Hole is the very bottom end of a canyon draining off the Sand Hills which flows into the Paria. All you'll see from the river is this lower end. At the very bottom of this drainage, and right next to the river, the seeping waters have eroded away the sandstone, making an alcove or cave-like feature shaped like an inverted key hole; thus the name.

This niche in the canyon wall is known as The Hole. Normally there's water seeping out at the bottom of the big dryfall.

where the water falls when it comes off the slickrock country above. Near the entrance to The Hole, you can set up camp on a little bench, which is completely under a big overhang. This would be a good place to camp for those hardy souls who prefer to travel without a tent. The seep will likely have water when you arrive, although it's not on anybody's *"best springs list"*. Upstream about 50m or so, is another seep, which had a good flow upon each of the author's visits.

It's in the area below the Adams Pump that the canyon begins to widen, and from The Hole down, it continues to open up even more. Between The Hole and Wrather Canyon there isn't anything special to see, except there are many places with scattered cottonwood trees which could make good campsites. Only problem is, the author doesn't recall seeing many good seeps.

Wrather Canyon

Wrather Canyon is one of the real gems of the Lower Paria River Gorge. It's a short side-canyon, only about one km long, but it has one of the most interesting & impressive arches in the world called **Wrather Arch.** There's also a spring not far below the arch, which provides water for a small year-round flowing stream in the lower part of the canyon. This is between mile P20 & P21 on the new BLM map.

As you approach this canyon from upstream, you'll be looking right into it. But as the stream inside Wrather comes near the Paria, it turns abruptly east and parallels the Paria for maybe 250m. You'll have to reach the very mouth of Wrather Creek before you can enter this drainage. Inside the canyon, a hiker-made trail runs up to and underneath the arch. Along the way is a good example of riparian vegetation. There are several huge cottonwood and box elder trees, water cress, mosses, cat tails, and other plants this author can't describe. It's a little green paradise in the middle of the desert.

Because the bottom of Wrather is so narrow and fragile, the BLM asks that hikers not camp in the canyon. There's not much space anyway. Instead, camp at the mouth of the canyon across the river to the north, and/or in one of several groves of cottonwood trees nearby. When you go up to the arch, take your empty water jugs to be filled. By not camping inside the canyon, you can also help preserve the good quality of water for those who follow in your footsteps.

Wrather Canyon Overlook Hike & South Rim Indian Route

For those with a little time who like climbing and want a break from trudging along in this seemingly endless gorge, here's a diversion. Take a hike to the canyon rim right above Wrather Arch.

From the campsites at the mouth of Wrather, head downcanyon about 750m. At about that point you'll be passing through an area of tall grasses, sort of like bullrushes. On the right or south side, will be a low bench which you can breach easily. Above this low bench is a triangle-shaped sandslide coming down from the southeast. Walk straight up the sandslide toward its apex. As of 2003, there was an emerging hiker's trail; follow it up. At the top is a steep gully coming down to the top of the sandslide. Climb right up this mini canyon or couloir, sometimes right in the bottom, or to the left side. This may be a little steep for some, but it's easier than it first appears because there are many good hand & footholds.

At the very top of the gully is the most challenging part of the entire hike. There are 2 short cliffs or dropoffs you must scale. The height is only about 3m each, and there are plenty of hand and foot

Map 31, Lower Paria River Gorge--Part 3
Wrather Canyon to Bush Head Canyon

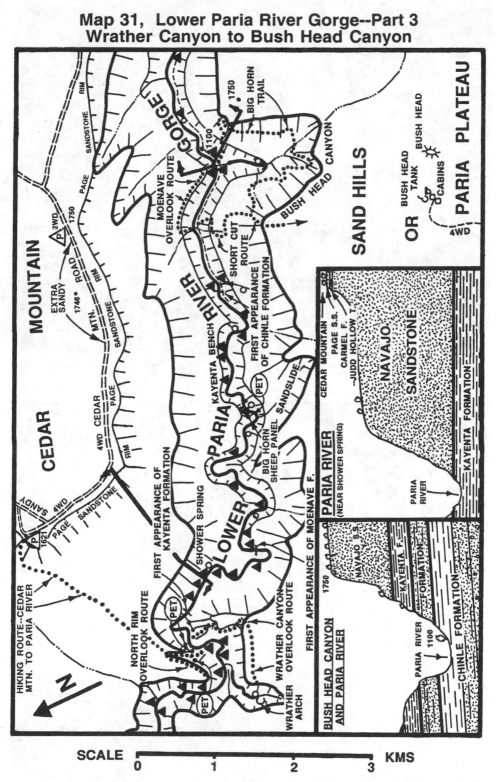

SCALE

0   1   2   3   KMS

From the canyon rim looking straight down on Wrather Arch. This is one of the largest and most unusual arches in the world. Its single support leg is on the right.

Underneath Wrather Arch, the single support leg on the left. Don't bypass this one.

holds, but the sandstone is a little crumbly. Just take your time, and test each handhold. The author had no major problem, but some may want a short rope to add a touch of security, or to lower packs on the return trip. Going down is a little more risky than going up, so if you have an extra short rope consider tying it off and leaving it there. If only one member of a group can get up, then all others should be able to make it.

At the top of the gully, make a hard right turn and head due west just a few meters, contouring around the corner on an emerging hiker's trail. You'll be just below some massive Navajo Sandstone cliffs. Shortly, you'll turn south, still bench-walking or contouring towards another minor fairly steep drainage. It comes down from the pass to your upper left. There's now a faint trail up this slope.

Upon arriving at the top, rim-walk west towards the edge of Wrather Canyon. You should reach the rim directly above the arch. It looks a lot smaller from above than when you're in the canyon, indicating the great height of the wall you're standing on. On one trip to the rim, the author spotted 3 desert big horn rams on the rim directly above the arch. This hike may be one of the best side-trips in the whole canyon. Take fotos of the arch from about midmorning through midday.

North Rim Overlook Hike & Indian Route

If you're a natural bridge watcher, here's a hike that will place you high on the north rim of the Paria directly across from the mouth of Wrather Canyon. From this overlook, you can see right up Wrather for one of the best views of the arch.

Begin at the campsites at the mouth of Wrather and walk downcanyon about 300m. As you pass the last corner, look straight ahead to the north and to the left a little, and you'll see a kind of crack canyon, similar to the fault-made cracks further upstream. It's shape and geologic origin become very clear when viewed from the south rim.

Head straight for the crack, passing where you can through the low cliff or bench made by one of the lower layers of Navajo Sandstone. Just as you're about to enter the bottom of the crack canyon, look to your right and at the corner, and you'll see a good panel of **petroglyphs.** In about the same area on your left or west, is a single rock art figure which is hard to see. To the author and others, this indicates an old **Indian trail or route**, as they normally made etchings along well-traveled routes. This is the only place in the canyon where you can go from rim to rim, with a quick river crossing in between. There's another panel of petroglyphs on the other side of the river (the author couldn't find this on his last trip?), at about the place you begin the hike up to the Wrather Canyon Overlook, lending more credibility to the idea that this is an old Indian trail or route across the canyon.

As you enter the narrow chasm, you'll be climbing due north. The way is easy at first, then it steepens and narrows. The upper part is almost vertical, but since it's right on the fault line, there was a buildup of minerals in the crack, which is now exposed. This new rock, different from the Navajo Sandstone, is harder and has numerous hand & footholds. So although it's nearly vertical, and somewhere between 12m & 14m high, it's quite easy to climb. Just at the very bottom of the pitch is a chokestone you must pass on the right. With a little help from a friend, most people should be able to chimney or wedge their way up this 2m-high obstacle. Take a short rope for less-experienced hikers, especially on the way down.

After the steep pitch, it's just a scramble to the rim where you'll then make a hard left turn, and walk southwest to a point overlooking the river and the mouth of Wrather Canyon. Late morning to midday, and in late spring or early summer, would be the best time for taking fotos of the arch. Take a telefo-

Left From the south-side canyon rim looking north at the old Indian trail or route to the river.
Right Shower Spring, one of the best waterholes in the Lower Paria River Gorge.

These petroglyphs are part of what the author calls the Big Horn Panel. This has to be the best rock art site in the Lower Paria River Gorge.

An aerial view looking downcanyon at the hanging sandslide to the right. It's about halfway between Wrather Arch and Bush Head Canyon. Just below the center of this picture facing southwest is the Big Horn Panel of rock art seen in the picture above.

to lens.

Another way to reach Wrather Arch and this part of the canyon is to come down this old Indian route from above. Read all about that under **Map 33, North Rim Hikes--Lower Paria River Gorge.**

Going downcanyon again. The next important stop is **Shower Spring,** 2 kms downcanyon from the mouth of Wrather and on the left or north side. It's at mile P22 on the new BLM map. Throughout the years this one has proved to be a good reliable waterhole. Water drips off a mossy ledge into a knee-deep pool (2003), thus the name. You'll have to look for it (and listen) behind some willows--just follow the trails in the area on the left or north side of the stream. This important spring comes out of the rock right at the contact point between the Navajo Sandstone above, and the Kayenta Formation below. This indicates the permeability of the Navajo, and the impermeability of the Kayenta. Across the river is a fine campsite.

Below Shower Spring, the canyon widens still further, and the Kayenta Bench becomes more prominently exposed. Between Wrather & Bush Head Canyons, there are several minor seeps or springs, including one which comes out of the wall on the south side of the river below a big sandslide in an upper basin above. As you near the cliffs below the sandslide, get out of the creek and on the bench to the left or northeast side. At the same time, be looking up to your left at the smooth wall covered with black desert varnish. There you'll see perhaps the best petroglyph panels in the canyon. It's covered with etchings of big horn sheep, thus the name, **Big Horn Panel.** About 1 1/2 kms below the hanging sandslide & rock art panel, is the last seemingly-reliable spring in the main canyon before reaching Lee's Ferry. There's also a place to camp near mile P25.

Bush Head Canyon, Transplanting Big Horn Sheep & the Big Horn Trail

The next major stop is **Bush Head Canyon,** between miles P26 & P27 on the BLM log map. Like Wrather, this one is very short, less than 1 1/2 kms from the river to its headwall. At the mouth of this canyon are several campsites, and best of all, normally good clear water. It may or may not be flowing down to the Paria when you arrive, but even if it does, it might be best to walk 700m-800m upcanyon to where a very good spring comes right out of the bottom of the Moenave Formation. The water in this little canyon is surely good to drink as-is, because cattle don't quite make it up that far. However, the water has a kind of swampy taste to it in the lower end near the river. This is caused by decaying cottonwood and box elder leaves lying in the creek bed. At the spring itself, it's *puro agua dulce!*

Immediately above the spring, is a dryfall and you can't go up any further in the bottom of the canyon. But, for the adventurous hiker who enjoys a little climbing, here's a fun side trip. The author calls it the **Big Horn Trail.** Actually there are no real trails involved, just a couple of routes to the canyon rim that are occasionally used by desert big horn sheep.

But the story behind the desert big horns must first be told. As indicated by the hundreds of petroglyph panels in the region, almost all of which show etchings of big horn sheep, one can conclude this magnificent animal has long been a part of the scene in this canyon & mesa country. But in the period of a little more than a century since the white man first began exploring the region, their numbers have gradually shrunk. Local ranchers believe the big horns caught diseases from domestic sheep and were hunted to near extinction. It appears they virtually disappeared in the Paria Canyon,

Looking downcanyon from the top of the Shortcut Route with Bush Head Canyon on the right.

sheep and were hunted to near extinction. It appears they virtually disappeared in the Paria Canyon, so it was decided to reintroduce desert big horn sheep to this gorge.

In July of 1984, the Arizona Game & Fish Department, in cooperation with the BLM, started to carry out the plan. Because of the overgrazed desert big horn sheep range on the south shore of Lake Mead, which is part of the Lake Mead National Recreation Area, it was decided to capture some of those sheep and place them in other areas suitable for their existence. The places chosen were the Lower Kanab Creek (between Kanab and the Colorado River), the Paria River Canyon and the Vermilion Cliffs.

Altogether, 53 sheep were captured in July of 1984, of which 16 were taken to the Kanab Creek area. The remaining 37 were taken to Lee's Ferry. Nineteen were taken to and released at Fisher Springs, not far west of Lee's Ferry, and up against the Vermilion Cliffs. The remaining 18 sheep were transported by helicopter to the Bush Head Canyon area and released.

In the Bush Head Canyon release, there were 11 females or ewes, and 7 males or rams. Of the 18, five females were equipped with radio-telemetry collars. These special radios have the ability to send out a signal, not only when the sheep is alive and well, but can also detect when the animal dies with a mortality sensor. The radio signals are then monitored periodically by aircraft.

In the weeks and months following the transplant, numerous flights were made over both release sites to monitor their movements. Very little movement or migration was detected at first, but in the time since, the herd of sheep at Fisher Springs has moved out along the base of the Vermilion Cliffs, with several going into the Marble Canyon region. Those at Bush Head, seemed to stay nearer the release site. About 8 months after the release, 2 sensors noted fatalities in the Bush Head area. In late February, 1985, with the help of a helicopter, the 2 big horns were found dead, apparently having fallen from icy cliffs.

After about a year's time, it was observed that the Bush Head sheep had started migrating, perhaps on a seasonal basis, to other locations along the Paria River and to the mesa top, or the Paria Plateau. But each time the Game & Fish people fly over the region, it's been found that the sheep stay pretty close to the initial release site, indicating that location is a good one. In November, 1984, a volunteer group from Arizona State University helped to build a slickrock water catchment basin somewhere on the plateau above Bush Head Canyon. In 11/2003, while hiking up the Dominguez Trail just above Lee's Ferry, the author saw at fairly close range, 2 groups of big horns totally 11 head.

Over the years, the author made several trips up from the bottom of the Paria, just to check out the ways these sheep were getting up & down the canyon wall from the river to the rim. On an earlier trip, he saw at close range, 3 big horns on the lip of Wrather Canyon, which sparked this curiosity. In the end, he found 2 routes from the river to the rim and to the Sand Hills rock feature called Bush Head.

Here's one way to the canyon rim. **See Map 31, Lower Paria River Gorge--Part 3.** From the very mouth of Bush Head Canyon, look southeast up the steep slope. You'll see a talus slope, then a green place with tall grasses and bullrushes, indicating a wet spot or minor seep just below the first bench. Head that way, straight up to the southeast. From the first little ledge, make your way up through several more benches and minor cliffs. Remember, you're heading for the big bench, just below the massive Navajo Sandstone wall. There's an easy way through each little bench, but you'll have to zig zag a bit, and route-find on your own to find the easier places to pass through. As you near the big terrace, bench-walk or contour to the left or east a little and into a minor drainage. On the other side of this gully is one last step or cliff to get through, which is again very easy. Once on top of this, bench-walk or contour first around to the west, then south, heading toward the big south wall of upper Bush Head Basin.

As you near the headwall, you'll have to walk down through a break in the top layer of the Kayenta to the mini valley below, then route-find back up to and into the most western of the 2 alcoves at the head of the canyon. Go straight for some trees, which appear to be near a spring (but there's no spring or water).

From the head of this second draw, turn right and walk due north, still contouring or bench-walking along the top of the Kayenta. In one little mini canyon, you'll come to a cliff where it appears that'll be the end of your hike; but from there simply walk uphill to the west, then down a little ramp to the bottom, thence again contour to the north.

As you near the area southwest of the mouth of Bush Head Canyon, you'll see in front of you another small canyon coming down from the left, or west, and a sandslide just beyond. Head up this canyon, but just into it, veer to the right or northwest, and route-find up through some minor cliffs. This part is nearly a walkup all the way to the rim.

From the rim, you might choose to walk due south about 2 kms to Bush Head, or the Bush Head Stock Tank. At that old stockman's camp are 2 old cabins, a stockade-type corral, and a small concrete dam, located at the base of a little slickrock valley. If there's been rain in the region recently, this stock tank will have some water. But don't count on drinking this, it's full of cow poop! Cattle graze this area during the winter months, making the water unfit to drink.

Back at the Big Horn Trail. The longer and more scenic route has been described. If you've come up this one, but want a shorter way down, take the **Short-cut Route** back to the river. Begin this one at the very last part of the first route described. Walk straight down the cliffy slope, but when it becomes less steep, veer to the left or northwest, and make your way around some of the intertongued beds at the contact point of the Navajo & Kayenta. There is no way of describing the route, except to say you may have to zig zag a little to reach the river. At one place, the author chimneyed down a 10m-high crack in one of the ledges. If he had walked still further west, he may have found an easier way and walked down through this bench.

As you work your way down this slope, you'll see a minor drainage below. Head for it. But just as you think you've got it made, you'll come to one last cliff. The author jumped down this one, but you can walk through it if you'll veer to the right and bench-walk to the east until you come to a mini-dugway, where you walk down to the north and to the river and trail.

Whichever route you go up or down, it'll involve route-finding. There are no serious obstacles, but you may have to do some zig zagging on either of these routes to find the easy way up or down through the Kayenta and Moenave Formations. Take all the water you'll need for the day, as there's none above Bush Head Spring, and you can't get to the spring from either of the routes just described. Also, take a lunch, as you can spend a day on this one. The author lost time exploring around for the Big Horn Trail, then went all the way to Bush Head Tank, finally returning via the Short-cut Route, arriving back at camp in just under 9 hours. Without the side-trip to Bush Head Tank, it

Map 32, Lower Paria River Gorge--Part 4
Bush Head Canyon to Lee's Ferry

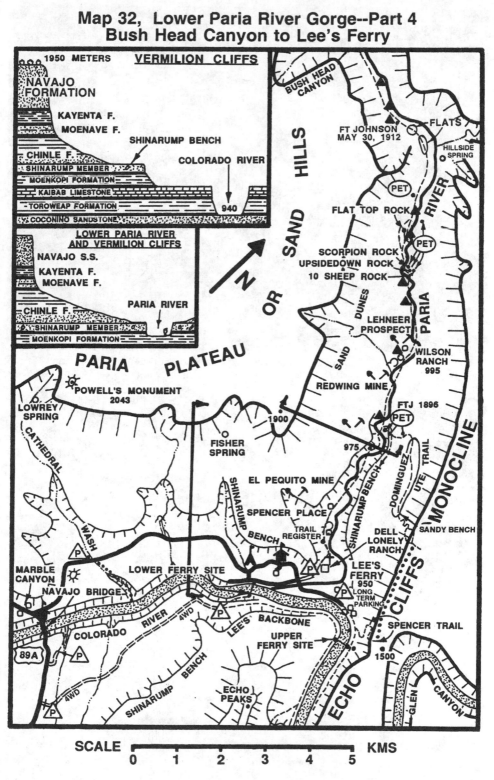

VERMILION CLIFFS

1950 METERS
NAVAJO FORMATION
KAYENTA F.
MOENAVE F.
SHINARUMP BENCH
CHINLE F.
SHINARUMP MEMBER
MOENKOPI FORMATION
KAIBAB LIMESTONE
TOROWEAP FORMATION
COCONINO SANDSTONE
COLORADO RIVER
940

LOWER PARIA RIVER AND VERMILION CLIFFS
NAVAJO S.S.
KAYENTA F.
MOENAVE F.
CHINLE F.
SHINARUMP MEMBER
MOENKOPI FORMATION
PARIA RIVER

N

PARIA PLATEAU

SAND HILLS OR SAND

BUSH HEAD CANYON
FT JOHNSON MAY 30, 1912
FLATS
HILLSIDE SPRING
PET
FLAT TOP ROCK
PET
SCORPION ROCK
UPSIDEDOWN ROCK
10 SHEEP ROCK
DUNES
LEHNEER PROSPECT
SAND
WILSON RANCH 995
REDWING MINE
FTJ 1896
PET
PARIA RIVER

POWELL'S MONUMENT 2043
LOWREY SPRING
1900
FISHER SPRING
975
CATHEDRAL WASH
EL PEQUITO MINE
SPENCER PLACE
TRAIL REGISTER
SHINARUMP BENCH
SHINARUMP BENCH
DOMINGUEZ
UTE TRAIL
SANDY BENCH
DELL LONELY RANCH
MONOCLINE

MARBLE CANYON
NAVAJO BRIDGE
LOWER FERRY SITE
P
P
LEE'S FERRY 950
LONG TERM PARKING
SPENCER TRAIL
89A
P
COLORADO RIVER
4WD
LEE'S BACKBONE
UPPER FERRY SITE
P
4WD
SHINARUMP BENCH
ECHO PEAKS
ECHO
1500
CLIFFS
GLEN CANYON

SCALE
0 1 2 3 4 5 KMS

193

Frank T. Johnson was the son of Warren Johnson. The Johnson's ran Lee's Ferry for many years.

Looking northwest. The square-shaped boulder on the right is called Flat Top Rock. It has petroglyphs right on top.

directly to camp, taking most of a day.

In 2003, the author came down the old Indian Route from the North Rim to the river, walked down-canyon to this Short-cut Route, then climbed to the top, rim-walked northwest to view Wrather Arch, went down the route describe earlier to the river near Wrather Canyon, and finally up the Indian Route back to his Chevy Tracker on Cedar Mountain. That took 9 1/4 hours.

While interviewing some of the old-timers in the region about the early-day history of the canyon, the late Mel Schoppman of Greene Haven (northwest of Page), told the author about a scheme by his father John, and Rubin Broadbent. It seems they were looking for ways to either get water up to their cattle on top of the Sand Hills, or take cattle down to the river below. They searched, and finally found a way off the plateau and down to the river at Bush Head Canyon. The route they made on horseback was along what has just been described as the Short-cut Route. They considered constructing a cat-tle trail, but it turned out to be too big a job. Years later Mel Schoppman also made it up through the cliffs on horseback. With a little scouting around, this is an easy walkup route.

According to everyone the author talked to, there are no routes up through the Vermilion Cliffs to the Paria Plateau between Bush Head Canyon and the Sand Hill Crack, discussed under **Map 36A**. Rock climbers could surely find a route, but it likely couldn't be climbed by ordinary hikers.

Now back to hiking down the Paria. As you leave Bush Head Canyon on your way to Lee's Ferry, you'll be walking along the south side of the river. You'll walk on an old cattle trail, which over the years has gradually gotten better and more distinct with the increase of hikers. Actually, from 3 or 4 kms above Bush Head, you can get on the south side of the river and stay there until you're in the area of the first of many prominent boulders with petroglyphs, as shown on **Map 32**. In this section of about 10-12 kms, you won't have to cross the stream once--unless you want to.

The reason for the trail winding its way up and above the river, is that in this part of the canyon the softer beds of the Chinle Formation are beginning to be exposed. When this occurs, the canyon auto-matically widens, and the cliffs made of the Navajo, Kayenta and Moenave Formations, begin to pull apart. As this happens, large boulders break off the canyon walls and roll down into the stream chan-nel. In this section, the stream channel itself is choked with these house-sized rocks, therefore it's been naturally easier to walk on the bench above, than right along the river.

About 1/2 km below Bush Head Canyon, you may see where **F.T. Johnson** left his inscription on **May 30, 1912**. It's on a boulder just south of the trail (to your right) with the etching facing north-west. No doubt, Frank was chasing cows! Farther downcanyon and just before you get back down to the river, look to the right or west to see a large boulder with rock art on the south side and top. That boulder is 6m-8m west of the trail.

Further along and about 750m below where you first reach the river, you'll be walking along a bench made of whitish sandstone. To your left 25m or so, you may see a red-colored boulder on top of the lighter slickrock bench. On top of that square-shaped rock are more petroglyphs. This is near mile P31. This the author calls **Flat Top Rock** on **Map 32**. From about that point, look up and to the east side of the river, and you can see a couple of boulders standing alone on the sandy hillside. One of these also has petroglyphs.

About one km below Flat Top Rock, and as you first cross over the river to the east side, are at least a dozen large rocks or boulders with panels of petroglyphs. These are between miles P31 & P32. One

This boulder is called Scorpion Rock. Can you see the scorpion on the left?

This is what the author calls 10 Sheep Rock. Every boulder in this area has rock art.

is called **Scorpion Rock**, because of a large scorpion-like figure on it. Another is **Upside Down Rock,** because half the glyphs are upside down. The rock must have rolled down the slope halfway through an etching party. These last 2 boulders are immediately left of the well-defined trail. Just around the corner and up the slope about 30m to your left, is another good one. This might be called **10 Sheep Rock**. It has, among other glyphs, 10 big horn sheep in a line. If you spend a little time there, you may find even more rock art. These *boulderglyphs* are some of the best the author has seen, and up till now, there's no paleface graffiti on them. There's a good campsite under 2 cottonwood trees just across the river and down a bit from these boulderglyphs, but you'd have to purify and drink river water.

The Wilson Ranch and old Uranium Mines

About 2 kms downstream from the petroglyphs, you may see at a point where the river turns east, some old fence posts, some minor seeps, and an old mine test hole called the **Lehneer Prospect**. Another 200m further and on your right as the trail turns south, is an old road running up on a bench. This looks like a rock wall. This may be part of the old **Wilson Ranch** (?). About 500m below that, you'll come to some large cottonwood trees on the west bank, where the old Wilson Ranch house once stood. It's between miles P33 & P34 on the BLM log map. The house foundations can still be seen, as well as a cement trough of some kind. At that point, and just behind you to the north, is the remains of a small wooden shack built next to a large boulder.

The Wilson Ranch was first built by Owen Johnson and Sid Wilson in about 1918. They gathered lumber from a sawmill on the Kaibab near Jacob Lake, and logs from Lee's Ferry, and hauled them in wagons about 8 kms upriver to this site. With this material, they built a rather large 2-room cabin, in the shape of an "L". According to the late George W. Fisher, each room measured about 6m x 8m.

It was Sid Wilson who lived there and claimed the rights to the place. Throughout the years, no one ever actually owned the ranch, but each person who lived there was able to claim and sell his squatter's rights. While at the ranch, Wilson ran some cattle, but worked at other jobs too. At one time he was the one who measured the water levels of the Paria and Colorado Rivers at Lee's Ferry.

In 1927, Wilson left and sold his rights to Pete Nelson, but Nelson didn't actually live at the place until after about 1930. In 1933, George W. Fisher bought out Nelson, and lived there until he was drafted into the military in 1944. The BLM, which in the days before 1947 was called the Grazing Service, allowed Fisher to run about 200 head of cattle during his stay at the ranch.

It was the Fishers who installed a rough wooden floor to the house and covered it with Navajo rugs. They also built a windmill and hooked it up to a small generator. The electricity first went to several batteries for storage, then was used for lights and a radio. They had a pump, which pumped water from the nearby spring to their house in a 10-cm (4") pipe. Water from the spring was also used to irrigate a small garden.

When the Fishers left in 1944, they sold it to a Navajo man by the name of Curly Tso, who lived mostly on the reservation. Curly had it for a number of years until his death, then his son sold it to the Grafs of Hurricane, Utah. Sometime while Curly owned the place, the house burned down. Then in 1974, the National Park Service bought out all the private holdings at Lee's Ferry, including the Lonely Dell Ranch. Since no one had any ownership papers on the Wilson Ranch, and it was part of the public domain, it just became part of the Paria Canyon--Vermilion Cliffs Wilderness Area. In 2000, this entire canyon became part of the Vermilion Cliffs National Monument.

The Wilson Ranch site. The house was located to the right of the trees in the background. The corral must be for wild horses because the highest logs are about 2m above the ground.

This old water pump is located just northwest of the Lonely Dell Cemetery.

Almost next to where the old ranch house stood is Wilson Spring. This spring usually has a good flow, but it seeps out of the hillside for about 30m and hasn't been cared for in many years, so you can't expect to get a safe drink there. You'd do better to go to the river for water. At one time part of the spring was developed and put into a pipe, and fenced off so cattle couldn't pollute it, but now the spring is full of cow pies and the water undrinkable. Immediately south of the willows, grass & trees, is a corral at least 2m high; it must have been used for wild horses!

Next to this corral is a rocked-up pit looking something like what mechanics used to get into when working underneath cars. Next to it is a pile of what appears to be uranium ore. This was likely part of the local mining operation. From there look south, and on a hill just to the west of the creek, can be seen a couple of mine tunnels. This was known as the **Red Wing Mine**, which dates from the uranium boom days of the early 1950's.

About 2 kms below the Red Wing, you'll see on your left a faint track running up the hill to the east. This hill is actually the Shinarump Bench, and the track is the beginning of the **Dominguez or Ute Trail**. Actually, the track you see is another 1950's uranium prospecting track, but it's apparently in about the same place as the old trail. Right where the trail begins to climb, you may see on a 1 1/2m-high boulder, more petroglyphs, including a **F.T.J. 1896.** This glyph was etched by Frank T. Johnson, who grew up at the Loney Dell Ranch and who helped run the ferry in the years after 1910. Read more on this Dominguez Trail along with **Map 34.**

About 600m below the beginning of the Dominguez Trail, and on the west side of the river, is another old mining road running upon the Shinarump Bench. There are no doubt other test prospects up there to the west. At the bottom of that road is a raised & sagging wooden platform with uranium ore stacked on top.

The Spencer Place

About 2 kms before you arrive at Lee's Ferry and the Lonely Dell Ranch is another old building with the remains of a very old car (from the 1920's) lying there rusting away. This is what the late George W. Fisher called the **Spencer Place.**

In the period between the 2 world wars, there were as many as 10 families living at Lee's Ferry, mostly in the vicinity of the old Lonely Dell Ranch. Most of them were polygamists; some of whom had been/or soon would be, excommunicated from the Mormon Church. One of these families belonged to Carling Spencer (no relation to Charles H. Spencer). It was from Carling Spencer that Fisher bought this old house or cabin in about 1940. Fisher put it on skids and dragged it up to the place where it's seen today. In those days it was simply called the Spencer Place. Fisher fixed the place up to live in part time when he wasn't up at the Wilson Ranch. Part of Fisher's time in those days was spent working on constructing roads in the area, because he couldn't make a living on ranching alone.

Less than a km below the Spencer Place is another wooden shack & corral, which are part of some of the later development of the Lonely Dell Ranch. This corral is used periodically today by cattlemen who still retain grazing rights in the area.

Just beyond this corral, and in the middle of a big flat, is a trail register where hikers are encouraged to sign in or out of the canyon (to get a count on visitor use). From that point continue straight ahead on the right or west side of the river. Soon you'll walk along a trail built along the face of a cliff. Immediately after that are the remains of several old water pumping schemes. Whenever dams were built to divert water to the fields at the Lonely Dell Ranch, they were soon washed out by floods. So later on, and to this day, water is pumped from the Paria to the orchards further on.

Just beyond the pump site is the cemetery, some old farm machinery and finally the Lonely Dell Ranch where you can see some old ranch houses. Beyond that is the day-parking lot with toilet, then nearly a km past it is the **long term parking lot.** That's where you leave your car if hiking this entire canyon. See map.

Lonely Dell Ranch

The Lonely Dell Ranch really started on December 23, 1871, when John D. Lee and wives Emma & Rachel arrived at the place late in the afternoon. Early the next morning, Emma looked around and made a comment about how lonely the place was, thus the name. It was John D. Lee who was sent to the Paria to make and run a ferry for the Mormon Church. Read more about this man in **The Story of John D. Lee and Mountain Meadows Massacre,** in the back of this book.

After Lee was captured in November of 1874 in Panguitch, the Church had to send help, because Emma Lee--wife No. 17, couldn't handle the job by herself. So they sent Warren M. Johnson to take charge and run the ferry service. That was in March, 1875. At first Johnson took his first wife, then about a year later, brought his younger second wife to the ferry. After he arrived, he built a large 2-level house, which stood until 1926.

At the time Johnson arrived, Emma owned the ferry and had squatters rights to the Lonely Dell Ranch. So she and the Johnsons both profited from the ferry service. But in 1879, the Mormon Church bought the ferry rights from Emma for a reported $3000. She then moved south into Arizona and eventually settled at Winslow, where she died in 1897.

Warren Johnson's family lived at the ranch and ran the ferry from 1875 until 1896. At that time the church decided he had completed his mission and released him. It had been a long struggle living at this almost-forgotten desert outpost for so many years. Just one of the hardships he had to suffer through, was the loss of 4 of his younger children.

In May 1891, a family passing through the area traveling from Richfield, Utah, to Arizona, told Warren about a child of theirs which had gotten ill and died in Panguitch. No one thought about it then, but 4 days later, one of the Johnson children became ill and died. A few days later other children were struck with the same sickness. All together, 4 Johnson children died between May 19 & July 5, 1891. The disease was diphtheria, which 3 other children got, but recovered from. One large grave stone, with all their names on it, can be seen in the cemetery today just north of the ranch houses.

The church replaced Warren M. Johnson with a man named James Emmett. Emmett arrived in 1896, along with his 2 wives. While he ran the ferry he talked the church into building a cable across the river, to which the boat could be fastened. This made things much safer and easier. Before that time there had been a number of accidents and drownings associated with the crossing.

While running the ferry, Emmett also did a little farming and ran cattle, part of which were in the House Rock Valley to the west. Even though that area was mostly public domain and open to all, he had troubles with the Grand Canyon Cattle Company (GCCC), which was run by B. F. Saunders and

Charles Dimmick. At one time in about 1907, Dimmick accused Emmett of stealing cattle, and it went to court. Emmett was found innocent.

But later, the GCCC got back at Emmett, by buying the ferry service from the Mormon Church in August 1909. Shortly thereafter, Emmett sold his land and property to this same company. At first the ferry was run by any GCCC cowboy who was staying at the Lonely Dell Ranch at the time. But things changed after less than a year, because the service was unreliable. In early 1910, the Grand Canyon Cattle Company hired the best men for the job--the sons of Warren M. Johnson.

Jerry Johnson arrived at the ferry in February, 1910, and was joined by his brother Frank in July, and both ran the ferry. It was these men and their families who lived at the Lonely Dell Ranch and assumed responsibility for the ferry until the Navajo Bridge opened across Marble Canyon in January, 1929. Actually the last ferry crossing was on June 7, 1928. That's when the boat tipped over with 2 cars on board. All 3 men running the ferry were drowned, and the boat floated down into Marble Canyon. Because the bridge was so near completion, the ferry was never replaced.

Because of the way the ferry was handled in 1909-1910, Coconino County became concerned about keeping this important link open. So the county bought the ferry service from the Grand Canyon Cattle Company in June 1910. Coconino County became the owner, but they hired the Johnsons to run it until the bridge opened.

In December of 1926, clothes drying near a stove caught on fire and burned down the 2-story Johnson home at Lonely Dell. It had been built by Warren M Johnson in about 1877 and had stayed in the Johnson family until it burned.

After the bridge opened, there wasn't much traffic in or around Lee's Ferry, but several polygamist families lived there during the 1930's. The Church owned the ranch for a time, then the polygamist families of Lebaron, Spencer and Johnson bought it. Still later on, the Church got it back, but then Leo & Hazel Weaver bought the Lonely Dell Ranch in the late 1930's and attempted, unsuccessfully, to run a dude ranch and raise Anglo-Arabian horses. While there, they constructed the long white stone building which sits just northeast of the cabin refuted to have been built by John D. Lee himself, and which is now called Emma Lee's (or Samantha Johnson) Cabin.

The Weavers stayed at Lonely Dell until the early 1940's, then moved out. Essy Bowers owned the ranch for a couple of years, then in 1943 sold it to a man name C. A. Griffin, a stockman from Flagstaff, who had a big herd of cattle on the Navajo Nation lands to the east. It was Griffin who first attempted to pump water out of the Paria onto farm land, rather than to build dams, which always washed out. In later years the LDS Church once again held title to the ranch.

In about 1963, Lee's Ferry was included into the Glen Canyon National Recreational Area, but the 65 hectares (160 acres) of private land remained private. In 1974, the private property of the Lonely Dell Ranch was bought by the U. S. Government and National Park Service. Lonely Dell Ranch was put on the National Register of Historic Places in 1978.

For a lot more detailed information about Lee's Ferry, read **Desert River Crossing,** by Rusho & Crampton; **Lee's Ferry,** by Measeles; and 3 books by Juanita Brooks: **John D. Lee, Zealot--Pioneer Builder--Scapegoat; A Mormon Chronicle: The Diaries of John D. Lee;** and **Mountain Meadows Massacre**.

If you're hiking up the Paria for more than one day, or doing the entire Paria River trip from the Whitehouse Trailhead, be sure to park at the large paved long term parking lot southeast of Lonely Dell instead of at the small visitor parking place at the ranch entrance.

This picture of the Warren Johnson Family was fotographed from a larger one located at an informa- tion board at the Lonely Dell Ranch parking lot (Glen Canyon NRA foto). It was taken by Frank Nims of the Stanton Survey in December, 1889. L to R: Mary, Jonathan, Polly, wife Permelia holding LeRoy, Jerry, Millie (Permelia?), Frank Warren, Laura Alice, Nancy, and Melinda. About 1 1/2 years after this foto was taken, 4 of these children (names are underlined) died of diphtheria. They are buried in Lonely Dell Ranch Cemetery with one tombstone.

Above Aerial view looking northeasterly down at the Lonely Dell Ranch (center) and Lee's Ferry to the upper right near the shadows. To the right & center is where rafters begin their trips down the Colorado River. On the far right is Lee's backbone.

Right The grave marker of John G. Kitchen, the man who created the Nipple Ranch in Kitchen Canyon.

JOHN G. KITCHEN
BORN IN CANADA
MARCH 25, 1830
DIED
JULY 13, 1898

KITCHEN

Farm equipment dating from the 1930's or thereabouts. These are located just south of the Lonely Dell Ranch Cemetery. The ranch buildings are located to the right a ways.

Part of the Lonely Dell Ranch built by Leo Weaver in about 1940. This stone building was used as part of his dude ranch operation. The National Park Service now uses it.

Depending on the source, this is either the Emma Cabin, built by John D. Lee--or the Samantha Johnson Cabin, located at the Lonely Dell Ranch. Some of the tools seen here date from the late 1800's. A cellar is on the far right in the background.

This is a blacksmith shop apparently built by Jerry Johnson in the late 1920's (?). For a time, this was used as a school.

Grave of the 4 Johnson children all of whom died of diphtheria in the summer of 1891.

The chimneys of 2 cabins is all that remains of the Upper Ferry Terminal.

The Warren Johnson home at the Lonely Dell Ranch. It burned down in 1926.
(New Mexico State Archives)

The Upper Ferry Terminal at Lee's Ferry in the early 1900's. Beyond is the south side of the Colorado River. You can still see some of the ruins at the ferry terminal today.
(Arizona State Library)

Ox teams pulling wagons up the dugway toward the Upper Ferry Terminal. (Arizona State Library)

The old wagon road leading to the Upper Ferry Terminal on the south side of the Colorado River. Straight ahead in the background, and zig zagging up the cliffs, is the Spencer Trail. To the left and out of sight on the other side of the river, is where the Paria enters the Colorado.

North Rim Hikes & Old Indian Route: Lower Paria River Gorge

Location & Access Featured here are some hiking possibilities from the high country on the north side of the Lower Paria River Gorge. Three parts of this area are known as East Clark Bench, Flat Top & Cedar Mountain. While there are several 4WD-type roads running up to this plateau from the Big Water area, the normal way to get there is to drive along Highway 89 about 5 kms east of the Paria Ranger Station & Visitor Center. Between mile posts 17 & 18, and directly across the highway from the start of the Cottonwood Wash Road, turn south. This is called the **Cedar Mtn. Road**. It's generally good for cars up to Cedar Mtn., but there is one little rocky place with a short sandy section below. However, the author's VW Rabbit & Tracker (using 2WD) did fine (in the months of October & November with a little moisture in the sand). Staying on the most-used road, drive a total of 17.5 kms (10.9 miles) to a **4-way junction**, then turn southwest into sandy country fit for 4WD's only--most of the time. Pass under the power lines at Km 20.9/Mile 13. At Km 26.7/Mile 16.6, turn right or northwest at a "T" junction near the rim and continue to Km 28/Mile 17.4, and park at 1621m as shown. This is the starting place for a hike along an old **Indian Route or Trail** to the river.

Or, if you drive southeast from the **4-way junction** on the Cedar Mtn. Loop Road, set your odometer at 0, then observe these distances from there. That loop road is sometimes graded up to the communications facility at Km 4.2/Mile 2.6, then it gets very sandy after Km 10.9/Mile 6.8, and less-used. If you have a 2WD only, it's best to go there after a good rain storm, or in the spring, fall, or winter when the sand has more moisture and is firmer. The author shifted into 4WD only a couple of times when he drove this loop road about 15 days after a pretty good rainstorm in mid-October of 2003.

In the **Flat Top** area, are side-roads out to the north side of Judd Hollow to some metal tanks & a trough, and down toward Bridger Point. See distances from the highway on the map. Both of these side-roads are sandy in places, but with a little moisture, even cars can be driven there. **But be sure to take a shovel!** Especially if things are dry.

Another possible way to reach the rim along the lower end of the Lower Paria River Gorge is from near Lake Powell. First head in the direction of Page, Arizona. Near the entry roads to Greene Heaven, leave Highway 89 between mile posts 555 & 556, and drive southwest on some pretty good well-used roads in the direction of Ferry Swale. When you leave the main roads near the power lines, watch out for deep sand.

Trail/Route The best hike here, and one for an experienced outdoor person, would be down an old **Indian Route** to the Paria. From the parking place at 1621m, walk west over the rim, hopefully following 6-8 cairns marking the route to the bottom of the steep Page Sandstone bench & rim. Once at the bottom, continue southwest about 2 kms to the canyon rim and a steep crack-like chute going down to the river. Use Wrather Canyon as a landmark to find this steep gully from the rim. Also, see **Map 31**, and read the nearby description of how to climb up from the river under the heading, **North Rim Overlook Hike & Indian Route.**

You can use this route to the Paria avoiding the fees, crowds & toilet problems at or near The Confluence. If you plan to take a big pack & camp in the canyon, include a short rope to lower packs in a couple of places, and to help beginners down & back up. Or, you can day-hike down this route to see some of the best parts of the Lower Paria River Gorge. Also, take the more detailed USGS maps for this hike. Once at the Paria, you can head downstream to Bush Head Canyon, cross the creek to see Wrather Canyon & Arch, climb the steep route up to the south rim of Wrather, or head upstream to the Adams Water Pump and/or Trail.

Here are some other hikes. From the southeast side of Cedar Mtn., you can route-find down into a side-canyon to a place called **Water Pockets**. However, you can't go too far as there are some big dropoffs halfway down. You'll also have some good views from the rim. From the north side of Judd Hollow and the metal tanks & trough, route-find down over the rim via some old ladders and a pipeline. Once into Judd Hollow, it's an easy walk down to the edge of the canyon for a look straight down at the old Adams Water Pump site located next to the river.

There are also some interesting rim-hiking possibilities from the end of the pretty good road down onto the south peninsula of **Bridger Point**. It's easy to get off the Page Sandstone Rim and to the very edge of the gorge. See **Map 30**. There might even be a route down into one of the 4 Crack Canyons from along the north rim. If you find one, please email the author.

From the usually-dry stock pond in Ferry Swale, it's an easy walk to the rim along the lowest part of the canyon. The Thousand Pockets area isn't so interesting, but the view from the area just southeast of Water Pockets is well worth the effort of getting there.

Elevations Cedar Mountain 1800m; bottom of gorge at Bush Head Canyon, 1100m.

Hike Length/Time Needed It's about 2 1/2 kms from the parking place at 1621m to the Paria, but finding the old Indian Route to the bottom may take a little time. Plan on staying all day, depending on how far you go once you reach the river. The other hikes to the rim would likely take about half a day, or less.

Water Take plenty in your car, but there should be some at the Bunting Well (?), Trough & Corral on top of Flat Top. Be prepared to purify it first, unless you can get the water before it reaches the cow trough.

Maps USGS or BLM maps Smoky Mountain & Glen Canyon Dam (1:100,000) for driving & orientation; perhaps the USGS maps MF-1475, A,B,C or D (1:62,500); and Bridger Point, Glen Canyon City, Wrather Arch & Water Pockets (1:24,000--7 1/2' quads) for hiking.

Main Attractions An unregulated way to reach the middle part of the Lower Paria River Gorge from the rim and different views of the canyon from either the north or south rims.

Ideal Time to Hike Spring or fall, and hopefully soon after some rains, as all road are made of sand. You'll seldom, if ever, see any mud out there.

Boots/Shoes Any dry weather boots for rim-walking, wading shoes if going to the canyon bottom.

Author's Experience In 2003, he drove his Chevy Tracker to the parking place at 1621m, climbed down to the Paria, heading downcanyon to Bush Head, climbed to the rim, rim-walked to an overlook of Wrather Arch, down the Wrather Canyon Overlook Route and back to his car, all in 9 1/4 hours. Next day, it was down to the river again, up Wrather Canyon to the arch, upcanyon past the Adams Pump, up the Adams Trail a ways, and almost to the 2nd Crack Canyon, and finally back to his car, all in 10 hours.

Map 33, North Rim Hikes & Old Indian Route: Lower Paria River Gorge

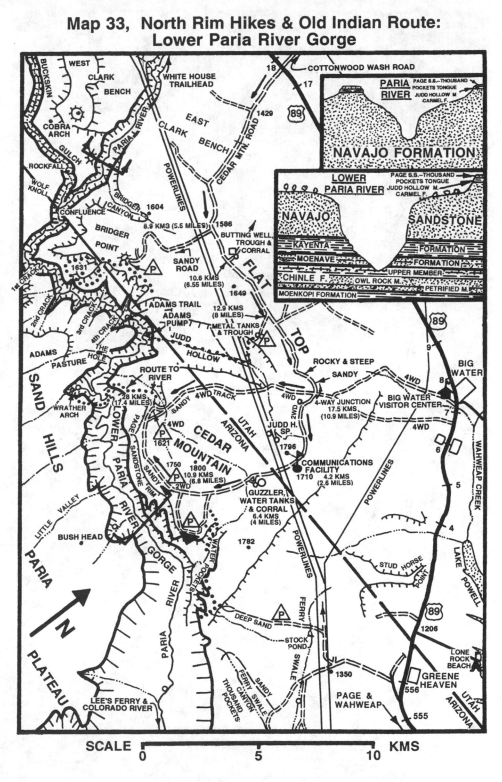

SCALE 0   5   10 KMS

Looking down at where the Paria meets Wrather Canyon (upper part). There's just a thin fin of rock separating the 2 canyons. To the left around the corner is the Indian route down to the river.

Left Looking down the steepest part of the old Indian route to the Paria River. It's easier than it first appears, but some may want a short rope to lower packs, or to help beginners down. **Right** From near the bottom of the Indian route looking back up toward the north.

Aerial view of the old Indian route to the Paria is just to the right of center. Wrather Canyon is to the left. Part of the Page Sandstone bench where you'll be parking, is to the upper right.

Left A small part of what this writer calls the Big Horn Panel, one of the best rock art sites around.
Right Looking up from the bottom of a steep pitch along the old Indian route from the river to the rim.

The Dominguez & Spencer Trails, and the Lee's Ferry Historic Sites

Location & Access Both trails featured on this map begin at Lee's Ferry. In 1776, Spanish padres Dominguez & Escalante, used the **Dominguez Trail** when looking for the Ute Ford (later called the Crossing of the Fathers) to cross the Colorado River on their historic journey back home to Santa Fe. This same trail (sometimes called the **Ute Trail**) was used by Navajos & Utes in the early days, when they would cross the Colorado River to trade with the Mormon settlers in southern Utah. The **Spencer Trail** was built by big-time promoter Charles H. Spencer, partly as a short-cut from Lee's Ferry to coal fields in the northeast, and partly to impress investors who were given the grand tour of his mining operations at the Ferry.

To get there, turn off Highway 89A at Marble Canyon/Navajo Bridge and drive northeast to Lee's Ferry. After 8.4 kms (5.2 miles) turn left or north and continue for another 350m and park at the Lonely Dell Ranch parking place. This is where you park if hiking to the Dominguez Trail. Or if climbing the Spencer Trail, park where they launch boats at the end of the road which is 9.3 kms (5.8 miles) from Highway 89A.

In addition to these 2 hikes at Lee's Ferry, another interesting side-trip would be to the south side of the Colorado River to the **Lower & Upper Ferry Terminal sites**. But don't do this without the *Lee's Ferry 7 1/2' quad,* which you can buy at the Navajo Bridge Visitor Center. To get there, drive east across Marble Canyon on the Navajo Bridge. From the bridge, continue southeast roughly 2 1/2 kms (1 1/2 miles). About halfway between mile posts 536 & 537, turn north and go through a gate (close it behind you please). From the gate you almost immediately have to have a HCV & 4WD. This route is used by Navajos going to the Lower Ferry site to fish, and they have churned up several of the steeper hillsides pretty bad, evidently using 2WD's and spinning like hell! Also, in several places, the road splits into a number of tracks; these were made by people looking for an easier way over some ledges, so stay on the most-used road. Finally, after 5.4 kms (3.35 miles), you'll come to the edge of a flat bench where you can look down on the Colorado to the left, and the 4WD road going down straight ahead. That's a good place to park, because beyond that the road does a lot of zig zagging and you can walk about as fast as driving. Park or camp there.

Trail/Route To hike the **Dominguez Trail**, walk from the Lonely Dell Ranch parking lot upstream along the Paria River Trail for about 5 kms. On the right, you will see an old mining track running up a minor slope to the east and through a break in the Shinarump Conglomerate Formation. It begins next to a boulder with some petroglyphs. Once on the bench, head southeast past another boulder with rock art, then go over a hill and down past a north-south running mining track. Cross it and head straight upslope to the east. There's nothing in the way of a visible trail here. Higher up, and on a 2nd bench, you'll come to a big sandy bench stretching out to the southeast. Walk southeast toward a low place on the canyon rim; either route-finding or following big horn sheep trails. At the south end of the sandy bench, head east straight upslope. When you reach the cliffs, you should pick up the constructed part of a trail as it zig zags up the slope, then turns south, at or near the ridge crest. There are 2 constructed cattle trails through the cliffs to the rim as shown; no doubt this was the work of the Johnsons when they were at the Lonely Dell Ranch.

The **Spencer Trail** begins just east of Lee's Fort. The bottom of the trail veers left from the more-traveled route to the Upper Ferry Terminal. Once on this path, you can follow it easily as it zig zags up the steep cliffs. If you'd like to do both trails together on the same hike, then walk up the Spencer, route-find north along the ridge crest, then head down the Dominguez. It's easier to locate the Dominguez Trail from the top than from the bottom.

Before heading up the Spencer Trail, spend some time exploring around **Lee's Fort.** There are several stone buildings in that area and you can pickup a map & guide at the parking lot. Among other things, you can see part of Spencer's old 1911 mining operation, including the **boiler**, plus the sunken remains of the stream boat, the **Charles H. Spencer**. Just upriver from that, is what remains of the **Upper Ferry Terminal.** There's more to see there than on the south side of the river.

From the suggested parking place on the south side of the Colorado River, walk down along the twisting road. After roughly 600m, be looking over the rim to the left for an old road running down to the river and the **Lower Ferry site.** This lower site is nearly one km below where the Paria meets the Colorado. This is a favorite fishing place for Navajos

Or, stay on the track going up along a dugway below Lee's Backbone. This old wagon road runs up along the chocolate-colored clay beds of the Moenkopi, then gradually descends to the river across the way from the rafters launching site at the end of the paved road. Beyond the gauging station & cable, the faint track crosses a flat area on its way to the **Upper Ferry site** and beyond.

Elevations Lee's Ferry, 950m; top of the Spencer Trail, 1450m; Dominguez Pass, 1500m.

Hike Length/Time Needed The Spencer Trail is about 2 1/2 kms, one way, and will take about 2-4 hours round-trip. From the trailhead to Dominguez Pass is about 8 kms, one way. Most could do this in 5 or 6 hours or more round-trip, returning the same way. If a loop-hike is made using both trails, it's close to 16 kms. With the ruggedness of the ridge-top, it'll likely take the average person all of one day to make the trip. If you're in a big hurry, you can walk the 4-5 kms to the Upper Ferry site (on the south side of the river) and back in 2 hours, but most people will want 4-5 hours for this hike. There are actually more things to see at the Upper Ferry Terminal on the north side of the Colorado than on the south side.

Water Always take it with you, but there is water available at several places around the Lee's Ferry area.

Maps USGS or BLM map Glen Canyon Dam (1:100,000) for driving & orientation; and Ferry Swale & Lee's Ferry (1:24,000--7 1/2' quad) for hiking.

Main Attractions Historic trails in an historic region, with fine views from the rim of the canyon.

Ideal Time to Hike Spring or fall. Summers are hot as hell, winter time can be pleasant.

Boots/Shoes Dry-weather boots, except waders for the walk up the Paria to reach the Dominguez Trail.

Author's Experience He first climbed both trails on separate trips, then in October, 1997, he parked at the end of the paved road at the boat launching site, and made the loop-hike suggested above in just over 5 hours. In 2003, and racing the setting sun, he made the top of the Spencer in 38 minutes. Later, on the Dominguez Trail, he spotted some new petroglyphs as shown, and 2 herds of big horn sheep totaling 11 head, on the sandslide below the pass. On his 2nd trip to the south side of the Colorado River and the 2 ferry sites, he parked at the suggest place and did the trip in just over 2 hours, but he was in a hurry. He also explored the Lower Ferry site the evening before.

Map 34, Dominguez & Spencer Trails, and the Lee's Ferry Historic Sites

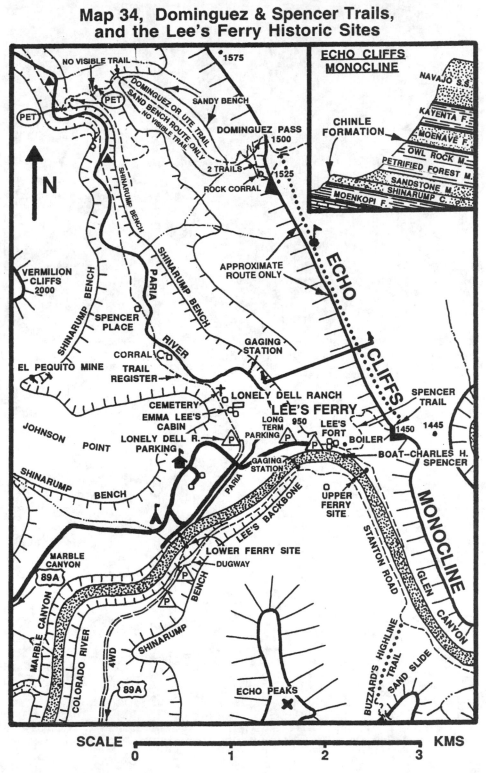

211

Aerial view looking east at the lower Paria River and the big sandy bench on which the Dominguez Trail is located. This trail or route, begins at the lower left, and proceeds diagonally to the upper right while crossing 3 sandy gullies before heading straight up to the rim.

From the lower northern end of the sandy bench looking southeast. The Dominguez Trail reaches the rim in the area of the gap between the 2 peaks in the upper right.

Above The Spencer Trail skirts to the left or north side of the boiler seen in the background. This trail zig zags up the slope in the distance. The boiler is the one used by Charles H. Spencer in 1911 & '12 in the hopes of extracting gold from the nearby Chinle clay beds.

Left Aerial view of the Lee's Ferry area looking eastward. Left of center is the Lonely Dell Ranch and Paria River. To the right is the Colorado River and the end of the road at the boat launching ramp. The Upper Ferry Terminal is in the shadows to the upper right, and the Spencer Trail runs up the slope in the upper half of this foto.

Spencer Trail
Is a historical route
and not maintained.
Hike at your
own risk.

Coyote Buttes

Location & Access Before going anywhere, read the part below about the **required permit system in the Coyote Buttes**. This map features a place called Coyote Buttes, which is a part of The Cockscomb Ridge immediately south of Wire Pass Trailhead (one entry point to the upper Buckskin Gulch). In the early 1990's, someone went there, made a motion picture, and showed it in Germany. Ever since, there's been a stampede of Europeans, mostly Germans, heading that way, along with American fotographers. The color & striations of some rocks, notably The Wave, is spectacular, making Coyote Buttes high on the gotta-go-to list for foto bugs.

To get there, you could come in from the south and Arizona. About halfway between Jacob Lake & Marble Canyon, and between mile posts 565 & 566 on Highway 89A, turn north and drive along the **House Rock Valley Road (HRVR)** to the **Wire Pass Trailhead**, a distance of 34.5 kms (21.4 miles). When conditions are dry, this is a good road for any car; when wet it can be slick in places (?). However, as of 2004, Arizona had improved the road on their side of the state line, so it isn't as bad as it once was. **See Map 36B, The Sand Hills & Paria Plateau Ranches,** for a look at the entire area including the HRVR.

But the more popular and most-used way to get there is to drive along Highway 89 about halfway between Kanab & Page. Immediately west of The Cockscomb, and between mile posts 25 & 26, turn south onto the same HRVR. Drive 13.7 kms (8.5 miles) until you reach the Wire Pass Trailhead on the right or west side of the road. This is also the most popular entry point to the Buckskin Gulch. This trailhead now has a large parking lot, public toilet, and you can camp there too, or anywhere else in the area. Hiking from Wire Pass Trailhead is the fastest, easiest and shortest way to reach the heart of Coyote Buttes and **The Wave**--the number 1 destination. Another nearby foto shoot is **Wave 2**.

Here are several other ways into Coyote Buttes via the House Rock Valley Road. Not far north of Coyote Spring is the beginning of a trail into the heart of the Buttes through **The Notch**. To get there, drive south from Highway 89 a total of 17.5 kms (10.9 miles), or north 30.6 kms (19.0 miles) from Highway 89A. As you near this area, watch for a big prominent notch, gap or pass in The Cockscomb to the east. Park where there's space, perhaps near the old rusty metal water tank 200m northwest of the HRVR. There are several places to park.

Another way to the southern end of the Buttes, and with the help of the recommended USGS maps listed below, and **Map 36B** in this book, locate your way along the HRVR, but turn east toward Coyote Spring, as shown. This turnoff is 21.3 kms (13.2 miles) from the north & Highway 89; or 26.9 kms (16.7 miles) from Highway 89A. Drive southeast about 500m and park on top of the hill before going down the steep dugway to a locked gate below. That gate keeps people away from the Northcott Ranch house at the spring. By parking there, you can walk around the ranch on the way to **Paw Hole** at the south end of the Buttes. If you have a 2WD car, this is one way into Paw Hole, **but it's longer and not recommended.**

The best way to Paw Hole, is to drive south from Highway 89 for 26.7 kms (16.6 miles); or 21.4 kms (13.3 miles) north from Highway 89A. At that point, a road heads east for 350m to Lone Tree Reservoir. If you have a 2WD, better park there; or if it's colder weather with moisture in the sand & you have some pretty good clearance, you might try going further--otherwise the road beyond is **very sandy** and for **4WD's only**. From **Lone Tree Reservoir**, drive ESE up hill for about 2.1 kms (1.3 miles), then turn left or northward at a "T" junction. After about another 1 1/2 kms (1 mile) you'll see a sign blocking the road asking that you walk from there. Paw Hole is 250m straight ahead. From there, the very sandy track heads east, just south of Paw Hole, towards the Poverty Flat Ranch.

Here's one way into the **Cottonwood Spring & Cove area**. Using **Map 36B**, turn east from the HRVR onto the Pine Tree Pockets Road. That junction is 32.8 kms (20.4 miles) from the north & Highway 89; or 15.3 kms (9.5 miles) from the south & Highway 89A. Immediately west of that junction is a corral. Head east in the direction of the ranch house at Pine Tree Pockets, but turn northeast at the windmill & metal water storage tank known as the **Corral Valley Well** (5 kms/3.1 miles from the HRVR). From there, you must have a **4WD or walk!** The name Sand Hills tells the tale!

When you reach the old **Poverty Flat Ranch house** (14.7 kms/9.1 miles from the HRVR), you could turn west to reach Paw Hole, but be warned--the sand around that place is incredibly deep, so you'll need a 4WD with low range to get there! Or head due north past the ranch, windmill & airstrip; later go through a gate (close it behind you please--that gate & fence separates 2 cow pastures) and up to a corral near the pass marked 1737m. The sand gets real deep on the north side of that pass (as of 2003, part of that road downhill to the north was a virtual canyon 3m deep due to a cloudburst!), so park your 4WD in some cedars where the parking symbol is shown (18.5 kms/11.5 miles from the HRVR).

Because of deep sand on all roads surrounding the Poverty Flat Ranch, the best time to go into that region, or anywhere else in the Sand Hills, is right after a good rainstorm, or in the winter season (late October through March) when there's normally more moisture in the sand. When deep sand gets really dry, even the best 4WD's have a hard time.

Trail/Route The normal starting point for the route to **The Wave** is the **Wire Pass Trailhead**. On the east side of the parking area is an information board & sign-in place. Read instructions, do what you have to do, then walk east across the road on an obvious trail and into the dry creek bed; or along a marked trail (there are 6 signs pointing out the way on this short trail, but when you get close to The Wave, BLM rangers kick over any stone cairns marking the route to this hard-to-find place--figure that!). If you stay on the trail, it will join the dry creek bed after about 200m. About one km from the trailhead, and as you're heading in a northerly direction, you should see an old road/trail and many footprints going up the steep hill to the right or east. Go up this hill (if you continue along the dry creek bed you'll soon be in the Buckskin Gulch). About 300m-400m from the creek bed will be the trail register for Coyote Buttes. Continue southeast on an old sandy road to the bottom of the first drainage, then veer left and follow tracks east over a low divide in this slickrock ridge. About 50m after you cross the little pass, veer right or southerly and route-find along the eastern side of the same north-south running ridge. Follow this map and other people's tracks as best you can over mostly slickrock.

Roughly 9/10's of the way to The Wave, you'll look down on a sandy valley with 3 medium-sized cottonwood trees, and not far beyond, a dry wash running out of Sand Cove, which is to the southwest. See the foto below which also shows a vertical crack-like feature behind or south of The Wave. This is something you can see for much of the way to The Wave. It's also the best landmark to shoot for. From the wash, you'll see 2 sandslides coming down from the south, also 2 trails; walk up one of these directly to The Wave. It's located about 200m from the dry wash, and about 50 vertical meters

Map 35, Coyote Buttes

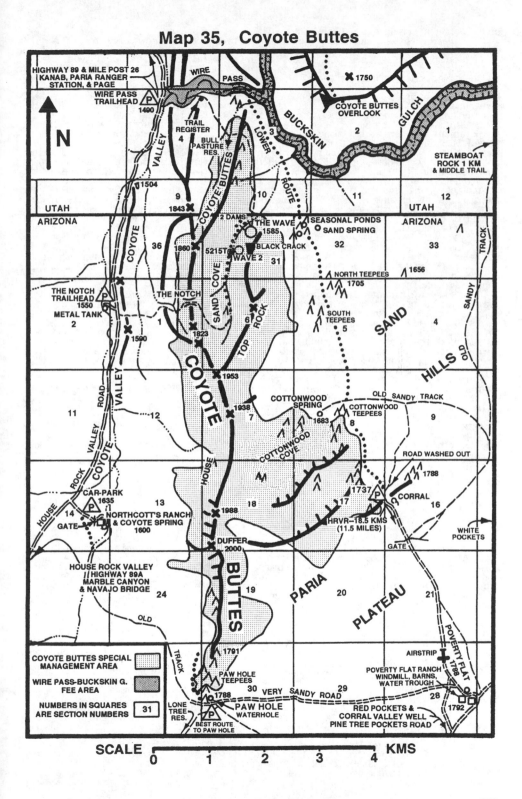

HIGHWAY 89 & MILE POST 26
KANAB, PARIA RANGER
STATION, & PAGE

WIRE PASS
TRAILHEAD P
1490

WIRE
PASS
BUCKSKIN
GULCH

X 1750

COYOTE BUTTES
OVERLOOK
2   1

STEAMBOAT
ROCK 1 KM
& MIDDLE TRAIL

TRAIL
REGISTER
4   BULL
PASTURE
RES.   3

LOWER

ROUTE

V 1504
V 1490
X 1843
9

COYOTE BUTTES

1   10

11   12

UTAH
ARIZONA

COYOTE

36

2 DAMS
X 1860   5215T
WAVE 2

THE WAVE
1585
BLACK CRACK
31

SEASONAL PONDS
SAND SPRING

32

UTAH
ARIZONA

33

THE NOTCH
TRAILHEAD P
1550
METAL TANK
2

X
THE NOTCH
X 1590
1

SAND COVE

TOP ROCK

X 1823
6

NORTH TEEPEES
1705

SOUTH
TEEPEES
5

1656

SAND

X 1953

X 1938
7

COTTONWOOD
SPRING
1683

COTTONWOOD
TEEPEES
8

OLD SANDY TRACK

9

HILLS

OLD

TRACK

11

COYOTE VALLEY ROAD

12

HOUSE

COTTONWOOD
COVE

ROAD WASHED OUT

1788

CAR PARK
1635 P
14
GATE
NORTHCOTT'S RANCH
& COYOTE SPRING
1600

13

COYOTE

X 1988

18

17

1737 P

HRVR—18.5 KMS
(11.5 MILES)

GATE

CORRAL
16

WHITE
POCKETS

HOUSE ROCK VALLEY
HIGHWAY 89A
MARBLE CANYON
& NAVAJO BRIDGE
24

DUFFER
2000

19

BUTTES

PARIA

20

PLATEAU

21

OLD

TRACK

X 1791

POVERTY FLAT

AIRSTRIP
1788

POVERTY FLAT RANCH
WINDMILL, BARNS,
WATER TROUGH

28
1792

PAW HOLE
TEEPEES
30   VERY SANDY ROAD   29

1788
LONE
TREE
RES. P
BEST ROUTE
TO PAW HOLE

PAW HOLE
WATERHOLE

RED POCKETS &
CORRAL VALLEY WELL
PINE TREE POCKETS ROAD

COYOTE BUTTES SPECIAL
MANAGEMENT AREA

WIRE PASS-BUCKSKIN G.
FEE AREA

NUMBERS IN SQUARES
ARE SECTION NUMBERS   31

SCALE   KMS
0   1   2   3   4

N

up the north end of a ridge called **Top Rock**.

Other nearby fotogenic sites are in Sand Cove and what some are now calling **Wave 2**. To get there, follow the dry wash into Sand Cove about 1000m (1 km), instead of climbing up to The Wave. Aim for the tiny cluster of buttes labeled **5215T** on the *Coyote Buttes 7 1/2' quad*. Wave 2 is 250m ENE of this butte, but 70m above it on a bench. Climb up steep slickrock. You can also get there by bench-walking southwest from just above The Wave, and into Sand Cove. At Wave 2, you want shadows, so be there just after the sun comes over the ridge to the east, maybe 9 am to 10 am; and just before the sun drops below the western ridge. Be at **Butte 5215T** around mid-day--you don't want shadows there. Butte 5215T has some nice color & striations on it's south side. See picture. This site even rivals The Wave and Wave 2. Other nice places are the North & South Teepees.

If you don't have a permit, you can still go to **The Teepees** which are outside of the **Special Management Area**. Instead of taking the trail to The Wave, continue down the Wire Pass drainage toward Buckskin Gulch for about another 800m or so, then look for one of several ways out of the canyon to the south. This will be just before you enter the Wire Pass Slot. Once out of the drainage, and on top of any high point, look SSE and you should see the North & South Teepees and other rocks near Sand Spring (dry) on the horizon in Section 5. Walk cross-country east, then south along the approximate route shown on the map. You can also get there by walking west from The Wave.

Another emerging trail into The Wave and Sand Cove, is through **The Notch**. From the HRVR near the rusty metal water tank, head east. You should soon pick up trail. On the first ridge, hop a fence, cross a sagebrush flat in the next valley going east; as you cross the flat you'll see a good trail/old road running up the south side of a little canyon. Once into that minor canyon, continue southeast on a trail, then veer north cutting across the bottom of The Notch. Here you'll see several BLM fiberglass signs marking the way. Soon you'll veer south and eventually reach The Notch. From there, veer right on a sandy trail contouring south, then east, and down into the slickrock valley called **Sand Cove**. Head northeast down the drainage to see Wave 2, but don't forget to see the foto op just south of the butte marked 5215T on the quad. Or, near the bottom of the drainage are a couple of old historic rancher-made sand-filled cement dams and maybe some water(?). About 150m below the ruins of the 2nd dam, veer right or south with all the other tracks, and climb up to The Wave.

The **easiest & recommended way to Paw Hole** is from **Lone Tree Reservoir**. If you have a 2WD, walk the road discussed above all the way. Paw Hole is a sometimes-water-filled natural pocket or depression surrounded by teepee-shaped rocks. From Paw Hole, you can also walk north along the west side of these teepees; and if you stay down in the sand, you can legally do this without a permit. On this map north of the road on either side of Paw Hole is wilderness, with the Special Management Area shaded. The other way there is from near Coyote Buttes. Walk southeast cross-country to avoid the ranch house and corrals (Northcotts own the buildings & water rights, but not the land near Coyote Spring). Once in Coyote Valley, stay left or east of the dry creek bed, to find the faded remains of an old road. Stay on this faint track all the way to Paw Hole.

From the road & pass north of the **Poverty Flat Ranch**, walk northwest into the area east of **Cottonwood Cove** and south of **Cottonwood Spring**. There you'll find the **Cottonwood Teepees**, but be careful wandering around--there are lots of small erosional fins of rock sticking up that go crunch when you step on them. Or if you don't have a permit, you could legally walk due north from the corral & pass to the North & South Teepees avoiding the Special Management Area.

Elevations Wire Pass Trailhead, 1490m; The Notch Trailhead, 1550m; pass near Cottonwood Cove, 1737m; high point in the Buttes, 2000m; The Wave, 1585m.

Hike Length/Time Needed It's less than 4 kms from Wire Pass Trailhead to The Wave, and if no stops are made, should take up to 1 1/2 hours; most people spend 4-6 hours for the entire hike. From the car-park near Coyote Spring to Paw Hole is about 5-6 kms and will take about 1 1/2 or 2 hours each way. From Lone Tree Reservoir to Paw Hole is about 3 1/2 kms in deep sand; this should take a couple of hours, or a little more, round-trip. From Wire Pass Trailhead to The Teepees via the Lower Route is about 7 kms and will take 1 1/2 or 2 hours one-way. From the HRVR to The Wave via The Notch Trail is only 3-4 kms, but may take 1 1/2 hours or more one-way. Time and distance to the Cottonwood Teepees area will depend on how far you can drive.

Water Always take plenty in your car and in your pack, especially if 4WD'ing north of Poverty Flat Ranch.

Maps USGS or BLM maps Kanab, Smoky Mountain, Glen Canyon Dam & Fredonia (1:100,000) for driving & orientation; Pine Hollow Canyon, West Clark Bench, Poverty Flat & Coyote Buttes (1:24,000--7 1/2" quads) for hiking. Sorry, The Wave and Coyote Buttes are exactly where 4 maps meet!

Main Attractions The Navajo Sandstone in the Coyote Buttes is colored red, yellow, white and maroon, plus it has interesting shapes and erosional features. The Wave seems to get all the attention, but Wave 2 & just south of butte 5215T, the various Teepees and other similar sites are great too.

Tips for Photographers Take plenty of film/memory cards. Use film that's heavy on reds & yellows; or pump up these colors on digital shots at home on your computer. Under exposing a little seems to bring out the colors on film. A Polaroid filter might help (?) with film cameras. The Wave has a NNW to SSE component, and you don't want shadows! So from early November to early February, be there between 10:10 am & 10:50 am for best results. A month on either side of these dates will give you a slightly larger window. In the 2 months before/after June 21, which is daylight savings time, be there from about 10 am to 2 pm. Also, be there on a day with 100% pure, clear, unfiltered & unadulterated sunshine--something that's difficult under the present booking & reservation system! **Write and complain! Read more below.**

Ideal Time to Hike April, May and early June, and September & October. Summers are pretty hot, plus there's desert haze. Winters can bring crystal clear skies and it's easier to get reservations or a walk-in pass, but it can also be pretty cold, plus there's a very small window for foto ops.

Boots/Shoes Running or athletic-type shoes that won't leave black scuff marks on rocks.

Author's Experience Once, he left his VW Rabbit at the Corral Valley Well and walked to Cottonwood Spring and back in 8 hours. Later he drove his Chevy Tracker to the pass & corral and spent 4 hours in that area. He walked from the Wire Pass Trailhead to The Teepees via the Lower Route and returned, all in 4 hours. He walked from the car-park near Coyote Spring to Paw Hole and back in 3 1/2 hours. Using The Notch Trail, he made it to The Wave and back in 3 hours, but was in a big hurry. Once he hurried into The Wave via the normal route but missed the best time frame with the sun. Round-trip was 2 hours, but you'll want lots more time than that. Another trip to The Wave via Wire Pass took 5 1/2 hours round-trip; but that also included a quick trip down the Buckskin for pictures. Walking most of the way to Paw Hole from Lone Tree Reservoir took 1 1/2 hours round-trip.

Permit Requirements for Coyote Buttes
Special Management Area--2004

Before going into the heart of Coyote Buttes, which is the shaded area on the map, you're supposed to have a permit. Below are the **latest rules & regulations** as outlined in a BLM handout for 2004. However, be warned! BLM policy can change at the drop of a hat, so see the website **www.az.blm.gov/paria** for the latest changes or updates!

Permits Required--US$5 per person. **Coyote Buttes North** (this includes **The Wave**, Wave 2 & Sand Cove)--20 people/day--10 with advanced reservations, 10 for walk-ins. **Coyote Buttes South** (Paw Hole & Cottonwood Cove)--20 people/day--10 with advanced reservations, 10 for walk-ins. Group size limit 6 people. Coyote Buttes are for day use only. No overnight camping permitted. Dogs and the use of horses are not allowed in the Coyote Buttes Fee/Permit Special Management Area. Campfires or burning of trash/toilet paper prohibited. Please carry out all trash. Guides, outfitters and certain organized groups require a separate Special Recreation Permit.

To Make Reservations There are 3 ways you can get one of the 10 reserved permits issued daily, up to 7 months in advance, for the North & South Coyote Buttes:

1. Online To quickly view available hiking dates, secure a reservation, and pay fees (credit card only), visit the Paria Canyon Project Website at: **www.az.blm.gov/paria.** If you do not have access to the internet or cannot obtain access at your local library, call the Arizona Strip Interpretive Association (ASIA) at 435-688-3246; or the Kanab BLM Field Office, 435-644-4600 and a staff member will access the web for you.

2. Mail Mail your request & payment of fees to: ASIA, Paria Project, 345 E. Riverside Drive, St. George, Utah, 85790. Or the Kanab BLM Field Office, 318 N. 100 E., Kanab, Utah, 84741.

3. Fax Fax your request & credit card payment (number?) to ASIA, Paria Permits, 435-688-3258. Or the Kanab BLM Field Office, 435-644-4620.

Permits for available hiking dates may also be purchased in person at one of several BLM office locations including Kanab, St. George and the Paria Ranger Station & Visitor Center near mile post 21 on Highway 89 about halfway between Kanab & Page.

Once your hiking date is reserved, a permit & map will be mailed to you, or you may choose to pick it up at one of the locations listed above.

To Get Walk-in Permits 10 Walk-in Permits for the **North Coyote Buttes** and **The Wave** are available every day for the **FOLLOWING DAY**. Between **March 15 & November 15**, drive to the Paria Ranger Station & Visitor Center located near mile post 21 on Highway 89. The Paria Station opens at 8:30 am. If more than 10 hikers are present, they will draw permits from a hat at 9 am. Walk-ins are not on a first come, first serve basis--all applications received before 9 am will be given the same priority. Few people go to the **South Coyote Buttes,** so they will give you a permit on the spot for the same day!

In the winter months, from November 16 to March 14 (always subject to change), obtain a walk-in permit at the Kanab BLM Office, 318 N. 100 E. Call 435-644-4600 for further information, or any changes in policy which is about a 100% possibility!

Comments on How to Change Public Policy on
Coyote Buttes Permit Reservation System

The above stated requirements for 2004 are constantly being reevaluated as this is being written and will surely be modified as soon as this book goes to press! In the opinion of this writer, that part of the BLM which sets the policy for Coyote Buttes is now being dominated by the lunatic fringe of the Southern Utah Wilderness Alliance (SUWA), an organization this writer has been a member of for many years.

The BLM policy of permits and especially reservations, has turned this into a first class bureaucratic nightmare, because a few radicals in the environmental movement want everyone to have a *true wilderness experience in the Coyote Buttes.* Another bunch out in California tried limiting the number of people going up Mt. Whitney on weekends too, but there was such public outrage they had to reverse themselves (now they've gone back to the nightmare!). For sure, those making the policy for Coyote Buttes have all been to places like The Wave, maybe several times, and all before this reservations system was set up. And since they work for the BLM, they have the right to go there anytime they want without getting a reservation or permit. They don't have to jump through all the hoops the rest of us are required to. It seems some BLM employees want to keep this place a big secret, and part of their own little private sanctuary. But remember, it's our land, not the BLM's!

One of the legitimate issues BLM policy makers worry about in allowing more people to visit The Wave, is that everybody walks right on the places they want to fotograph. In time, some black-soled shoes may leave scuff marks--but none have ever observed by this writer as of the fall of 2003. Even if scuff marks do occur, the next rainstorm wipes them away--this is soft sandstone, remember! Instead of asking hikers to just wear soft-soled shoes into the area, this writer suggests everyone remove shoes entirely while at The Wave; that way 500 people a day could visit the place and would do no more harm than with the present policy. Beyond The Wave, there are few other places in Coyote Buttes where walking all over colorful rocks would have a detrimental effect, but some policy makers use this argument to justify their actions. What this present policy seems to be doing is creating a type of forbidden fruit, which everyone wants to taste, just to see if it's really poison. In the end, and with this type of bureaucracy in place, people will just go out there anyway, with or without a permit, and not pay the user-fee.

Here are more suggestions this writer offers the BLM.

1. Have everyone pick up a one-day user-fee permit when they arrive at the Kanab BLM office, the Paria Ranger Station & Visitor Center; or with the increased fee collections, install a small trailer house at Wire Pass Trailhead and have a seasonal ranger sell permits there. That person could also inform hikers on proper ethics in the more sensitive areas, and recommend other places to get great pictures. That person could also make periodic hikes to The Wave to make sure everyone has a permit. This would eliminate the Soviet-style bureaucratic nightmare of getting reservations.

2. Charge $5 a day for a user-fee per person, and have no limitations on visitor numbers. If it turns cloudy, they can buy another permit and go out again the next day with better light & sun. If things get too crowded on weekends or holidays, charge a higher fee for those days.

3. Install a sign at the entrance to The Wave asking that all shoes be removed. A solar-powered toi-

let could also be placed near The Wave, but out of sight, to eliminate that potential problem.
4. The BLM should erect a line of cairns or markers of some kind to show the way to The Wave-- instead of kicking them over like rangers are doing now! That way everyone would stay on one narrow path instead of wandering all over the place. The route to The Wave seems to be the only place on earth, or in any wilderness area, where the custodians don't want to make an easy-to-follow trail!
5. For every rule or regulation the BLM makes, someone has to be hired to go out and enforce it. By eliminating the reservation system, more money could be used for onsite personnel to educate the public on the potential problems.
6. Since the Utah Olympics, there have been 20 permits issued each day for The Wave (North Coyote Buttes), 10 of which have been walk-ins. But in talking to no less than a dozen hikers who have been there, none saw anywhere near that many people out there. Rumors say that some wilderness radicals are grabbing up reservations with no intention of going to the Buttes (?). They just want to keep people out. Or, fotographers are reserving 3 or 4 days in a row to insure they have a sunny day (?). This is another good argument for eliminating the reservation system.
7. For those who want a *true wilderness experience*, go to a million other places! By eliminating the reservation system, everybody who gets a permit will likely go and enjoy it. And Europeans who come from halfway around the world will at least have a fighting chance to see The Wave.

Why not try a new policy with no quotas and see what happens. If there ever were crusty fins at The Wave, they are now long gone--so little if any more damage can occur. The only problem that could occur is that fotographers may have to direct traffic to get their shots. And the only thing that will be lost is the *true wilderness experience* as defined by SUWA. Please keep in mind, this world is getting smaller by the day, and the population getting larger. So we're all going to have to get used to the idea that some special places, like The Wave & Coyote Buttes, are going to be popular destinations, even though they're in a wilderness area. Also, there are at least a million other places, just on the Colorado Plateau, where people can enjoy solitude. The way it is now, with 20 people allowed to visit The Wave daily, can this be called a true wilderness experience? Not quite!

This writer has never heard of anyone trying to deny tourists the right to go to Delicate Arch in Arches N. M. when they wanted to, just so there wouldn't be so many people in their picture. There's never been anyone try to limit the number of tourists walking all around Bryce Canyon's hoodoos, just so some can have a wilderness trip. Same with Zion Narrows! In most of our national parks, better facilities have been created to handle bigger crowds and more traffic.

This writer would much rather be at one of these places with a crowd, than to be required to make reservations 7 months in advance. People still have to walk 4 kms to The Wave, and the access road will remain dusty or muddy, so the herd heading that way will never be that large.

If you feel the same way about this nightmarish reservation and/or quotas system as this writer, please write a letter with your opinions to the BLM, 345 East Riverside Drive, St. George, Utah, USA, 84770, Tele 435-688-3246; or to the Kanab BLM Office, 318 North, 100 East, Kanab, Utah, USA, 84741, Tele 435-644-4600; or the Utah State Headquarters of the BLM, 324 South State Street, #301, Salt Lake City, Utah, USA, Tele 801539-4010.

The BLM sets public policy on your public land, so please write letters or make telefon calls. If they don't hear from you, they think everyone approves of what they're doing. In the past, the BLM has been more responsive than some other government agencies (especially the BLM) when it comes to incorporating public comment into policy; hopefully that same trend will continue.

This picture shows part of The Wave which is always in shadows. It's located immediately west of that part seen in the foto on the opposite page above.

Looking NNW at The Wave seen at about 10:35 am in late November. This has become one of the most sought-after fotographic scenes around in recent years. Please wear shoes that don't leave scuff marks, because you'll be walking right on the place you intend to fotograph.

Looking northward at the South Teepees, one of the nicer scenes around.

About 9/10's of the way to The Wave, you should come to this sandy flat with 3 cottonwood trees. See the dark crack in the upper middle part of this picture? The Wave is below and to the right of that crack. Get up to The Wave via one of 2 sandy slopes in the center of this picture.

People are now calling this feature Wave 2. You can get there by contouring southwest from The Wave; or by going up the drainage into Sand Cove and turning left or east from the little butte marked 5215T on the *Coyote Buttes 7 1/2' quad*. Climb 70m upslope to the east to get there. You want shadows, so be around in the morning and/or later afternoon. (Lars Janssen foto)

Paw Hole is in the center of this picture, below and to the right of the butte on the left. It was dry in December, 2003 because of the drought, but it normally has water in the fenced-off area in the center of this foto. Best way to get to Paw Hole is via Lone Tree Reservoir.

In the upper part of this foto is Butte 5215T on the *Coyote Buttes 7 1/2' quad*. This is the south side of that butte looking north. It's is in the lower end of Sand Cove and is one of the nicer places in Coyote Buttes for taking pictures. Be here in the middle of the day--no shadows wanted.

The Sand Hill Cracks & Bonelli Spring Indian Trails, the Condor Release & History of the Sand Hills Ranches

Location & Access The Vermilion Cliffs is the wall of rock rising prominently north of Highway 89A. You'll see it as you drive between Jacob Lake, and Marble Canyon/Navajo Bridge & Lee's Ferry. Along this entire escarpment are only 3 easily climbable routes up through the Navajo Sandstone part of the cliffs. One route is up past a seep called **Bonelli Spring**. Because there are petroglyphs along the way, and Anasazi ruins on top, the author is calling this the **Bonelli Spring Indian Trail.** To get there, drive along Highway 89A roughly halfway between Jacob Lake & Marble Canyon/Navajo Bridge. Between mile posts 560 & 561, turn off the highway and first drive west, then go through a wire gate--please close it behind you. From that gate, head east parallel to the fence for 200m, then turn left or north for a total of 2.4 kms (1.5 miles). At that point is a road junction; this is the wilderness boundary and the Honeymoon Trail. Stop & park, and walk from there--or about 200m to the west where the old road continues to head north.

The other 2 routes up through the Vermilion Cliffs are called the **Sand Hill Cracks.** There's some confusion on which route is actually called the Sand Hill Crack. The author was told by several people years ago that this name applied to the twin canyons north of the old stone building at **Jacob Pools.** However, on the *Emmett Hill 7 1/2' quad,* it's the smaller, less-conspicuous crack just to the east that's labeled Sand Hill Crack. This writer is now calling that the **Eastern (Sand Hill) Crack.** To get to both of these old Indian trails, turn north from Highway 89A between mile posts 557 & 558. Drive through the unlocked wire gate, closing it behind you. Continue north on a good sandy road for 3.1 kms (1.9 miles). There you'll find the old ranch house & corrals called Jacob Pools (which is on a small piece of private land). Park at the old stone building, which is on the Honeymoon Trail, as well as the southern boundary of the **Paria Canyon--Vermilion Cliffs Wilderness Area.**

Trail/Route From the Honeymoon Trail & wilderness boundary below **Bonelli Spring,** walk north along an old sandy road to and past some livestock watering troughs. Further along, this old track ends near the bottom of a sluffed-off section of the Vermilion Cliffs. From there, follow a trail along the plastic pipeline, which brings water from Bonelli Spring down to the troughs. When you come to the first steep part, veer left into a gully to avoid the first cliffs. Just above these cliffs is a flatter area, then steeper talus. From there, you can barely see Bonelli Spring, which is about halfway up the cliff face and at the base of the Navajo Sandstone part of the wall.

There are 3 parts to Bonelli Spring; the western seep has 3 cottonwood trees; the middle part has a square mine-like tunnel with water inside; and the eastern seep which seems to be dry like the one on the west. From the easternmost-spring with the half-buried engine & water pump, climb due north up the steep talus slope to the vertical Navajo wall, which has a panel of petroglyphs, indicating this was a route for aborigines. From there, turn left or west and make your way to another protruding wall, which is the bottom part of a steep crack. Scramble up that narrow defile on all-4's. At the plateau rim are several stone Anasazi Indian ruins and 3 cement watering troughs. Read the history of Bonelli Spring below.

Sand Hill Cracks Walk north up an old unused track from **Jacob Pools** to the base of the cliffs just below Hancock Spring. Once there, don't go left on the little trail with old pipe coming down from spring--instead, turn 90° east and look for some stone cairns marking the beginning of a big horn sheep & hiker's trail up to the top. After a short distance, you'll find what is now a pretty good trail marked with stone cairns all the way. It gradually turns left and heads due north up through the vari-

Looking north at the stone building at Jacob Pools. The Sand Hill Crack is seen in the background to the right. That's the route with the pinnacle.

Map 36A, The Sand Hill Cracks & Bonelli Indian Trails, the Condor Release & History of the Sand Hills Ranches

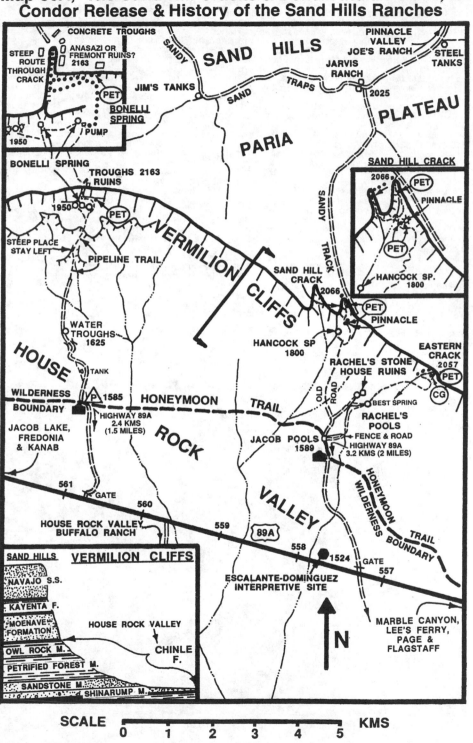

CONCRETE TROUGHS

STEEP ROUTE THROUGH CRACK

ANASAZI OR FREMONT RUINS? 2163

SAND HILLS

PINNACLE VALLEY JOE'S RANCH

STEEL TANKS

JARVIS RANCH

JIM'S TANKS

SAND TRAPS

2025

PET

BONELLI SPRING

SAND

PLATEAU

PUMP

1950

PARIA

BONELLI SPRING

TROUGHS 2163 RUINS

1950

PET

SAND HILL CRACK

2066

PET

PINNACLE

STEEP PLACE STAY LEFT

PIPELINE TRAIL

VERMILION

SANDY TRACK

PET

SAND HILL CRACK

HANCOCK SP. 1800

CLIFFS

2066

PET

PINNACLE

WATER TROUGHS 1625

HANCOCK SP 1800

EASTERN CRACK 2057

HOUSE

TANK

RACHEL'S STONE HOUSE RUINS

PET

WILDERNESS BOUNDARY

P

1585

HONEYMOON

TRAIL

OLD ROAD

BEST SPRING

CG

JACOB LAKE, FREDONIA & KANAB

HIGHWAY 89A 2.4 KMS (1.5 MILES)

ROCK

RACHEL'S POOLS

FENCE & ROAD

JACOB POOLS 1589

HIGHWAY 89A 3.2 KMS (2 MILES)

561

GATE

560

HOUSE ROCK VALLEY BUFFALO RANCH

559

89A

VALLEY

HONEYMOON

WILDERNESS

558

1524

GATE 557

TRAIL

BOUNDARY

SAND HILLS

VERMILION CLIFFS

NAVAJO S.S.

KAYENTA F.

MOENAVE FORMATION

HOUSE ROCK VALLEY

CHINLE F.

ESCALANTE-DOMINGUEZ INTERPRETIVE SITE

MARBLE CANYON, LEE'S FERRY, PAGE & FLAGSTAFF

N

OWL ROCK M.

PETRIFIED FOREST M.

SANDSTONE M.

SHINARUMP M.

SCALE

0 1 2 3 4 5

KMS

ous breaks in the cliff. When you reach the base of a prominent spire or pinnacle, look around its western base to see several panels of petroglyphs. Walk around this pinnacle on the left or west side, then head straight up the steep drainage behind it. As you near the top, look closely at the wall to the right or east to see more rock art. Because of the existence of these petroglyphs, we can surmise this is another old Indian trail. At the top of the cliffs are the Sand Hills or Paria Plateau. On the rim is an old sandy track you can use to walk to the Jarvis Ranch & Pinnacle Valley.

To reach a 3rd old Indian route, called here the **Eastern (Sand Hill) Crack,** you could walk northeast from Jacob Pools on an old road in the direction of several springs called **Rachel's Pools.** From the clay beds below the ruins of Rachel Lee's old stone house (which is just above the green area), walk east to the main spring as shown on this map. Or, you can bypass the ruins of Rachel's old house and walk east from the stone building at Jacob Pools on another old road paralleling a fence. After 500m, the road turns north into a minor canyon. This washed-out track leads up to the main spring. From that spring, look up to the left to see an emerging hiker's trail marked with cairns heading north up the steep slope. Walk up this to a bench, then head up a sandy slope at the base of the steepest cliffs. From there, this cairned trail heads southeast, then zig zags up to the bench below the final Navajo cliffs, then cuts back to the north. Finally, you'll reach the crack itself with signs of a constructed cow trail. From there, head east up the steep gully. Watch closely on both sides of the crack; there are 6-7 panels of petroglyphs, plus several etchings of early-day ranchers and/or travelers. One of these reads: *G.M. Wright, 20 Apr. 1894.* From the top, you could return the same way, or head northwest and return via the other Sand Hill Crack & Hancock Spring.

Elevations Trailhead for Bonelli Spring, 1585m; top of Paria Plateau, 2163m; Jacob Pools, 1589m; top of Sand Hill Crack, 2066m; top of Eastern Crack, 2057m; Jarvis Ranch, 2025m.

Hike Length/Time Needed It's about 6 kms from the Honeymoon Trail to the Sand Hills via **Bonelli Spring,** but in places it's steep and the going slow. It may take roughly 4-5 hours for the average person to do this hike round-trip. From Jacob Pools to the top of the **Sand Hill Crack** is about 3 to 3 1/2 kms. Round-trip could take 3-5 hours, or about half a day for the average person. From the rim to the Jarvis Ranch is about 5 more kms, so from Jacob Pools to the ranch and back, about 17 kms round-trip; this will be an all-day hike. From Jacob Pools to the top of the **Eastern Crack** will take 2-4 hours round-trip.

Water Take your own on all hikes. But there's water in the hole in the wall which is Bonelli Spring, lots of good water at Hancock Spring, and some at the main spring at Rachel's Pools.

Maps USGS or BLM maps Glen Canyon Dam (1:100,000) for driving & orientation; Emmett Hill & One Toe Ridge (1:24,000--7 1/2' quads) for hiking & driving; or one of the 4 MF-1475 maps A, B, C or D (1:62,500).

Main Attractions Petroglyphs & cowboy etchings along 3 old Indian routes to the top of the Sand Hills, great views from the rim, and historic Jacob & Rachel's Pools which John D. Lee helped put on the map.

Ideal Time to Hike Spring or fall, but you can hike year-round.

Boots/Shoes Lightweight but rugged hiking boots.

Author's Experience He climbed to the top of the Bonelli Spring Trail 3 times in 3 to 4 1/2 hours each, round-trip. Three trips to the top of the Sand Hill Crack and back took 2-3 hours each. One trip in 1987 was to the steel tanks east of the Jarvis Ranch, in 6 1/2 hours round-trip. His 3 hikes up to

The ruins of Rachel Lee's stone house just above the western-most spring at Rachel's Pools. This site is about one km northeast of the stone building at Jacob Pools.

Left From near the top of the Sand Hill Crack looking south at the pinnacle, with Jacob Pools in the far background. **Right** These petroglyphs are on the western base of the pinnacle seen to the left.

the Eastern Crack took less than 2 1/2 hours each, round-trip.

History of the Bonelli Spring Development

Most of the history in this chapter on the Sand Hills comes from the late Dunk Findley who lived in Kanab for most of his life.

The Bonelli Spring was unknown and unused by white men until the early 1900's. Sometime after about 1916, Alex Cram, who owned a large ranch in the lower House Rock Valley, began to develop this minor seep. He blasted a square hole in the bottom of the Navajo Sandstone cliff in order to increase the flow and to better capture the water. Sometime later, he traded his grazing rights to a man named W.J. Mackelprange for 2 horses.

Later, and in the early 1930's, a Basque sheepman named Bonelli from Flagstaff, Arizona, came into the country and bought the water rights to the spring. Prior to this time it may have been called Death Tanks, because there was never much water there (one source says the name Death Tanks referred to another little seep just downhill from Bonelli Spring?).

Bonelli brought sheep with him, but needed a better waterhole. After considering his options, he bought pumping equipment & pipe, then set to work to construct a pumping station, pipeline, and troughs, in order to pump water from the spring up to the plateau rim to several cement troughs. His operation was successful, and he had water on the rim for about 4 years. His sheep were on top of the Sand Hills in the summers, down under the cliffs in House Rock Valley during the winter season.

But in 1936, the newly established Grazing Service (forerunner to the BLM) ran him out. Bonelli had apparently not been in the area long enough before the Taylor Grazing Act was passed in 1934, and wasn't eligible for a permit to run livestock in that part of the country. So after 4 apparently successful years, he had to abandon the operation.

At the site today, you'll see a half-buried pump & motor, and some hoses & wire at the eastern-most spring. The middle spring is the only one which has a large enough flow to get a drink out of today. It's shaped like a huge square mine tunnel, which was blasted out of the lower Navajo. Inside are etchings of cowboys like *Mel Shoppman-1941*, a mossy pool of water and a plastic pipe running down to the troughs in the valley below. Better be careful drinking this water--in 11/2003, the author observed hoof prints of big horn sheep inside this tumb-like tunnel. At the 3rd seep, or wet spot to the west, 3 cottonwood trees grow, but no sign of water.

Above the pump and near the big wall, are scattered odds & ends of the water pumping operation. On the Navajo wall itself are several small etchings or petroglyphs. On the rim of the plateau are 3 cement troughs, still in very good condition, looking like they were constructed last month. Also right on the rim and south of the troughs, are 4 or 5 structures that look a lot like stone corrals; but on closer inspection, you'll see small window portals in the higher walls. This is actually the remains of a small village or perhaps a hunting camp likely built by a group of aborigines called Virgin Anasazi. No doubt those people established this settlement because of the existence of the spring and a route from the top to the flats below. Because of the altitude of 2163m, they probably tried growing corn and other crops--but likely failed. There are probably dozens of structures like these all over the Sand Hills.

Down below in the House Rock Valley, and along your hiking route, are half a dozen watering troughs and a small overflow pond. Cattle graze this area is the winter season, which is from November through April each year. You'll likely find water in these troughs during the winter months, but perhaps not during the summer season.

Left This is the man-made tomb-like hole in the cliff that is now the Bonelli Spring. The plastic pipe takes water down to troughs in the valley below. **Right** Inside the short tunnel at Bonelli Spring. On the walls inside, are the signatures of several old timers who ran cattle & sheep in this area.

Almost covered by sand, the motor and pump at Bonelli Spring. These were used to pump water from the spring up to some watering troughs on the rim of the Sand Hills.

Map 36B, The Sand Hills & Paria Plateau Ranches

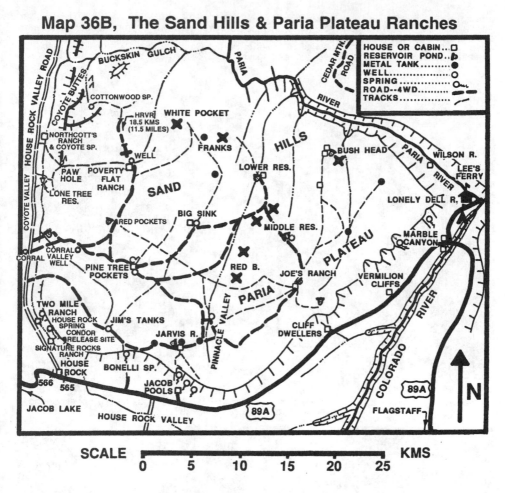

SCALE

0   5   10   15   20   25   KMS

History of Jacob & Rachel's Pools

In May, 1872, Rachel Woolsey, one of John D. Lee's wives, was moved into the area now known by various names such as The Pools, Jacob Pools, or Rachel's Pools. Her first shelter was a mud & willow shack, not much better than what Indians lived in. On June 2, a group of men from the Powell Survey came through the area, and fotographed the scene (see the foto below).

Later in the fall of 1872, John D. started building a better house. He hired a stone mason named Elisha Everett to help, since the home was to be made of rock. It was mostly completed on Christmas Day of 1872. It measured 9 x 11 meters, had 2 doors, 2 bedrooms, a kitchen, a parlor and a wooden roof. Nearby was a cellar. The ruins of this rock house can still be seen just above the westernmost spring called Rachel's Pools. In the same area, and just below the springs, are numerous rock walls, apparently used as fences or pens to hold livestock. This location is 32 kms west of Lee's Ferry, and was set up to be a way-station for Mormons who were heading south to settle in Arizona. It was one day's travel between these 2 waterholes.

One day by wagon to the west, was another site of interest, which goes back to the spring and summer of 1873. This is the resting place or way-station along the **Honeymoon Trail** called **House Rock Spring & Signature Rocks**. At, or just below House Rock Spring, are a number of interesting sites. There's a grave of a young woman named May Whiting and a number of ruins of fences and old stone structures of some kind. If you walk east up the drainage about 400m from the grave site, and up against the canyon wall, you'll see a tunnel which is House Rock Spring. From there, and all along the cliffs to the west for 300m you'll see dozens of emigrantglyphs, or signatures of some of the earliest Mormon settlers who were heading to the Arizona Territory in the very first year Lee's Ferry was in operation. Many of these signatures date from early June, 1873.

To get there, drive along Highway 89A roughly halfway between Marble Canyon/Navajo Bridge & Jacob Lake. Between mile posts 565 & 566, and next to the house & corrals known as House Rock, turn north onto the House Rock Valley Road destined for Coyote Buttes, Wire Pass & Highway 89. After 6 kms (3.7 miles) (42.2 kms/26.2 miles from the north and Highway 89) turn right or east toward some old ranch buildings, corrals & water tank. From the barn & corrals, continue east crossing a dry wash. About 150m beyond the dry wash, turn left or north. Continue due north until you reach the end of the road west or below House Rock Spring. This is 2.2 kms (1.35 miles) from the main road.

One of half a dozen ruins on the rim of the Sand Hills or Paria Plateau just above Bonelli Spring. This was actually a small village.

Left The cement watering troughs on the rim of the plateau above Bonelli Spring. **Right** Looking down the crack in the cliffs between Bonelli Spring, and the ruins & troughs on top of the Sand Hills. This was a foggy, rainy day, with the plateau rim schrouded in clouds.

Cars with reasonable clearance can just about get there. Be aware that the area of the barn & corral, and the area where you may be parking below House Rock Spring, are on 2 separate pieces of private land. If you see any signs like **"No Trespassing", then Stop**. In that case, you could likely park along the House Rock Valley Road and walk. In the future, the Vermilion Cliffs National Monument may purchase this land (?).

Back at The Pools. At the end of the sandy road coming up from the highway, is what is called **Jacob Pools**. It's about 1 or 1 1/2 kms southwest of Rachel's Pools. At that location are a couple of corrals and a rather well-built stone building. Information as to when this structure was built is scarce, but most of the old-timers around believe it was built in the early 1900's when the Grand Canyon Cattle Company ran cows throughout the entire House Rock Valley. In those days, B. F. Saunders was running things. It may have been both a way-station and a ranch house on the road running to Lee's Ferry. Be aware that Jacob Pools is on private land with cattle there in the winter months.

Reestablishing California Condors to the Vermilion Cliffs

The release of 6 California Condors to the Vermilion Cliffs on **December 12, 1996,** marked the beginning of the reestablishment of these rare birds into the wilds of the American Southwest. This has been a cooperative effort between the BLM, National Park Service, Arizona Game & Fish, the Peregrine Fund at the World Center for Birds of Prey in Boise, Idaho, the San Diego Wild Animal Park and the Los Angeles Zoo.

The release site is located about 2 kms east of the House Rock Valley Road in Section 14, T39N, R3E. There's a parking place & verandah located 4.5 kms (2.8 miles) north of House Rock and Highway 89A. Look ENE, and you'll see white streaks of bird manure running down the highest Navajo Sandstone wall. That's the release site, plus it's a favorite roosting place for many birds. Nearby is a large cage where new birds are brought to acclimatize before actually being released.

Here's the number of condors that have been released over the years: 1996--6 birds; 1997--13; 1998--9; 1999--7; 2000--12; 2001--0; 2002--11; and for 2003--8 birds. This makes a total of 61 releases from captivity. Since the start of the program 23 birds have died: 3 were shot; 5 were killed by coyotes; 1 struck a powerline; 4 died from lead poisoning; 3 were killed by eagles; 1 starved to death; 2 were lost; 3 were captured and returned to the captive breeding program; and 3 are unaccounted for. Read more below.

For additional or updated information, see the website **peregrinefund.org;** then click *Conservation Projects, & Condor Fact Sheet.*

California Condor Fact Sheet--October 1, 2003

Scientific Name: *Gymnogyps californianus* **Population low:** 22 individuals in 1982 **Current World Population-Wild & Captive:** 220 individuals **Life span:** Unknown, possibly up to 60 years. **Wingspan:** Up to 3 meters **Weight:** Averages 7 1/4 to 10 1/2 kgs **Body Length:** 1.2 to 1.4 meters **Range:** Occurred historically from British Columbia south to northern Baja California and in other parts of the southwestern United States. **Maturity:** Condors reach sexual maturity and attain adult plumage and coloration by 5-6 years of age. Breeding is likely between 6-8 years of age. **Reproduction:** One egg every other year if nesting cycle is successful. Instead of having many young and gambling that a few will survive, the condor produces very few young and provides an extensive amount of parental care. Average incubation period for a condor egg is about 56 days. **Nest Site:** Usually in a cave on a cliff or a crevice among boulders on a steep slope. **Young:** Nestlings fledge (leave nest) full grown at six months of age, however, historically juvenile condors may be dependent on their parents for more that a year. Reintroduced condors are released on their own and must learn to forage and survive alone. **Sexes:** There is no sexual dimorphism (observable difference in size or appearance) between males and females. **Feeding:** Condors are strict scavengers. Unlike Turkey Vultures, condors do not have an exceptional sense of smell. They instead find their food visually, often by investigating the activity of ravens, coyotes, eagles, and other scavengers. Without the guidance of their parents, young inexperienced juvenile condors may also investigate the activity of humans. As young condors learn and mature this human directed curiosity diminishes. **Reasons for decline:** The main reason for the decline of the condors was an unsustainable mortality rate of free-flying birds combined with a naturally low reproductive rate. Most deaths in recent years have been directly or indirectly related to human activity. Shootings, poisoning, lead poisoning, and collisions with power lines are considered the condors' major threats. **Identification points to look for:** Numbered wing tags, white or mottled triangle under wing, no feathers on head, and head color black in juveniles or orange/pink in adults, not dark red as in Turkey Vultures.

Current Condor Numbers
16 December 2003

Wild Population of California Condors			-83
Arizona (Paria--Vermilion Cliffs)	-36	Baja California (Mexico)	-5
Southern California	-22	Central California	-20

Detailed information is available here on each of the condors that have been released in Arizona. **Condors in Field Pens Awaiting Release** -- -23

Arizona (Paria--Vermilion Cliffs)	-15	Baja California (Mexico)	-0
Southern California	-0	Mentor bird in Field Pen	-1
Mentor bird in Field Pen	-0		
Central California	-6		
Mentor bird in Field Pen	-1		

Captive Population of California Condors			-124
World Center for Birds of Prey-Boise, ID	-50	Los Angeles Zoo	-38
San Diego Wild Animal Park	-36		

TOTAL CALIFORNIA CONDOR POPULATION--220

Contacts: The Peregrine Fund---Tele. 928-355-2270; Arizona Game & Fish, Flagstaff---Tele. 928-

774-5045; BLM, St. George, Utah---Tele. 435-688-3200; National Park Service---928-638-7756.
If you should observe a condor please report your sighting to The Peregrine Fund biologists at 520-355-2270 or email us at *AZcondors@aol.com*. Helpful information would include date, time, location, number of birds observed, and wing tag numbers if possible.

The Sand Hills Ranches

Included along with 3 hikes to the top of the Vermilion Cliffs, is a short history of some of the ranching activity which has taken place for more than a century on top of the Sand Hills or Paria Plateau.

In the region between the Buckskin Gulch, the Lower Paria River Gorge, the Vermilion Cliffs, and The Cockscomb (to the south this is known as the East Kaibab Monocline), is the Paria Plateau. For the most part, this is a moderately high and very isolated corner of the Colorado Plateau, which is extremely difficult to get to. The local name, the Sand Hills, tells the whole story.

The top layer of the Plateau, for the most part, is made up of sand, which has eroded away from the Navajo Sandstone Formation. This is primarily the reason it's almost a no man's land. It's not only difficult for a man to walk around, but it's also difficult for horses; to say nothing of the problems people have in getting around in a 2WD car or pickup. This is 4WD country!

Actually, you can sometimes get around up there with a 2WD vehicle, but you have to do it when the sand is either wet or frozen, or both. Winter is the best time. Another method some of the old-timers used, was to let about half the air out of their tires, which put more rubber to the road. As they left the sandy parts, they'd have to hand pump the tires back up again. For those without a 4WD vehicle, it's highly recommended you forego any visits to this little hideaway in the desert.

Joe's Ranch or The Ranch

Joe's Ranch was one of the first to be set up in the country, and because of the difficulty in travel, the isolation, and the total lack of any live running water or permanent springs, it has always been a kind of hardship post. The only real springs around are Two Mile and Coyote, located at the western edge of the Sand Hills, and in House Rock and Coyote Valleys.

This ranch got its name from Joe Hamblin, one of 3 sons of Jacob Hamblin; Walt, Ben & Joe were their names. According to the late Dunk Findlay, Joe Hamblin had worked with John W. Powell on one or more of his surveying parties (but not the early river expeditions), had been in the area before, and returned later to build the ranch. The year he went there was 1884, and since it was the only ranch of any kind in the Sand Hills, it was always just called **The Ranch or Joe's Ranch,** by local cowboys and sheepmen. Joe Hamblin had cattle, as well as sheep & goats.

No one alive today knows how long the Hamblins had the ranch and the squatters rights, or in what year it was sold to Johnny Adams, the second owner. The late Dunk Findlay seemed to think it was in 1926 when Johnny Adams bought most of the squatters rights in the Sand Hills from Nephi, son of Joe Hamblin. Johnny Adam's herds grazed most of the Paria Plateau range for many years. Adams is the one who devised the scheme to pump Paria River water up onto the lower or northern end of the Sand Hills. It was in the winter, spring & summer of 1939, that he and his workers cut the trail, laid down the pipe and installed the pump. However, because the drought ended just at that time, he never used the pump. Read all about that scheme under **Map 30**, showing the **Adams Trail.**

It was during the time Johnny Adams was at The Ranch in 1934, that the Taylor Grazing Act was passed. In the years after that legislation, the Sand Hills was broken up into 2 or more different grazing areas, much to the consternation of the old-timers. Other cattlemen got in on the western part of the Sand Hills range, and fences were erected. This changed the whole setup.

Quoting now from a letter written to the author by Dunk Findlay: *The only water Adams had was at the Ranch, and the Middle and the Lower Reservoir. There was no other water on the Plateau. Other people had to graze when there was snow on the ground. That's when the sheep and goats were in there. Most times it served only as a winter range other than around the Ranch. That is why it was not over grazed.*

After many years of riding the Sand Hills range, and after having developed many of the stock tanks and ponds seen there today, Adams finally sold out. According to Dunk Findlay, Adams was somehow forced out, partly because of The Depression, and maybe the drought (?). The man in the middle was Jim Jennings, who foreclosed on Adams, but then A.T. Spence, a cattleman from Phoenix, ended up with much of the Sand Hills range in 1941. Spence built cement cores to some of the little stock ponds and brought in several metal tanks, although he owned the place just a short time. In 1944, Dunk's father, Merle Findlay bought out Spence.

Dunk remembered: *The Ranch was a permanent ranch used year-round by Hamblin, Adams, Spence, and the Findlays. There were several times the cattle had to be moved away on account of lack of water, that's why we drilled a well. After the Taylor Grazing Act, there was no place to move; before that, cattle were moved any place there was water on the public domain. No one owned anything then.*

Once the Findlays had it, Dunk and his brother Lynn did most of the work around the range. After Merle died in 1960, these 2 brothers split up the range; Dunk to the west, and Lynn to the east in the area around Joe's Ranch house. Actually, throughout the years each man or family who ran cattle or sheep on the range, did some work on it. One bit of work which had little to do with ranching was the building of an airstrip at Poverty Flat, located just east of the southern end of the Coyote Buttes. The man who built that and the only one to ever use it was Rowd Sanders.

Developing a water system was of primary concern on the Sand Hills range. As stated before, there was never any live running water on the entire plateau. The range itself was excellent, due to the altitude, which ranged up to about 2200 meters. But because of the water problem, it was virtually impossible to take or have enough livestock there to overgraze the place.

In the early 1950's, the Findlays drilled a well in the lower northern end of Pinnacle Valley, with a drilling rig they bought just for that job. A bit later they sold the drilling equipment to Fay Hamblin and Floyd Maddox, who drilled the second well at Poverty Flat. A third well was drilled by Roy Woolly at Pine Tree Pockets (locally it's just called Pines), which for many years was a kind of ranch headquarters for the western part of the Sand Hills range. Throughout the years, and since about 1950, eight wells in all have been drilled.

The Findlays were heavily involved with the development of a number of slickrock water basins or rainwater stock tanks, and they installed a number of metal tanks for water storage, etc. Dunk and a man named John Rich also installed 4 or 5 pipelines, which ran water from several of the wells downhill to the north by gravity, to other water storage tanks, so cattle could be spread out on the range more evenly.

In 1962, just after the Findlay brothers had divided the range, Lynn sold his part to John Rich (he's the one who still owns the facilities at Jacob Lake), who called his outfit the Vermilion Cliffs Cattle Company. This was the part with the old Joe's Ranch house on it. Dunk held onto his part until March 1, 1980. That's when he sold his grazing rights to the Ramsay Cattle Company, along with about 500 head of cattle. Dunk recalls the times and said: *We had 80 acres [about 30 hectares] of patented land at the Ranch. Adams got this after the survey; before that it was just a squatters claim. We had around 16 or 18 state sections leased, on the Ranch.*

Shortly thereafter and still in 1980, Two Mile Corporation took over, and obtained grazing rights to the entire Paria Plateau. Actually, the name Two Mile Corp came about after they bought out Dunk Findlay and the Vermilion Cliffs Cattle Co. The next owner to all the Sand Hills range was Kay Sturdevant of Springville, Utah. Here's what he remembered about the place:

Two Mile Corp belonged to a guy from Texas who bought out Dunk Findlay. That's the way I remember it. Then they went into bankruptsey, or receivership, and Jay Wright & Mark Stevenson bought it out of bankruptsey, but I can't remember just how long they had it. Then we bought the ranch in 1992; all the grazing rights and the private land. We called it Two Mile Ranch, Inc.

While we were there we had about 62 miles [100 kms] of pipeline. We got the existing lines back up and into operation. It was a rundown deal. We put in all new pumps on the wells, and changed everything over to propane. We done quite a bit of improvement. Then we sold it in late 1999 to a man named Gelbaum. That new ranch of Gelbaum's is called Kane Ranch LLC. The way I understand it, he put the Kane Ranch and Two Mile Ranch together under this business heading.

Long-time ranch foreman JR Jones of Kanab adds more information about the days of Kay Sturdevant: *They had a BLM permit to run up to 1500 head of cattle, but they actually had closer to 1200-1300. They ran cattle on the Sand Hills year-round, with their winter range being in the north, just south of the Buckskin Gulch and the Lower Paria River Gorge; their summer range in the higher & cooler south half of the Plateau. This is all BLM land, except for about 20 state sections; and the quarter section [160 acres or 65 hectares] at Joe's Ranch, which is still private.*

The present Kane Ranch headquarters is located at Two Mile Spring near the head of House Rock Valley. Normally the ranch has only 3 full-time employees, including JR Jones as foreman. Also one cowboy, and the waterman who lives at Pine Tree Pockets most of the time. The waterman makes frequent sorties out to the various wells to pump water to storage tanks, and keeps an eye on the range & facilities. In the spring and fall, JR hires part-time help to move cattle around.

In early 2004, JR said: *The drought kinda caught up with us so we just sold the cows off 'till it starts rainin' again and we get some feed. We sold 'um this past summer and fall (2003), but we still have some strays around. I'm the only one out there now. When I see some cattle, I'll get some help to get 'um.*

Jarvis Ranch

The Jarvis Ranch came about and had something to do with the grazing rights changes back in the mid to late 1930's as a result of the Taylor Grazing Act. Dunk Findlay said: *Jarvis never got a permit to run cattle--he was not there in the priority period. Jarvis was working for Walt Hamblin (Fay's dad) when the BLM finally gave him a small allotment of three or four sections.* According to Dunk Findlay, they never had many cows, maybe 15 or so, but they built a rather fine ranch house there anyway, which is just north of the Sand Hill Crack. That was in 1935.

The Jarvis house isn't just a line cabin or a bunk house, but quite a nice home. It's still used today by cowhands when they're in the area working cattle. It's painted white, has five good-sized rooms and a propane gas lighting & cooking system. There's even a refrigerator, which is run on propane. Water was collected by the use of roof rain gutters and down-pipes, which funneled rainwater into a cistern below the house. There's surely water in the tank today, but it won't be drinkable.

When A. T. Spence got a hold of the ranch in 1941, he (according to Dunk Findlay) used the *house for his main headquarters. He had built the house at the lower reservoir, and it and the house at the Ranch were used as line cabins. Spence added two more rooms to the original Jarvis house.* He said not to spoil a good thing he put hard wood floors in then too.

After Dunk and his brother divided the range, Dunk made this house his headquarters. It was Dunk Findlay who put the propane lights and refrigerator in the house in about 1962. He installed the metal tank next to the barn, and pumped water to it from the Pinnacle Valley Well. This was done by a small portable gasoline engine.

The Jarvis place also has a good barn which is still used today. Behind the barn are a couple of

other metal water tanks, and just to the west, a dam which can catch a lot of water--if and when big storms occur. Near the house is a fruit cellar for storage. The whole ranch site is situated in a part of the Sand Hills called the Dark Forest. It's a P/J covered region, with very healthy and rather large trees.

Rachel Lee's willow & mud shack on June 2, 1872. In the picture are John D. Lee, 2 small sons and a daughter. (Arizona Hist.Society)

The ranch house at Pine Tree Pockets in the western part of the Sand Hills.

The Jarvis Ranch house as seen in 1987. It looks like new, but it was originally built in 1937.

This is one of hundreds of signatures at Signature Rock, which is near House Rock Spring. The one above is suppose to be *JD Lee Dec 25 1871,* but it appears someone has vandalized it.

Left The tomb of *May Whiting, Daughter of Edwin & Mary Whiting, 1862--1882.* In the far background is where House Rock Spring is located. Along the walls in the upper right is where Mormon emigrants heading for Arizona left their signatures. **Right** This tunnel is now House Rock Spring. In the early 1900's, someone mucked-out this tunnel to better capture what little water there is at this spring.

The Henrieville CCC Camp

Civilian Conservation Corps (CCC's) camps were built and operated throughout the United States in the 1930's for the purpose of building roads, trails, fences, catchment basins or stock ponds and other conservation projects on public lands. Most of them were in the west. They were organized and run by the US Army in cooperation with the Forest Service, the Division of Grazing or Grazing Service (BLM after 1947) and/or the National Park Service.

The **Henrieville CCC Camp #2529, Division of Grazing #33,** was located northeast of Henrieville immediately south of present-day Highway 12, the paved road running between Bryce Canyon National Park and Escalante. It was located just below where the old Smith Ranch was originally situated. Regarding the location, Iris Smith Bushnell had this to say about the place: *The old Smith Ranch was settled by my grandfather, James Edward Smith, Sr. He was probably there in the late 1800's (?). The CCC camp was located about a quarter mile [400m] below where the Smith Ranch was. They used to live up there in the summertime; they'd raise a garden and had their cattle. I guess grandpa just abandoned the place. There wasn't anyone at the ranch when the CCC camp was built.*

Most older people in Bryce Valley know something about the camp, but maybe the best source is from one of the enrollees. Most of the story below was told to the author by Darrel Blackwell who lives in Layton, Utah.

That CCC camp was 7 miles [11 kms] up the canyon from Henrieville, and that road ended right at the camp. The road then is exactly where the paved highway is today. The next thing above the CCC camp was The Blues. In later years, they built that road and it went on up over the top into Escalante.

They had 3 or 4 barracks for the men, and there was 15 to 20 men in each barracks. Then they had the mess hall and the administration building. Now that camp was set up for the Division of Grazing [Grazing Service]. Some camps were run by the Forest Service, some by the Park Service, and the one in Henrieville was run by the Division of Grazing. And of course they had their office building, and then the army people that supervised the kids when they weren't workin', they had their own building. Then they had work shops where they kept their trucks & tools--the motorpool. They also had an infirmary or sickbay--a barracks-type place. They also had a little PX or store where you could buy candy or cigarettes. Then they had a recreational building where they had their educational programs. You see, they had educational programs for most of those kids, because most of 'um got in the CCC's before they was graduated from high school. The educational advisor for that camp was from Ogden, Utah.

Then they had their wash house where they had toilets & showers. You had to go to a different building to shave & shower. The showers, toilets and wash basins was located in a buildin' just below the barracks. You had to get up and go quite a little ways from the barracks, maybe a 100 feet [30m] or so.

I don't know for sure, but I would imagine there was about 150 or 200 people in the camp at any one time. You see, the Division of Grazing, they had their own personnel, their foremen, then of course the army had their people that took care of the camp stuff.

In each barracks they had a leader and an assistant leader. I was a leader, and we slept at the head of the barracks right at the door. It was our responsibility to keep order in the barracks, and make sure it was kept clean. Then when we went out on the job in the mornin', we had a foreman that was generally an older guy that was a local person [these were called LEM's--Local Experienced Men] from some of those towns around the area. These foremen lived in the camp in barracks where the army guys lived. And each foreman was assigned a leader and an assistant leader. So it was our responsibility to watch over the men, make sure they worked, make sure everything was OK. Each foreman had, depending on the project that was goin' on, probably 15 to 20 men.

The foremen were hired by the CCC's. Most of the foremen at our camp was from over around Panguitch & Circleville. The guy who was our foreman was really old. He was a butcher who used to live in Panguitch. When we'd go out to cut posts, and when guys would get scattered out, he'd go over and lay down under a cedar tree and have a nap. He had most of us guys from Kentucky that knew how to handle an ax and knew how to cut timber.

Then we had a guy in the camp that was a night guard. It was his duty to patrol the camp at night, then he'd come into the head of the barracks ever' mornin' and wake the leader and assistant leader up, then it was their responsibility to go down through the barracks and get the guys up and washed and have them get ready for breakfast. In the CCC's, we never had guard duty like in the army.

Then we had a sergent who had some duties over the whole camp. He was a regular CCC enrollee like the rest of us. His duties was to go with the officers and inspect the barracks, and go to town in an army truck and get the mail. He was over the clothing and PX too. We just called him Sergent. He stayed there all the time to oversee what was goin' on around camp and in the kitchen. That camp was organized about as well as anything I've ever been in. They had everything covered, and everything worked pretty good.

There was 3 guys who were regular army in our camp. Most of the time I was there, we had an army captain, and we had a lieutenant--I think he was a 2nd lieutenant. I guess they were full-time army people, and they knew the ropes, and of course they handled all the clothing and food and stuff. Then there was a doctor. He was in charge of the clinic or sickbay. If we ever had any serious health problems, they'd send us to Fort Douglas [next to Salt Lake City]. A lot of our supplies come out of Fort Douglas too. At that time Fort Douglas was a big army post.

Don Chynoweth, grandson of Arthur Chynoweth, was a small boy when the Henrieville camp was up and running. He recalls one experience at the camp: *My grandmother Rose, Arthur Chynoweth's wife, used to do the laundry for the CCC's boys in Henrieville. And when she'd get the clothes done she'd put'um in boxes & baskets, and take 'um back to the camp in a rubber-tired wagon with a team. On one trip, me and my cousin Wayne, rode with her up to the CCC Camp. We got there about noon, took the clothes and dropped them off, and they invited us into the mess hall and said, "here, have your dinner with us". Now in them days we didn't have a lot of food--it was hard to get hold of; so I remember they were cooking these great big pork chops in metal treys. I never saw so much food! I can remember that so well.*

Now back to Darrel's story. *Some of those kids were from back east and they'd get homesick. They'd send 'um way out here and some had never been away from home before. And some of 'um had never been off concrete or blacktop--those guys from Brooklyn and Youngstown, Ohio, and those big cities, and they would get homesick and some of 'um would try to go home. They called it, "goin'* over the hill". "Oh, he's gone over the hill", they'd say. And I guess they just let 'um go; we'd have a few of 'um try to go over the hill and get home, some of 'um never could make it. But if they did, they'd get a dishonorable discharge just like in the military. If you got one of those dishonorable discharges, you was in pretty bad shape!

There was another camp at Bryce Canyon, but that wasn't part of ours. That Bryce Canyon camp, I think was a part of the camp from Zion [National Park]. The bigger camps would send out these people to setup temporary spike camps. The Bryce camp didn't seem to be a really big one but I remember the foreman up there was from Henrieville. Later on, when I was drivin' that mail contract I used to haul food and milk and stuff into that Bryce Canyon camp. But it wasn't a big camp like Henrievilles. They lived in buildings not tents, and they was up there quite a while. They worked on the trails in Bryce Canyon National Park.

We had a spike camp at Pipe Springs, which was in northern Arizona west of Kanab & Fredonia. Then there was one over on the Sevier River about 5 miles [8 kms] south of Panguitch on Highway 89. It was pretty close to where you turn off Highway 89 goin' east toward Bryce Canyon--about a mile or so south of there. We had quite a few guys over there. We stayed in the main camp and drove out ever' mornin' from the Henrieville Camp into Dry Valley and Butler Valley, and down into the upper part of what they called The Gut.

Afton Pollock of Tropic, son of Sam Pollock, contradicts some of this information, in part because he lived there throughout the life of the CCC camp, and Darrel didn't. Regarding spike camps, many of which were only in one spot a week or two, here's what Afton remembered: They had a little spike camp on Watson Ridge near that CCC or BLM corral, and in the winter of 1936-37, the CCC boys brought 14 ton of cottonseed cake there for my Dad. They arrived on Christmas morning, 1936. An army cat driven by Hasle Caudil opened a road out there through snow up to my arm pits! They erected a big army tent and put the cottonseed cake in it, then I'd come in from Death Valley and pickup this cottonseed cake, put it on mules and haul it down to our sheep. That spike camp was just south of where that corral is today.

There was another little spike camp down by Round Valley [near Round Valley Neck and Round Valley or Rush Bed Seep], and another one over at the head of Cottonwood Wash by that stockade corral just south of Grosvenor Arch. It wasn't very big, they must have had 25 men there. I remember that because my brother and I came up through there with a herd of sheep in about 1936, and these boys was there workin' in that corral. They had tents for sleeping, a tent for a kitchen and a latrine. They also had a couple of spike camps out on Deer Range [along the Skutumpah Road] and in that country. They may have had one down there about halfway between Deer Creek & Crack Spring along the Paria (?).

Now back to Darrel's story again. Then there was another big camp in Escalante just over the hill from where we were, but you couldn't go up through The Blues where the highway is today. You had to go up to Bryce, then north to Widtsoe and east clearn the hell of over Table Cliff Mountain and Barney Top in order to get to Escalante. That camp built a lot of that road goin' over to Boulder in 1937. Escalante was a big camp like ours.

We built a corral in Butler Valley and also put a windmill in there with storage tanks for water. We done quite a lot of work out in Kodachrome Flats and Round Valley. We built that road startin' in Butler Valley that goes down into The Gut and Wahweap country. In them days you couldn't get very far, there was washes, and it just wasn't passable. It was when they started workin' on Glen Canyon Dam that they started opening up that Cottonwood Wash road so you could drive down through there.

We built a lot of fences for the Division of Grazing to help keep cattle out of certain places. And corrals and wells. We built that catchment near the Kodachrome Turnoff, but it filled up with sediment. We built a little monument there, DG 33 is what they called it. We spelled the name out in rock on the face of it. Originally it may have covered 4 or 5 acres, then it just filled up with those floods. We also built that corral on Watson Ridge [now it's generally called the BLM Corral].

Jack Chynoweth of Tropic says; they also had a little spike camp at Round Valley Seep, just south of the trailhead parking for Round Valley Draw. They developed that seep so water could be put into a large watering trough for cattle. They were the ones who blasted a hole in the sandstone wall nearby to keep their perishable foods in.

Darrel again. While in the main camp, we'd have to go out and watch the flag go up and down, and go out and do calisthenics before breakfast, and go out and stand at retreat and watch the flag go down--it was run by the army and it was strict! I'll tell you one thing, the army personnel that run our camp, the ones who took care of the boys after they'd get off work in the evening, they were 10 times stricter than the army was in World War II! I was in World War II, and the CCC camp had a lot stricter standards than the army. I mean they were more strict in the barracks on cleanliness, and more strict on everything. They held daily inspections in those barracks, and boy if they came through and flipped a quarter and if it didn't bounce off the bed, you was in trouble! You'd be on KP [Kitchen Patrol] on the weekend when you should be in town goin' to a dance!

In those days there wasn't no television; in fact, you'd have to have a damn good radio to get any kind of reception! You couldn't hardly get nothin'. But them little towns of Henrieville, Cannonville and Tropic, they used to have a dance ever' Friday night. They was great for that. Then a lot of times when people would get married--the locals, they'd have a wedding dance. And so the CCC camp would send a truck or two to town, and we'd always go down to those dances. Then they'd pick us up and bring us back. Goin' to dances was big in them days. Friday night was the big night down there, because they had a dance in one town one Friday night, then the next Friday it would be in the next town. And the CCC's were welcome to come and participate and dance.

We didn't have many picture shows, that recreational director was a guy named Dirk from Ogden, and he was the educational advisor. In the first camp I was in at Mammoth Cave, Kentucky, they had a rec. building where they showed movies. In our rec. hall you could play pool, or play ping pong, but mostly it was an educational-type thing, where you could go to school and learn a lot of stuff.

The pay wasn't bad for them days. One reason for setting up the CCC's was to help families who had no jobs. Most families got $25 a month, that was sent home to 'um; and their enrollee got only 5 bucks a month--$30 was your monthly pay unless you was a leader or assistant leader. A leader got $45 a month--he got $20, and the rest went home to the family. An assistant leader got $36. And they paid off in cash ever' 30 days. They'd have a big table laid out with them army blankets on it and they had the cash. All the enrollees got was the $5, and they'd send the rest to your home--but all you had to buy was toothpaste and candy and cigarettes. Ever'thing else was furnished.

The CCC's was a good organization and that's where I learnt most of the skills that I used in the contractin' business. When you'd first get to the CCC camp, the first thing you knew, they'd put you in a great big truck and put 25 men on it and send you out in the hills. Or put you up on a D-9 Cat that you'd never seen before in your life and make an operator, cat-skinner, out of ya. A lot of those guys that was in the heavy equipment stuff, the ones that stayed around there, ended up workin' for the state road department.

I think the Henrieville camp was set up around 1934; it was there when I arrived. I got there in the winter of 1936 & '37. I was there 18 months, because you could only sign up for 18 months, then you had to get out and let somebody else in. But I was around even longer than that. You see, I got married to a local girl and stayed there in Henrieville--I was there 30 years after that. I got married just a short time after I got out of the CCC's. The camp closed down in the winter of 1939-40 when the World War tactics got so bad in Europe. At that time I was drivin' the mail contract out of Henrieville to Panguitch, and I used to deliver milk and mail up to that camp. But they closed it down and then they drafted most of those people. Most of the guys went from the CCC's right into the army.

There was 7 CCC boys who married local girls. One guy lives over here in Ogden, Hasle Caudill, he drove a cat, a cat skinner, and he married Rhoda Chynoweth. Hobart Feltner of Cannonville married a Twitchell girl. He was a cook and he was there most of the time I was. Then there was Willy Bryant who lives down in Riverton. He was a truck driver, and he married Elma Mangum. There was another cook named Hamby who married another Twitchell girl. He's dead. Walter Livinguth was an assistant leader, and he married a Smith girl from Henrieville. Ora Shafer was a senior foreman. He married Rhoda Henderson and she still lives down in Cannonville. The family I married into were really strict Mormons. In fact, my father-in-law was bishop for 17 years. That was Harvey Chynoweth.

When I got out of the CCC's, I went home first, of course--they shipped me home, then I came right back out to Henrieville. They closed all the camps just before the beginning of the war--they figured they didn't need the CCC's anymore and they needed the boys in the army instead.

Hobart Feltner of Cannonville contributed a little more information: I got there October 12, 1936, at 5 o'clock. I was in 22 months. The camp was about 2 years old when I came in [It opened in about 1934]. Darrel Blackwell came in 6 months after I arrived.

Those buildings didn't have any insulation--there was no insulation in the damn things. They was just boarded up. It was pretty cool in them buildings in winter, I can tell you that. You see, in 1936 & '37 is when that big snow storm came here, and you could walk over a fence and anything else! I told the guys, if this is the kind of stuff we're going to have around here, I'm not a goin' to be around next year!

Hasle Caudill, another enrollee and presently of Ogden, remembered a few more things. The camp had both a basketball & baseball team that went around to different towns, mostly in the summer, and played pickup games. When Hasle arrived, they had a team of work horses at the camp. In some places, they pulled fresno scrappers, but the camp's big cat put them out of work. To transport the boys around to different jobs, they used one of 8 or 10 1936 Ford 1 1/2 ton flatbed trucks equipped with wooden sides & benches (see foto).

When the big snow storm came on Christmas Day, 1936, they had to load one of the trucks with several 50 gallon barrels of water so they could get out to the cat. He then drove the cat to Watson Ridge opening a road so the CCC's could haul cottonseed cake out to Sam & Afton Pollock's sheep herds. He then broke a number of trails with the cat so feed could be spread out for the sheep. In some places, the snow as up to an man's armpits.

In 1939, just before Hasle left the CCC's, and just before the Henrieville Camp closed, he & Ora Shafer and others, built a rough road above the camp up through The Blues going in the direction of Escalante. Years later the state came in, improved it, and made it into the good paved state highway we have today.

If Rhoda Henderson Shafer's memory is correct, the camp closed down in the winter of 1939-'40, and the men & equipment were taken to Hurricane near St. George. She and her husband Ora then moved into the camp as caretakers. This was in the spring of 1940. In the fall, the Shafer's left as other people came in & started tearing the buildings down. No one knows where the lumber went to.

Willy Bryant, one of the former enrollees at the Henrieville CCC Camp, has a couple of large photographs of the camp and men. On each of these are inscribed: **CCC Co. 2529, Camp DG [Division of Grazing]--33, Henrieville, Utah, May 20, 1938.** Also inscribed on the picture of the men is: **Lt. C. W. Callahan, Commanding; Mr. H. L. Dirks, Educational Advisor; Lt. L. J. May, Junior Officer; and Mr. Lionel Chidester, Project Superintendent.** Both pictures were taken on May 20, 1938 by Erwin Photo.

To get to this camp site, drive eastward toward Escalante from Henrieville's post office on Highway 12 for 10.2 kms (6.35 miles). Park on the highway where the valley begins to narrow and walk down a side-road toward the creek. About the only thing left to see is the rock foundation of the flagpole. This is now in a sea of tall sagebrush.

One of the trucks belonging to the Henrieville CCC Camp. It's loaded with a compressor. The building behind is the motorpool. That building is seen in the lower left hand corner of the picture above on the opposite page.
(Hasle Caudill foto)

The Henrieville CCC Camp. L to R: The motorpool, officer's quarters, infirmary, mess hall, offices for the army & Division of Grazing (DG), and on the far right are the barracks which housed the enrollees. The latrines & showers are the fartherest to the right. In the center can be seen the flag-pole, the base of which is the only thing that is easily visible today. (Willy Bryant foto)

The Henrieville CCC Camp basketball team. (Hasle Caudill foto)

Above Inside the army-style barracks of the Henrieville CCC Camp--army cots, footlockers & wool blankets.

Middle The CCC's baseball team.

Right This is the cat or bulldozer belonging to the Henrieville CCC Camp. Rex Thompson is the cat skinner (driver). Most conservation projects in the area were done with this cat, but some work was done with a team & fresno scrappers. (Hasle Caudill fotos)

Left A 1936 Ford flatbed truck hauls CCC enrollees out to work on various conservation projects, mostly in the Bryce Valley area. **Right** Unidentified enrollee with the Henrieville CCC Camp's team of work plugs. They were hardly used in the time Hasle Caudill was there from 1936-'39. Caterpillar bulldozers put these horses out of work. (Hasle Caudill fotos)
Below Morning and evening all the enrollees, at least while in the main camp, were required to stand at reveille & retreat and watch the flag go & down. Looking south towards the creek and barracks. Behind the camera is the infirmary. (Willy Bryant foto)

Sheep and Sheep Shearing Corrals

An interesting part of the history of Bryce Valley is the story of sheep and a couple of sheep shearing corrals. The first sheep to arrive in the Paria River Country may have been brought in by Olie Alhstrom. He brought them from Sanpete County in central Utah in about the mid-1890's (?). From that point on, and up until the mid-1940's, or at about the end of World War II, there were literally thousands of sheep roaming and overgrazing the entire country.

It seems the first corral built for the specific purpose of shearing sheep was located at the bottom of Rock Springs Bench next to Rock Springs. This may have been set up as early as the late 1890's (?). The **Rock Springs Shearing Corral** site is located about 1 1/2 kms west of Wallace Ott's Corral and along Rock Springs Creek. See **Map 15, Road Map to Rock Springs Bench & Hikes.**

In the life history of Sam Pollock (compiled by his son Afton Pollock of Tropic), he states that he first started herding sheep for R. F. Shumway in August, 1901. In his story, Sam tells of one sad experience that happened a few years later: *In the spring of 1915, I exchanged shearing dates with my father-in-law Johnny Davis. His sheep were so poor that he could not meet his date. This new date made it so I could get my fat & stronger herd to the shearing corral on the 1st & 2nd days of May [at that time, they used hand clippers to shear the sheep and the shearing corral was at Rock Springs]. On the 3rd of May, we pulled out and arrived at Little Creek [Bench] where we spent the night. It started to rain, turning to sleet and snow about 3 am. My brothers Joe and Woodruff, along with Oscar LeFevre, were with the sheep. By morning there was a foot of snow and 300 dead sheep. The sheep kept dying and by noon there were 300 more dead. I met the herders about noon and we began building fires as there was plenty of wood and timber nearby. We built 50 fires and kept them going all night. Some of the sheep crowded the fires until they were burning to death, and some were smothered. After it was all over, we had 900 dead sheep and most of them were ewes ready to lamb. Some of the sheep would freeze to death while still standing and be dead when they fell over. This together with the winter loss made 1350 sheep lost. With the loss of lambs to be born, the total loss was about 2100 head. Sheep sold for $5 per head then, which would have been around $10,650 we were in debt......*

According to Afton Pollock: *The Rock Springs Shearing Corral site is about 3/4's or a mile west from where Wallace Ott's Corral is. There's a spring and that's why they built the corrals there. I used to get keg water there for camp. There's still evidence of the corrals--some posts and old planks and other things, still there. This was the first shearing corral in the country, then Promise Rock Corral came after that. They had a set of troughs they watered their sheep in from this spring, and that's just below where the corral was which was on the south side of the draw [creek].*

When you go down that draw, there's some big ledges on the north and part of that ledge has caved off. Now there are 2 big boulders and a bunch of names carved on 'um. The names include George Shakespeare, Will Shakespeare, a Graf, some Littlefields, Willis' and Chynoweths--quite a few names in there. My Dad's name is there from 1936. One date is from1904, another from 1906 and one in 1908. So that's about the time that shearin' corral was running on Rock Springs Bench.

They used to take team & wagons in there to haul things, and the route they used to get from Rock Springs to Cannonville is about the same as they use now. From the corrals, they went east then north to Watson Ridge, then the road went west across Little Dry Valley and down Road Holler [Hollow] to the Paria River then came up to the old Diamond T Ranch [the original John Wesley Mangum Ranch] and on to Cannonville. Road Holler is between Little Dry Valley and Shepherd Point.

I suppose they stopped shearing out there at Rock Springs in the late 1910's, or by about the end of World War I. Then they came up here to Promise Rock because W. J. Henderson had property there, and then they started shearin' at Promise Rock.

Just after Sam Pollock first got into the sheep herding business, a man by the name of William Jasper Henderson of Cannonville (brother of Jim Henderson who once owned the Nipple Ranch), built another shearing facility just southeast of Cannonville on some ground he owned. This became known as the **Promise Rock Shearing Corrals.** Afton Pollock made a few telefon calls around Bryce Valley to find out how this place got it's name (Lula Chynoweth Moore & Desmond Twitchell contributed information). Here's what he found--edited slightly for this book:

William J. Henderson was part of the original group called by Brigham Young in the mid-1870's to settle Bryce Valley. While on their way, part of that group stopped in a grove of trees for a rest. One young man named John Henry laid down underneath a tree and fell asleep. A young lady named Avilda March Diana Hickman thought it would be fun to see John's reaction to a surprise shower bath and threw a bucket of water all over him. He, John Henry in turn jumped up, grabbed the girl and gave her a bath in the nearby creek. This little event started a budding romance which was in full bloom by the time they reach the site that would later be called Cannonville. A short time after arriving at their new home, the young couple decided to explore the area and climbed up on top of this large flat rock. They saw the bishop working in the nearby field and soon asked him if he would come up on the rock and marry them. The bishop consented, and the marriage ceremony was performed. Ever since that day in 1877, this unusual red rock outcropping has been called **Promise Rock***.*

Wallace Ott recalled the place: *They'd bring sheep out there to shear 'um so they could load the wool and take it down to the train in Marysvale.*

Afton remembered even more: *W. J. Henderson had 2 herds of sheep, and he had 2 sons who had sheep. He owned property by Promise Rock and that's why he built the shearin' corrals there. The original corral, the one where they used hand clippers, was first set up in the early 1900's (?). You notice on these pictures, they had the old hand clippers, and a grinding stone to sharpen 'um with. But the one I remember when my Dad [Sam Pollock] was shearin' sheep there, was a more modern one. After a few years, they build this other building where they had a tractor with a long belt attached, and that powered newer clippers [which ran off belts & gears]. They had 20 booths, and up to 20 shearers could work there at a time. When I was a kid about 6 years old, that would have been in about 1925, the modern corral was in good shape. I'd say that second more modern shearing corral was built in about 1920.*

[Later on] I'd been on a mission in 1940, and I came home in 1943. Dad had me deferred [held out of the draft] because the wool was a necessary item for the troops, and they needed the wool for blankets and clothing, but I was a 23-year-old healthy young man and the war was goin' on, so I enlisted in the Air Force. I flew 75 missions over Burma and China, then when I come home in 1945, I went out with the sheep until October of 1946, then Dad sold his entire herd. He was the last one in the

valley to have sheep. He sold 'um to some people down in Long Valley. The spring of 1946 was the last time that Promise Rock Shearin' Corral was used. Just before that time, the Alhstroms went out of the sheep business, John Johnson went out of the sheep business, also Wallace Houseston and Sam Graf got out of sheep herding, and Dad was the only one left at the end of the war.

Wallace Ott and 2 other gentlemen here in Tropic had a little herd of about 800-1200 sheep, something like that, but they didn't shear'um at that shearin' corral; they brought 'um up here to Tropic and they had a little one-stall shearing place. Then they sold their sheep and went into the cow business.

There's signatures of sheepmen on all sides of Promise Rock, and on top of it. On the southeast side of Promise Rock there's a nice arch.

Promise Rock is made of the Gunsight Butte Member of the Entrada Formation, same as what you find in Kodachrome Basin just to the southeast. This large outcropping consists of several minor peaks rising above the sagebrush flats between where the upper Paria River and Henrieville Creek meet. The corrals & barn site is 300m south of the southwestern part of this big red rock outcropping. On the northwest side of this southwestern peak are lots of old sheepmen's signatures.

Promise Rock and all the land surrounding it are private, but none of the land owners are willing to allow access to the public. Check at the Cannonville visitor center for any late developments.

About the time World War II began, the sheep business in Utah started a steep decline. One reason for this was that many small-town country folk moved to the cities where they could get good paying jobs created by the war. That was a lot better work than spending months on the range herding sheep! Another reason was better roads & trucks which made it easier to haul sheep and/or supplies around. By the end of the war almost all herds in the Paria River Country were gone. Today nothing is left of these shearing facilities but a few cedar posts from the corrals themselves, and other posts which supported the roof of the shearing barn at Promise Rock.

This is all that remains of the Promise Rock Shearing Corral. It wasn't used after 1946. Promise Rock is seen in the background to the north. On the north side of the highest point you see, is a big wall with dozens of signatures of local sheepmen. Those signatures that are still visible date from just after 1900.

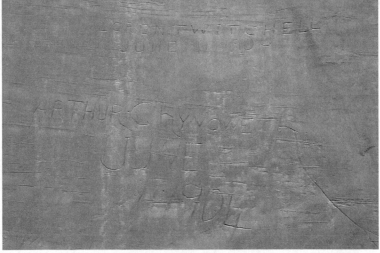

This is just part of the Promise Rock sheepmen's signature panel on the north side of the rock seen above. Here we see Loren Twitchell, 1906; he hauled lots of the equipment out to the Old Oil Well on the Rush Beds in 1929. And Arthur Chynoweth, 1904; he was an early resident of Pahreah.

The 2 fotos above were said to be of the Promise Rock Shearing Corrals, but the background is different. They certainly were taken in the early 1900's somewhere? (Cheri Schofield fotos)

Right Sam Pollock left, and his brother Lorem, packing up and moving camp somewhere in the lower Cottonwood Wash. Notice the sheep in the background. (Afton Pollock foto)

Hermon helped his father with the sheep between the years 1920 - 1937.

Afton Pollock thinks this is the shearing corral at Rock Springs (?). This picture would have been taken in the early 1900's. (Herman & Afton Pollock foto)

This picture shows Sam Pollock, 2 sheep dogs, and sheep in the background to the right. The peak in the distance looks like Castle Rock in the lower end of Cottonwood Wash. (Afton Pollock foto)

The Story of John D. Lee and the Mountain Meadows Massacre

A book on the Paria River, including Lee's Ferry, cannot be written without including the story of the life of John D. Lee. Nearly all Utah and Arizona residents know of him, but people from other parts of the country probably haven't. This chapter is a brief summery of Lee's life, and is intended to let the reader understand events leading up to the Mountain Meadows Massacre and why John D. Lee was sent to the lower Paria River to establish Lee's Ferry. The author used, with permission, a book by Juanita Brooks, **John Doyle Lee, Zealot-Pioneer Builder-Scapegoat,** as the primary source for this chapter.

John D. Lee was born on September 12, 1812, in Kaskaskia, the capital of the territory of Illinois. He lived in Illinois throughout his youth, and at age 16, left home to fend for himself. His first job was a mail rider, which lasted 6 months. He had various jobs in the several years until he got married, which was on July 24, 1833, at age 21. He married Agatha Ann Woolsey, the first of 19 women he would marry during his lifetime.

It wasn't long after this he became a convert to the Mormon Church. During the first 5 years of marriage, he was a missionary part of the time and had various jobs. In the period after 1838, he and the Mormons migrated to Missouri. As you might imagine, when the Mormons rode into that state proclaiming parts thereof to be their Zion, the reception wasn't too cheery. They had problems, and later had to leave, winding up in Illinois and eventually in Nauvoo where they built a temple.

Because Lee was a very religious man and totally devoted to the Church, he became one of the unofficial leaders. Because he was so good at things like farming, building homes, and working with machinery, he was called upon throughout his life to go out and help settle new colonies. He was never a high-ranking church authority, but was a major cog in the church settlement program for about 30 years.

From Nauvoo, Illinois, the Mormons headed for the Missouri River in the winter of 1946-47 and the region around Council Bluffs, Iowa, and near present-day Omaha & Florence, Nebraska. Since it would take a year or two to get all the Mormons to Utah, they needed to set up several temporary encampments enroute, in preparation for the long haul to the Great Basin. John D. was much involved in building these temporary settlements.

While in Iowa, the Mormons were called upon to send a battalion of soldiers to California. This they did, but the church President Brigham Young asked Lee to follow the group to Santa Fe, and collect the soldiers pay and bring it back to their families, who needed it a lot more than did the soldiers.

Because Lee was needed along the Missouri River area in Iowa and Nebraska, he was not chosen to accompany the first Pioneer Party to Utah in 1847. He instead followed in June of 1848. Upon arriving in Utah and the Salt Lake Valley, he immediately began to build a home for his wives. By the time he left Nauvoo, he had 10 wives; Brigham Young 17.

In one of the church meetings on December 2, 1850, in which Lee attended, Brigham Young mentioned they were going to send a group of volunteers south to what is now Cedar City, and establish an Iron Mission. There was a group of Englishmen who had the knowledge and skills to do the iron work, but they needed support in the venture. After the meeting, Young told Lee, that when he had asked for volunteers, he meant Lee. Young said, *"If we are to establish an iron industry there, we must have a solid base of farming to help support it."*

The next thing Lee knew, he was the leader of a small group heading for southern Utah in the dead of winter. On December 11, 1850, the wagons rolled out. Lee took 2 of his wives. As one can imagine, it wasn't an easy journey. There was no road, just a trail, and snow was deep at times. They arrived at the present-day site of Parowan in February of 1851. Parowan was the first of several new settlements Lee was to set up in the next 20 years.

Things went well for Lee and the church for several years, but in 1857 things began to change. News of an impending crisis came to the leaders of the church on July 24, 1857. This was the 10th anniversary of the landing of the Pioneer Party in the Salt Lake Valley. They had a big celebration up Big Cottonwood Canyon southeast of Salt Lake City. During the afternoon festival, 2 men rode up the canyon with news that, *"all mail routes to the east were canceled, and an army was enroute to put down the rebellion in Utah."* According to the Mormon version of events, there was no rebellion, unless you consider it a rebellion for all the church authorities to have too many wives!

With this news, the church leaders and the people became a little hysterical, and there was a call to arms. Since the Mormons had been run out of several eastern states, they gradually became better prepared, in a military sense. The church in Utah was organized not only into wards and stakes (religious groupings), but also in the event of an emergency, such as trouble with the Indians, they were organized into military companies and battalions as well. So preparations began, and in a way, Utah was almost in a state of martial law.

In many ways things went on as normal. But there began to be a very deep distrust for all non-Mormons. There were wagon trains crossing Utah all summer long, most of which were heading for northern California. But those who came late in the season usually went to California via the southern route. This route ran close to present-day Highway 91 and Interstate 15.

Since Salt Lake City was at about the halfway point between the populated eastern states and the coast, it was an important place to stop, rest and restock supplies. However, because of the impending arrival of Johnston's Army, the leadership of the church issued orders to all settlements not to sell food stuffs to any gentiles (non-Mormons). The church leaders also went to great pains to convince the various Indian leaders to join the Mormons to help rappel the US Army. The Indians were told to join the Mormons and help fight Johnston's Army, or the army would kill all the Indians as well.

One can imagine the hardships this must have created for those unlucky travelers who were caught up in the middle of this Utah problem. One of these groups of wagons was called the **Fancher Train.** It was a loosely knit group of several independent elements who had joined forces in Utah to travel in greater safety. The leader was Charles Fancher. He had crossed the country in 1855, selected and made arrangements to buy a large tract of land, and returned east in 1856 to bring his family and friends to join him to settle in California. They had a reported $4000 in gold coins, a large herd of cattle & horses and 11 well-stocked wagons. There were 11 families, with 29 children; a total of 65 people. Traveling with the Fancher Train was a group of horsemen with their supply wagons. They called themselves the **Missouri Wildcats.**

Map 37, John D. Lee's Country

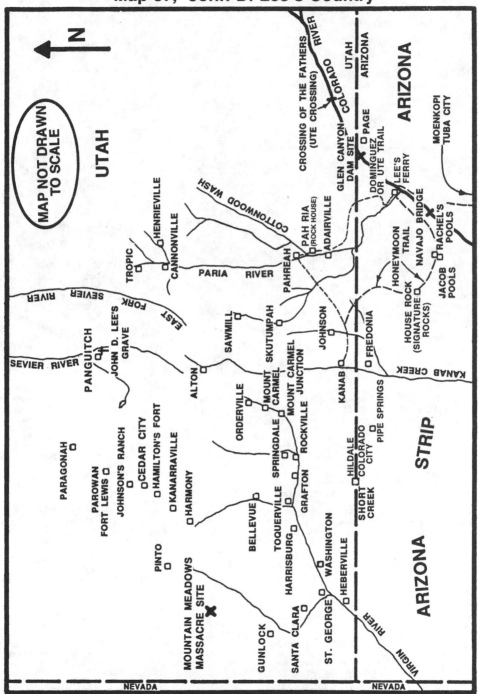

Adapted from Juanita Brooks' book, *JOHN DOYLE LEE--Zealot, Pioneer Builder, Scapegoat*

This picture of John D. Lee is thought to have been taken in about 1875 when Lee was 63 years old. (Arizona Historical Society)

Quoting now from Juanita Brooks' book on John D. Lee: "*This group all arrived in Salt Lake City on August 3 & 4, and mindful of the fate of the Donner Party in 1846, decided to take the southern route. They followed a few days behind President George A. Smith on his journey south ordering the people to keep their grain and not to sell a kernel to any gentile. The Fancher Train was well-to-do; they had cash to pay or goods to trade, but no one would sell. The attitude of the Mormons all along the way was one of belligerence and hostility, aggravated by the attitude of the group of "Missouri Wildcats", who spoke of the Mormon leaders with scorn, and boasted of what they had done in Missouri.*" This was the way things shaped up in Utah in the late summer and early fall of 1857.

As the Fancher Train moved south through the state, one thing after another aggravated the situation. The Mormons wouldn't sell them anything, and the emigrant train, especially the Missouri Wildcats, did or said things to upset the Mormons. Finally the emigrants arrived in Cedar City, the last place on the road to California to get provisions. Since the locals wouldn't sell them anything, it's been said some of the Missourians helped themselves to some of the gardens. The local Mormon police tried to arrest some members of the party, but were just laughed at. So things continued to get worse.

"*In the Sunday service at Cedar City on September 6, 1857, Stake President Isaac C. Haight spoke with bitterness of the coming of Johnston's Army, which he called an armed mob, and made pointed reference to the Fancher Train which had left only the day before. Following the regular service, a special priesthood meeting [men only] was called at which time the problems connected with the Fancher Train were discussed. Were they mice or men that they should take such treatment? Should they let such braggarts come into their midst and boast of the indignities they had heaped upon them in Missouri and Nauvoo? Should a man who would boast that he had the gun that 'shot the guts out of Old Joe Smith' go unpunished?*" Such were the feelings of the people in Cedar City.

Finally at the meeting, a resolution was passed to the effect that "*We will deal with this situation now, so that our hands will be free to meet the army when it comes.*" But then there was more discussion. Some wanted to do away with the emigrants who were the chief offenders; others preferring to let them all go and prepare themselves for the real war with Johnston's Army. Another resolution was presented to the effect that they should send a rider to Brigham Young in Salt Lake City seeking his council. It was passed, and they sent a rider (who returned late, and after the big event was over).

Still later a third resolution was passed, that of sending a messenger to John D. Lee at Harmony asking him to come and manage the Indians. At that time, Lee was an "*Indian Farmer*", or agent, and was second in command. Jacob Hamblin was the agent, but since he was in Salt Lake City, it was Lee who was called upon for advice. Lee had gotten on well with the Indians, and it's been said he spoke at least a few words of their language.

In the meantime, the Fancher Train had proceeded to a high meadow in the northern part of the Pine Valley Mountains. This was barely one day's drive from Cedar City. This place was called, and would always be known as, **Mountain Meadows.** They made camp near a spring and had plans to stay awhile to let their cattle recuperate, and until the weather got cooler, so they could cross the desert in more comfort.

Meanwhile back in Cedar City, things were happening at a rapid pace, with horsemen hurrying back and forth between Cedar City and Parowan, and between Mountains Meadows and Cedar City. At that time, there were 3 men who were the most important leaders in the area: William H. Dame from Parowan was appointed colonel commanding all the Iron County military. Isaac C. Haight was the Stake President who lived in Cedar City, and John D. Lee, who was the acting Indian agent, in the absence of Jacob Hamblin.

The Mormons were successful in getting the Indians on their side at this time. It seems both groups had no need for these emigrants, but for different reasons. A band of Indians had followed the Fancher Train south from Holden in central Utah, and had hoped the Mormons would help them attack the wagon train, and steal the cattle and other needed items. This same band of Indians joined others in the area of Cedar City, and had asked Lee to join them for an attack at Mountain Meadows. It seems that Lee had gone back home to Harmony to set things in order, and promised the Indians he would return on Tuesday, September 8.

But the Indians were ready for action, and knowing they and the Mormons were on the same side, made a predawn attack on the emigrant camp on the morning of September 8. The emigrants were caught by surprise, but were well-equipped and repulsed the attack. Later, Lee stated that 7 white men were killed, along with several Indians. When Lee joined the Indians on Wednesday the 9th, they were upset and excited. They insisted the Mormons join them to make another attack immediately. Lee wanted to go south and get help from the Santa Clara and Washington settlements, but about that time a group of settlers from those communities came, and they decided to send a messenger to Haight in Cedar City. Lee left at 2 pm.

In Cedar City, the bell rang out for the militia to gather. A statement was read that some of the emigrants had been killed, and they wanted volunteers to help bury them. But according to Brooks' story, a Nephi Johnson indicated a deception on the part of Isaac C. Haight. Johnson later suggested that Haight had said something to the effect that, *"Lee had suggested that they withdraw and let the emigrants go, and Haight sent word to Lee to clean up the dirty job he had started, and that he had sent out a company of men with shovels to bury the dead, but they would find something else to do when they got there."*

During the night of Wednesday the 9th of September, the military unit from Cedar City arrived at the Fancher camp. But at the same time, 3 emigrants had left camp under the cover of darkness and had gone to Cedar City to ask for help from the Mormons. As they neared their destination, and while watering their horses in a small stream, they were attacked by members of the Mormon Militia. One man was killed, and the other 2 scattered. It was later learned the remaining 2 men were killed by Indians at the Santa Clara crossing, down the Virgin River a ways. Again in Cedar City, the Mormon leaders gathered for council. It was decided to send John M. Higbee to Parowan in the night for advice from William. H. Dame.

Higbee returned the next day, Thursday the 10th, and delivered the message from Colonel Dame to Lee near the emigrant camp. The message indicated he should compromise with the Indians, allowing them to take all the cattle, then allow the emigrants to go. But then in the same message, Dame indicated if things couldn't be worked out, *"save women and children at all hazards".* Lee was in a predicament, and with conflicting orders. What to do? Years later Lee insisted, *"that he had written orders to the effect that the emigrants must be decoyed from their shelter and all who were old enough to testify slain".* Later in court, a man named Klingensmith testified that *"Lee's instructions came through Higbee from Dame at Parowan".* Klingensmith must have overheard the conversation between Higbee and Lee, *"Orders is from me to you that they are to be decoyed out and disarmed, in any manner, the best way you can."*

So there Lee was faced with a decision. The Indians and Mormons both wanted revenge. The Mormons felt they had rights to some kind of blood atonement, for the way the Missourians had treated them back in Far West and Nauvoo. The Indians also wanted some of the cattle; and the Mormons knew the Fancher Party was a wealthy group and had all those wagons and household goods. Greed must have been a factor in what was to be the final decision.

Lee along with a William Bateman, carried a white flag into the emigrant camp and negotiations began. Lee told them that if those guilty men would come back to Cedar City and face charges, they would all be given protection. But to do this, they would all have to show good faith and give up their arms. This the emigrants did, but ever since, people have wondered why they would give up their weapons (?). The day was **Friday, September 11, 1857.**

After the agreement was reached, all rifles and other weapons of the emigrants were loaded into one wagon, along with all the children under the age of about 10 years (17 in all). This wagon moved out in front. Then a second wagon was loaded up with the emigrants who had been wounded in the previous Indian attack. Some said there were 2 men and a women; others stated there were some older children as well.

Following the second wagon, were the women and older children walking in an unorganized group. Following them were the emigrant men, walking in single file, each escorted by an armed member of the Mormon Militia.

The idea was to save the small children, but have no witnesses. The first wagon went way out in front, so they couldn't see anything. Lee walked just in front of the second wagon, which was at least 500m behind the first. When the first wagon was just out of sight, somewhere near the marching men, the signal was given, *"Do your duty. Instantly all the guns were fired, and at the same moment the Indians leaped from their ambush and fell upon the women and [older] children. The teamsters with Lee, and their assistants killed the ones in the second wagon and threw the bodies out into the brush beside the road."* The plan was carried out to perfection, and it was over in a hurry. It was estimated 120 people were murdered.

Just after the massacre, the Indians stripped the bodies for clothing and valuables. Then Lee issued the order to let the Indians have what they had, but take no more. They were to return to their camp where some beef was ready for supper. The men of the Mormon Militia then heard several speeches by Higbee, Lee and others, to the effect that they had defended Zion and their families well, and that they had carried out "God's wishes". The men were then ordered to stay the night and bury the bodies before leaving for home the next morning.

The wagon with the rifles and children moved on up the valley to the Hamblin Ranch where Rachel Lee (Mrs. Lee No. 6) was living. She cared for the children and put them to bed. Lee came later, and during the night, Haight and Dame came to the ranch. The next morning, they all went back to Mountain Meadows and saw the ghastly site. The bodies were still being buried, and in the same holes the emigrants had dug previously to protect themselves from the Indians.

Then there was an argument between Haight and Dame about the orders given. The orders were confusing alright! This is the way Juanita Brooks stated part of the argument in her book.

"We must report this to President Young," Dame was saying.
"How will you report it?" Haight wanted to know.
"I will report it just as it is, a full report of everything."
"And will you say that it was done under your orders?"
"No"
Haight was furious with rage.
"You know that you issued the orders to wipe out this company, and you cannot deny it! You had better not try to deny it! If you think you can shift the blame for this onto me, you're fooled! You'll stand up to your orders like a man, or I'll send you to Hell Cross Lots."

About this time Lee interrupted to tell them it was done now and that they should go on from here. When the men finished with the burial, they gathered at the nearby spring and washed up. Then they all gathered around and Isaac C. Haight addressed the men. They were to say nothing to anyone and block it from their minds. Then they gathered in a circle, with Dame, Haight, Lee and Higbee at the 4 corners, and pledged they would never discuss it with anyone. Finally everybody left, including Lee, who wouldn't return to Mountain Meadows until the day he died.

A few days later they all met in Cedar City, and since John D. Lee was closest to Brigham Young, he was assigned to travel to Salt Lake City with the news of the killings. He left September 20, and arrived on the 29th. He reported the event to Brigham Young, which was written down by Wilford Woodruff. At that time John D. reported it as a job done by Indians.

The emigrant children were put into different homes and cared for. As far as they were concerned, it was Lee and the other Mormons who had saved them from the Indians--the Indians being the ones who killed their parents. The wagons and other contraband were placed in the Bishop's Warehouse to be given out to needy Mormon families.

In the months and years after the massacre everything went about as normal, given the circumstances. Lee took wife No. 17, a 22-year-old girl from England, on January 7, 1858, when he was age 46. This was Emma Batcheler, the one who would accompany John D. to the lower end of the Paria River in 1871, to set up a home at Lonely Dell, later to be known as Lee's Ferry.

Later on, Lee was involved in setting up the Cotton Mission on the Santa Clara River, near present-day St. George. While in the area, John D. stopped in Washington (just east of St. George), and bought some land, including a house in town, where he soon had 2 of his wives. And speaking of wives, still later in 1858, Lee seemed to be courting a young girl named Mary Ann. He apparently proposed to her, but she refused. She even wrote 2 letters of protest to Brigham Young. In January of 1859, he mentions in his diary, that she wanted instead to marry John D's oldest son, which she did.

It was in August of 1858, and after peace had finally been arranged between the Mormons, and Johnston's Army & the Federal Government, that a George A. Smith and James McKnight, both church officials, went to southern Utah, and made out 2 reports on the massacre. The reports didn't amount to a hill of beans, because everyone remained silent.

In the meantime, Lee lived at the fort in Harmony most of the time, where he had about 4 of his wives. Since there were lots of travelers passing through Utah at that time, he took advantage of the situation and set up a caravansary or way-station, to accommodate the wagon trains. Harmony was in the right place. They got most of their business in the fall and early winter. For a couple of years after the massacre, things went well for John D., but then things gradually changed.

According to Juanita Brooks, in *"April [1859] word came that Judge Cradlebaugh was on his way to investigate the Mountain Meadows Massacre, accompanied by a force of two hundred soldiers. Jacob Forney, the new Indian agent, came ahead to gather up the surviving children that they might be returned to their relatives in the east. They took Charley Fancher from the Lee household, although he was reluctant to go, and in line with the policy followed by all who had kept any of the children, Lee made out a bill to the government for his care."* With this, the beginning of the federal investigation, John D. Lee went into hiding, and was on the run for most of the next 18 years.

Judge Cradlebaugh and his group arrived at Cedar City in May of 1859, and set up camp in a big field about 2 1/2 kms from town. His assignment was to *"collect and bury the bones of the slain emigrants, and to arrest as many participants in the massacre as he could catch.*

The judge brought warrants for the arrest of a half-dozen of the leaders, and he wanted information concerning others who were involved. He found the local people reluctant to talk, for none knew anything for a certainty, and if they did, they would not betray their brethren into the hands of the enemies of the church. A few did want to talk, but feared the consequences. At least one participant came to the judge secretly late at night and told the story of that tragic day, giving some names and details, and begging for protection and anonymity. The burden of the crime was more than he could bear."

Because many of the participants were either in hiding or had gone to different states, the judge was unable to make a single arrest. There was eventually a reward of $5000 offered for the arrests of Dame, Haight, Higbee, Klingensmith, or Lee. But no one ever turned any of them in. After spending a month in the area, the judge gave up and returned to Salt Lake City.

In the years of 1860 & '61, things went quite well for John D., considering. He had 2 homes; one in Harmony, the other in Washington, and nearly all the wives he wanted. Both places were opened as caravansaries & taverns, and business was good.

Right at the end of 1861, there was a stormy period which lasted from December 25 until the beginning of February, 1862. This was a disaster for everyone in the region, and especially for John D. Lee and his families. The fort they had been living in at Harmony was made of mud bricks, and it literally melted away. During the first part of February, they were all trying to move out of the Harmony Fort and into some new dwellings at nearby New Harmony. But before they could all get moved, the roof of part of the building caved in, killing 2 of Lee's children.

Down at Washington, things were just as bad. John D. had just recently erected a molasses mill, which had earned him good money the previous fall. It had been swept away in the flood, and the machinery buried in sand & mud. Because of this 40-day storm, it took Lee about 4 full years to get back to the financial position he had been in before the floods.

In 1866, John D. finally was on his feet again and doing better. In that year he took his last wife,

Ann Gordge, who was from Australia and just 18 years of age. Later in the same year, he lost his first bride, Aggatha, who died of a lingering illness. This was a sad occasion for Lee, and seemed to be a sort of beginning of the end for him.

It was about this time that the people of Harmony began giving him untold misery. *"Whisperings about the massacre continued; the stories became more numerous and highly colored. In many ways his neighbors showed their disapproval--by turning their cattle into his grain fields, interfering with his water ditches, and making snide remarks to his wives or children.* He always attended church, he was first to fill the assignment made by Brigham Young to get out poles for the new telegraph line, he was prompt in paying his tithes. At Parowan and Cedar City, he was often called upon to speak at church, and at Kanarra he was held in high esteem. Perhaps his very industry, his driving use of his family and hired help, his shrewd trading, his ability to amass property and to live well made his neighbors all the more critical of him."

In the fall of 1867, he made a trip to Salt Lake City with a herd of goats belonging to Brigham Young, his adopted father. When he returned in December, he found his estate falling apart. Without Aggatha, and with his 2 oldest sons away on missions, there had not been the same enthusiasm as had been the case earlier.

It was also in the late 1860's, that trouble began to brew for Brigham Young and the church leadership, and since John D. was always a strong supporter of the President, he began to feel the pinch as well. In 1868, there appeared in Salt Lake City a new publication, the **Utah Magazine.** This, as it turned out, was a voice for those who were becoming discontented with the church leaders and their policies. Some of the unrest resulted in a number of excommunications in the northern part of the state. Many of these people wanted to be members of the church, but were simply critical of the leaders; thus they were booted out of the church.

The original complaint against Young was, he got too involved with their financial dealings; but later they condemned Young for condoning murder. During this period, there were some mysterious deaths in Salt Lake City. Dr. K. Robinson was assassinated in 1866; John V. Long, former secretary of Brigham Young, was found dead in a ditch in April, 1869; and Newton Brassfield was murdered on one of the main streets of Salt Lake in April 1866. These men were part of the group generally known as the **Godbeites,** after it's chief spokesman, W. S. Godbe.

One of their worst complaints about Brigham Young was that he gave public recognition to men who had participated in the Mountain Meadows Massacre. The **Utah Reporter**, published in Corrine (in the middle of northern Utah's gentile country), *"ran a series of open letters addressed to Brigham Young, demanding that those guilty of that outrage be brought to justice. The articles were signed by 'Argus,' who claimed to have lived in Southern Utah and learned the facts from some of the participants."*

During the winter of 1869-70, Lee defended Brigham Young by visiting many communities in southern Utah, to as far north as Fillmore, and by making speeches in Young's behalf.

In September of 1870, Brigham Young led a small group of men to explore areas east of the southern Utah settlements. Lee joined this group, and was assigned the job of locating the best route (as they were heading into new country without roads), and making camps along the way. William H. Dame was in charge of preparing meals.

Their route went through Panguitch, south to Roundy's Station (now called Alton), then down Johnson Canyon. At some point along the way, Brigham Young had a private talk with John D. He was urging Lee to move. Quoting again from Juanita Brook's book, Young said, *"I should like to see you enjoy peace for your remaining years. Gather your wives and children around you, select some fertile valley, and settle out here."*

Along the way they met, and were joined by John W. Powell. The party traveled east from the bottom of Johnson Canyon to the Paria River. They got as far as the Peter Shirts' (Shurtz) farm at Rock House, which just after that time was called Pah Ria on Utah state maps, and found a small patch of green corn and some squash. Lee was not impressed and made the statement, *"I wouldn't bring a wife of mine to such a place as this."* After the visit to the Paria River, they came to the conclusion there was little there to attract future settlements, and left. On their return, the party surveyed and laid out the site of Kanab, to be settled by some of those same men (one group had already tried to settle Kanab in about 1865, but had left on account of the Black Hawk War). After the lots were numbered, the settlers each drew a number from a hat to select their home site.

Brigham Young wanted Levi Stewart to set up a sawmill to make lumber to build Kanab. Levi stated he had worked with Lee before and would like to have him as a partner again. John D. reluctantly said yes, out of sheer obedience to the Church leader. The group then returned to the southwest Utah settlements via Pipe Springs.

Lee immediately set to work to sell his property and settle accounts. He put up for sale and sold his holdings in Harmony, but kept the Washington property, leaving several of his wives there until he could get back later. He started the trip to Kanab with wife Rachel and her children, 4 wagons, and 60 head of stock. The route taken was up through the canyon via Rockville, then over the plateau, and finally down to Kanab. It took 10 days to travel the very rough 150 kms.

From Kanab, they went east to what is today Johnson, about 16 kms east of Kanab. They then went north up Johnson Canyon to a moderately high grassy valley now called Skutumpah. This was to be their new home, but they were to live temporarily a little above Skutumpah where the sawmill was to be located. It was about 15 kms to a site on Mill Creek where they built a camp. It was in late October, 1870, that he first built a cabin for Rachel.

When the engineer and surveyor arrived, they quickly set up the sawmill, but almost immediately it broke down. Someone would have to return to Parowan for a new part. With Rachel safe in the new cabin, Lee left to get other members of his family. He met a second family group at Pipe Springs--it was one of his son-in-laws and several children, along with 3 wagons and 40 head of cattle. At that time, in mid-November, 1870, he was handed a letter which had to do with his excommunication from the Mormon Church! It was dated October 8, 1870. At that time he mentioned it to no one.

The group went straight for Skutumpah, set up a tent for a temporary home, and went upcanyon to Rachel's cabin. Help from Kanab finally came in early December, and they worked fast and furious, because of the coming winter. The work at the sawmill was so fast the wagons coming and going from Kanab couldn't keep up. On December 13, news came of a disastrous fire in Kanab; the fort had burned to the ground, and 6 members of the bishop's family were killed. That ended the winter logging operation in the upper Skutumpah area.

John D. left Rachel and the others, and made a trip back to Washington, where he had a cold reception from his other wives and children. The next morning he went to St. George to speak to Brigham Young, who was in his winter home, about his excommunication. He pleaded his case saying that he had been loyal to him and the church, and that now he was being singled out to bear the guilt of the massacre. He also stated that the decision to attack the Fancher Train was a mutual agreement between the highest church leaders in the area. After the meeting, Lee left and returned to Harmony, where he was invited to speak in church on Christmas Day, 1870.

Upon his return to Washington, he received a note from a high church official, stating, *"If you will consult your own safety & that of others, you will not press yourself nor an investigation on others at this time least you cause others to become accessory with you & thereby force them to inform upon you or to suffer. Our advice is, trust no one. Make yourself scarce & keep out of the way."*

After these kind words, and on January 2, 1871, John D. set out once again for Skutumpah, this time with Caroline (Mrs. Lee No. 4), and her 8 children. It took them 15 days to reach Skutumpah this time, because of the heavy snows and poor travel conditions. Upon arriving, the whole family set to work cutting trees and sawing lumber in order to build and finish a large home for Caroline. When that was completed, they dismantled Rachel's cabin, and reconstructed it again down at Skutumpah. By the first of March, they began the third house, but about that time, Emma, wife No. 17, came up in an empty wagon. She was distressed, trying to decide which way to go--whether to stay with John D. or leave him for someone else. She decided to stay with her husband.

Soon after this and as the sawmill was roaring full blast, Lee sold his interest in the site. With all the lumber he needed, he continued to work at Skutumpah until he had finished 4 homes, each with wood floors, shingle roofs, and glass windows. In June, 1871, he made another quick trip back to St. George to attend to business. While there he worked to sell out his Washington property, and bring the rest of his family to Skutumpah.

Enroute, and in Johnson Canyon, he met Isaac C. Haight, who was also in hiding and laying low. Together they went to Kanab, but waited outside town, while Jacob Hamblin and John Mangum brought them food, and more importantly, news. The news this time was that the federal authorities were clamping down on polygamists, and they were advised to transfer all their property to their wives. Lee set out to do this at once, naming Rachel Woolsey, Polly Young, Lavina Young, Sarah Caroline Williams, and Emma Batchelor as recipients. All of his other wives had deserted him by that time. But the real heartbreaking news was that he was ordered by the church to take one or 2 of his wives, and move down to the Colorado River at the mouth of the Paria River. That was in August of 1871.

This was John D. Lee's greatest decision. But he would obey. He had 5 wives; which 2 would he take? He was heading for some wild country, and would end up in the middle of the desert and be in country controlled by Navajos. Problems would be immense, but even though he had been excommunicated, he still had the secret backing of Brigham Young. After all, it was Young who had ordered him to go.

The first wagons rolled out of Skutumpah in November of 1871. It consisted of 3 wagons, 57 head of livestock of various kinds, and Caroline and her family. At their first camp in lower Johnson Canyon, Jacob Hamblin joined them. He knew the country better than anyone, and he and Lee had a long discussion on the best route to take. It was decided to have the wagons head down what was to be called later the Honeymoon Trail, while John D. and 14-year old son Ralph, would take the cattle to the new settlement of Pah Ria, and drive them straight down the canyon.

At the Paria River, which maps of that era labelled **Pah Ria**, he met Tom Adair and John Mangum, and was happy to have these 2 men join him. The going downriver was more difficult than anyone had anticipated. *"They spent 8 days on the trail, much of the time in water. Two days and one night they traveled without stopping because there was no place to camp. When their provisions were gone, they shot a cow that had become hopelessly mired in quicksand and cut steaks from her, living for the next few days on a meat diet."*

Upon arriving at the mouth of the Paria, they found no wagons. Brigham Young had sent out a work crew to build a road, but neither the work crew nor Caroline had reached the Paria. Adair and Mangum returned up the Paria River to Pah Ria via the Dominguez or Ute Trail, while Lee and Ralph headed around the Vermilion Cliffs hoping to meet their wagons enroute. Because it was unfamiliar country, John D. got lost, and ended up returning all the way to Skutumpah.

The next day John D. and wives Emma and Rachel, and several wagons, headed out to find Caroline. Below Johnson, they found one broken-down wagon, and knew she had gone to Kanab instead. She had changed her mind, and had decided to go and stay there the winter and to give birth to another child, rather than go into the wilderness alone.

Back on the road again, the new contingent made it to the Colorado River on December 23, 1871. (At Signature Rocks next to House Rock Spring, John D. left his mark in the rocks, **J.D. Lee Dec 25 1871.** This tells us that someone's diary is wrong, or that the 25th, which is hard to read, is really another date, maybe Dec. 21?). The next morning, when they all had a chance to look around, Emma said, *"oh what a lonely dell"*. And forever more the name of the small settlement or ranch at the mouth of the Paria River has been called Lonely Dell.

The first thing they did at the lower Paria River was to build a house. The first shelter was a dugout up against the hill and made of rock. It would later be a cellar. The second was a rock building with a door and 2 windows. When the 2 shelters were finished, John D. rode upcanyon a ways to check on his cows. When he returned, he found Emma with a new baby, which was born on January 17, 1872. They named her Francis Dell Lee.

The very next day, January 18, they saw Navajos across the river. The Indians wanted Lee to help them across. John D. and Rachel first had to work on one of John W. Powell's boats, which had been left there in 1869 on his first Colorado River trip. After repairs, Lee & Rachel made the first ferry crossings. It took 3 trips to get all the Navajos across. They later made some trades, Lee and his families ended up with blankets, cloth for making clothing, and other needed items. The Navajos got 2 horses, a mule and a colt.

In April, 1872, a group of miners came into camp, and the Lee family helped accommodate them. Emma cooked, in exchange for their help in building up the place, and for some needed tools. It was at about this time it was decided they would build 2 places; one at Lonely Dell, the other at the springs known as The Pools, or Jacob Pools, and later Rachel's Pools. The 2 places were 32 kms apart, and Jacob Pools would be a welcome stop for travelers who were making the long journey from Utah to Arizona. It must be remembered that Lee was sent there to set up a ferry and provide food, shelter and accommodations for travelers, many of who would be Mormons. The church at that time was expanding into Arizona, and Lee, although officially excommunicated, was instrumental in this expansion.

By early May 1872, Rachel moved. The first shelter at Jacob Pools was made with mud & willows, and didn't give much shelter. On June 2, a group of engineers of the Powell Survey, passed through the area and fotographed Rachel's first little willow shack. This was a different group than Powell's river expedition.

In was on July 13, that Major Powell and his survey crew landed at Lonely Dell with the boat Cañonita, and were out of about everything except coffee & flour. Emma cooked for them and both groups shared what they had; the expedition members enjoying Emma's vegetables.

John D. was in and out of Lonely Dell and Jacob Pools. He had to help build shelters and go north & west to get supplies from the settlements. This was all fine, because as long as he was on the move, it would be difficult for the authorities to track him down. At that time the federal people were always after the "cohabs", or polygamists, and a bit later they were after Lee for his involvement in the Mountain Meadows Massacre.

In October 1872, a small military group out to explorer & survey the Colorado River made it to Lonely Dell and met Mrs. Lee No. 17, but no John D. They explored up the Paria River, but one of their group drowned. That full story is told in the hiking section in the Lower Paria River Gorge.

On December 16, 1872, a man named Heath came with a load of lumber for the purpose of building a ferry. While he and a crew were in the process of building a boat, John D. was at Rachel's place making a fine home. He had hired Elisha Everett to help on the rock work, for there was no other material there with which to build. This new home was mostly completed on Christmas Day, 1872. It measured about 9 x 11 meters, had 2 doors, 2 bedrooms, a kitchen, a parlor and covered with a wooden roof. Nearby was a cellar. If you're there today, you can still see the remains of this 1872 dwelling, just above the western-most spring north of Jacob Pools. Most people call this place at the springs Rachel's Pools, as opposed to Jacob Pools, which is about a km SSW of her home site. At least the USGS maps put Jacob Pools out in the valley a ways, and on what was likely the actual route of the Honeymoon Trail. See the hiking section and **Map 36A,** for the location.

The ferry boat was completed by January 11, 1873. Counting the Lee family and work crews, there were 22 people in all at the ferry site, and they all took a ride in the new boat, which they called "The Colorado." A little later, on February 1, a group of 12 men used the ferry for the first time. They were heading south to explore the Little Colorado River country for the church. From February 1873 until about November 1874, John D. Lee was the ferryman at what then and now is called **Lee's Ferry.** The first company of settlers on their way south arrived in April, 1873. They were charged $3.00 a wagon, and $.75 a horse for the service. For those who didn't have the money, payment could be made in food or supplies, so things worked out well for the new ferryman.

In the summer of 1873, a message came from Kanab that a unit of 600 soldiers were on their way to Lee's Ferry to set up a permanent camp. This spooked Lee pretty bad, so he swam a horse across the Colorado River, and headed south to Moenkopi. While at Moenkopi, John D. met Jacob Hamblin and later they made a deal for a swap. They agreed to trade places; Lee's or rather, Rachel's home and holdings at The Pools, for Jacob's claim at Moenave, near Moenkopi. In the fall, Jacob would help Rachel make the move down into Arizona. As it turned out, the story of the soldiers coming to Lee's Ferry wasn't true.

For about a year, things went well and uneventful. Then came the fall of 1874. A Sheriff named Stokes had warrants for the arrest of eight men who were the leaders of, and had participated in, the Mountain Meadows Massacre. By then the name of John D. Lee was at the top of the list. The Sheriff was partly familiar with Lee's habits, and was aware of where his wives lived. At the time, Caroline lived in Panguitch. It was on a visit to this wife, that Lee was captured. This was in early November of 1874. They took John D. to Beaver in a wagon. He was there in jail from November 10, until July 23, 1875, when the trial for the massacre at Mountain Meadows began.

At the trial, the indictment included William H. Dame, Isaac C. Haight, John D. Lee, John M. Higbee, George Adair Jr., Elliot Wilden, Samuel Jukes, P.K. Smith, and William Stewart. Because everybody involved had sworn to secrecy, no one would testify except Philip Klingensmith. As it turned out Klingensmith's testimony was rather accurate and precise. The defense made the point, *"that while Lee was present and might have participated, he was there by command of his superiors, both military and ecclesiastical, whose orders in this time of military rule would be death to disobey. While they admitted the facts of the massacre and all its unbelievable horror, they placed the responsibility upon the Mormon Church and its doctrine that men were justified in 'avenging the blood of the Prophets' as a part of their duty to God."*

In the end it was a hung jury. The 8 Mormons being for acquittal, the 4 gentiles for conviction. This meant another trial. This time Lee would be held in Salt Lake City. But this meant hardship for his families. Rachel left Moenkopi for the Utah settlements; Caroline was in Panguitch; Lavina and Polly remained at Skutumpah; and Emma stayed on at Lonely Dell. As for the ferry, the church sent Warren Johnson and his family to Lonely Dell to take charge of that operation.

John D. Lee left Beaver on August 9, 1875, and was taken to Salt Lake City. He was kept in the state penitentiary, which at that time was in the area of present-day Trolley Square. As one might expect, Lee was a model prisoner, and ended up with many privileges. At various times he taught other inmates how to read, was a kind of doctor, and was even entrusted with some keys to the place. For some reason, he was released on May 11, 1876, on $15,000 bail. He was to appear in Beaver 4 months later for the trial.

In the period before the second trial, John D. traveled around visiting his various wives and families. He was at Lonely Dell in August. His sons had tried to talk him into going to Mexico to escape, but he insisted by doing so he would be admitting guilt. In late August of 1876, he left the Lee's Ferry and headed for Skutumpah via the Dominguez Trail. Just after he left, a messenger came via the Honeymoon Trail, with word from the church authorities counciling Lee to jump bond and leave the country. The church would assume the full responsibility to the bondsmen. But he missed the message.

In Beaver, the second trial began in September, 1876. For some reason the atmosphere of this trial was totally different. Twelve jurors were selected, all in good standing in the Mormon Church. During the trial, 7 witnesses were called, again all good members. They were all now willing to talk about the whole thing. The witnesses told of John D. Lee's participation, and that of Klingensmith's, but he had immunity since he had turned state's evidence. They also spoke of how Haight and Higbee were involved, but they were both dead at the time of the 2nd trial. It was very clear that something had been worked out so that everyone pointed the finger at John D. Lee. To resolve the issue, it seems clear that it was necessary to have a scapegoat, so that life for the church could go on as normal. Lee never did take the stand or defend himself. He sat through the trial in silence.

At the end and when the jury came back, the statement read, *"Guilty of murder in the first degree."* Lee immediately wrote to Emma for more money, to take the case to a higher court. His attorney, W.W. Bishop felt he had been sold out. Meanwhile 2 petitions were circulated in southern Utah, asking that the Governor give him clemency. The Governor said he would consider the move if Lee would speak up and tell all, and make an attempt to implicate those above him. But Lee remained silent, and there was no clemency.

So on March 23, 1877, John D. Lee was taken back to Mountain Meadows, the scene of the crime. There were a number of people there, including James Fennimore, the fotographer who Lee had known and made friends with at Lonely Dell. A foto of the place shows John D. sitting on his coffin. Lee was blindfolded, but his hands were free, when the 5 shots were fired. He fell back in the coffin and it was closed and loaded into a wagon. He was then carried to Panguitch and buried in the cemetery just east of town and south of the Highway 89.

To get to Mountain Meadows today, drive west out of Cedar City toward Beryl Junction and Enterprise, then turn south on State Highway 18 running toward St. George. About halfway between Enterprise & Central, and between mile post 31 & 32, is the turnoff to Mountain Meadows. From St. George, drive north toward Veyo & Central and in the direction of Enterprise. Just off the paved road to the west is a new memorial built on a hill overlooking the valley. This was built in 1990. From this hillside overlook, drive west down a good gravel road to a new monument where a number of those killed were buried. The original plaque placed there in 1932 read:

MOUNTAIN MEADOWS
A FAVORITE RECRUITING PLACE ON THE OLD SPANISH TRAIL
In this vicinity, September 7-11, 1857, occurred one of the most lamentable tragedies in the annals of the West. A company of about 140 Arkansas and Missouri emigrants led by Captain Charles Fancher, enroute to California, was attacked by white men and Indians. All but 17, being small children, were killed. John D. Lee, who confessed participation as leader, was legally executed here March 23, 1877. Most of the emigrants were buried in their own defense pits.

The first monument at Mountain Meadows was erected in May 1859 by Brevet Major James H. Carleton and 80 soldiers of the first Dragoons from Fort Tejon, California. Assisting were Captains Reuben P. Campbell and Charles Brewer, with 270 men from Camp Floyd, Utah. The bones of about 34 of the emigrants were buried where the monument is now. The remains of others were buried 2 1/2 kms north near the place of the actual massacre.

The original monument, consisting of a stone cairn topped with a cedar cross and a small granite marker set against the north side of the cairn, was not maintained. The Utah Trails & Landmarks Association built a protective wall around what remained of the 1859 monument and, on September 10, 1932, installed a bronze marker. That marker was replaced with another one on September 15, 1990.

In 1990, there was a new memorial erected on a hill overlooking Mountain Meadows with the names of those who died in the massacre. Along the paved path to this monument are several plaques recounting the story of the massacre, plus a map showing all the historic sites. During that dedication ceremony for the new plaque, no apologies were given and it seemed everyone, especially the Mormons, were trying to put this one behind them as far as possible. It also seems that whoever made the new plaque was trying to put the blame for the massacre as far behind them as possible too.

On September 11, 1999, another ceremony took place at the grave site, this time dedicating a new monument which replaced the one built in 1932. Located there today is a large parking lot & toilet facility, a paved trail across a small stream, and a large memorial structure with several plaques. This is the last of 4 monuments commemorating the site.

Breaking News: On March 25, 2004, Washington city officials stated they will honor several of the city's founding fathers by placing statues of them in front of the city museum. One of the 5 will be that of John D. Lee. The dedication ceremony will take place on May 7, 2004. Members of the Mountain Meadows Association are not exactly happy about this policy. Washington is just east of St. George in southwestern Utah.

Mountain Meadows, March 23, 1877. John D. Lee sits on his coffin (far left) awaiting execution by a firing squad. At his left, the Deputy U.S. Marshal reads the death warrant. On horseback in the background are Lee's sons. They were kept at a distance as it was feared they would attempt a last minute rescue. The firing squad is hidden under the canvas at far right. (Library of Congress foto)

This is the tombstone of John D. Lee, which is in the northeast corner of the Panguitch, Utah, Cemetery. To get there, drive along Highway 89 immediately east of Panguitch. Between mile posts 130 & 131, turn south at the cemetery sign, and drive a short distance.

This foto was taken in November, 2003. It shows the new monument located at the main burial site in Mountain Meadows. On the hill above to the left or east, is another memorial with signs & maps showing the layout of the historic sites in the valley.

History of Ghost Towns along the Paria River

Bryce Valley Ghost Towns

One of the best sources for the history of the first settlements in the upper Paria River drainage, known today as Bryce Valley, is **The Geology and Geography of the Paunsaugunt Region-Utah,** by Herbert E. Gregory. Most of the following account is adapted from his early geologic explorations and travels throughout the region.

In the 1860's & 70's, there were surveying parties traveling across parts of the upper Paria and Escalante Rivers, and they noted several large valleys which looked promising for settlement. One of the surveyors was A. H. Thompson, who said the upper valley of the Paria River was well-watered, had good soil, and a good climate. He also noted there were coal beds close by and good range for grazing livestock.

Because of such reports, the first pioneer white settlers in the upper Paria Valley were the families of David O. Littlefield and Orley D. Bliss, who on December 24, 1874, laid out farms near the junction of the Paria River and Henrieville Creek. With the arrival of eight additional families in 1875, the original cluster of log houses at the base of the red cliffs grew into a small settlement called **Cliff Town**. Since those earliest days, the name gradually changed to **Clifton**. The old Clifton townsite is located about 3 kms due south of Cannonville.

One of the new settlers, Ebenezer Bryce, who is said to have come to Clifton in 1875 or '76, decided they needed more room and looked for another location to farm. He selected a site farther upstream in what was known then as Henderson Valley. This new settlement was first called **New Clifton**. Bryce, in association with Daniel Goulding and others (1878-80), constructed an irrigation canal 11 kms long, planted orchards, and took up livestock raising.

It was during this time, and when Eb Bryce ran cattle into the canyons to the west, that Bryce Canyon received it's name. An early-day saying around the region, which Bryce is given credit for, makes a statement about herding cattle into the area which is now called Bryce Canyon National Park. That statement was, *It's a hell of a place to lose a cow!*

Bryce left New Clifton in 1880, while Goulding left in 1883. They sold their holdings to Isaac H. Losee, Orville S. Cox, and Ephriam Cottall. They renamed the site **Losee** or **Loseeville**. The Losee townsite is located about 3 kms due east of present-day Tropic, in what is now called East Valley.

Now back to Clifton. About 2 years after settlement, the people in the little settlement of Clifton found themselves too closely hemmed in between the cliffs and the bank of the Paria, and their farmland in the process of being carried away by flood waters. So in 1877 Clifton was mostly abandoned, with most of its settlers going to a new site about 3 kms north. This new town was named **Cannonville**, after a high-ranking dignitary of the Mormon Church, George Q. Cannon.

While some of those who abandoned Clifton went to and settled Cannonville, 3 families headed east instead, and settled on Henrie Creek, about 8 kms east of Cannonville. This is present-day **Henrieville** and **Henrieville Creek**, named in honor of James Henrie, then-president of the Panguitch Stake of the LDS Church. An interesting side note, the first time any of these towns were named on a map of the state of Utah was in 1884. Cannonville & Henrieville were both on that map. The first time the name Losee appeared on any state map was in 1893.

In 1886, Seth Johnson, Joseph & Eleazer Asay, Richard C. Pinney, and other stockmen took up

This is the new monument about Losee or Loseeville. It's located next to the main road in East Valley east of Tropic, and near the Losee Cemetery.

Map 38, Bryce Valley Coal Mines & Ghost Towns: Georgetown, Clifton and Losee

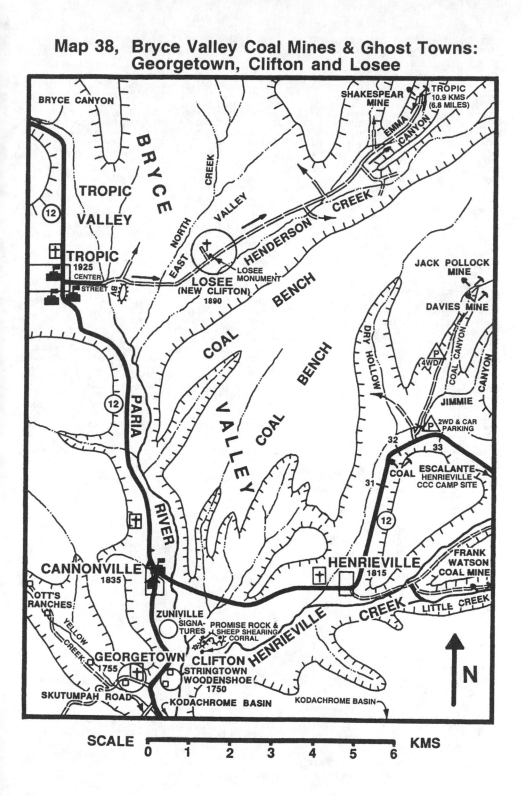

BRYCE CANYON

BRYCE

TROPIC VALLEY

(12)

TROPIC
1925
CENTER
STREET

SHAKESPEAR MINE

TROPIC
10.9 KMS
(6.8 MILES)

EMMA CANYON

NORTH CREEK

EAST VALLEY

HENDERSON CREEK

LOSEE MONUMENT

LOSEE
(NEW CLIFTON)
1890

COAL BENCH

COAL BENCH

JACK POLLOCK MINE

DAVIES MINE

COAL CANYON

CANYON

DRY HOLLOW

JIMMIE

P
4WD

P
2WD & CAR PARKING

32

33

COAL

31

ESCALANTE HENRIEVILLE CCC CAMP SITE

(12)

COAL VALLEY

COAL BENCH

PARIA

RIVER

(12)

CANNONVILLE
1835

OTT'S RANCHES

YELLOW CREEK

ZUNIVILLE

SIGNA-TURES

PROMISE ROCK & SHEEP SHEARING CORRAL

HENRIEVILLE
1815

FRANK WATSON COAL MINE

HENRIEVILLE CREEK

LITTLE CREEK

GEORGETOWN
1755

SKUTUMPAH ROAD

CLIFTON
STRINGTOWN
WOODENSHOE
1750

KODACHROME BASIN

KODACHROME BASIN

N

SCALE   0   1   2   3   4   5   6   KMS

lands on lower Yellow Creek about 5 kms southwest of Cannonville and thus became the pioneer settlers of **Georgetown.** Like Cannonville, this new ranching community was named after George Q. Cannon.

It was during the early 1880's, Cannonville became the center of prosperity for the entire valley. That's where a Mormon church was built, and where the most prosperous cattlemen lived. Later on, in the early 1890's, people were beginning to move out of Georgetown on account of the lack of water. Shortly after 1894, the town was so small, it became part of the Cannonville Ward of the LDS church. A year or two later, it was all but deserted except for a ranch or two.

About the same time Georgetown was thriving, there were some families who moved back into the areas left abandoned in the former Clifton settlement. Perhaps it wasn't totally deserted in the first place (?). In the late 1880's and/or early 1890's, this small area received the nickname of **Stringtown.** It seems there were a number of separate ranches strung out along the road between Cannonville & Georgetown; thus the name Stringtown. It was never incorporated into a town or an organized LDS ward or congregation.

If you talk to old-timers in the Bryce Valley about early-day settlements, they will always mention the name **Woodenshoe.** The man who knew a little more about it than anyone else, was the late Kay Clark of Henrieville. He recalled stories and history of his grandfather, Owen W. Clark. After the Clarks had moved into, then out of, the Clark (or White House) Cabin on the lower Paria, then had attempted to resettle at Adairville, then moved north again to Pahreah for several years. That place wasn't as promising as they had hoped, so again they moved, this time north to what was then Stringtown, which was actually part of Cannonville at the time. They lived there until 1896, then sold the farm to some Dutch people. This family was poor and often wore wooden shoes; thus the name Woodenshoe was attached to the area of the original settlement of Clifton.

Another interesting story about an early Bryce Valley settlement comes from Wallace Ott of Tropic. When he was just a wee small boy of 3 or 4 years of age, he remembered an event and place just south of Cannonville, in the same general area as Clifton, Stringtown and Woodenshoe. It seems that in about 1914 or '15, there came into the valley a wagon train of Mormons who had fled Mexico. It was in August of 1912, that the Mormons of Chihuahua and Sonora had to leave, because of the Mexican Revolution and Poncho Villa. It must have taken them a couple of years to make it north to the Paria Valley, otherwise Wallace, who was born in 1911, wouldn't have remembered the event.

They came in the late summer or early fall and asked if it was OK to make a temporary camp about one km south of Cannonville. Permission was granted and they simply made a half circle with their wagons and camped for the winter. They were the poorest people Wallace had ever seen. Many were of large polygamist families and the church had to help out for a time. In the spring, they all set out in different directions looking for new homes. In the meantime, their camp had gotten the local nickname of **Zuniville.**

Going back in history for a moment. By 1886, the increasing population of the valley was using about all the land the available water would irrigate, but north of Cannonville there remained a large fertile valley of unirrigated land that was otherwise suitable for cultivation. To increase farmland, in 1889 the people of Cannonville revived an old scheme outlined by Ebenezer Bryce back in 1880. That plan was to divert water from the East Fork of the Sevier River on top of the Paunsaugunt Plateau (the high country just west of Bryce Canyon National Park) through a ditch or canal that would pass over the Pink Cliffs to the land in the upper Bryce Valley.

At the instigation of William Lewman, the locally financed Cannonville & East Fork Irrigation Company was organized. A reservoir site was selected and a survey made for a feeder canal about 16 kms long. Maurice Cope was made boss of the project, and work began May 15, 1890. Anticipating the successful completion of the project, James Ahlstrom, C.W. Snyder and others, began building houses on land that the proposed ditch was intended to water. In 1891 a townsite was laid out which was later called **Tropic,** allegedly after its fine climate. On May 23, 1892, the new-found water was flowing through the townsite and onto the adjoining fields. This date marks more than a century of continuous habitation of Tropic, which is truly a man-made oasis.

This is south of Cannonville in the area of Clifton looking northeast. In the distance to the left is Table Cliff Plateau & Powell Point; nearer & on the right is Promise Rock (the darker colored rock).

The first time the name Tropic was displayed on any state map of Utah was in 1902. However, that name was placed where Losee was situated out in what is now Easy Valley, and the name Losee was placed where Tropic is today.

The canal from the East Fork, known locally as the **Tropic Ditch,** is still used today, as it is the lifeblood of Tropic. It took 2 years of voluntary labor and hard work by 50 men, women and boys from Cannonville and the neighboring communities to finish the project. It was mostly hand work with pick & shovel. The only payment received was a reliable water supply and a better place to make a home. On the plateau, the canal can be seen about 100m south of Ruby's Inn as you drive toward the entrance to Bryce Canyon National Park; or in the lower end of Tropic Canyon, as water comes out of Water Canyon and along the Mossy Cave Trail. The water is put into a pipe somewhere near the parking lot next to the highway at the end of **Water Canyon.**

Today in the area of Georgetown, you'll find the cemetery just north of the road. It's still used today by some people who reside in Cannonville. It has some old graves dating from the late 1800's. A little further down the road to the west, you'll see the remains of an old ranch, but this one dates from the early 1900's, and isn't that historic. However there are a couple of old 1920's cars hidden in the sagebrush out back. Just across the road from this old homestead (to the northwest), are the foundations of an even older home, complete with the remains of a wooden pipeline.

There's nothing remaining of anything historic in the area of Clifton, Stringtown or Woodenshoe, however there are 2 very old cabins east of the paved road as you drive south out of Cannonville. They are out in the fields a ways and are clearly visible from the road. These may date from the later days of the Woodenshoe era, and are still used today as barns for livestock, and storage.

If you drive due east out of Tropic and past the *"BV"* on the hillside, you'll be in the general area of New Clifton or Losee. There's nothing there today except the old **Losee Cemetery**. The author counted 7 tombstones, only 3 of which could still be read. Two belonged to young children, the other an older woman. They all had died in 1889 or 1890.

To get to the cemetery, drive east out of Tropic on Center Street, over a low hill and to about the middle of East Valley. Once there, locate a narrow lane running north from the main graveled road. That lane takes off 3.3 kms (1.95 miles) from the main highway in Tropic. At the beginning of that lane is a new monument to the early settlement of New Clifton & Losee. About 250m north of the main road and to the right 100m in the middle of a field, is the small cemetery site with a meter-high fence around it. If you park on the road, then walk to the site and disturb nothing, no one should care if you cross that private land. Local farmers occasionally find stones or other old debris in the Losee area, but this graveyard is really the only thing to see.

Middle Paria River Ghost Towns

What is believed to be the very first white settler to make a home anywhere in the Paria River drainage was a man named **Peter Shirts** (sometimes spelled Shurtz). His homestead has always been known as **Rock House,** but later this same area was called **Pah Ria** on some older maps of the state of Utah. Today, most people believe the location of his home was in or near what is now called **Rock House Cove.** More below. Most of this information about Shirts comes from an unpublished family document, **History of Peter Shirts and his Descendants,** by his grandson Ambrose Shurtz.

Peter was born in 1808 in St. Claire, Ohio. He married for the first time in 1831, then became a

The entrance to the Georgetown Cemetery south of Cannonville.

Mormon convert in 1832. In 1835, he worked on the Mormon Temple in Kirkland, Ohio, and became a high ranking church leader in 1844. Later he lived in Nauvoo, Illinois, where he worked on the temple there. He came to Utah in 1849, and became part of a group to settle in Parowan in 1851. In 1852, he helped build Shirts Fort just south of Cedar City. With John D. Lee, Shirts helped settle the area around what is now known as St. George, then helped survey the site for the future Las Vegas in 1855. He was apparently not part of the Mountain Meadows Massacre and was not a polygamist. Peter had 4 wives altogether, but only one at a time.

Shirts migrated to the Paria River in the spring of 1865 with his family--a wife and 2 children. The presumed site is about 8 or 9 kms downstream from what would later be known as the second Pahreah townsite, and on the east side of the river. In the back side of a cove, it's been said, he built his home up against a cliff, behind which was a cave. He walled up the front part with rocks, partly because rocks were so abundant, and logs weren't; and partly it's been said, so the Indians couldn't smoke him out. The roof of the home was covered with flat slabs of rock, called flagstone, of which there is an abundant supply in the area. He enlarged the rear end of his cave to store grain & produce. This is how the place got the name Rock House.

One story says he built his house right over a ditch, so he could have water if under attack. But in the story told by Ambrose, Peter dug a hole down to the water table right in the floor of his home. After he raised a good crop that first year, the Black Hawk War broke out, and hostilities erupted between the Indians and Mormon white settlers all over Utah.

On November 12, 1865, Erastus Snow, one of the leaders of the Mormon Church, wrote to all settlers in the region reminding them of the impending crisis and to obey their church military leaders. One of the main events signaling the beginning of the Black Hawk War, was the killing of a Dr. Whitmore and Robert McIntyre by Indians at Pipe Springs, located west of Kanab, & Fredonia, Arizona. This happened in January of 1866. At the time of that attack, Peter Shirts was already besieged by Piute Indians, who killed or ran off all of his livestock. A militia force stationed in St. George, under the command of Col. MacArthur, attempted to rescue Shirts, but deep snows prevented a speedy march.

The military didn't get to the region until later, but in the meantime Shirts had outlasted the Indians, and by winter's end, was apparently in better condition than his attackers, who were half starved. He talked to the Indians, explaining that since they had run off and/or killed his oxen, he could no longer plow his ground. When the militia finally arrived, they found Shirts behind a plow pulled by 6 Piutes. Shirts and his family returned with the militia, or were removed unwillingly, to Toquerville. On March 10, 1866, he gave a report of his adventures to Erastus Snow.

According to one story (2 or 3 versions exist) of the history of Rock House, March 1866 was the last time anyone lived at the Shirts Homestead. Later, on December 7, 1869, Jacob Hamblin guided a small group of settlers to explore possible sites for a settlement of some kind on the Paria River. It seems that some of that group stayed there in the area of Rock House.

However, there's a little different story about Rock House, as told by Herbert E. Gregory, the geologist who did a lot of exploring in that part of the country in the 1920's. He claims that Shirts stayed right there on the land for 3 full years, instead of being marched off by the Mormon Military in March of 1866 (perhaps he went back after reporting to Snow in Toquerville?). He then packed up and hightailed-it for the San Juan River. Gregory also states that Rock House was relocated in 1871 (perhaps late 1869 or early 1870?) by 6 families, who did well for a short time. In 1872, 11 more families came in and grew corn & sorghum. Gregory quoted someone as stating: In 1874, trouble with the ditches, [no doubt caused by floods] caused the 15 families at Rock House to relocate above the hogsback

Left Thomas Washington Smith Jr, the son of the second & last bishop of Pahreah. (Thayne Smith foto) **Right** Samuel Chynoweth moved to Pahreah in the fall of 1892 and lived there for 15-20 years with his 4 sons; Will, Sam, Arthur and Harvey. Since 1892, they have been one of the most important families in the history of Pahreah and Bryce Valley. (Mary Jane Chynoweth Fuller foto)

Map 39, Middle Paria River Mines and Ghost Towns: Rock House, Pah Ria, Pahreah & Adairville

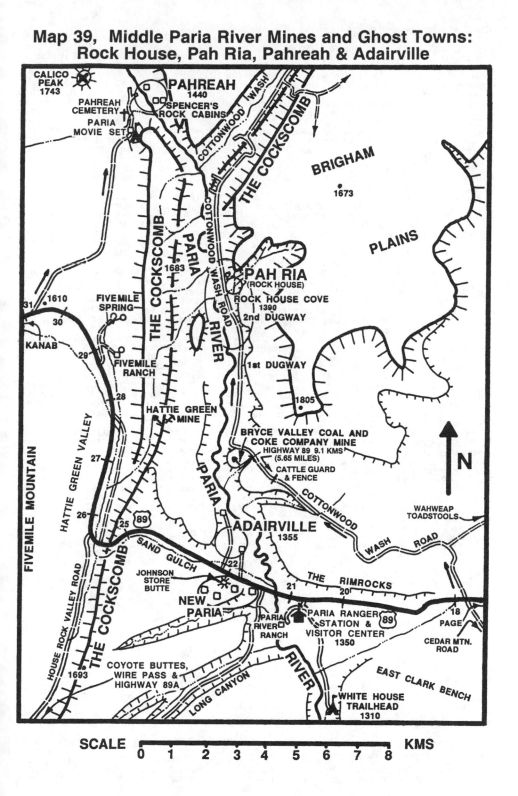

CALICO PEAK 1743
PAHREAH 1440
PAHREAH CEMETERY
SPENCER'S ROCK CABINS
PARIA MOVIE SET
COTTONWOOD WASH
THE COCKSCOMB
BRIGHAM 1673
PLAINS
THE COCKSCOMB
PARIA RIVER
COTTONWOOD WASH ROAD
1683
FIVEMILE SPRING
PAH RIA (ROCK HOUSE)
ROCK HOUSE COVE 1390
2nd DUGWAY
31 1610
30
KANAB
29
FIVEMILE RANCH
1st DUGWAY
28
1805
HATTIE GREEN MINE
27
HATTIE GREEN VALLEY
FIVEMILE MOUNTAIN
PARIA RIVER
BRYCE VALLEY COAL AND COKE COMPANY MINE
HIGHWAY 89 9.1 KMS (5.65 MILES)
CATTLE GUARD & FENCE
26
25
89
COTTONWOOD
WASH ROAD
WAHWEAP TOADSTOOLS
SAND GULCH
ADAIRVILLE 1355
JOHNSON STORE BUTTE
22
THE RIMROCKS
21 20
HOUSE ROCK VALLEY ROAD
THE COCKSCOMB
NEW PARIA
PARIA RIVER RANCH
PARIA RANGER STATION & VISITOR CENTER 1350
89
18 PAGE
CEDAR MTN. ROAD
1693
COYOTE BUTTES, WIRE PASS & HIGHWAY 89A
LONG CANYON
PARIA RIVER
EAST CLARK BENCH
WHITE HOUSE TRAILHEAD 1310

N

SCALE
0 1 2 3 4 5 6 7 8 KMS

[The Box], at the present site of Pahreah.
    To finish the story of Peter Shirts, he apparently was in the Cedar City area in the late 1860's, then by 1877, was wandering alone around the Four Corners area. He attempted to settle on lower Montezuma Creek near the San Juan River. According to the Reeves Survey (**Utah Historical Quarterly, Spring, 1998**), he was at the Mitchell Ranch on September 4, 1878, and ended up guiding the Reeves crew for 2 weeks. Also, some of the Hole-in-the-Rock Expedition members met him in the same place during the winter of 1879-80, then he was with his son Don Carlos in Escalante in 1882. In the spring of that year he left with his burro packed with supplies and headed for Fruitland, New Mexico. Later that same year he got sick and died. He apparently is buried in the Fruitland cemetery.
    Now going back to that first settlement on the Paria as told by various sources. It was in December of 1869, when Jacob Hamblin was sent by the Mormon Church to guide a group of settlers in organizing an Indian farm on the Paria River. According to a family history written by Thomas W. Smith, Jr. (the father of Thayne Smith of Kanab) in 1948, the group was headed by his father Thomas W. Smith, Sr. This history was told to him by Elizabeth J. Smith who was born in 1861. Her story is very similar to that told by Gregory, the geologist.
    Elizabeth contends that Peter Shirts came there with Ezra Meeks, both of whom were interested in mining, and may have been the first to locate what later became known as the Hattie Green Copper Mine not far west of Rock House.
    Hamblin's or Smith's group (?) included John Mangum and his son Joseph; Jacob, James, Joseph, and J.H. Heath; Allen F. Smithson, Thomas W. Smith, Sr; and James O. Wilkins who was a son-in-law to John Mangum (from **Red Hills of November**, p131). Thomas Adair was there, but may have come in with a 2nd group (?). At first this group did well. They built homes, a rock guard house, where men could cook and have safe lodging, and corrals. By March, 1870, they had 2 1/2 kms of ditches and 800m of fence built, and had 8 Indians there helping and learning about agriculture. Some of the first information about this settlement comes in the form of a letter from Jacob Hamblin to Erastus Snow of the LDS church. It was dated March 27, 1870.
    The location where this group settled was at or near the place where Peter Shurtz had his farm or camp. This was 8 or 9 kms below the later settlement which is called Old Pahreah today. On an 1871 map of Utah, it shows a place called & spelled **Paria** located near the Utah-Arizona state line and on the west side of the creek about where Adairville would later be situated. But that is not a good map! However, on an 1874 map of Utah, and one of better all around quality, it shows **Pah Ria** several kms below The Box, where the Paria cuts through The Cockscomb, and on the east side of the river. This would be the approximate location of Peter Shirts' place.
    In the story of John D. Lee, Juanita Brooks mentions a trip to the Paria River in September of 1870 by John D. and Brigham Young. Along the Paria near Peter Shirts settlement, they found some green corn and squash, but Lee didn't like the looks of the place and refused to take any of his wives to go there to live. The people there at that time must have been part of the Hamblin-Smith group.
    In the diaries of John D. Lee, **A Mormon Chronicle: The Diaries of John D. Lee**, he mentions he was in the Pahreah settlement on Sunday, March 3, 1872. In an evening meeting led by Jacob Hamblin, a branch of the church was organized with Allen F. Smithson to preside, and John Mangum as his 1st councilor. Throughout that time period, Lee was calling the place, the **Pahreah settlements**. He often passed through Pahreah on his way between Skutumpah and his Lonely Dell Ranch at Lee's Ferry via the Dominguez Trail.
    Herbert E. Gregory thinks that after about 3 years, they were driven out by floods, and couldn't get water in their ditches and onto their fields. At that time, about 1873 or '74, they relocated; some went downstream as did Tom Adair, to settle at what would later be known as **Adairville**, while others went north through The Box of the Paria and founded another settlement site.
    An interesting side-note, the 1874 map of Utah also shows **Molly's Nipple, Lake Adair and Swallow Park** for the first time. The 1875 map looks the same as in 1874, but the 1879 version shows Adairville on the east side of the river (people today think it was mostly on the west side), and **Pahreah** above The Box in it's present location. An 1893 map shows Pahreah and Adamsville (a typo error?). Other maps up through 1915 show Pahreah & Adairville (or Adamsville), but on the 1922 version, both are missing. On a 1930 map, both are shown again, but not on later maps.
    The second townsite of **Pahreah** did very well at first. They grew fruit & nut orchards, vineyards, vegetable farms, sorghum and raised cattle & sheep. In 1877, Pahreah was large enough to have an organized LDS (Mormon) ward by itself, and was part of the Kanab Stake (a group of regional wards of the LDS Church). According to Thomas W. Smith's family story: *Allen F. Smithson was appointed as the [Pahreah] ward's first bishop. He was the father of Elizabeth J. Smith, mother of the writer of this story. Thomas W. Smith, Sr. was the ward's second and last bishop.*
    Pah Ria/Pahreah seems to have been organized as a branch of the Kanab ward in March of 1872, then later, and at the second townsite with lots more settlers, it became a full ward of the church.
    According to most accounts, by the spring of 1884, the number of people living at Pahreah reached an all-time high. At that time, there were 47 families including 107 members of the Mormon Church, plus a number of other cattlemen and about 20 Piute Indians living there.
    But then came a series of floods, the first of which was in 1883. It was followed by the severe winter of 1883-84, then more flooding in the summer of 1884, which washed away farm houses and fields and converted the shallow stream channel into a wash that extended in places from canyon wall to canyon wall. This spelled doom for Pahreah and people started leaving. By September of 1884, only 48 people remained. The next year, 1885, the church ward was disbanded. By 1892, only 8 families remained. Incidentally, *Pahreah* is a Piute word meaning *muddy water*.
    We know that John W. Mangum, the son of John Mangum, was there from the late 1870's through the mid-1890's with a short stay in Arizona during the mid-1880's. The original Smith family of Thomas W. Smith, Sr. was there into the 1890's, as he was buried there in the cemetery in 1892. Susan R. Smith stayed on and was buried there in September, 1897. See the picture of the memorial in the Pahreah Cemetery. It lists the graves of 13 people buried there. They were Smiths, Smithsons, Twitchells and one Mangum.
    The Chynoweths were an important family in Pahreah during its waning years. According to Will Chynoweth's daughter, Mary Jane C. Fuller, Sampson Chynoweth left England in late 1870, and settled at the mining town of Junction south of Marysvale, Utah. Between 1887 & 1892, they were in Antimony and in the cattle business. In the fall of 1892, they moved to Pahreah with a herd of cattle. That fall, Will Chynoweth left his signature in 1892 at the bottom of the Lower Trail in Hackberry

Above John W. Mangum, the son of John Mangum, one of the original settlers at Pahreah. J.W.M. lived at Pahreah from 1870-'76, and from 1891-'95. Six of his 13 children were born in Pahreah during those 2 time periods. He died in Cannonville in 1920. (Twila Mangum Irwin foto)

Top Pahreah in the early 1900's. Looking south toward The Box of the Paria on the left. To the right of the highest peak is the Paria Movie Set. Notice the rip gut or stake & rider fence in the foreground. (John H. Johnson & Ferrell Brinkerhoff foto) **Above Right** Sam Chynoweth and his young wife Edith in Lethbridge, Alberta. Sam got into some kind of trouble and lived in Canada--British Columbia and Alberta--for about 35 years before returning to Henrieville in about 1934. No one around Bryce Valley knows anything about that part of Sam's life. (Lula Chynoweth Moore foto)

Canyon. Harvey Chynoweth was born in Pahreah in 1893, and we know at least some of the family was there in 1901. By 1916, Will Chynoweth was there, and that's when he met his wife, who was just passing through. Sampson Chynoweth died in Henrieville in 1920.

In Sam Pollock's unpublished life story, he states that in August of 1901, and as a boy of 16, he and a fellow by the name of Butler, were returning from wrangling cows in the House Rock Valley with the clothes on their backs and a couple of tired, lame horses. They walked into Pahreah barefoot leading their steeds, and were helped by some of the folks. Sam recalled the Chynoweths, Twitchells, and his uncle Seth Johnson as living there at the time. Not far north of Pahreah at the Dugout Ranch, William

Top Unidentified people and house in Pahreah in the early 1900's. (John H. Johnson & Ferrell Brinkerhoff foto) **Above** Arthur Chynoweth, his wife Rosella (Rose) holding baby Rhoda, and Hazel (3 years old) at Pahreah in 1922. (Don Chynoweth foto)

Swapp was living. Further along, they left one poor horse at the John W. Mangum Ranch, which at that time was just west of Shepherd Point, about 3 kms south of Cannonville. Tommy Richards later bought it and called it the Diamond T Ranch.

In the years following the original exodus, people came and went, but mostly left for greener pastures. However, even in its declining years, Pahreah received a post office on July 26, 1893, and Emily P. Adair became the first postmaster. Finally things got even worse, and the post office closed on March 1, 1915.

In 1912, promoter Charles H. Spencer brought his miners up from Lee's Ferry, and tried unsuccessfully to extract gold from the colorful Chinle clay beds. This was after the gold mining failure at Lee's Ferry. In 1921, Spencer once again returned to Pahreah, this time to do some surveys for a proposed dam to be located in The Box of the Paria River just downstream from the Pahreah townsite. Add this to the long list of failures for Spencer.

Throughout the early 1900's, there were only one or 2 families living in or around Pahreah at any one time. Their sources of income were from farming & ranching, and supplying sheepmen who had large flocks in the region during the winter months.

In the History of Marian Mangum, written by himself and documented in the Mangum family history book, **John Mangum: Revolutionary War Soldier**, he tells a story of his life in Pahreah beginning in about 1914, after he and the family had been wandering around Idaho and other places:

My father [John Wesley Mangum], John [Long John William Mangum] and I bought the ranch that was once the town of Pahreah in Kane County, where I grew up. The old town had been abandoned several years before and there were only 3 of the old houses remaining. The floods that came down the Pahreah Creek had washed away the land that once was building lots and left high banks.

We 3 farmed together and could raise about anything we wished to plant. We raised molasses cane and made molasses. My father always did the boiling of the molasses in a large vat which was set over a fire in a rock pit. One had to know his business to make good molasses, and Father really did know how. When it was time to cut the cane and make it into molasses, we all worked, children and all. Father always cooked the last batch of molasses into candy. Then we would all get together and have a candy pulling party under the big mulberry trees. One summer we made eight hundred gallons of molasses.

We raised wagon loads of melons, both watermelons and cantaloupes or muskmelons. Some of the watermelons grew so large a man could hardly lift them. We had a black cow that loved the melons. Every night the children would cut a tub full of melons and feed them to the cow. She would eat all the melons, letting the juice run back into the tub, then she would drink the juice.

In 1924 we went to Oregon..... Marian never states exactly who went to Oregon, but it seems it was just himself. It seems the father, John Wesley Mangum, went to Cannonville, but his brother, known to most people in the area as Long John (because he as so tall and lanky), may have stayed on at Pahreah, living there either full or part-time.

John (Long John) William Mangum and his only son, Herman, lived in the Pahreah area, including the Dugout and Fivemile Ranches, until the mid-1930's, then left for Idaho. In about the same time period as Long John, Jack Seaton was around and he ranched and was the sheepman supplier for awhile. According to Leola Scheonfeld of Kanab, Jack lived in a dugout just southwest of Pahreah for several years. Then on April 2, 1932, Jack Seaton traded his holdings at Pahreah for a home & land in Horse Valley southeast of Henrieville. This trade was with Jim Ed Smith. For 3 full years, Jim Ed Smith, along with his son Layton, lived in Pahreah.

Iris Smith Bushnell of Henrieville, one daughter of Jim Ed Smith, lived at Pahreah part of the time in the early & mid-1930's as a young girl. Here's some of what she remembered:

I was about 10 or 11 years old when Dad & Mother bought that place and we moved down there. Pahreah was a kind of stopping-off place for the stockmen around there. There was a lot of old rock houses and sheds that was left after the floods came and most people moved away. We lived in one of the places. It was a little old log cabin with a room on the back made of lumber. That was the kitchen. The kitchen must have been built with that lumber Dad brought down from the old oil well in the upper Rush Beds.

Dad and Layton, who was my oldest brother, lived there the year-round. They had cattle and a farm, and they raised quite a lot of alfalfa. Dad also went around to the old homes that belonged to the people who left, and fixed 'um up. He had about 10 or 11 of those old log & rock houses fixed up for the stockmen to store their food & supplies in. He charged a little for rent, and he took care of everything for 'um. He made a little money on that.

The rest of the family lived here in Henrieville and we'd go to school here in the winter time. When school was out in the spring, which was usually in April, Dad would come up the creek in a wagon and get us and take us down there. We'd stay down there in the summer and in September he'd bring us back up here to go to school.

At Pahreah, there were lots of fruit trees, including a big mulberry next to the house, but it was nectarines that I remember most. In the summer they raised beautiful melons. We fattened pigs on watermelons. We also had some grape vines, and they did real good too. We were there for several years,

The Jim Ed Smith family at Pahreah,1933. From Left to Right: Marjorie, Flora, Jim Ed, Deward (small boy), Nellie (mother), Alta Rea (little girl), Doris, Laura and baby Ronald, and Iris Smith (Bushnell). The cabin to the right was the last place to be lived in at Pahreah. It had an extension on the back made with lumber brought down from the Old Oil Well in the Upper or Northern Rush Beds. The cabin to the left is where the girls slept in summer. (Iris Smith Bushnell foto)

then Dad traded Pahreah for a ranch that's down here just south of Cannonville on the Paria Creek.

Layton Smith recalled the family sold [perhaps traded?] their holdings at Pahreah to Roy Twitchell in March of 1935, after living there only 3 years. Roy was old then and most of the work was done by his son Cecil, and a couple of stepsons. The Twitchells stayed on for about 4 years, but it was a tough life. Finally, after the long winter of 1938 & '39, the Twitchells apparently just walked off the land and left the country.

Charley Francisco, presently of Tropic, along with his father Charles Edward Francisco, then went down to Pahreah in the spring of 1939 and started planting crops and cleaning ditches. In the meantime, it seems that a man named Burge bought the land for back taxes (?). Burge was from somewhere in the east and never lived at Pahreah. Instead, he collected some rent money from the Franciscos.

Charles E. Francisco and his boy Charley were in & out of Pahreah in the 1930's and knew the country. Charley remembered Charles H. Spencer coming back to Pahreah (with a daughter in her 20's) in the early 1930's (Wallace Ott says Spencer was there in 1932, the year the Lindbergh baby was kidnapped) and was again working on a scheme of some kind. Spencer was old then and was trying to find someone who wanted to lose more money with another of his gold mining adventures.

Charley Francisco remembered Spencer and Old Pahreah: *We lived up here in Henrieville, and the first time I went down there, they had big vats of mercury--we called it quicksilver then--and that quicksilver got away from 'um and nobody knows where it went. It was a semi-truck load, and that cost a lot of money! They was tryin' to collect gold & silver from them clay beds.*

Jim Ed Smith had built granaries, and stables big enough for 20 head of horses. He had a wonderful place there at Piaria [Pahreah]. All the cowboys & sheepmen left their supplies right there in them big cellars--there was 6 or 8 or 'um. The CCC boys made some of them cellars at Piaria, and the sheepmen used them for their warehouses. That's where the sheepmen headquartered in winter. From Piaria, they went in every direction--but they'd come back once in a while for their supplies--and Jim Ed Smith supplied feed for all their horses. They'd have a big string of pack mules they packed all their supplies back out to their camps with. They only had to come in there every 3 weeks or so and they'd stay over night.

Dad was down there all the time for about 3 years. At that time our family lived up here in Henrieville, and went down to Piaria in summer, but we had to come back to go to school in winter. We raised everything--we had alfalfa, a lot of corn, we raised everything to feed other people's livestock in winter. That country was their winter range. If those cattle would get snowed-in and weak, they'd die before spring, so those guys would gather all the weak ones and herd 'um to Piaria and my Dad would feed 'um. Dad fed a lot of cows for the Kanab ranchers the same way. He'd feed 4 or 5 cows, and they'd give him one. Otherwise the cows would have died.

That cabin Jim Ed Smith lived in and the one the BLM tore down piece by piece and moved back from the river [it burned down in the winter of 1994-'95, but the chimney is still there] was the one we lived in. I graduated from the 8th grade while I was there at Piaria in the summer of 1939. I had to leave school early that spring and go down there with my father and didn't graduate, so they sent me school material and I done it that summer so's I could graduate. At that time I was goin' to school in Cannonville. I was about 17 years old when we finally left Piaria. Me and my father were the last ones to farm there. Everybody had gone, and the mining had gone. If I'm not mistaken, I think we finally left Piaria after the summer of 1941. When the war started, then everybody left the country to get work.

Calvin C. Johnson of Kanab, mentions an interesting event at Pahreah during the summer of 1943. Movie makers went there and filmed a picture about Buffalo Bill and Geronimo. They had 300 Navajos, plus Joel McCrae, Anthony Quinn and Maureen O'Hare. They built a little dam across the Paria inside The Box to back water up during the shooting. You may still see parts of that dam.

The hills around Old Pahreah are very colorful, mostly due to the Chinle clay beds, and because of that, the place became a favorite for movie makers during the 1950's & '60's. For one movie, *Sergeants Three*, they built a model town which later became known as the **Paria Movie Set.** This was in 1962. That fake town was built in a little valley about 1 1/2 kms south of the site of Old Pahreah. The last movie to be made there was in 1973. In 1998, a big flood came down the valley and damaged the set, so between 2000 & 2002 someone partially built another one in the same place. It was rebuilt because this is on the tourist circuit for which Kanab & Kane County depend.

At Old Pahreah today, is part of a corral, some fence posts, the chimney of the old cabin that was the last to be lived in, evidence of old ditches & canals and a couple of rock cellars. About 400m southeast of the chimney of the cabin the Smith's lived in, are several rock structures and some remains of the sluicing operation dating from Spencer's time in 1912, 1920 and evidently in 1932. One of these rock buildings is in relatively good condition.

To get to **Old Pahreah,** drive along Highway 89 about halfway between Kanab & Page. Between mile posts 30 & 31, turn north and drive 7.6 kms (4.7 miles) to the new Paria Movie Set, and a small campground with toilets & picnic tables (but no water). Just up the road to the north at Km 8.4/Mile 5.2, is the Pahreah Cemetery on the left. In 2003, descendants of the original Smith family who settled Pahreah, erected a new iron fence & gate, plus new tombstones. The original grave markers were unreadable and removed. The one large tombstone monument lists 13 people buried there. Another 800m beyond the cemetery, is the end of the road at the edge of the river. Park at or near the sign, and walk east across the river to the sites mentioned above. Wear an old pair of shoes, or remove shoes, to wade in the usually ankle-deep water of the Paria River.

To reach the original settlement site on the Paria River which was first called **Rock House,** and/or **Pah Ria** or **Pahreah;** or **Rock House Cove** as it's now called on some maps, drive along Highway 89 about halfway between Page & Kanab. Between mile posts 17 & 18, turn north onto the Cottonwood Wash Road. Drive 15.1 kms (9.4 miles). There you'll see a cottonwood tree on the right next to the road. Just east of that is Rock House Cove. It's in the western part of Section 4, T42S, R1W, on any USGS map.

That cottonwood tree is near the north end of a 200m-long line of tamaracks. They're so large, they're almost like trees, but someone set fire to them in about 2000 (?), and what you see today is a lot of younger chutes. No one can say for sure if this is the Peter Shirts Homestead, or if it's part of the settlement of Pah Ria, but those tamaracks are (were) the biggest this author has seen, and in a line too straight to have occurred by accident. The author has never found any sign of the rock house, but most people who have seen the cove are convinced this is indeed part of somebody's early homestead dating back to the 1860's or '70's. However, it's very probable the tamaracks got there later, because they were first known to exist in St. George only after 1880. The late Kay Clark, formerly of Henrieville, once stated he remembered a pile of rocks towards the south end of that line of tamaracks, but they're not visible today.

As for the people who farmed this part of the Paria shortly after Shirts, all of their farms, ditches, barns and homes, have all been washed away by floods. In fact, that entire valley, which ranges in width from 600m to 800m, is a virtual river flood plain today.

Adairville is another of the tiny farming & ranching settlements along the middle Paria River. The site of this little cluster of ranches is just north of mile post 22 on present-day Highway 89, about halfway between Page & Kanab. This place is just east of The Cockscomb, whereas Old Pahreah is just to the west of this same cockscomb ridge.

All sources seem to agree that Adairville was first settled in 1873 or '74, by a group of cattlemen, led by Tom Adair. Some of these settlers came down from Rock House/Pah Ria, where Adair had originally settled. In the beginning, Adairville was prosperous, as they farmed the land, planted gardens and raised livestock. According to Gregory, there were 8 families at Adairville in 1878, but they had some of the same problems as the earlier settlers had upstream at Rock House/Pah Ria, and later at Pahreah. They had some floods, which lowered the creek bed, and they couldn't get water to their fields. Also, water in the river in the heat of summer didn't always reach their settlement. Water in the Paria is reliable down to where it crosses The Cockscomb, but below The Box, it gradually seeps into the sands and disappears during early summer. So in 1878, those 8 families left, most of whom went upstream to resettle at Pahreah.

In the years after 1878, there was nearly always a rancher or two in the area. The late Kay Clark, said his grandfather Owen Washington Clark, built the cabin, which was later known as the **White House,** in 1887. This is downstream one km from where the Lower Paria River is today (all that's left of that homestead today is a pile of rocks that appear to be the remains of a chimney on a bench on the east side of the river). After a year or so there, they moved upstream to the area of Adairville and lived there for a couple of years. After that, the family moved upstream to Pahreah for a while, then on up to Bryce Valley in the early 1890's. Read more about the history of the White House in the hiking section under, **Map 29, Buckskin Gulch & Paria River Loop Hike.**

After the Clarks left Adairville, it's not certain just what happened to the place for a number of years, but the late Elbert (Farmer) Swapp of Kanab, remembered some of the later history. Elbert believed the land around Adairville was abandoned from the 1890's until the 1930's. However, the Cross Bar Land & Cattle Company filed on water rights in the area in 1912 according to courthouse records.

Finally the Adairville area was homesteaded by Charley Cram & Charley Mace in the 1930's, but they sold out to Elbert & Orson Swapp in the early 1940's. From that point on, the Swapps have owned most of the land south of Highway 89. The Swapps built the brick & cement ranch house just southwest of the Paria Ranger Station & Visitor Center in the 1940's. Most people refer to this as the **Paria River Ranch.**

Some of the land just north of the highway, and right where Adairville was founded, was homesteaded in the late 1930's by Sandal Findlay. He later sold out to Fay Hamblin and Floyd Maddox. Finally, the Frosts bought them out, and have owned that land ever since, leasing it to the MacDonald family in the 1980's. After Merrill MacDonald passed away, his sons got out of the ranching business. Just south of the place MacDonalds used to lease, is the Hepworth place. It's just north of the former rest area along the highway and northeast of the Johnson Store Butte. In the 1990's, Hepworth also leased some farm land from the Frosts, in conjunction with his public lands grazing rights.

Today, there's nothing left to see at the original Adairville townsite, except perhaps for some of the old trees just west of the Hepworth place, and just north of mile post 22 and Johnson Store Butte. In there someplace is one *grave of a Mrs. Goodrich who died in childbirth,* according to Sam Pollock's story, but it's private land, and permission would have to be granted before entering.

South of Highway 89 and Johnson Store Butte, are now 6 or 8 new homes forming a rural settlement generally called **New Paria.** Those people commute to Page or Kanab to work each day, or are retired. Halfway between mile posts 21 & 22, and on the south side of Highway 89, is the **Paria River Resort**. This appears to be a kind of dude ranch with a small campground, restaurant and horseback riding.

The last cabin to be lived in at Pahreah. The part of this cabin made of lumber was the kitchen. That lumber was brought down from the Old Oil Well in the Rush Beds by Jim Ed Smith and Long John Mangum in about 1932. Some of that oil well lumber was used to build the house at the Fivemile Ranch near the Hattie Green Mine. (Iris Smith Bushnell foto)

IN MEMORY OF

	BORN			DIED		
THOMAS W. SMITH	DEC.	23	1815	DEC.	28	1892
SUSAN R. SMITH	SEPT.	2	1813	SEPT.	10	1897
MARY L. SMITH	AUG.	11	1866	SEPT.	10	1880
ELLEN SMITH	DEC.	23	1882	DEC.	26	1882
TABITHA S. SMITH	MAR.	8	1871	JAN.	22	1883
WILLIAM W. SMITH	OCT.	13	1819	DEC.	7	1884
MARTHA A. R. MANGUM	JAN.	26	1849	JULY	4	1890
RUPERTA A. TWITCHELL	JAN.	10	1877	FEB.	15	1879
JOHN S. TWITCHELL	APRIL	1	1891	SEPT.	10	1891
DENNIS A. SMITHSON	MAR.	2	1878	SEPT.	2	1879
ALLEN F. SMITHSON	FEB.	11	1816	SEPT.	27	1877
MARGARET L. SMITHSON	MAY	20	1866	MAY	10	1883
SUSAN E. R. SMITHSON	SEPT.	16	1865	JAN.	24	1883

This is the memorial plaque at the Pahreah Cemetery not far north of the Paria Movie Set. The death dates on this plaque gives a small history of the town of Pahreah.

Left Will Chynoweth in what looks like a foto studio setting in 1903. Will was born in 4/1876 in Junction, Utah, making him 27 at the time. (Mary Jane Chynoweth Fuller foto) **Right** Harvey Chynoweth was born in 10/1893 at Pahreah. That was one year after the Samuel Chynoweth family moved there. This picture was taken in about 1915. (Lula Chynoweth Moore foto)

This picture shows Arthur Chynoweth and his 2 sons in 1924. Art was born in Junction, Utah, in 1/1884, and died only 2 years after this foto was taken. Lloyd is on the left, with Lawrence on the right. This foto was taken in Henrieville. (Don Chynoweth foto)

Left Elije Moore, a long time resident of Henrieville. He ran cattle down in the Wahweap country to as far as Lone Rock and the Colorado River which today is Lake Powell. He may have been one of the first to see the Wahweap Toadstools. (Lula Chynoweth Moore foto) **Right** The late Herm Pollock of Tropic. He found these Anasazi pots in some ruins on West Clark Bench in 1937 while herding sheep. In the end, some of these pots went to museums at BYU in Provo, the University of Utah in Salt Lake City, and to Southern Utah State U. in Cedar City, Utah. (Afton Pollock foto)

About the only thing left at Old Pahreah today is this cellar. In the background and left of the 2 cottonwood trees, is the chimney which was once part of the last cabin to be lived in at Pahreah.

The Paria Movie Set located along the road to Old Pahreah. It's the colorful Chinle clay beds, seen in the background, that made this a favorite place for movie makers for many years.

Aerial view looking southwest where Pahreah once was. Near the bottom and to the left a little, is where Charles H. Spencer's mining operation & stone buildings are found. In the upper part of the foto is the Paria Movie Set. To the right is upstream; to the left is The Box of the Paria River.

Another aerial shot, this time looking down on the rounded Rock House Cove (lower half of foto), located 8-9 kms downstream from **Old Pahreah**. See the road, and the "Y"-shaped line of tamaracks. This could only have been planted by farmers. It's in this area that the settlement of **Pah Rea** was first laid out in 1870, and first appeared on Utah state maps in 1874.

Geology of the Paria River Basin

While most people aren't really interested in geology, it's only a matter of time and one or more trips to the Colorado Plateau, before many get hooked. All you have to do is look at a map of the lower 48 states, and you'll see that many of our national parks and monuments are found on the Plateau.

The Colorado Plateau is a vast physiographic region covering the southeastern half of Utah, the northern half of Arizona, the northwestern corner of New Mexico, and the western fifth of Colorado. In other words, it covers the middle third of the Colorado River drainage system.

What makes the Colorado Plateau so unique are the flat-lying rocks. During millions of years while the sediments were being laid down, the land remained relatively flat. Sometimes it was below sea level or was under the waters of a freshwater sea or lake. But always it remained relatively flat, even during this last time period when the entire region was uplifted to create what we have today. And what we have is a colorful and majestic canyon country unequaled anywhere.

Because much of the Plateau is dry and has very little vegetation, the rocks are laid bare, and can be examined by all. This is why so many people become interested in geology when visiting this part of the country.

The Paria River drainage is near the middle of the Colorado Plateau, and has at least its share of unique geologic wonders. The Paria begin at Bryce Canyon National Park and Table Cliff Plateau, and ends at Lee's Ferry on the Colorado River. In between are canyons like Bull Valley Gorge, Deer Creek, Round Valley Draw, the Buckskin Gulch, and the Lower Paria River Gorge. Perhaps the most interesting geologic feature of all is The Cockscomb. All these areas combine to make a fascinating geology field trip.

Geologic Formations and Where They're Exposed

If we follow a line from the top of the Table Cliff Plateau & Powell Point, south to Lee's Ferry on the Colorado River, we'll pass along all, or most, of the formations which are exposed in the drainage. Let's begin at the top of the Table Cliff and run down through the different formations, and where they are prominently seen. At the end of this list are 3 formations which are exposed in Kaibab Gulch, just west of the Buckskin Trailhead. Two of these are not exposed along the lower Paria River.

Tuff of Osiris It's found only on top of Table Cliff Plateau just north of Powell Point. It's of volcanic origin, as is the Aquarius Plateau, located further north and east.

Variegated Sandstone Member--Claron (formerly the Wasatch) Formation This is usually considered the top of the Claron Formation, and seen only in a few places on the rim of Bryce Canyon N.P. and on top of Table Cliff Plateau. It's more weather resistant, therefore a capstone.

White Limestone Member--Claron Formation This is prominently seen all along the rim of the Pink Cliffs in Bryce Canyon, the Sunset Cliffs on the west side of the Paunsaugunt Plateau, and the upper part of Table Cliff Plateau. This and the Pink Limestone below, look nothing like ordinary limestone.

Pink Limestone Member--Claron Formation Seen on the lower slopes of Table Cliff and on Canaan Peak, as well as in Bryce Canyon. In this member are found the famous **Hoodoos**, for which Bryce Canyon is famous. It's the same member as is seen in all the Pink Cliffs, the Sunset Cliffs, and in Cedar Breaks National Mon. This crumbly limestone formation is full of iron, which gives it its color.

Pine Hollow Formation An indistinct mudstone strata immediately below the Pink Cliffs of Bryce Canyon and Table Cliff Plateau.

Canaan Peak Formation Another indistinct formation below the Pinks at the bottom of the Table Cliff Plateau. Made up of cobble, pebble, and sandstone conglomerate.

Kaiparowits Formation A slope-maker, made of sandstone, limestone, siltstone and clays, and is seen most prominently east of The Cockscomb, or between Henrieville and the pass between Table Cliff Plateau and Canaan Peak.

Wahweap Formation This is a cliff-making formation, most prominently exposed as the east side ridge of Cads Crotch, one of the features of the upper end of The Cockscomb. It's a brownish-yellowish sandstone, mudstone, siltstone and shale.

Straight Cliffs Formation This formation is another cliff-maker. It's best seen as the highest ridge of The Cockscomb east of Cottonwood Wash. It also forms the western ridge of Cads Crotch, which is the eastern of the 2 valleys within the larger structure called The Cockscomb.

Tropic Shale The name tells the tale; it's mostly the blueish gray clay beds you see around the town of Tropic, the type location. It's also the grays you see above Henrieville on the way to Escalante. That area is called **The Blues**. Another location is in the lower end of the main valley of The Cockscomb, the Cottonwood Wash. You'll be driving along this gray clay area in the bottom 16 to 18 kms of the Cottonwood Wash Road. It begins just north of Highway 89, and is slick as hell when wet.

Dakota Sandstone This one is mostly a light brown sandstone, which makes a prominent cliff, but it also has siltstone and some shale. You'll see this as one of the prominent and intermediate ridges within The Cockscomb Valley which in this case is called Cottonwood Wash. It's the first prominent ridge just west of the gray Tropic Shale.

Henrieville Sandstone The type location for this one is near the town of Henrieville. It's seen in only a few areas, from the head or northern end of The Cockscomb, up through Butler Valley and at the head of Round Valley Draw. It's a yellow cliff-making massive sandstone. It's best seen at the Butler Valley Arch, more commonly known as **Grosvenor Arch**. It's that part of the wall from the top of the arch down to ground level. The Dakota Sandstone is immediately above at the top of the arch.

There's a question on whether or not the **Morrison Formation** is exposed in this area, especially along The Cockscomb. In the lower end of The Cockscomb, the author sees no gap between the Dakota and the top of the Entrada, but there may be a thin layer of Morrison in there somewhere. Some reports place it there, but those are not detailed reports. Thompson & Stokes leave it out in their report.

Escalante Member--Entrada Sandstone An indistinct, and mostly white sandstone member of the Entrada Formation seen in the upper slopes of Kodachrome Basin and west of Cannonville.

Cannonville Member--Entrada Sandstone This is a mostly fine-grain reddish-brown to buff-colored sandstone. Its type location are the slopes around Cannonville, but it's also prominently exposed in Kodachrome Basin. It's the white upper slopes and cliffs you see above the more scenic red sandstone in the park, and west of Cannonville.

Gunsight Butte Member--Entrada Sandstone This is the reddish brown sandstone layer you see in

Geology Cross-Section
Table Cliff Plateau to Lee's Ferry

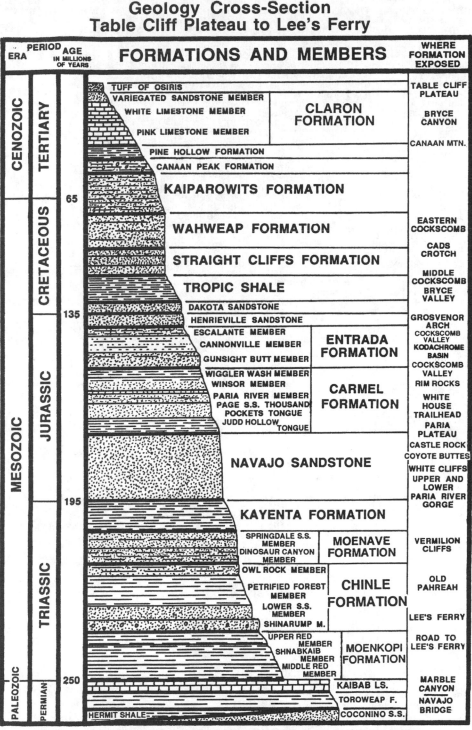

ERA	PERIOD	AGE IN MILLIONS OF YEARS	FORMATIONS AND MEMBERS		WHERE FORMATION EXPOSED
CENOZOIC	TERTIARY		TUFF OF OSIRIS		TABLE CLIFF PLATEAU
			VARIEGATED SANDSTONE MEMBER		
			WHITE LIMESTONE MEMBER	CLARON FORMATION	BRYCE CANYON
			PINK LIMESTONE MEMBER		CANAAN MTN.
			PINE HOLLOW FORMATION		
			CANAAN PEAK FORMATION		
MESOZOIC	CRETACEOUS	65	KAIPAROWITS FORMATION		
			WAHWEAP FORMATION		EASTERN COCKSCOMB
			STRAIGHT CLIFFS FORMATION		CADS CROTCH
			TROPIC SHALE		MIDDLE COCKSCOMB BRYCE VALLEY
		135	DAKOTA SANDSTONE		
			HENRIEVILLE SANDSTONE		GROSVENOR ARCH
	JURASSIC		ESCALANTE MEMBER	ENTRADA FORMATION	COCKSCOMB VALLEY KODACHROME BASIN
			CANNONVILLE MEMBER		
			GUNSIGHT BUTT MEMBER		COCKSCOMB VALLEY
			WIGGLER WASH MEMBER	CARMEL FORMATION	RIM ROCKS
			WINSOR MEMBER		WHITE HOUSE TRAILHEAD
			PARIA RIVER MEMBER PAGE S.S. THOUSAND POCKETS TONGUE JUDD HOLLOW TONGUE		PARIA PLATEAU
			NAVAJO SANDSTONE		CASTLE ROCK COYOTE BUTTES WHITE CLIFFS UPPER AND LOWER PARIA RIVER GORGE
		195	KAYENTA FORMATION		
	TRIASSIC		SPRINGDALE S.S. MEMBER DINOSAUR CANYON MEMBER	MOENAVE FORMATION	VERMILION CLIFFS
			OWL ROCK MEMBER	CHINLE FORMATION	OLD PAHREAH
			PETRIFIED FOREST MEMBER		
			LOWER S.S. MEMBER		LEE'S FERRY
			SHINARUMP M.		
			UPPER RED MEMBER SHNABKAIB MEMBER MIDDLE RED MEMBER	MOENKOPI FORMATION	ROAD TO LEE'S FERRY
PALEOZOIC	PERMIAN	250			MARBLE CANYON
			KAIBAB LS.		
			TOROWEAP F.		NAVAJO BRIDGE
			HERMIT SHALE	COCONINO S.S.	

ADOPTED FROM: BUSH--GEOLOGY MAP OF THE VERMILION CLIFFS-PARIA CANYON
SCALE 1:62,500, MAPS USGS MF-1475 A, B, C, & D

the Cannonville Slots southwest of Cannonville and in Kodachrome Basin. In this member, are found most of the **sand pipes** in Kodachrome Basin. Another good place to see this one is in The Rimrocks, which is just north of Highway 89 and Paria Ranger Station & Visitor Center. There it's the white cliffs which form the bulk of The Rimrocks. This is just above the colorful Winsor Member of the Carmel Formation. In this location it's mostly white with some reds at the bottom. You can also see this member in the bottom part of the Cottonwood Wash immediately east of the road. It's the white sandstone monoliths you see standing up alone like icebergs. The **pedestal** parts of the **toadstools** you see in The Rimrocks and along Wahweap Creek are made of this fine-grained white sandstone.

Wiggler Wash Member--Carmel Formation The type location for this strata is in the southern part of Kodachrome Basin where it's a thin gypsum layer, just below the red Gunsight Butte Member.

Winsor Member--Carmel Formation This is a mostly sandstone layer you can see just north of the Cottonwood Wash Road in the southern part of Kodachrome Basin. It's largely indistinct there, but the author believes this is the very colorful beds of clayish-looking deposits you see just north of Highway 89, between the eastern side of The Cockscomb to just east of the Paria Ranger Station & Visitor Center (?). These are the purple and white banded layers forming the lower part of The Rimrocks.

Paria River Member--Carmel Formation These are indistinct beds of mostly sandstone, mixed with thin layers of siltstone, as well as some limestone & gypsum. This one may be seen between the Paria Ranger Station & Visitor Center, and the White House Trailhead.

Thousand Pockets Tongue--Page Sandstone This is a massive sandstone layer, once considered the top part of the Navajo. It's type location is in the area just east of the top of the Dominguez Trail & Pass, in the lower end of the Paria. It's the smooth white sandstone you see at the White House Trailhead and around the town of Page, Arizona. White House Spring comes out of the bottom of this tongue. (On the BLM map-guide-booklet, Hiker's Guide to Paria Canyon, it shows a geology cross section on page 31. It shows the Temple Cap Sandstone immediately above the Navajo. However, in the source they used, the UGMS Bulletin 124, 1989, it states, the Temple Cap Sandstone exists only to the west of Johnson Canyon, which is a few kms east of Kanab.)

Judd Hollow Tongue--Carmel Formation This tongue separates the Page Sandstone from the Navajo below, and is easily seen all along the Cottonwood Wash. It's the first layer above the massive white and yellowish Navajo Sandstone on the west side of the road. You'll also see it as you walk downstream from the White House Trailhead and into the Lower Paria River Gorge. The type location for this member is in Judd Hollow, which is just above where the old Adams Pump still sits in the middle part of the Lower Paria Gorge.

Navajo Sandstone This formation is probably the most famous and most prominent of any formation on the Colorado Plateau. This is the one in which many of the fantastically narrow slot canyons are made. It is a massive sandstone, up to 600m thick, and is considered by many to be one large fossil sandune. It was created by wind-blown sand, therefore it has lots of crossbedding. The Navajo is seen as the White Cliffs between Highway 89 and Cannonville, and in the narrows of Bull Valley Gorge, Round Valley Draw, upper Deer Creek, Castle Rock & Yellow Rock, the Buckskin Gulch, and the Lower Paria River Gorge. It's the Navajo Sandstone which forms the fantastic slopes and colors of the **Teepees** and **The Wave** in the Coyote Buttes. It's also seen as the top-most part of the big cliff making up the Vermilion Cliffs just south of the Sand Hills or Paria Plateau. Elsewhere, you see the Navajo in the big walls of Zion National Park, all the canyons of the Escalante, throughout the San Rafael Swell, Robbers Roost Country, in the Moab area, and all across the Navajo Nation, which is the type location.

Kayenta Formation Wherever you see the Navajo, you'll see this one just below. Frankly, the author can't remember seeing a geology cross section without these 2 together. The Kayenta is usually a deep reddish brown formation made of mudstone, sandstone and siltstone layers. It normally forms the series of benches just below the Navajo.

Moenave Formation This is the red cliff-maker just below the Kayenta, and above the Chinle clay beds. To the east of the Echo Cliffs Monocline (just east of Lee's Ferry and running south), this one phases into, and is called the Wingate Sandstone. But between the Paria and Zion National Park, it's the Moenave filling the same or similar slot. This formation forms the lower cliffs just above the talus slopes along the Vermilion Cliffs and in the bottom end of the Lower Paria River Gorge.

Owl Rock Member--Chinle Formation An indistinct mostly sandstone layer just below the Moenave cliffs along the base of the Vermilion Cliffs and just above the varicolored banded slopes around Old Pahreah, the Paria Movie Set and in lower Hackberry Canyon.

Petrified Forest Member--Chinle Formation This is the same formation where all the petrified wood is found in northern Arizona. It's also full of petrified wood along the Paria in Utah. This is the very colorful and fotogenic banded layers of clay you see around the site of Old Pahreah and the Paria Movie Set. It's this red, purple, green, pink and white layered formation which has attracted movie makers to Old Pahreah throughout the years. It's also seen in lower Hackberry Canyon behind the Frank Watson cabin.

Lower Sandstone Member--Chinle Formation Another indistinct sandstone bed in the lower part of the Chinle. Probably best seen in the lower end of the Paria around Lee's Ferry and just above the prominent Shinarump Bench.

Shinarump Conglomerate Member--Chinle Formation A white and very course sandstone and pebblestone conglomerate, which forms a very prominent ridge, cliff or bench throughout Utah and northern Arizona. It's white only when disturbed, otherwise it's covered with desert varnish and very dark-colored (**desert varnish** covers many smooth vertical canyon walls such as those made from Navajo or Wingate Sandstone. It occurs when rain washes minerals from other formations down on some walls. After evaporation, all that's left is a coating of iron-rich minerals that resembles black varnish). In other parts it's called the Black Ledge; because of desert varnish. It's best seen around Lee's Ferry, where it forms what is called Lee's Backbone, which is on the south side of the Colorado River. This member is also full of petrified wood and in some places, uranium. All the uranium mines in the area of Lee's Ferry are in this formation.

Moenkopi Formation This is the chocolate brown-colored strata you'll see all across Utah and Arizona, wherever the Chinle's Shinarump Member is found. It makes up the slope below the Shinarump and is composed of clay beds along with sandstone and siltstones. You drive on it as you make the side-trip to Old Pahreah. It's also seen along the road running between the Navajo Bridge/Marble Canyon, and Lee's Ferry.

Kaibab Limestone This formation is seen at the land surface just west of the Buckskin and Wire Pass

Trailheads, and on Buckskin and Fivemile Mountains. It's the capstone along the rim of Kaibab Gulch (that part of the gulch, wash or canyon just above the Buckskin Trailhead). It's this limestone which forms the top layer throughout the House Rock Valley. You are driving atop the Kaibab as you approach Marble Canyon and Lee's Ferry along Highway 89A from either direction. It forms the top layer in Marble Canyon, as seen at the rest stop & visitor center at Navajo Bridge. You can also see the Toroweap and Coconino Formations in Marble Canyon if you stop at the Navajo Bridge on your way to Lee's Ferry.

Toroweap Formation   In the Paria drainage, this formation is only seen in Kaibab Gulch, just upcanyon from the Buckskin Trailhead, where the channel cuts deep into Buckskin Mountain.

Hermit Shale   This is the lowest or oldest of all formations found in the Paria River system. It's the red rock seen only in the very bottom of the Kaibab Gulch, just upcanyon above the Buckskin Trailhead. Normally the Coconino Sandstone is in that slot, but it's missing in Kaibab Gulch. However, the Coconino is seen just emerging in Marble Canyon below the bridge.

Above This is the boiler used by Charles H. Spencer during his mining activities at Lee's Ferry between 1910-'12. It's the same as the one shown in the Mining Chapter of this book. In the background left is the Colorado River with Lee's Backbone rising above the boiler.

Left This picture was taken at Pahreah sometime after Spencer was involved with trying to remove gold from the Chinle clay beds starting in 1912. Sitting on top of some of the mining equipment is Rose Chynoweth, wife of Arthur on the right; and Laura Moore Babb on the left. Arthur and Rose Chynoweth lived there until about 1922. (Iris Smith Bushnell foto)

Mining History: the Paria River Drainage

Coal

Not a lot of mining has occurred in the drainage of the Paria, but in the early days of settlement, coal was mined in various places and used mostly in the blacksmith trade. If you look at the maps of Bryce Valley Coal Mines & Ghost Towns, and the Middle Paria River Mines & Ghosts Towns, you'll see coal mines near each of the former or present townsites. Most of the coal mining has occurred in the upper reaches of the Paria northeast of Tropic and north of Henrieville.

The coal mined in Bryce Valley comes from the bottom part of the Straight Cliffs Formation, while that coming from the mine above Adairville, comes from the Dakota Sandstone. There are also coal beds in the Tropic Shale, but they're so thin it has always been uneconomical to mine.

The most northerly coal mine in the valley is usually called the **Shakespeare Mine,** but sometimes it's referred to as the **Emma Canyon Mine.** It's located about 11 kms northeast of Tropic, in a little side-drainage of Henderson Valle, called **Emma Canyon.**

The late Herm Pollock believed it was his grandfather William W. Pollock and his brother Jack, who may have been the first to dig coal out of this mine. They were among the earliest settlers to the valley and both were blacksmiths. They needed coal to do their work; on the other hand, Obe Shakespeare, longtime Tropic resident, told the author he never knew coal in his life, until an uncle started mining it not too many years ago. Bryce Valley families always used cedar (piñon/juniper) wood in their stoves, even though coal was there for the taking.

After the earlier blacksmith days, nothing happened in the coal mining business until the late 1930's. This is when Lewis and Vern Ray (father & son) came into the valley from Orderville, and filed on the mineral rights to the coal in Emma Canyon. They mined coal for 5 or 6 years, until about the mid-1940's, then sold it to Alton and Vernal Shakespeare. They were the ones who did more mining than anyone. They shipped it to as far away as St. George and Panguitch, but most of it stayed in the valley. The mine was active until perhaps the late 1950's, then business slowed down and it was not used after about 1960. One person thought the state closed it down because of water and safety problems (?).

Finally in 1964, Alton Shakespeare sold the old Shakespeare Mine for a reported $75,000 to a man from Denver. This new owner was hoping to invest more money in the business and make big profits, but nothing ever happened to the scheme, and coal hasn't been mined there since.

The Shakespeare Mine is located in the bottom part of the Straight Cliffs Formation, where there's a total of nearly 4 meters of coal in 4 separate seams.

To get to this site (in the NW corner of Section 22, T36S, R2W), drive east out of Tropic on Center Street toward the old townsite of Losee in East Valley. There are several side roads, so follow this map in a northeast direction and straight into Emma Canyon. Stay on this main road, which is generally good for any car. From Tropic to the mine is 10.9 kms (6.8 miles).

In the area north of Henrieville are the **Pollock & Davies Mines.** These are both in the Straight Cliffs Formation, and presumably across the narrow canyon from each other (?). Old timers in Henrieville called the one place the **Jack Pollock Mine.** He was one of the earliest settlers in Henrieville and he used the coal for blacksmithing. Today there is little or no evidence this old mine ever existed, but the one just across the canyon did operate for a while and is clearly visible. This was the **Davies Mine.** The author was told these are 2 separate mines, across the canyon from each other, but has only seen the mine on the east side of the canyon. Maybe there was only one mine that had 2 names (?).

Left This is an adit or tunnel in Emma Canyon and is likely part of the Shakespear or Emma Canyon Mine. **Right** The remains of a chute at the Davis/Pollock Mine in Coal Canyon.

Map 40, Mine Locations of the Paria River Drainage

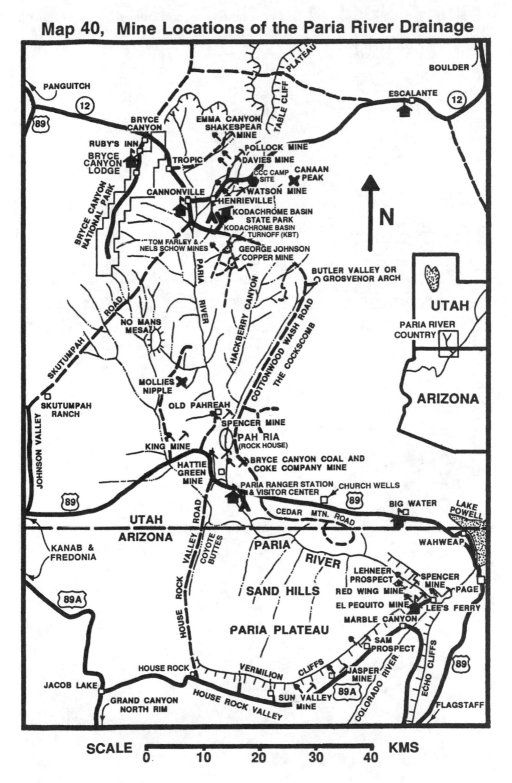

BOULDER

PANGUITCH

12

ESCALANTE

12

TABLE CLIFF PLATEAU

BRYCE CANYON

EMMA CANYON
SHAKESPEAR MINE

POLLOCK MINE

RUBY'S INN

DAVIES MINE

BRYCE CANYON LODGE

TROPIC

CCC CAMP SITE

CANAAN PEAK

BRYCE CANYON NATIONAL PARK

CANNONVILLE

HENRIEVILLE

WATSON MINE

KODACHROME BASIN STATE PARK

KODACHROME BASIN TURNOFF (KBT)

TOM FARLEY & NELS SCHOW MINES

GEORGE JOHNSON COPPER MINE

BUTLER VALLEY OR GROSVENOR ARCH

PARIA RIVER

HACKBERRY CANYON

ROAD

UTAH

PARIA RIVER COUNTRY

NO MANS MESA

THE COCKSCOMB

COTTONWOOD WASH ROAD

ARIZONA

SKUTUMPAH

MOLLIES NIPPLE

SKUTUMPAH RANCH

OLD PAHREAH

SPENCER MINE

PAH RIA (ROCK HOUSE)

KING MINE

JOHNSON VALLEY

BRYCE CANYON COAL AND COKE COMPANY MINE

HATTIE GREEN MINE

89

PARIA RANGER STATION & VISITOR CENTER

CHURCH WELLS

89

BIG WATER

LAKE POWELL

UTAH

CEDAR MTN. ROAD

ARIZONA

KANAB & FREDONIA

COYOTE BUTTES

PARIA

RIVER

WAHWEAP

89A

HOUSE ROCK VALLEY ROAD

SAND HILLS

LEHNEER PROSPECT

RED WING MINE

SPENCER MINE

PAGE

EL PEQUITO MINE

LEE'S FERRY

PARIA PLATEAU

MARBLE CANYON

SAM PROSPECT

89

HOUSE ROCK

VERMILION

CLIFFS

ECHO CLIFFS

JACOB LAKE

JASPER MINE

COLORADO RIVER

GRAND CANYON NORTH RIM

HOUSE ROCK VALLEY

SUN VALLEY MINE

89A

FLAGSTAFF

N

SCALE

0   10   20   30   40

KMS

Wallace Ott of Tropic recalled a time he took Byron Davies up **Coal Canyon** and showed him the veins of coal. That was in the early 1940's and after Davies had tried, apparently unsuccessfully, to mine coal from a mine down around Adairville. It was Davies who did some mining here in the 1940's. He ran a shaft into the beds from 30m to 50m, but didn't have the money to go into mining big time. The Davies Mine has one vein nearly 3m in thickness; another about 2m thick. The mining that was done was more for a promotional scheme than anything else. Davies, Ott and others, including Alfred Foster, organized the Garfield Coal Company in about 1960, but nothing has happened.

To get to these old mines, which are supposed to be nearly side by side, drive north out of Henrieville on Highway 12 in the direction of Escalante. After about 5 kms, and between mile posts 32 & 33, turn left, or northwest. The mines are almost due north of that point in Coal Canyon, which is between Jimmie Canyon & Dry Hollow. **See Map 38, Bryce Valley Coal Mines & Ghost Towns.** From the highway drive west only about 30m on a graded road, then turn right or north onto a rough dirt track. From there continue north crossing a dry wash for which you may need at least a HCV (cars should be parked there at the dry wash). Continue north for a total of 2.6 kms (1.6 miles) to a fence, gate & washout. Stop and park there--don't attempt to go further as there are nearly a dozen washouts between there and the mines. From there it's about 2 kms to the site (located in the north half of Section 36, T36S, R2W). The Davies Mine is on the south side of the canyon, and there is still a pile of coal and a chute at the site. Across the canyon, you can just barely make out a faint line indicating the possible location of the Pollock Mine (?).

Not far south of the mines in Coal Canyon is another old coal mine one old-timer called the **Jack Pollock Mine** (?). Maybe Jack Pollock had several mines, one near each town (?). It's immediately east of Highway 12 between mile post 31 & 32, north of Henrieville. No one in Henrieville today knows much about the history of this mine, except that one cold winter day, 2 boys from Henrieville, went into the mine and started a fire to get warm. When they left, they failed to put out the fire properly and it started the coal burning. Later the state of Utah had to send men and equipment down to cover the shaft and smother the fire. You can still see some of the coal from the highway.

There's supposed to be another old coal mine not far east of Henrieville. If you hike on some old roads about 5 kms east of town and into Little Creek, you may see the **Frank Watson Mine.** This is the same man who built the cabin in the lower end of Hackberry Canyon. After he left the Hackberry country, he went to Henrieville for a while, then ran a small store out on Watson Ridge just south of Kodachrome Basin. His hottest seller was rot-gut whiskey known locally as *Jamaica Ginger*. After he left the store, he started working a coal mine in Little Creek, but he apparently only worked that for one winter. The author walked up Little Creek in December of 2003 but never saw anything resembling a mine. And no one in Henrieville today seems to know anything about it or whether or not it exists (?). It's possible a cave-in has occurred hiding the entrance (?).

In the Adairville area, and not far north of Highway 89 & the Paria Ranger Station & Visitor Center, is another old abandoned coal mine. About 2 1/2 kms due north of the site of Adairville, and in a small side-canyon just east of the Paria River, is the site of the **Bryce Canyon Coal & Coke Company Mine.** This old mine is located in the center of Section 21, T42S, R1W, and in the Dakota Sandstone. See **Map 39, Middle Paria River Mines and Ghost Towns.**

This mine was first opened in the late 1930's by Byron Davies of Cannonville. It's been said he took some good coal out by truck in the direction of Kanab, but apparently he couldn't find a market for it. They mined it for just a couple of years, then sold it to David Quilter in about 1940. No mining ever

From the rim of a short side-canyon, looking down on what's left of the Bryce Canyon Coal & Coke Company Mine. Seen here is a tunnel and a collapsed loading chute.

took place after that and it was abandoned.

To get there, drive along Highway 89 to between mile posts 17 & 18, about 5 kms east of the Paria Ranger Station, then turn north onto the Cottonwood Wash Road and drive 9.1 kms (5.65 miles). At that point you'll be about 600m west of the only fence & cattle guard around. Park right on the road at or next to a dry creek bed. From where you park, walk southwest about 100m and look right down on the mine, which has one collapsed shaft and a tumbled-down loading chute. Continue south along the east side of the drainage, which by then is a small canyon, and locate a route down the steep slope to the mine. While on the rim, notice what you're walking on. At that point is a broken-up shaley limestone bed which has literally billions of fossil shells roughly 140 million years old. These clam-like shells range in size from your fist down to marble-size.

Copper

Prospecting for copper has been carried on at a number of places in the Paria River drainage, but only a small amount of low-grade copper ore was ever shipped from the **Hattie Green Mine.** The history of this mine goes back to the late 1800's. It was March 8, 1893, that George J. Simonds filed a claim or notice of location on what was called the Hattie Green. Just a few days later, there were several other locations registered in the area just to the north. They were the Silver Queen and Gold King claims which are about one km north of the Hattie Green and evidently on top of The Cockscomb (?). These were filed by several members of the Ahlstrom family. In the same time period, Tom Levy, Oren Twitchell and Murphy Alexander filed on what was called the Red Bird Claim. This was just south of The Box of the Paria. Of all these claims, only the Hattie Green saw any mining activity.

According to the late Kay Clark of Henrieville, 2 brothers named Clint & Pat Willis, worked this mine in the late 1910's and early 1920's. They are the ones who did most of the work on the tunnels and adits (test pits) you see, and who lugged out most of the copper ore. Kay Clark did some poking around the place and filed on the old claims in the 1960's, but nothing came of that.

To get to the Hattie Green, located in Section 18, T42S, R1W, stop on Highway 89, just south of mile post 28. Then walk due east across the gully, and locate a track first running east, then south, then north inside a minor draw within The Cockscomb. From where you turn north, it's about one km to the mine, which sits atop The Cockscomb Ridge on the right. You can also drive there from a point just north of mile post 28, but if you see signs indicating **No Trespassing--then stop!** There is some private land to cross before reaching the mine, but heretofore, the owners seem to care less (?). Read more on route details in the hiking section under **Map 27, The Hattie Green Mine Trail & Fivemile Ranch.**

At the mine there are 2 tunnels, one coming in from the east side, the other from the west. The west-side tunnel has wooden tracks which small ore cars rolled on within the mine. Deep inside are branch tunnels running left & right. Inside the east-side tunnel is a wooden doorway, a shaft going down to a lower tunnel, and an old hand-cranked wooden hoist. Take a headlamp or large flashlight to explore these tunnels--which you will do at your own risk! Right on top of the ridge is an ore heap with the turquoise-colored stained rocks still lying there. There are also 3 other adits or test prospects in the area.

There was another attempt to mine copper about halfway up **Rock Springs Bench,** which is south and a little east of Kodachrome Basin. This one is located in the SE1/4 of the NW1/4 of Section 35, T38S, R2W. A rough track leading to 2 shafts leaves the main road next to a 5m-tall rock pinnacle, as

Left One of 2 closely-spaced shafts at the George Johnson Copper Mine on Rock Springs Bench. Sitting is Afton Pollock and his son Steve. This one has a ladder going down, but only a fool would use it! **Right** This is the squy or arasta just downhill to the east from the Tom Farley & Nels Schow Mines. Far right is Wallace Ott; next to him is Afton Pollock, 2 of Bryce Valley's oldest.

shown on **Maps 15 & 22**. It was called the **George Johnson Mine** and about the only guy around in 2004 who knew much about it was Wallace Ott of Tropic. Here's some of what he remembered:

One of those guys who started that mine was named George Johnson. He had a store in Tropic. and he opened up the first mine back before the turn of the century--in the 1890's sometime. George's brother Sixtus Johnson was there too, along with John Johnson who was their younger relative. George hired some guys to dig a shaft 100 feet [30m] deep and that shaft has still got water in it [dry in 2004]. They were after copper and lead--mostly copper, and a little silver. This was called the George Johnson Mine. He's the one that put up the money, but he never actually did any of the digging.

The last time anyone worked out there was in about 1935. I was there part of the time they was diggin' it. They done all their drilling by hand; of course that was Navajo Sandstone and it wasn't all that hard. The guy who done the drilling was Byron Davies, and he had done mining up at Eureka. [Mining and following those veins wasn't easy]. You would start down on a vein and get down maybe 10 or 15 feet [3m to 5m], then it would go off in a different direction.

Byron would go down in the shaft, then they had a pulley-like thing fixed so they could send a 25 gallon bucket down on a cable, then he'd load the rock and a horse would pull it up and dump it. The one that run the horse and pulled the rock out was Clyde Johnson; he was my cousin. They'd a gone down to 100 feet [30m], but they didn't quite make it that far because the water got the best of 'um.

When Byron would blast, he always blasted a kind of a shelf out of the way so that when the bucket was goin' up, he's sit back in this little hole, so if that bucket or cable broke loose, or a rock fell, it wouldn't hit 'im. Then he'd drill again and blast, and of course he'd have to put a long fuse on it--they didn't have electric caps then--so he could get in the bucket and they'd pull 'im out, then the blast would go off. Then they'd have to wait till the smoke and dust got out of there. The smoke from the fuse and dynamite was poison, so they had to wait awhile before he'd go back to work. They put that 2nd shaft down in about 2 weeks. Those shafts are still there, open and dangerous!

The only money I know of that was made from that mine, and I don't know if they paid their expenses or not, was by 2 guys from Cannonville who had a big truck. They went out on that bench and gathered up a lot of ore that was layin' around, with lead and copper, and loaded it up. They loaded that truck several times and took it up to the mill in Midvale, and put it through that mill and they got a little money out of it. But the people that run the mill said it wasn't quite high enough grade, so they quit. They hauled quite a little ore up there, but there wasn't any real money made on it. Loren Twitchell was the one who owned the big White truck. He was in this country truckin' for quite a few years haulin' posts and wood and stuff. And the guy that helped him was Mayben Johnson. Clyde Johnson and Byron Davies were workin' for George Johnson.

Lead

There were 2 small insignificant lead mines in the upper part of the Paria drainage. The site is at the southern end of Watson Ridge, just west of Ott's Corral & Rock Springs Creek, and in the NW1/4 of the SE1/4 of Section 22, T38S, R2W. The mine entrances are 75m apart and 200m west of the Rock Springs Bench Road; while the squy or arasta is 15m west of the same road. See Maps 15 & 22. Wallace Ott described the mines as we walked around the place:

They tried to mine it just after the turn of the century. It was a lead mine. Nels Peter Schow was the first one. He dug that tunnel that goes in on the south. Nels told me, he took some powder and another man out there, and after mining awhile, Nels reached down to pick up a rock or something and that other guy who had a pick, run that pick right through Nel's hand. And of course, they was here with only a wagon and they took him to town in that. This would have been in the early 1900's and a

This is the shaft that once was the Tom Farley/Wilford Clark Lead Mine. Just downhill to the east is the squy or arasta where the lead ore was ground up.

little before I was born in 1911.

Then in about 1945, Tom Farley came into this country from Arizona near the Mexican border and camped near that mine for one summer. Wilford Clark and his son Kay was grubstak'in 'im. I think they had a claim on it. They was a feedin' Tom while he was workin' at the mine. Tom was tellin' me about the vegetables they brought out here. He had a new .22 rifle and he was always out huntin' rabbits; there used to be quite a lot of rabbits out here. He was eatin' rabbits and that garden stuff the Clarks brought out.

Tom brought the ore down from the shaft on top of the hill to this squy [arasta] which is this round cemented place where he ground up the ore. He had a little motor to run the squy to drag a big rock around in a circle to grind the ore into a powder, and another little motor to pump water up from Rock Springs Wash. After he'd grind a while, he'd wash the ore out with his hose and down into a chute made with big planks. The chute was lined with burlap and that burlap would catch that heavier metal, then when he figured it was loaded with metal, he's stop the water and let it drain and take up the burlap and wash it out in water and he got quite a lot of pure lead. He had a seamless sack and was going to take that lead up to the mill in Murray [near Salt Lake City] to have it tested.

*I'd call the mine on the south side of the hill the **Nels Schow Mine**, that's the tunnel. And the shaft on top is the **Tom Farley/Wilford Clark Mine**.*

Manganese

Another mining operation took place not far south of Kitchen Corral Point and along the Nipple Ranch Road. This was the **King Mine** and its primary mineral was manganese.

According to Calvin C. Johnson of Kanab, this operation first began sometime in the late 1930's. It was on November 15, 1939, that John H. Brown filed a claim and started mining. It was soon found they couldn't separate the manganese from the bentonite clays of the Petrified Forest Member of the Chinle Formation. After Brown gave up, several Johnson brothers from Short Creek, Arizona (this place is now called Colorado City, Arizona & Hildale, Utah), worked it for 6 or 8 months. This was in the early 1940's. Then it was abandoned for about a decade.

In 1954 or '55, a bigger outfit came in with a man named Bennett in charge. In the year or two they worked the area, they spent upwards of $250,000 to develop it. They made five small dams in the one little canyon where most of the mining took place. They then built another dam across Kitchen Corral Wash and caught flood water; plus they used water from some nearby springs. They then pumped this water up the canyon to the five reservoirs, and used the water in the attempt to separate manganese from the clays. At the height of the operation, 20 to 25 local men worked there. But they also had trouble with separation, and soon closed down.

To see this old abandoned mine, drive along Highway 89 about halfway between Page & Kanab. Right at mile post 37, turn north onto the Nipple Ranch Road and drive 5.5 kms (3.4 miles). At that point a road runs northeast into a minor canyon. Drive about half a km from the main road and park under a large cedar tree. From there, you can walk upcanyon on an old & partly washed out road about 200m to the old ponds, one mine tunnel, and some loading chutes (it's in the middle of Section 2, T42S, R3W). When you return to the Nipple Ranch Road, turn northwest and drive to Km 7.1/Mile 4.4 (from Highway 89), and on your right or east about 150m, you'll see some mining scars and an old loading chute on the nearest hillside.

This loading chute on the Nipple Ranch Road is part of the King Manganese Mine.

Uranium

In the very bottom end of the Paria River Canyon in the vicinity of Lee's Ferry, and along Highway 89A just under the Vermilion Cliffs, are a number of uranium mines & prospects. These all go back to the 1950's uranium boom days.

If you're coming downcanyon out of the Lower Paria River Gorge, you'll pass the **Red Wing Mine** about 6 1/2 kms up from Lee's Ferry, and about half a km south of the Wilson Ranch site (in the north half of Section 3, T40N, R7E). This mine has 2 tunnels, 13m & 17m long. The adits were tunneled into the Shinarump Member of the Chinle Formation, but the vegetal trash heaps (derived from vegetation such as logs) where the uranium is concentrated, are right at the contact point of the Shinarump above and the Moenkopi below. About half a km upcanyon from the Wilson Ranch is another adit, called the **Lehneer Prospect.** Not much happened there.

Near Lee's Ferry is the **El Pequito Mine.** It's found about 2 kms west of the Lonely Dell Ranch, at the head of a minor canyon just north of Johnson Point. El Pequito is in the Shinarump, but at the contact point of the Moenkopi. Mineralization occurs in an old stream channel in the Shinarump. This mine is found in the northwest corner of Section 14, T40N, R7E.

Going southwest from Lee's Ferry, you'll find the **Sam Prospect** in the southeast corner of Section 2, T39N, R6E. It's about 3 kms west of Vermilion Cliffs Lodge, along Highway 89A, and on the south side of Badger Creek. This adit is in the upper part of the Petrified Forest Member of the Chinle Formation. Not much went on there.

Further along to the southwest, is the **Jasper Mine** in the southwest corner of Section 27, T39N, R6E. It's about half a km northeast of Cliff Dwellers Lodge, and about 100m from the highway. It too was located at or near the contact point of the Shinarump and Moenkopi. They found small amounts of many minerals, including copper staining, but not much else.

The only real uranium mine in these parts was the **Sun Valley Mine.** It's 5 kms southwest of Cliff Dwellers Lodge, and in the south half of Section 6, T38N, R6E. At the time it was studied by Lane & Bush, this mine was owned and operated by Intermountain Exploration Co. The mine was started in 1954 during a period of intense uranium exploration in the area. An inclined shaft was sunk on a Shinarump outcropping, with the ore being on the contact with the Moenkopi. Several hundred tons of high grade uranium ore was shipped before the shaft was filled with mud from a flash flood. Later, a vertical shaft was sunk, and a drift was driven to connect with the old, sand-filled workings, but there was no further production. The Sun Valley Mine has been worked in recent years on a sporadic basis.

Today all of these old mines and prospects are included in the new Vermilion Cliffs National Monument.

Gold

The story of gold mining along the Paria River is also the story of Charles H. Spencer. As one writer put it, *"he seemed to enjoy the pursuit more than the gold itself, especially when it meant spending other peoples money looking for it."*

Spencer first arrived in the Colorado River country in 1909, where he set up an operation on the lower San Juan River far upstream from Lee's Ferry on the Colorado. There he was trying to separate gold from the Wingate Sandstone. While there, a couple of prospectors told him about the possibilities of finding gold in the Chinle Formation at Lee's Ferry, and that coal existed north of the Colorado River a ways. With that tip, he made tracks for Lee's Ferry, arriving there in April, 1910.

On arriving at the Ferry, Spencer looked things over and decided the Chinle clays 300m from the river could be a possibility. He speculated that a boiler could power a high pressure hose, which could wash the clays & shales down to the river where gold could then be recovered with the help of an amalgamator. But his first job was to send his men out to look for the promised coal field. It was found in a side-drainage of Warm Creek called **Crosby Canyon**, about 45 kms upstream in Glen Canyon.

While the hunt for coal went on, Spencer began experimenting with power dredging at Lee's Ferry. At first he used wood to power the boiler. He then set up power hoses to wash the gold-bearing clays down to a sluice and amalgamator at the river. Gold is indeed in the Chinle, but it's in the form of very fine dust. The method used to separate the gold from the clay, was to run the muddy water over the amalgamator which had mercury in the bottom. The mercury was supposed to absorb and trap the gold, allowing other materials to pass over. But instead, the operation merely clogged the amalgamator, and the mercury did not absorb the gold. While chemists worked on the problem, Spencer was thinking about how to get the coal from Warm Creek to Lee's Ferry.

At first it was thought coal could be brought in by mule, using an old trail called the **Dominguez or Ute Trail,** which entered the canyon about 5 kms above from the Ferry. Because of the extra distance, it was decided to make a shortcut route directly above the operation on the Colorado. So in the fall of 1910, Spencer and his men constructed the **Spencer Trail** from the river to the top of the cliffs. From there it was hoped they could head northeast with mules for the Warm Creek coal fields. But the trail was never used to bring in coal; instead, it was more of a promotional scheme than anything else. Spencer finally decided to bring coal downriver in a boat.

The next job was to build a wagon road right down the dry stream bed of Warm Creek to the Colorado River. While workers were building the road, others were building a barge on the banks of the river. This all went well; they brought coal down the canyon, loaded it onto the barge, then floated it down to Lee's Ferry. But then the problem was to get the barge back upstream.

This problem, it was thought, could be solved by a tugboat of some kind. So with more investors money, a 9-meter-long tug boat called the **Violet Louise,** was purchased and brought to Lee's Ferry. As it turned out, it was far too underpowered to push a large barge upstream against the current. The current wasn't that fast, but pushing a barge wasn't easy.

While Spencer worked on problems at the Ferry, the managers of the Chicago company he worked for, ordered a steam-powered boat from San Francisco. The boat was built in 1911, dismantled, and shipped by train to Marysvale, Utah, the end of the railway line at the time. It was then put onto large wagons for the remainder of the 320 km trip to the mouth of Warm Creek. There it was reassembled in the spring of 1912 and it was the biggest thing to sail the Colorado River above the Grand Canyon. It measured 28m x 8m, was powered by a coal boiler, and had a 4-meter-wide stern paddle wheel. Even though this part of the project wasn't one of Spencer's ideas, the boat was named the **Charles H. Spencer.**

The next problem was to find a crew for the boat. This wasn't easy in the middle of the desert, but they found a crew anyway, with a fellow by the name of Pete Hanna at the helm, the only crew member who had any experience with boats. They loaded the deck full of coal for the trial run. But almost immediately, they hit a sandbar. Then another. Finally Hanna turned the boat around and allowed it to sail down the river backwards, which gave it better maneuverability. They spent one night in the canyon, then finished the 45 km run to Lee's Ferry the next morning.

They then had to figure out how to get the steamer back upstream against the current, which was stronger than anyone had expected. Hanna decided to keep most of the coal which had been brought down on board, to insure passage back up to Warm Creek. This was a good move, because they barely made it back to Warm Creek. They again loaded the boat as full as possible, and returned to Lee's Ferry, where it sat for a couple of months. All this, while the chemists and the workers figured out what to do about separating the gold from the Chinle clays.

Finally it was decided to try something different. They ended up towing the original barge upstream with the Spencer. This worked fine. They then loaded both the barge and the steamer with coal. The barge was then allowed to drift downstream with several workers guiding it around the sandbars, with the Spencer following. This worked fine too, and it appeared they had this part of the gold mining problem solved. The only thing left to do, was to find a successful way to get the gold out of the clay. This Spencer was never able to do, and the steamboat had made its last run.

Spencer left Lee's Ferry later in 1912, bound for the nearly abandoned settlement of Pahreah. Meanwhile, the steamship Charles H. Spencer sat on the river tied to the bank. In 1915 the combination of high water and piles of driftwood, put the boat on its side and it sank in one meter of water. Later, parts were stripped off and taken away, and some of the lumber from its decks was used for various projects. Today, you can just barely see the sunken remains of the boat and its boiler just upstream from Lee's Fort, at the bottom end of the Spencer Trail. Nearby is the boiler used for mining, and parts of the stern paddle wheel. Just north of the boiler one can still see scars where they operated the power sluicing machinery. The best sources of information about the history of Lee's Ferry is found in the books, **Desert River Crossing** and **Lee's Ferry**. See **Further Reading**, in the back of this book for more details.

From Lee's Ferry, Spencer moved his operations to Pahreah. He was accompanied by Herbert A. Parkyn. The new dream was to extract gold from the same Chinle clays at Pahreah, but they failed at that too. They did however set up some stone buildings at Pahreah, and tried some sluicing. These sites are still there at Old Pahreah today. Several attempts were made to refinance new schemes, including building a dam across The Box of the Paria River just below the Old Pahreah townsite, but that too failed to bring in more money. That was in 1921. In 1932, he again returned to Pahreah to look things over, this time with his daughter, but nothing came of that.

Charles H. Spencer was in and out of Pahreah and Lee's Ferry all his life, but he never made a dime from any of his big-time mining schemes.

This boiler, belonging to Charles H. Spencer's mining operation, is heading for either Lee's Ferry or Pahreah (?). It appears there are several ox teams with wagon loads of supplies coming down a narrow canyon. (John H. Johnson & Ferrell Brinkerhoff foto)

Above Charles H. Spencer right (facing camera) working with vats of mercury trying to extract gold from Chinle clays at Pahreah. Charles Edward Francisco is in the middle of the picture with his back to the camera. **Right** Spencer's mining operation at Pahreah. Some of this stuff is still there today. **Below** Ox teams pulling wagons with mining supplies, apparently from Lee's Ferry to Pahreah. All fotos were taken at Pahreah in 1912. (John H. Johnson & Ferrell Brinkerhoff fotos)

This stone cabin & cellar at Old Pahreah were built by Charles H. Spencer in 1912. He was trying to extract gold from the Chinle clay beds behind the camera. These are located on the east side of the Paria River and in the southeastern part of what was the farming community of Pahreah.

This is the boiler Charles H. Spencer used while at Lee's Ferry. This foto was probably taken in 1911-'12 when mining was in full operation. This boiler is still at Lee's Ferry near the bottom of the Spencer Trail, and where the steamship Charles H. Spencer is sitting in the waters of the Colorado. (This picture was taken from an information board at Lee's Ferry--National Park Service foto)

Lee's Ferry Fort, as it's known today, was build in the summer of 1874 as a trading post. This is the largest building at Lee's Ferry today. Nearby are 3 other stone buildings; the American Placer Corp office or Post Office (?), the Spencer Bunkhouse, and the USGS Residence. At the parking lot next to the boat launching ramp, you should find a small booklet with map on sale showing all the sites.

The steamship **Charles H. Spencer** as it appeared in August, 1915. Today, all you'll see is the half-submerged boiler and other parts in the clear water of the Colorado River. There's a sign marking the place just below the beginning of the Spencer Trail, and along the path to the Upper Ferry Terminal. (USGS foto?)

Map 41, Bryce Valley and Skutumpah Road Ranches

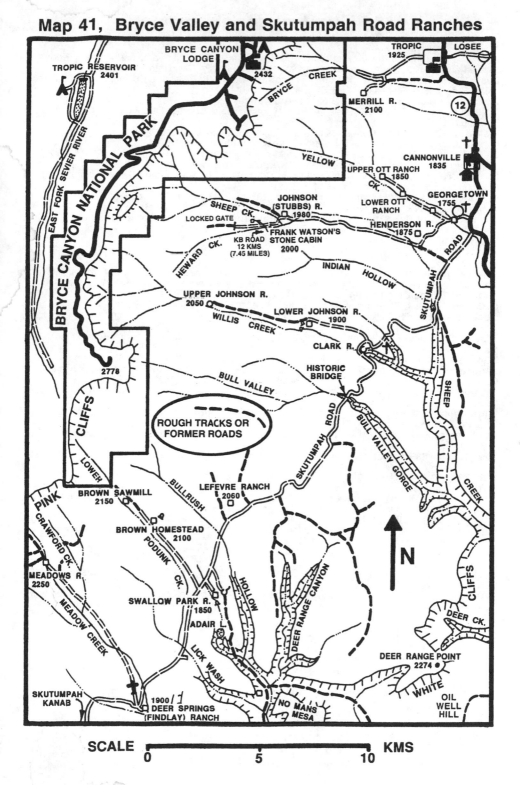

TROPIC RESERVOIR
2401

BRYCE CANYON
LODGE

TROPIC
1925

LOSEE

BRYCE CREEK

2432

MERRILL R.
2100

12

EAST FORK SEVER RIVER

BRYCE CANYON NATIONAL PARK

YELLOW

CANNONVILLE
1835

UPPER OTT RANCH
1850

GEORGETOWN
1755

SHEEP CK.

JOHNSON
(STUBBS) R.
1980

LOWER OTT
RANCH

LOCKED GATE

HEWARD CK.

FRANK WATSON'S
STONE CABIN
2000

KB ROAD
12 KMS
(7.45 MILES)

HENDERSON R.
1875

INDIAN HOLLOW

SKUTUMPAH ROAD

UPPER JOHNSON R.
2050

LOWER JOHNSON R.
1900

WILLIS CREEK

CLARK R.

2778

BULL VALLEY

HISTORIC
BRIDGE

SHEEP CREEK

CLIFFS

ROUGH TRACKS OR
FORMER ROADS

SKUTUMPAH ROAD

BULL VALLEY GORGE

LOWER

BROWN SAWMILL
2150

BULLRUSH

LEFEVRE RANCH
2060

N

PINK

CRAWFORD CK.

BROWN HOMESTEAD
2100

PODUNK CK.

CLIFFS

MEADOWS R.
2250

DEER CK.

MEADOW CREEK

SWALLOW PARK R.
1850

HOLLOW

DEER RANGE CANYON

ADAIR L.

LICK WASH

DEER RANGE POINT
2274

SKUTUMPAH
KANAB

1900

DEER SPRINGS
(FINDLAY) RANCH

NO MANS
MESA

WHITE

OIL
WELL
HILL

SCALE

0   5   10

KMS

Further Reading

History Books
A Mormon Chronicle: The Diaries of John D. Lee--1848-1876, Edited and Annotated by Robert G. Cleland and Juanita Brooks, University of Utah Press, Salt Lake City, Utah
Desert River Crossing, Historic Lee's Ferry on the Colorado River, 3rd Edition, Rusho-Crampton, Tower Productions, Salt Lake City & St. George, Utah.
Emma Lee, Juanita Brooks, Utah State University Press.
Golden Nuggets of Pioneer Days--A History of Garfield County, Daughters of Utah Pioneers, Panguitch, Utah.
History of Kane County, Daughters of Utah Pioneers, Kanab, Utah.
John Doyle Lee, Zealot-Pioneer Builder-Scapegoat, Juanita Brooks, A.H. Clark Co.
John Mangum: Revolutionary War Soldier, Mangum Family History Compiled by Dallas Mangum.
Lee's Ferry, A Crossing of the Colorado River, Measeles, Pruett Publishing.
Lee's Ferry and Lonely Dell Ranch Historic Districts, (a booklet) Grand Canyon Natural History Association, South Rim-Grand Canyon, Arizona.
Mountain Meadows Massacre, Juanita Brooks, University of Oklahoma Press.
Some Dreams Die, Utah's Ghost Towns, George A. Thompson, Dream Garden Press.
The Red Hills of November: A Pioneer Biography of Utah's Cotton Town, Andrew Karl Larson, The Deseret News Press, Salt Lake City, Utah.
Utah Ghost Towns, Stephen L. Carr, Western Epics.

Geology
Chinle Formation of the Paria Plateau, J. P. Akers, Masters Thesis, University of Arizona, 1960.
Geology of Bryce Canyon National Park, Lindquist, Bryce Canyon Natural History Association.
Geology of Kane County, Utah, Doelling, Davis & Brandt, UGMS Bulletin 124, 1989.
Geology of Table Cliff Region, Utah, Bowers, Bulletin 1331-B, USGS, 1972.
Geology of Utah's Parks and Monuments, Sprinkel, Chidsey & Anderson, Utah Geological Association, Salt Lake City, Utah.
Mine and Prospect Map, Vermilion Cliffs, USGS Map MF-1475-D, Miscellaneous Field Studies (also contains maps A, B & C).
Map-Geology of the Kaiparowits Plateau, Carter & Sargent, USGS Map I-1033-K.
Sandstone and Conglomerate-Breccia Pipes and Dikes of the Kodachrome Basin Area, Kane County, Utah, Cheryl Hannum, Masters Thesis, Brigham Young University, 1979.
Stratigraphy of the Dakota and Tropic Formations, Lawrence, Bulletin 19, Utah Geological Survey, 1965.
Stratigraphy of the San Rafael Group, Southwest and South Central Utah, Thompson & Stokes, Bulletin 87, UGMS, October 1970.
The Geology and Geography of the Paunsaugunt Region, Utah, Gregory, Professional Paper 226, USGS.
The Kaiparowits Region, Gregory & Moore, Professional Paper 164, USGS.

Magazines and Unpublished Manuscripts & Family Histories
A Brief History of Early Pahreah Settlements, Thomas W. Smith (Thayne Smith of Kanab, Utah).
An Episode of Military Exploration and Surveys (A survey party's account of riding up the Paria River Gorge), The United Service, Vol. 5, Number 119, October 1881.
Biography of John G. Kitchen, J. G. Kitchen Jr., Kanab, Utah,1964.
California Condors, Updates on restocking public lands with condors: from Arizona Desert Digest, Arizona Game & Fish Department, and The Peregrine Fund.
Desert Bighorn Sheep Restocking, Arizona Game & Fish Department, Wildlife Surveys & Investigations, 1984.
First Motor Sortie into Escalante Land, Breed, National Geographic Magazine, September, 1949.
History of Deer Spring Ranch, Graden Robinson, Kanab, Utah.
History of Peter Shirts [Shurtz] and his Descendants, Ambrose Shurtz, 1963, unpublished family history, but available at Special Collections, BYU Library, Provo, Utah. (Soon a real book may be published?)
Historic Utilization of Paria River, Reilly, Utah Historical Quarterly, Vol. 45, Number 2, 1977.
Lee's Ferry at Lonely Dell, Juanita Brooks, Utah Historical Quarterly, Vol. 25, 1957.
Samuel & Emily Pollock, compiled by Afton Pollock, Tropic, Utah.
Things That Remind me of my Brother: Herman Pollock, compiled by Afton Pollock, Tropic, Utah.
Vegetation and Soils of No Man's Mesa, Utah, Mason & others, Journal of Range Management, January, 1967.
William Chynoweth: An American Cowboy, Mary Jane Chynoweth Fuller, Orem, Utah

Other Guidebooks by the Author

Books listed in the order they were first published.
(Prices as of July, 2004. Prices may change without notice)

Climber's and Hiker's Guide to the World's Mountains (4th Edition), Kelsey, 1248 pages, 584 maps, 652 fotos, ISBN 0-944510-18-3. US$36.95 (Mail Orders US$40.00).

Utah Mountaineering Guide (3rd Edition), Kelsey, 208 pages, 143 fotos, 54 hikes, ISBN 0-944510-14-0. US$10.95 (Mail orders US$13.00).

China on Your Own: and *Guide to China's Nine Sacred Mountains*, Kelsey, **Out of Print.**

Canyon Hiking Guide to the Colorado Plateau (4th Edition), Kelsey, 320 pages, 118 hiking maps, 185 fotos, ISBN 0-9605824-16-7. US $14.95 (Mail orders US$17.00).

Hiking and Exploring Utah's San Rafael Swell (3rd Edition), Kelsey, 224 pages, 32 mapped hikes, plus History & Geology, 198 fotos, ISBN 0-944510-17-5. US$12.95 (Mail orders US$15.00).

Hiking and Exploring Utah's Henry Mountains and Robbers Roost, *Including The Life and Legend of Butch Cassidy,* (Revised Edition), Kelsey, 224 pages, 38 hikes or climbs, 158 fotos, ISBN 0-944510-04-3. US$9.95 (Mail orders US$12.00).

Hiking and Exploring the Paria River, *Including: The Story of John D. Lee & the Mountain Meadows Massacre,* (4th Edition), Kelsey, 288 pages, 38 mapped hiking areas from Bryce Canyon to Lee's Ferry, ??? fotos, ISBN 0-944510-21-3. US$11.95 (Mail Orders US$14.00).

Hiking and Climbing in the Great Basin National Park--*A Guide to Nevada's Wheeler Peak, Mt. Moriah, and the Snake Range,* Kelsey, **Out of Print.**

Boater's Guide to Lake Powell (4th Edition), *Featuring: Hiking, Camping, Geology, History & Archaeology,* Kelsey, 288 pages, 256 fotos, ISBN 0-944510-10-8. US$13.95 (Mail Orders US$16.00).

Climbing and Exploring Utah's Mt. Timpanogos, Kelsey, 208 pages, 170 fotos, ISBN 0-944510-00-0. US$9.95 (Mail Orders US$12.00).

River Guide to Canyonlands National Park & Vicinity, Kelsey, 256 pages, 151 fotos, ISBN 0-944510-07-8. US$11.95 (Mail Orders US$14.00).

Hiking, Biking and Exploring Canyonlands National Park & Vicinity, Kelsey, 320 pages, 227 fotos, ISBN 944510-08-6. US$14.95 (Mail Orders US$17.00).

Life on the Black Rock Desert: A History of Clear Lake, Utah, Venetta B. Kelsey, 192 pages, 123 fotos, ISBN 0-944510-03-5. US$9.95 (Mail Orders US$12.00).

The Story of Black Rock, Utah, Kelsey, 160 pages, 142 fotos, ISBN 0-944510-12-4. US$9.95 (Mail Orders US$12.00).

Hiking, Climbing & Exploring Western Utah's Jack Watson's Ibex Country, Kelsey, 272 pages, 224 fotos, ISBN 0-944510-13-2. US$9.95 (Mail Orders US$12.00).

Technical Slot Canyon Guide to the Colorado Plateau, Kelsey, 288 pages, 307 fotos, ISBN 0-944510-20-5. US$13.95 (Mail Orders US$16.00).

This is the stone house or cabin that is thought to have been built by Frank Watson probably in the early 1920's. It's located southwest of Cannonville along Heward Creek, and about 50m northwest of the road. Drive slow and look hard; in 2004, it was behind a couple of small piñon/juniper trees. Read the driving instructions under Hackberry Canyon and the Watson Cabin.

Distributors for Kelsey Publishing

Primary Distributors All (or most) of Michael R. Kelsey's books are sold by these companies. Please call or write to one of these when ordering any of his guidebooks.
Alpenbooks, 4602 Chennault Beach Road, Suite B-1, Mukilteo, Washington, USA, 98275, Website alpenbooks.com, Email cserve@alpenbooks.com, Tele. 425-493-6380, or 800-290-9898.
Brigham Distribution, 156 South, 800 West, Suite D, Brigham City, Utah, 84302, Tele. 435-723-6611, Fax 435-723-6644, Email brigdist@sisna.com.
Books West, 5757 Arapahoe Avenue, D-2, Boulder, Colorado, USA, 80303, Tele. 303-449-5995, or 800-378-4188, Fax 303-449-5951, Website bookswest.net.
Liberty Mountain, 4375 W. 1980 S., Suite 100, Salt Lake City, Utah, 84104, Tele. 800-366-2666 or 801-954-0741, Fax 801-954-0766, Website libertymountain.com, Email sales@libertymountain.com.
Treasure Chest Books, 451 N. Bonita Avenue, Tucson Arizona, USA, 85745, Tele. 928-623-9558, or 800-969-9558, Website treasurechestbooks.com, Email info@treasurechestbooks.com.

Other Distributors
Anderson News, 1709 North, East Street, Flagstaff, Arizona, USA, 86004, Tele. 928-774-6171, Fax 928-779-1958.
Canyonlands Publications, 4860 North, Ken Morey Drive, Bellemont, Arizona, USA, 86004, Tele. 928-779-3888 or 800-283-1983, Fax 928-779-3778, Email books@infomagic.com.
Crown West Books (Library Service), 575 E. 1000 S., Orem, Utah, USA, 84097, Tele. 801-224-1455, Fax 801-224-2662, Email jimproc@attbi.com.
High Peak Books, Box 703, Wilson, Wyoming, USA, 83014, Tele. 307-739-0147.
Recreational Equipment, Inc. (R.E.I.), 1700 45th Street East, Sumner, Washington, USA, 98390, Website rei.com, Mail Orders Tele. 800-426-4840 (or check at any of their local stores).
Online--Internet: amazon.com; adventuroustravelers.com; btol.com (Baker-Taylor); Ingrams.com; Bdaltons.com; borders.com (teamed with amazon.com).

For the **UK, Europe, and the rest of the world** contact: **Cordee,** 3a De Montfort Street, Leicester, England, UK, LE1 7HD, Website cordee.co.uk, Tele. Inter+44-116-254-3579, Fax Inter+44-116-247-1176.
For **Australia** and **New Zealand: Macstyle Media,** 20-22 Station Street, Sandringham, Victoria, Australia, 3191, Website macstyle.com.au, Email macstyle@netspace.net.au, Tele. Inter+61-39-521-6585, Fax Inter+61-39-521-0664.

This is what's left of the steamship *Charles H. Spencer*. This sign and remains are immediately below the trail that runs upriver to the Upper Ferry Terminal at Lee's Ferry.